Introduction to FORTRAN IV Programming:

USING THE WATFOR COMPILER

GOODYEAR COMPUTER SERIES

JOHN M. BLATT

Professor Applied Mathematics
University of New South Wales
Sydney, Australia

Introduction to FORTRAN IV Programming:

USING THE WATFOR COMPILER

Goodyear Publishing Company

Pacific Palisades, California

© 1968 by Goodyear Publishing Company
Pacific Palisades, California

Printed in the United States of America

Library of Congress Catalog Card No.: 68-8969

Current printing (last digit):
10 9 8 7 6 5 4

PREFACE

This preface explains what the book is intended to do, and the ways in which it differs from other FORTRAN IV programming books. Some knowledge of the subject is necessary to understand this preface fully. Beginning students are advised, therefore, to skip this preface and start Chapter I immediately; Chapter I assumes no prior knowledge whatever. Teachers and more advanced students may wish to read the preface first.

This book provides a new approach to the teaching of FORTRAN programming. In our opinion, the teaching of the language rules of FORTRAN should not be separated from practical experience in FORTRAN programming, including debugging of the resulting programme. Programming, in FORTRAN or any other language, is very much a practical skill which requires practical experience.

Yet, in the past it has often been felt necessary to defer actual programming experience until a very large fraction of the FORTRAN language has been taught as a language, with its own vocabulary, spelling, punctuation, and syntax. Furthermore, many FORTRAN books attempt to teach the FORTRAN language with little reference to what goes on inside the computer, either during the process of compilation, or during execution of the object programme. In our view, this is poor teaching practice and tends to make FORTRAN programming appear much more formidable to the beginner, than it really is. However, there has been a difficulty in the path of giving the beginner in FORTRAN programming rapid access to a machine: that difficulty is the nature of the FORTRAN READ and WRITE statements, with their associated FORMAT statements. The formatted READ and WRITE are a major stumbling block for students, and are copious sources of errors even for experienced programmers.

Fortunately, a trend has appeared recently towards special student compilers, which are a *super-set* rather than a subset of FORTRAN; which are specially designed to give fast throughput of student programmes; and which provide easily readable diagnostic messages. The most prominent compiler in this class is WATFOR. It is a superset of FORTRAN, in the sense that it provides "free" READ and PRINT commands *in addition to* the ordinary FORTRAN formatted READ and WRITE statements. FORTRAN compilers of this type are ideally suited to student teaching, but as yet there is no FORTRAN book written specially to be used with such compilers. This is the function of the present book.

Part A of the book is a quick introduction to FORTRAN programming, with the intention of getting the student onto the machine as rapidly as possible. Indeed, Chapter I by itself contains enough information so that students can submit very simple jobs after reading only that one Chapter. Chapter II is devoted to the arithmetic assignment statement, Chapter III to flow control (GO TO, STOP, logical IF, flow-charting, and related matters), Chapter IV to free input and output under WATFOR, Chapter V to the structure of the input deck, and Chapter VI to the interpretation of the printed output, including the meaning of diagnostic messages. The WATFOR diagnostic messages are collected in Appendix B, thereby eliminating the need to issue separate mimeographed material to students.

There are *two kinds of exercises* in the book: (1) *Drill exercises,* which can be done with pencil and paper, without going to the machine, and (2) *Programming exercises,* which are meant to be full programmes, to be written by the student, punched up onto cards, and debugged by use of actual machine output. *Answers to all drill exercises* appear in the book, in Appendix C. Answers to the *programming* exercises will be made available in a separate booklet, to teachers only.

All drill exercises in Part A, as well as a number of programming exercises, should be completed by the student before going on to Part B.

In Part B, we give a complete account of the entire FORTRAN IV language, starting from fundamentals. Chapter VII, the first Chapter of Part B, contains an account of how information is stored inside the machine, using the IBM/360 as an example. We feel strongly that many FORTRAN language terms cannot be appreciated properly without knowing a bit about what goes on inside the machine. It takes very little effort to learn enough about the way information is stored inside the machine, to make the FORTRAN language rules much more comprehensible, and correspondingly easier to remember.

The sequence in Part B is didactic in nature, starting with fundamentals and proceeding in stages to more complicated matters. We start with the storage of information in the machine (Chapter VII), the corresponding rules for FORTRAN constants (Chapter VIII) and FORTRAN variables (Chapter IX). FORTRAN arithmetic is discussed in Chapter X, including a brief discussion of round-off errors and error accumulation. Chapter XI gives the more elaborate FORTRAN flow control features, in particular the DO statement; this chapter completes the preliminary discussion of programme flow control in Chapter III. Built-in Functions and Arithmetic Statement Functions are introduced in chapter XII, Array Storage and its use in Chapter XIII, and Subprogrammes of various types in Chapter XIV. Chapter XV gives a full discussion of FORTRAN input-output organization, including transfers to and from magnetic tapes and disks. Note that the FORMAT statement, that bugbear of FORTRAN programming, is introduced only at this stage of the book: it is not required earlier, and we feel that only at this stage is a beginning student likely to find the FORMAT statement meaningful and not too difficult to learn. Students should be asked at this point to revise their earlier exercise programmes, by substituting formatted I/O for the "free" I/O statements used heretofore. This is the *one and only* alteration required to go from student FORTRAN, such as WATFOR, to the production versions of FORTRAN. *Everything else which has been learned is standard FORTRAN language material, which need not be changed in any way.*

There is more to computer programming than understanding the rules of a programming language, such as FORTRAN, and writing programmes in that language. Chapter XVI is devoted to *programme planning and debugging.* In our view, nine tenths of good programming is planning and debugging.

The last chapter, Chapter XVII, is devoted to a short discussion of machine language and assembly language programming. We do not give enough to enable the student to programme in assembly language (that would be another book!), but we say enough to make him appreciate just what the advantages of FORTRAN are, and just where FORTRAN programming could be replaced profitably by assembly language programming.

We have provided large numbers of worked examples of actual programmes, using and illustrating the FORTRAN language features under current study. We have taken considerable care to use examples of practical importance wherever possible, rather than special "made" examples. Questions of importance in numerical computation, such as the number of significant figures, the possibility of arithmetic overflows, the machine time required by various techniques, are all given major emphasis in these discussions.

There are five appendices. Appendix A contains a dictionary of FORTRAN. Appendix B is an annotated list of the diagnostic messages put out by the WATFOR compiler. If every student runs to an instructor or tutor every time he gets a diagnostic message from his computer run, the load on the teaching staff becomes unbearable. The annotations in Appendix B are designed to reduce this load. A student who gets the error message DO-1 from his WATFOR run is told, in appendix B, that this means ILLEGAL TRANSFER INTO THE RANGE OF A DO LOOP. But he is also told, right at this point: "Have you forgotten to insert, in your programme, the final CONTINUE statement for a DO loop? If so, the compiler thinks the DO loop is still going strong." These annotations are not guaranteed to work in all cases. But they work often enough to make a great deal of difference in running really large classes in computing.

Appendix C contains the *answers to all drill exercises* in the text. Appendix D summarizes and discusses the various "dialects" of FORTRAN. In Appendix E, we summarize our experience with organizing large classes in computing (2000 first year students at the University of New South Wales). We then discuss monitor control systems, and problems associated with them.

Last but not least, it is my great pleasure to thank Mr. A.J. Guttmann for checking the sample programmes and answers to exercises; to thank him as well as Mrs. A.V. Nikov and Mr. N. Shiraev for reading the manuscript and making a number of helpful comments; and to thank Mrs. Anne Stuart for typing the manuscript.

John M. Blatt

TABLE OF CONTENTS

PREFACE

PART A

This, first part of the book gives enough of an introduction to FORTRAN IV programming to allow the student to prepare small programmes, punch these programmes onto cards to make up an acceptable input job deck, and to understand and interpret the printed output from the machine run.

A number of programming exercises appear throughout Part A, including some very simple exercises at the end of Chapter I. Students should do as many of these exercises as possible, the more the better, before starting on Part B of the book. "Doing" an exercise means all of:

1. Writing down a flow diagram,

2. writing down the FORTRAN coding,

3. preparing an input job deck,

4. repeated computer runs, to "debug" the programme until it works properly.

Chapters I through VI contain enough information to do all this; but it requires practical experience to really learn this material. No amount of theoretical reading will enable you to play the piano; the same is true of programming the computer.

CHAPTER I

COMPUTERS AND COMPILERS

The ordinary commercial or scientific electronic computer of today is not an electronic brain but a machine that does calculations on data (numbers given to it) by obeying a sequence of instructions that also must be given to it. It does not "think" but merely obeys the given instructions without either "will" or "common sense" of its own. It is a high-speed electronic moron.

The computer can add, subtract, multiply and divide; it can "read" data and print out results consisting of numbers, letters and various other symbols and it can transfer symbols from one place in the computer to another. In order to attempt to solve any problem on a computer the problem first must be analysed into these elementary steps and instructions given to the computer in a language that this particular computer has been constructed to read and obey. This is called "programming" the computer. In the form just described it is called "machine language programming" because each different model of computer, or "machine", usually is constructed to read and obey its own "machine language".

From the logical viewpoint a computer under the control of a machine language programme operates in the following way:

1. The computer's "memory" is "cleared", that is, each cell or location for storing numbers is cleared of whatever it may have contained before and then has a zero stored in it;

2. the programme suitably punched onto cards is put in the card reader and "loaded" into the computer, that is, the computer reads card after card and stores the contents into consecutive locations in its memory;

3. the computer begins to "execute" the programme, that is the computer obeys the first instruction of the programme (now in the memory), then the second instruction and so on;

4. the computer obeys the instructions in a sequence that the instructions themselves may arrange; some instructions reached in this sequence may be for the computer to read data from a data card, others may be for it to print results on the printer, so the "input card deck" must contain not only the programme cards but also, following them, all the data cards that will be required;

5. the computer continues to execute the programme, obeying instruction after instruction, until
    - i)   it reaches a "stop" instruction
    - or ii)   it reaches a "read" instruction and there is no card in the card reader
    - or iii) it reaches a "print" instruction and there is no paper in the printer
    - or iv) the operator switches off the computer.

This form of computer operation was quite common about 1950 but now certain standard and very elaborate master programmes called "compilers" are available that make programming much easier and programme execution more automatic. The FORTRAN master programme is such a compiler.

The student's programme need no longer be written in machine language, but may be written in FORTRAN (the "source language"), a language similar to that of ordinary mathematics.

Using the master programme FORTRAN, the computer operates in the following way (this describes the WATFOR version of FORTRAN):

1. The FORTRAN compiler is first loaded into the computer and the computer then operates under instructions in the compiler; under these instructions, the computer then reads the student's programme (the "source programme") written in the FORTRAN language;

2. as each card of the source programme is read, its content is reproduced ("listed") in one line on the printer, so that the programmer can see what was actually read from the card; the lines are numbered consecutively for easier reference;

3. after each card has been read, its content is checked to see whether it is a grammatically correct FORTRAN instruction, i.e., consistent with the FORTRAN rules of vocabulary, spelling, punctuation, and syntax; if it is not, the next line on the printed output contains an error message ("diagnostic") that tells the programmer which rules of FORTRAN grammar were broken; grammatically wrong instructions are ignored;

4. each grammatically correct FORTRAN instruction is translated from FORTRAN to machine language (the "object language");

5. the resulting machine language programme (the "object programme") is stored in a section of the computer memory not occupied by the compiler itself;

6. this translation process continues until a special card is read, containing the symbols (*) $ENTRY in its first 6 columns; this card tells the master programme that it has finished translating the last source language statement of the source programme; the translation process is now terminated, and the object programme is executed; if execution of the object programme requires the reading of numerical (or other) data, the "data cards" must be placed in the card deck immediately following the $ENTRY card; unlike execution of a true machine language programme, the object programme does not run "unattended", rather, the master programme keeps a paternal eye on what goes on, and prints out "execution time error messages" whenever something goes wrong (e.g., an attempt is made to divide by zero); less paternally, the master programme stops execution altogether if the time taken on the computer becomes excessive (e.g., more than 10 seconds), or if the number of printed output pages becomes excessive (e.g., more than 4 pages of output). Typical student programmes should not require more than a few seconds on the computer, nor more than one or two pages of output. A student programme which exceeds these limits is probably in a "loop", i.e., is obeying the same set of commands over and over again, without end and without sense. You will find that it is surprisingly easy to write programmes which loop indefinitely.

(*)   The precise nature of this "control card" differs from one computer installation to another. In some places, the control card is //DATA in the first 6 columns, rather than $ENTRY.

7. after programme execution is finished (whether because the machine finished your programme, or because you were stopped by the master programme), the master programme calls for the input cards of the next student job. FORTRAN keeps on processing student job after student job, until all jobs in the "batch" are finished.

To illustrate these concepts, we now present two simple FORTRAN programmes.

The first programme is for the calculation of compound interest on a principal; let P be the principal, R the yearly rate of interest (in percent), and Y the number of years during which interest accumulates. Then the value V of the investment after Y years is $V = P(1 + 0.01R)^Y$. The factor 0.01 is to convert the percentage rate R into a fraction. The programme is designed to read numerical values of P, R, and Y from a data card, to compute the value of V, and to print out the values of P, R, Y, and V. Computation then stops.

The source language programme, given below, consists of five FORTRAN statements, each of which is written onto a separate line; when punched onto cards, each FORTRAN statement appears on a separate card, *starting in column 7 of the card,* i.e., columns 1 through 6 remain blank; the use of columns 1 through 6 is discussed in Chapters III (statement numbers) and V (comment cards, continuation cards). Punching of cards is discussed in Chapter V, section A. The programme reads:

```
READ,P,R,Y
V=P*(1.0+0.01*R)**Y
PRINT,P,R,Y,V
STOP
END
```

The FORTRAN command READ,P,R,Y tells the compiler to produce an object programme which expects to find a data card in the card reader, this card containing the numerical values of P, R, and Y, in that order. As soon as the execution phase starts, this data card is read, and the numerical values of P, R, and Y are stored inside the memory of the machine, available for future use. The READ command and the data cards are discussed in Chapter IV, B. (*)

The next FORTRAN command, V=P*(1.0+0.01*R)**Y, tells the compiler to produce an object programme which multiplies the value of R by 0.01, adds 1 to this, raises the sum to the power Y, multiplies the result by P, and stores the overall result into memory location V. The symbols + and − are used just as in ordinary arithmetic. The symbol * stands for multiplication, and must be used whenever a multiplication is desired; it must not be omitted. For instance, 0.01R would be grammatically incorrect FORTRAN, and would give rise to an error message from the compiler. The symbol ** stands for raising to a power. Parentheses are used as in ordinary mathematics, i.e., operations within parentheses are carried out first, before other operations. These matters are discussed in detail in Chapter II.

The third FORTRAN command, PRINT,P,R,Y,V, tells the compiler to produce an object programme which, at that point during the execution phase, orders the printer to print one line, this line containing the numerical values of P, R, Y, and V, respectively, in that sequence. The PRINT command, and the form in which the numbers are printed out, are discussed in Chapter IV, A. Both the READ and PRINT commands, in the forms given here, are specific to WATFOR; standard

(*) It is possible to write numerical values of P, R, and Y directly into the source language programme, through statements such as P=1500.0, for example. See Chapter IV, beginning of Section B, for the reasons in favour of using a READ statement and data cards, instead.

FORTRAN commands for reading and printing are more complicated, and are given in Chapter XV.

The FORTRAN command STOP tells the compiler to produce an object programme which stops execution at this point. The "job" is then considered finished, and the machine proceeds to the next "job" in the "job stream".

The FORTRAN instruction END is a signal to the compiler that the source language programme ends here, i.e., translation from source language to machine language ceases at this point.(*)

Our second little FORTRAN programme is intended to find the two roots of the quadratic equation $ax^2+bx+c=0$. We shall use the letter D for the combination

$$D = b^2 - 4ac$$

The two roots x_1 and x_2 are given by

$$x_1=(-b + \sqrt{D})/(2a)$$

$$x_2 = (-b - \sqrt{D})/(2a)$$

Again, the programme is meant to read input numbers (in this case, the values of the coefficients A, B, and C) from a data card; we then compute D, and from it, the values of X1 and X2; input numbers as well as results are then printed out, and thereafter computation stops. This source programme, given below, consists of seven FORTRAN statements:

```
READ,A,B,C
D=B**2-4.0*A*C
X1=(-B+D**0.5)/(2.0*A)
X2=(-B-D**0.5)/(2.0*A)
PRINT,A,B,C,X1,X2
STOP
END
```

We note the following additional points: First, it is not necessary for variable identifier names to be single letters, such as A, B, C, or D. More complicated names are permitted, for instance the two-character names X1 and X2. Variable identifier names are discussed in Chapter II; they may have up to 6 characters, the first of which must be alphabetical (a letter of the alphabet); subsequent characters may be either alphabetical (letters) or numerical (one of the digits 0, 1, 2, 3, 4, 5, 6, 7, 8, or 9; note the distinction between the digit 0 (zero) and the letter O (Oh); these are different characters). For the moment, avoid use of the letters I, J, K, L, M, or N as starting letters of an identifier name (see chapters II and IX).

The expression D**0.5 tells the compiler to produce an object programme which raises the value of D to the power 0.5, i.e., which computes the square root of the value of D.

(*) Note the distinction between STOP and END: STOP must be translated into machine language; the translated command is an actual instruction to the machine during the execution phase. END is a signal to the compiler, and is never translated into a machine instruction. The instruction END must appear as the last source language statement of every FORTRAN programme.

The slash / is used to denote division.

The two little programmes above are only source language programmes. They are not complete *machine jobs*. To make up an acceptable *job* to be run under control of the FORTRAN compiler (in its WATFOR version), certain additional cards are needed, which we shall now describe briefly; a more complete exposition appears in Chapters V (control cards) and IV (data cards).

1. *The first card of the job deck* must be the *job card;* this card tells the master programme that a new job starts here, and gives accounting information, such as the name of the subject, the name of the student, the student record number of the student, and the name of the tutorial instructor. The job card is not the same everywhere, and it is necessary to make sure of the precise format of the job card demanded at your computer installation. For example, in some installations the symbols $JOB in the first four columns of the job card are replaced by the symbols // PROGRAM in the first nine columns of the job card. All *control cards*, including the job card, are punched starting with column 1 of the card; whereas FORTRAN source language cards are punched starting in column 7 of the card (except for statement numbers etc., see Chapters III and V). The job card is discussed in Chapter V, B.

2. The second control card comes immediately *after* the source language cards, i.e., immediately after the FORTRAN card with the instruction END. This second control card usually contains the symbols $ENTRY in its first six columns. But in some installations this is altered, for example to // DATA. For simple programmes, the control card $ENTRY duplicates the function of the FORTRAN statement END: both signal the end of the translation phase, and the start of the execution phase. In more advanced programming, the functions of END and $ENTRY are different, see Chapter XIV.

3. The third additional card required for a complete job deck is a *data card* to be read during the execution phase, by the translated version of the FORTRAN command READ. This card must come *after* the $ENTRY card, which signals the start of the execution phase. Data cards are discussed in Chapter IV, B. For the moment, suffice it to say that the data card must contain ordinary decimal numbers, as many numbers as there are quantities to be read from the card; different numbers must be separated from each other on the card by at least one blank column; negative numbers are preceded by a minus sign, with no blank between the minus sign and the number to which it belongs (but there is at least one blank before the minus sign). No plus sign is required for positive numbers, but a plus sign does no harm.

4. In some installations, an *end-of-job card* is required as the final card of every job; the usual format of this card is: $IBSYS in the first 6 columns. Not all installations require this card; you must find out the rules for your own installation.

As illustrations, we now give the *complete input decks* for our two simple jobs. For the job card, we assume that the subject number is 10.001, that the name of the student is Brown, the record number of the student is 68235179, and that the name of the tutorial instructor is Jones. For the first job, we assume that the principal sum is 1500.00, the rate of interest is 5 percent, and the interest is to accrue over 20 years. The complete job deck is:

```
$JOB              10.001         BROWN              68235179  JONES
      READ,P,R,Y
      V=P*(1.0+0.01*R)**Y
      PRINT,P,R,Y,V
      STOP
      END
$ENTRY
      1500.0    5.0     20.0
$IBSYS
```

For the second job, we assume that the same student name etc. apply; and we supply the numerical values 2.1 for A, 5.2 for B, and 1.12 for C as the coefficients in the quadratic equation $ax^2+by+c=0$.

```
$JOB              10.001         BROWN              68235179  JONES
      READ,A,B,C
      D=B**2-4.0*A*C
      X1=(-B+D**0.5)/(2.0*A)
      X2=(-B-D**0.5)/(2.0*A)
      PRINT,A,B,C,X1,X2
      STOP
      END
$ENTRY
      2.1     5.2      1.12
$IBSYS
```

The *printed output* produced by the machine is discussed in Chapter VI. It starts with a listing of the job card itself, followed by a listing of the FORTRAN source language cards and of the $ENTRY card. Thereafter comes the execution phase printed output, produced by the translated version of the PRINT statement. For both little programmes given here, this is just one line of print, containing input numbers and computed numbers.

If you wish to try your hand at some simple programmes, which can be done with the information now at your disposal, the exercises at the end of this Chapter are suitable.

The concepts illustrated in these simple programmes are discussed more fully in Chapters II through V; Chapter VI contains a discussion of the printed output, including error messages (diagnostics) for erroneous programmes. The information in Chapters II to VI is not necessarily in logical order, but rather in a sequence designed to be easier to understand than strictly logical order would be. For much the same reason, the information in these early Chapters is deliberately incomplete. Part B of the book completes the information, but it is neither necessary nor desirable that you should read the whole book before putting the first programme on the computer. On the contrary, computer programming is a practical skill which is best learned through practice on the computer.

Optional Exercises for Chapter I:

1. A rectangular brick has side lengths A, B, and C. Write a programme to read these three numbers from a data card, compute the volume V=abc of the brick, and print out the values of A, B, C, and V.

2. Same as problem 1, but compute not only the volume V but also the surface area S=2(ab+bc+ca) of the brick. Print out A, B, C, V, and S.

3. The monthly payment on a debt of amount DEBT is given by the value of PAYMNT; the interest rate is PERCNT percent per month. The three numbers DEBT, PAYMNT, PERCNT are read from a data card. We then compute the interest charge for the month: CHARGE=0.010*PERCNT*DEBT, where the factor 0.010 is required to convert the percentage to a fraction. We also compute the debt reduction: REDUCE=PAYMNT-CHARGE. Finally we compute the residual debt: RESIDU=DEBT-REDUCE. All input numbers and result numbers are printed out. Note the use of identifier names which remind us of the meaning of the quantity, e.g., DEBT rather than just D, PAYMNT rather than just P, etc. This can be of great help in programming.
Note also that all these identifier names start with letters other than I, J, K, L, M, or N; this is necessary at this early stage.

4. When two resistances R_1 and R_2 are connected in parallel, the net resistance R of the combination is given by $R = R_1 R_2 / (R_1 + R_2)$. Write a programme to read values of R1 and R2 from a data card, compute R, and print out R1, R2, and R.

5. A worker receives an hourly wage of amount RATE, and works a number of hours given by HOURS. His superannuation rate is SURATE (this is a fraction, not a percentage, of his wage); his rate of tax withholdings is TXRATE, also a fraction of the wage. The programme reads the four numbers RATE, HOURS, SURATE, TXRATE from a data card. We then compute the gross pay for the day: GROSS=RATE*HOURS, the superannuation deduction: SUDDCT=SURATE*GROSS, the tax deduction TXDDCT=TXRATE*GROSS, and the take home pay: PAY=GROSS-SUDDCT-TXDDCT. All input numbers and computed numbers are printed out.

6. Similar to problem 5, except that we allow for possible overtime OVTIME. The input numbers are now: RATE, HOURS, OVTIME, SURATE, TXRATE; and the gross pay is given by: GROSS=RATE*HOURS+1.5*RATE*OVTIME. The subsequent computations are unchanged.

7. A body in uniformly accelerated motion, with initial speed u and acceleration a, travels a distance s in time t. The distance is given by: $s = ut + \frac{1}{2}at^2$. The programme is to read values of U, A, and T from a data card, compute S, and print out the values of U, A, T, and S.

8. The area of an ellipse with semi-major axes a and b is given by A=πab, where π=3.14159. Write a programme to read values of A and B from a data card, compute the area AREA, and print out A, B, and AREA. Note that we use a new identifier name for AREA: different quantities, such as A and AREA, must be given different identifier names in the FORTRAN programme.

8

CHAPTER II

ARITHMETIC STATEMENTS

A. Constants and Identifier Names

Information is stored in the machine in binary form, as sequences of the binary digits 0 and 1. Each complete sequence of binary digits fills a "memory location" in the machine. However, in FORTRAN programming you need not be concerned (at this early stage) with how numbers look inside the machine, or just where they are stored inside the machine. You can give numbers to the machine in FORTRAN programmes as ordinary decimal numbers. The master programme carries out the conversion between decimal and binary number forms.

The decimal numbers 3.0, 3.00, and 3.000000 are all equal in the machine. The number 2.999999 is also the same, since numbers are stored to a limited number of significant digits only (approximately seven significant decimal digits). Unless otherwise specified (see Chapter VII), all numbers written *with a decimal point somewhere* are treated as real numbers in decimal form, truncated to approximately 7 significant digits.

We often wish to put a number into some particular memory location in the machine, and to use the content of this memory location for further calculations. It is important to distinguish between a *memory location* and the *content of this memory location*. You may think of the memory location as a "pigeon hole", which can accommodate exactly one number at a time. During execution of a calculation, the content of a given memory location often changes.

Memory locations are given "names" in FORTRAN programming. These names are called "identifiers". For example, the identifier HEIGHT is the name of a memory location in the machine. The memory location named HEIGHT may contain the number 5.89 at one time, the number 6.89 at another time, and so on.

Identifiers are composed of *characters*. The ten decimal digits 0, 1, 2, ..., 9 are called *numeric characters;* note that we use a narrow 0 to indicate the numeral "zero", to distinguish it from the alphabetic character "oh", written as O. The 26 letters of the English alphabet, A,B,C,...,M,N,O,P,...Z, together with the dollar sign $, are called *alphabetic characters.* An *alphameric character* is a character which is either alphabetic or numeric. Certain other characters will be introduced later.

DEF: An *identifier* consists of one alphabetic character, followed by at most five (5) alphameric characters next to each other (without intervening blanks).

Examples: Some grammatically correct identifiers are: HEIGHT, AREA, AREA1, AREA2B, B78O0T, $3A5. The character string 5AW is *not* an identifier, since the first character is numeric, not alphabetic. The character string VELOCITY is *not* an identifier, because it contains more than six (6) characters. In practice, the restriction to no more than six (6) characters is the most likely source of errors in inventing identifier names.

9

The identifier name of a memory location serves two separate purposes in the FORTRAN language:

1.   The identifier name is used to refer to the memory location in question

2.   The identifier name tells what type of information is stored in the particular memory location so named.

For the time being, the only information which we shall wish to store into a memory location will be an ordinary real number, truncated to approximately seven (7) significant digits; at a later stage (see Chapter VII) we shall be interested in storing other types of numbers (integers, complex numbers), as well as numbers with more significant digits, and completely non-numerical information.

DEF: In the absence of an explicit declaration to the contrary, any identifier name starting with an alphabetic character *other than* I, J, K, L, M, or N is a *real number identifier.*

DEF: The content of a memory location named by a real number identifier is a real number, truncated to approximately seven (7) significant digits.

Note: Identifier names starting with any one of I, J, K, L, M, or N are reserved for integers, rather than real numbers. We shall not use integer arithmetic for the time being.

Examples: Some real number identifiers are: HEIGHT, AREA, WIDTH, $3A5. The grammatically correct identifier name INDEX is *not* a real number identifier, since the name starts with the letter I.

Note: In this connection, it is desirable to emphasize the rule, stated earlier, that real number *constants* must be written *with a decimal point* as part of the character string; thus, the character strings 3.0, 3.000, 2.999999, and 3. all denote the same real number (equal to three within machine accuracy); but the single character 3 is interpreted by FORTRAN as the *integer* 3, rather than the *truncated real number* 3.000000.

The distinction emphasized here is particularly relevant in division. The result of dividing the truncated real number 7.000000 by the truncated real number 4.000000 is 1.750000, to machine accuracy. But omission of the decimal points from the input numbers would be catastrophic! Division of the integer 7 by the integer 4 within FORTRAN gives rise, not to the real number 1.75, but rather to the *integral part* of that number, i.e., the result of this "division" is the integer 1.

This feature of FORTRAN represents a copious source of programming errors. However, one does get used to it after a while; since FORTRAN programming has very real advantages over machine language programming, it is worth while to learn to live with the rules of FORTRAN programming.

Violations of the rules relating to the *type* of the information stored in a memory location are among the most frequent mistakes made by beginning programmers. Whenever your programme misbehaves, such violations are among the first things which you should suspect, and check into.

B. Initial Values, Assignment Statements

At the start of the execution phase (phase 6 in Chapter I) the contents of all the memory locations in the machine are unknown (that is, they contain whatever has been left over from the preceding student job in the batch of jobs). Thus, before the content of a named memory location can be used in your calculation, your programme must set the initial value with which you want to start the calculation.

One method to put something into a memory location is the *assignment statement,* of which a simple example is:

HEIGHT = 5.89

In the execution phase, this statement has the effect of storing the decimal number 5.89 into the memory location named by the identifier name HEIGHT.

It is important to realize that the equality sign "=" in the assignment statement does *not* imply a mathematical equality at all! Rather, the assignment statement represents an instruction to the computer to put the quantity to the right of the equality sign, into the memory location named by the identifier on the left of the equality sign. For example, consider the following assignment statement:

HEIGHT=HEIGHT+1.5

In the execution phase, the effect is as follows: The current value of HEIGHT is extracted from the memory location by that name. The decimal number 1.5 is added to this. These two steps are called *evaluating the arithmetic expression to the right of the = sign.* Finally, the result is stored into the memory location HEIGHT, thereby obliterating the number previously stored there.

If the two FORTRAN statements above appear in immediate sequence at the beginning of a programme, the contents of the memory location HEIGHT are:

Unknown   at the time execution starts
5.89   after the first statement has been executed
7.39   after the second statement has been executed

DEF: The general *assignment statement* has the form *"NAME=wfae"*, where *"NAME"* is any grammatically correct identifier name, the symbol = is used to denote assignment, and "wfae" stands for a "well-formed arithmetic expression" (see the next Section).

C. Well-Formed Arithmetic Expressions

We have already met two examples of arithmetic expressions: (1) A single number, e.g., the number 5.89 in the assignment statement HEIGHT=5.89, and (2) The result of a single addition e.g., the expression HEIGHT+1.5 in the assignment statement HEIGHT=HEIGHT+1.5.

More generally, an arithmetic expression is an instruction to the machine to carry out some arithmetic operation or operations so as to get a result which is a number. The arithmetic operations are denoted by:

+   for addition

-      for subtraction

*   for multiplication (the * must *not* be omitted: A*B is different from AB)

/   for division

**   for raising a number to some power

For example,

A+B   means the sum of the values of A and B

A-B   means the difference of the values of A and B

A*B   means the product of the values of A and B (whereas AB is simply another identifier name, *not* the product of A and B)

A/B   means the quotient obtained by dividing the value of A by the value of B

A**B   means the number obtained by raising the value of A to a power given by the value of B

If only a single arithmetic operation is to be carried out, that is all there is to it. If several arithmetic operations are required to get the result, it may be necessary to use parentheses to specify uniquely what is wanted: for example, consider the two arithmetic expressions

(A/B)*C   and   A/(B*C)

If the values of A, B, and C are 24.0, 2.0, and 3.0, respectively, then the first expression gives the result (24.0/2.0)*3.0=12.0*3.0=36.0, whereas the second expression gives the result 24.0/(2.0*3.0)= 24.0/6.0=4.0.

Operations contained within parentheses are always carried out first; if there are parentheses within other parentheses, the innermost parentheses are evaluated first.

In order to avoid the need for large numbers of parentheses, there are a number of parenthesis omission rules. For example, when parentheses are omitted in the above example, i.e., when we write A/B*C, then the operations are carried out reading from left to right, i.e., the compiler translates this expression as (A/B)*C, *not* as A/(B*C). The full, formal rules are given below; but for a quick orientation, it suffices to know that the rules for parenthesis omission are similar to ordinary mathematical notation; that is, multiplication and division take precedence over addition and subtraction, so that A*B+C/D is understood as (A*B)+(C/D), *not* as A*(B+C)/D; and raising a number to a power takes precedence over everything else.

Parentheses must not be omitted if their omission would result in two arithmetic operation signs appearing right next to each other. For example, A*(-B) is grammatically correct FORTRAN, and tells the machine to produce an object programme which multiplies the value of A by the negative of the value of B. But A*-B is grammatically incorrect (an "ill-formed" rather than a "well-formed" expression), since two arithmetic operation signs, the * and the −, appear next to each other. The exponentiation (raising to a power) sign ** is treated as a single symbol for the purpose of this rule, i.e., ** is not considered as two multiplication signs next to each other.

This quick survey of the FORTRAN rules should suffice for a first orientation. In the remainder of this Chapter, we present the formal rules for FORTRAN arithmetic expressions; this material must be learned eventually, but can be omitted in a first reading.

DEF: A *well-formed arithmetic expression,* or *wfae,* is defined by the following rules:

1. A number is a wfae;

2. A grammatically correct identifier name is a wfae;

3. If W is a wfae, then (-W) is a wfae whose value is the negative of the value of W. The parentheses are necessary in general; but we shall give rules later on to allow omission of parentheses in many special cases.

In all subsequent rules, W and V are taken to be wfae;

4. (W+V) is a wfae whose value is the sum of the values of W and V;

5. (W-V) is a wfae whose value is the difference between the value of W and the value of V;

6. (W*V) is a wfae whose value is the product of the values of W and V;

7. (W**V) is a wfae whose value is the value of W raised to a power given by the value of V;

8. (W/V) is a wfae; *if* all identifier names involved in W and V are real number identifiers, and *if* all numerical constants other than exponents are written as character strings containing a decimal point explicitly, *then* the value of the wfae (W/V) is the quotient obtained by dividing the value of W by the value of V.

Note: (W/V) is a wfae even if the stated conditions are not satisfied. But the *value* of (W/V) is then not necessarily equal to the result of an ordinary division. For example, (7/4) is a wfae; but the *value* of this wfae is not 1.75, but rather the *integer part* of 1.75, that is, the integer 1. The other operations, described by rules 3 through 7, inclusive, give the expected results even without these precautions; but division must be used with care. It is advisable to avoid division altogether in the early stages of learning how to programme in FORTRAN.

Note: In general, we advise against the use of integer constants (strings of numerical characters *without* a decimal point) at this early stage; however, there is one *exception* to this rule: Integer constants *should* be used as *exponents* whenever an integral power is wanted. For example,

X**3   is preferable to   X**3.0

The reason is this: although these two formulae are equivalent mathematically, the machine does different things with them. To evaluate X**3, the machine multiplies X by itself, and the result once more by X. To evaluate X**3.0, the machine takes the *logarithm* of X, multiplies this logarithm by the real number 3.0 (which could well be 2.999999 in the machine !), and then takes the anti-logarithm of the result. Not only does this take longer, and give less accuracy, but it even fails altogether if X happens to be negative.

The full rules for the evaluation of (W/V) appear in Chapter X. For the time being, the partial rules given here are sufficient.

By repeated application of these 8 rules, quite complicated wfae can be built up. For *example,* the following is a well-formed arithmetic expression (wfae):

$$(((B/2.0)**A)+(((C-D)/8.5)**3))$$

In usual methematical notation, this wfae would appear as

$$\left(\frac{b}{2}\right)^a \quad + \quad \left(\frac{c\text{-}d}{8.5}\right)^3$$

If the mathematical formula must be written entirely on one line, without the use of horizontal fraction bars, it might appear as

$$(b/2)^a \quad + \quad ((c\text{-}d)/8.5)^3 \qquad \text{or as} \qquad (b/2)**a + ((c\text{-}d)/8.5)**3$$

It is obvious that conventional mathematical notation employs much fewer parentheses, and is easier to read. *Some* parentheses are required even in conventional mathematical notation: for example, we could not write $c\text{-}d^3$ when we *mean* $(c\text{-}d)^3$; if c=9 and d=2, then $c\text{-}d^3$=9-8=1 whereas $(c\text{-}d)^3 = (9\text{-}2)^3 = 7^3 = 343$. But the number of parentheses required in the usual mathematical notation is kept down to an irreducible minimum.

In FORTRAN also, there are several rules which allow us to omit most of the parentheses; these rules are quite similar to the rules of ordinary mathematical notation. For the purpose of stating these rules, the arithmetic operations in the definition of a wfae above are given hierarchical ranks, ranging from the highest rank, 3, to the lowest rank, 1. We note that there are two separate "minus" operations, the "unary minus" (-W) defined by rule 3, and the "binary minus" (W-V) defined by rule 5; these have different ranks in the hierarchy below.

TABLE: HIERARCHY OF ARITHMETIC OPERATIONS

Hierarchical Rank	Operations	Defined by rules no.	Standard Order of Operations within this hierarchy
3	**, - (unary)	7, 3	right to left
2	*, /	6, 8	left to right
1	+, - (binary)	4, 5	left to right

In terms of this table, the *parentheses omission rules* are

DEF: *Parentheses omission rule 1:* Unless specified otherwise by use of parentheses, operations of superior rank in the hierarchy are performed before operations of inferior rank.

DEF: *Parentheses omission rule 2:* Unless specified otherwise by use of parentheses, operations of equal rank are performed in the sequence given in the last column of the Table. That is, operations of rank 3 are performed in the same sequence as reading the expression from right to left. Operations of rank 2 are performed in the same sequence as reading the expression from left to right. Operations of rank 1 are performed in the same sequence as reading the expression from left to right.

DEF: *Parentheses omission rule 3:* The outermost parentheses of a wfae can be omitted altogether.

DEF: *Parentheses omission rule 4:* If omission of parentheses would result in two arithmetic operators appearing immediately adjacent to each other, the parentheses must be retained.

Rule 4 limits the extent to which we can omit parentheses. For example, we *must not* omit the parentheses in the wfae A**(-3), since omission of the parentheses would result in the ungrammatical ("ill-formed") arithmetic expression A**-3. The operator ** (exponentiation) *must not* appear immediately adjacent to the operator - (unary minus).

Examples: We now give a number of examples to illustrate and explain these rules:

1. The wfae -W**6 involves two operators of hierarchical rank 3. It is therefore read from right to left: W is raised to the power 6 *first,* and then we take the negative of the result. Thus -W**6 is equivalent to -(W**6), and is different from (-W)**6.

2. 2**3**4 is to be read from right to left, also. It is therefore equivalent to 2**(3**4) = 2**81, and is different from (2**3)**4 = 8**4 = 4096.

3. A/B*C involves operations of rank 2, and is therefore performed in the sequence obtained by reading from left to right. That is, the division A/B is carried out *first*, and the result is multiplied by the content of memory location C. Thus A/B*C is equivalent to (A/B)*C and is different from A/(B*C).

4. A-B+C involves operators of rank 1, and should therefore be read from left to right. B is subtracted from A *first,* and C is added to the result. Thus, A-B+C is equivalent to (A-B)+C, and is different from A-(B+C).

5. The wfae given as an example before the Table of the hierarchy of operations can now be written in the simplified form (B/2.0)**A+((C-D)/8.5)**3. This is also the simplest form which we can achieve with ordinary mathematical notation, if we forego the use of horizontal fraction bars.

6. A-B/D**H+G**E*F is a wfae containing operators at all levels of the hierarchy. According to the hierarchical rules, the operations of rank 3 are performed first, i.e., we start by doing the exponentiations. If we insert parentheses to indicate this, the more explicit form of the wfae becomes: A-B/(D**H)+(G**E)*F. Thus we raise the value of G to the power given by E, and *then* multiply the result by the value of F. We raise the value of D to the power given by the value of H, and *then* divide the result into the value of B. The operations of lowest rank, that is the operations + and - in this wfae, are performed last of all.

Note: When in doubt about the sequence of operations in the absence of parentheses, it is simplest to use parentheses. However, it is hard to keep track of large numbers of parentheses, and correspondingly it is easy to make programming errors by omitting a final right parenthesis, or inserting a superfluous parenthesis; such errors are frequent not only in writing the programme with pencil on paper, but also when punching the programme onto cards. Thus, it is well worth while to become familiar with the parenthesis omission rules, and to employ them in programming.

DRILL EXERCISES FOR CHAPTER II:

1. Which of the following are grammatically incorrect real variable identifiers, and why?
   KILLER, 123GO, K123, DASTARD, $$$$, PROFESSOR, MAD, DOG, LOTTERY, LOTTRY, WHATINHELL, BE WARY, BEWARY.

2. Which of the following numerical constants do *not* represent truncated real numbers, and why?
   23., 23.000, 23, -23, -23., -23.000.

3. Write correct wfae to represent the following mathematical expressions, in each case first in completely bracketed form, then with maximum use of the parentheses omission rules:

   a) $A - \dfrac{B}{C+D}$

   b) $\dfrac{A-B}{C+D}$

   c) $\dfrac{A}{C+D} - B$

   d) $\dfrac{A}{C} - \dfrac{B}{D}$

   e) $\dfrac{A}{C+B/D} - E$

   f) $\dfrac{(A-B)(D-F)}{(A-C)(D-G)}$

   g) $3x^4 - 2x^2 + 1.34x - 2.5$

4. Which of the following assignment statements result in the real number 1.5 being stored in memory location FRED to machine accuracy?

   a) FRED=3/2

   b) FRED=3./1.+1.

   c) FRED=3./2.

   d) FRED=1.+2./2.

   e) FRED=(1.+2.)/2.

   f) FRED=0.75*2.0

   g) FRED=2.*0.7499999

5. Which of the following are well-formed arithmetic expressions involving real numbers only?

   a) CAT/MOUSE

   b) 3./NUMBER

   c) 3./ZNUMBER

   d) ZNUMBER1/ZNUMBER2

   e) BOY+GIRL

   f) CAT1*−CAT2

   g) LION1*(−LION2)

CHAPTER III

PROGRAMME FLOW CONTROL

A. Statement Numbers, "GO TO" Statement

Unless otherwise specified, a FORTRAN programme will be executed statement after statement in sequence, until the last statement is encountered. This would be much too restrictive, and there are a number of commands in the FORTRAN language to enable the programmer to tell the computer to execute statements in some other sequence.

To make this possible, it is necessary to give "labels" to FORTRAN statements. These are positive integers, ranging from 1 to 99999. They are referred to as *statement numbers*.

DEF: To number a statement, the statement number (which is an integer between 1 and 99999 inclusive) must appear on the card in columns 1 through 5. If the statement number has less than 5 digits, the number is "right-adjusted" within this "field"; that is, the last digit of the statement number always appears in column 5. Column 6 of the card must be blank. The numbered statement itself starts in column 7 of the card. No two statements can have the same statement number.

Thus, if we wish to number the assignment statement HEIGHT=5.89 with the statement number 1000 the card must read:

    1000 HEIGHT=5.89

where the numeral "1" appears in column 2 of the card, and the first character "H" of HEIGHT appears in column 7 of the card.

A later statement, in which HEIGHT is assigned a different value, might be numbered 2000:

    2000 HEIGHT=HEIGHT+1.5

Suppose that we use this value of HEIGHT to do some series of calculations, followed by a print-out of the result. We now wish to perform the same set of calculations again, with the value of HEIGHT increased by 1.5. Rather than writing the whole set of FORTRAN commands once more, we may write at this point.

    GO TO 2000

DEF: The *unconditional transfer* statement has the form GO TO *Number* where *Number* is the statement number of some FORTRAN command in the programme. The effect of this statement, in execution, is that the next instruction obeyed is the instruction numbered with the statement number *Number*.

In our example, the effect of the GO TO 2000 statement is that the next instruction obeyed is the instruction numbered 2000, i.e., the assignment statement HEIGHT=HEIGHT+1.5. Thus, the first time HEIGHT is set, in statement number 1000, the value of HEIGHT is 5.89. We then reach statement 2000, where we reset HEIGHT to 5.89+1.5 = 7.39. After some time, we reach the transfer statement GO TO 2000. At this point, the computer is told to obey statement number 2000 next. This resets HEIGHT to 7.39+1.5 = 8.89. Sometime later, we reach the GO TO 2000 statement the second time. This sends us to statement number 2000, which is now obeyed by the machine for the third time, resetting the value of HEIGHT to 8.89+1.5 = 10.39; and so on.

It is neither necessary nor desirable to number every statement. Numbers *must* be assigned to:

1.   statements to which control transfers take place; and

2.   statements immediately following a GO TO statement;

If a statement of the second type does not carry a statement number, then there is no way by which the flow of the programme can ever lead to that statement! (Explain!)

For all other statements, statement numbers are purely optional.

B.   Well-Formed Logical Expressions

Notice that we have already succeeded in producing a "looping" programme! We go round and round this loop, each time increasing HEIGHT by 1.5, without ever coming to a stop. Or rather, we stop only after we have exceeded the time limit imposed by the master programme.

To avoid such never-ending loops, we require "conditional transfers". Before explaining these, we need the concept of a "logical expression". A typical example of a well-formed logical expression (abbreviation: wfle) is (A.GE.B); this is read as "A is greater than or equal to B", and it can have only two possible values: .TRUE. if the content of memory location A is actually greater than or equal to the content of memory location B; and .FALSE. otherwise.

It is important to distinguish clearly between a well-formed *arithmetic* expression and a well-formed *logical* expression. The two are constructed according to different rules, and assume different values. A well-formed *arithmetic* expression is constructed according to the rules of Chapter II, and its value is always a *number*. A well-formed *logical* expression must be constructed according to the rules appearing below and its value is not a number at all, but rather is one of the two possibilities .TRUE. or .FALSE.

DEF: *Well-formed logical expressions (wfle)* are defined by the following set of rules. In these rules, W and V represent any two well-formed *arithmetic* expressions (wfae), and P and Q represent any two well-formed *logical* expressions (wfle).

1.   (W.EQ.V)   is a wfle which assumes the value .TRUE. iff ("if and only if") the numerical values of W and V are *equal.* The period signs before and after the alphabetic characters EQ are required.

2.   (W.GE.V)   is a wfle which assumes the value .TRUE. iff the value of W *is greater than or equal to* the value of V.

3. (W.GT.V) is a wfle which assumes the value .TRUE. iff the value of W is *greater than* the value of V.

4. (W.LE.V) is a wfle which assumes the value .TRUE. iff the value of W is *less than or equal to* the value of V.

5. (W.LT.V) is a wfle which assumes the value .TRUE, iff the value of W is *less than* the value of V.

6. (W.NE.V) is a wfle which assumes the value .TRUE. iff the value of W is *not equal* to the value of V.

7. (P.AND.Q) is a wfle which assumes the value .TRUE. iff *both* P has the value .TRUE. and Q has the value .TRUE. Note that P and Q here are wfle, not wfae.

8. (P.OR.Q) is a wfle which assumes the value .TRUE. iff *at least one* of P and Q has the value .TRUE.

9. (.NOT.P) is a wfle which assumes the value .TRUE. iff P has the value .FALSE. (negation of P).

Note: One must distinguish between a well-formed logical *expression* and its *value*. The well-formed logical expression (A.GE.B) may take the value TRUE. or .FALSE., depending upon the current numerical contents of memory locations A and B. For example, if the current content of A is 7.1 and the current content of B is 5.3, then the wfle (A.GE.B) has the current value .TRUE. . If, at a later stage in the execution of the programme, the number 18.7 is stored into memory location B (say by an assignment statement), then the wfle (A.GE.B) assumes the value .FALSE.

Example: Clearly, quite complicated wfle can be built up by repeated application of these rules. Consider the wfle:

(((TRUMAN.GT.HITLER).AND.(PROF.EQ.(DAMNED+DOG))).OR.(SAINT.NE.DEVIL))

Let the current contents of the storage locations TRUMAN, HITLER, PROF, DAMNED, DOG, SAINT, and DEVIL be, respectively, 102.5, 23.8, 2.5, 1.2, 1.3, 8.9, and 8.9. Then (TRUMAN.GT.HITLER) has the value .TRUE., and so does (PROF.EQ.(DAMNED+DOG)); on the other hand, (SAINT.NE. DEVIL) has the value .FALSE. The wfle as a whole has the value .TRUE., since the part before the .OR. has the value .TRUE. (see rule 8 above).

Note: The comparison operator .EQ., testing for equality of the values of two arithmetic expressions, can easily give misleading results, and should be used with great caution. The trouble is that real numbers in the machine are not exact, but are truncated to a limited number of significant digits (approximately 7 significant decimal digits). When arithmetic calculations are carried out with such numbers, the result is in general only approximate, not exact. For example, the sum of 1.2 and 1.3 may turn out to be 2.499997 in the machine, rather than 2.500000. If this happens, the comparison (PROF.EQ.(DAMNED+DOG)) gives rise to the incorrect value .FALSE. . Only in integer arithmetic (see Chapter X) can one be sure of exact results. *The comparison operators .EQ. and .NE. should be used only with integer arithmetic.*

Unlike arithmetic expressions, logical expressions should always be kept simple. "Tricky" wfle often give rise to programming errors, and should be avoided. The FORTRAN language contains parentheses omission rules for wfle, which are given in small print below, for the sake of completeness. But these rules are not needed for simple student programmes, and can be skipped in a first reading of this Chapter.

Just as for wfae, there is a hierarchy of operations for the operations involved in evaluating wfle. This hierarchy appears in the TABLE below:

TABLE III. 1. HIERARCHY OF LOGICAL OPERATIONS

Hierarchical Rank	Operation	Defined by rule number
5	Evaluation of all arithmetic expressions, by rules of Chapter II.	
4	.EQ.,.GT.,.GE.,.LE.,.LT.,.NE.	1,2,3,4,5,6
3	.NOT.	9
2	.AND.	7
1	.OR.	8

In terms of this table, the parentheses omission rules for wfle are:

DEF: Parentheses omission rule 1: Unless specified otherwise by use of parentheses, operations of superior rank in the hierarchy are performed before operations of inferior rank.

DEF: Parentheses omission rule 2: Unless specified otherwise by use of parentheses, operations of rank 4 in the table are performed in the same sequence as reading the logical expression from left to right.

DEF: Parentheses omission rule 3: In logical assignment statements, but not in logical IF statements, the outermost parentheses of a wfle can be omitted altogether. (See later for these two types of statements).

DEF: Parentheses omission rule 4: Two logical operators may appear in sequence (without intervening parentheses) only if the second one is the logical operator .NOT.; if omission of parentheses would result in a violation of this rule, the parentheses must be retained.

Example: With these rules, it turns out that all parentheses can be omitted from our earlier example of a wfle, to wit, we may now write:

TRUMAN.GT.HITLER.AND.PROF.EQ.DAMNED+DOG.OR.SAINT.NE.DEVIL

According to the hierarchy, the first operation performed is the evaluation of the wfae DAMNED+DOG; next, the computer performs the comparison operations of hierarchical rank 4, i.e., the computer evaluates the wfle TRUMAN.GT.HITLER, PROF.EQ.(DAMNED+DOG), and SAINT.NE.DEVIL; next comes the operation of rank 2, i.e. the operation .AND.; last of all, the computer evaluates the result of the logical operation of rank 1, i.e., the operation .OR. As it turns out, this agrees precisely with the order of evaluation specified by the many parentheses before.

Nonetheless, the earlier warnings stand: Avoid complicated logical expressions in the first place, and don't be too eager to omit parentheses even if the rules allow it. The parentheses in a wfle help greatly in reading the expression, and thereby aid in avoiding programming errors.

20

C. The Logical "IF" Statement

The *conditional jump* statement IF can be used to test whether some wfle is .TRUE. or .FALSE., and alter the programme flow correspondingly. A simple example is provided by the following sequence of two statements, the first of which is the IF statement:

```
IF (A.LT.0.0) A= −A
B=A**0.5
```

This sequence has the following effect during execution of the object programme:

1. If the content of memory location A is negative, the wfle (A.LT.0.0) has the value .TRUE., and this causes the rest of the IF statement to be obeyed by the machine; that is, the command A= −A is actually executed.

2. On the other hand, if the present content of A is zero or positive, then the wfle (A.LT.0.0) has the value .FALSE., and this causes the remainder of the IF statement to be *skipped*. In this second case, the command B=A**0.5 is the next command obeyed by the machine.

We note that this particular sequence of two statements ensures that we do not attempt to take the square root of a negative number: If A is negative initially, the command A=−A is obeyed, with the result that the content of storage location A is replaced by its negative, which is then a positive number. If A contains a positive number, or zero, initially, the command A=−A is skipped. In either case, by the time the machine obeys the command B=A**0.5, the content of storage location A is a non-negative number.

DEF: The *logical IF* statement has the form IF *(P) S* where *P* stands for any well-formed logical expression (wfle), and *S* stands for any executable statement other than another logical IF statement or a DO statement. The terms "executable statement" and "DO statement" will be defined later on; for the present we note that assignment statements and GO TO statements are both permitted statements *S* in the form IF *(P) S*. In execution of the object programme, the statement *S* is obeyed if *P* has the value .TRUE.; the statement *S* is skipped if *P* has the value .FALSE.

This definition of the logical IF, or conditional jump instruction, may appear very limited, since only one command is immediately affected by the IF, namely the command S. In fact, however, the logical IF is a most powerful statement. All that is required is to have an *unconditional* jump statement GO TO as the statement S. The unconditional jump is then executed if and only if the condition *P* is satisfied (if and only if the wfle *P* has the value .TRUE.).

Example: Let us use the earlier example, with its infinite loop, as an illustration. Suppose we wish to stop the set of calculations as soon as HEIGHT becomes greater than or equal to 97.8. This can be done as follows (note that 97.8-1.5=96.3):

```
1000  HEIGHT=5.89
2000  HEIGHT=HEIGHT+1.5
      ...  (OTHER FORTRAN STATEMENTS USING THE CURRENT VALUE OF HEIGHT)
3000  IF (HEIGHT.LT.96.3) GO TO 2000
      STOP
```

Let us follow through this example in detail. HEIGHT is set to 5.89 when statement number 1000 is obeyed. HEIGHT is immediately reset to 5.89+1.5=7.39 by execution of statement 2000. We then obey the other commands (which are not written explicitly) using the value 7.39 for HEIGHT. When we reach the logical IF statement, statement number 3000, we evaluate the wfle (HEIGHT.LT.96.3); since memory location HEIGHT contains the number 7.39 at this moment, the wfle has the value .TRUE.; we therefore *obey* the command GO TO 2000. The next command executed by the machine is command number 2000. This has the effect of increasing the value of HEIGHT to 7.39+1.5=8.89. The other FORTRAN statements are now executed once more, but with HEIGHT equal to 8.89. When we reach statement number 3000, the wfle still has the value .TRUE.; hence we obey the command GO TO 2000, once more, and proceed to increase HEIGHT to 8.89+1.5=10.39. This process of going around the loop continues many times. When HEIGHT has the value 95.89, the wfle (HEIGHT.LT.96.3) is still true, and we still obey the command GO TO 2000. Execution of the command number 2000 causes HEIGHT to increase to 95.89+1.5=97.39. The other FORTRAN commands are obeyed with this new value of HEIGHT. However, when we now get to statement number 3000, the wfle (HEIGHT.LT.96.3) has the value .FALSE., since 97.39 is not less than 96.3. Therefore the command GO TO 2000 is *skipped,* and the next command obeyed by the machine is the command STOP. As expected, we have the definition:

DEF: In the execution phase, the statement STOP causes execution of the object programme to be terminated. The FORTRAN master programme resumes full control, and starts reading in the next student job.

Thus, we are no longer in an infinite loop. Furthermore, we have stopped at the right point: if we had gone back to statement 2000 once more, the new value of HEIGHT would have become 97.39+1.5=98.89; this would have exceeded the desired upper limit 97.8 (see the statement of the desired condition at the beginning of this *Example).*

D. Clean Coding

Although the loop in the above example is coded correctly, and results in calculations being performed with values of HEIGHT equal to 7.39, 8.89, 10.39, ... 95.89, 97.39, and only these values of HEIGHT, nonetheless the above is an example of *bad coding.* The value of HEIGHT set initially by statement number 1000, that is the value 5.89, is not used at all in the calculations; furthermore, the number which appears in the explicit condition (HEIGHT.LT.96.3) is misleading to the casual reader, since in fact the last value of HEIGHT used inside the loop is 97.39, which exceeds 96.3; the true condition for termination of the loop is that the value of HEIGHT to be used in the calculations should stay below 97.8=96.3+1.5.

This coding may appear only slightly awkward, and is certainly not actually wrong. Nonetheless it is most important to get into good coding habits early. Student exercise programmes containing only a handful of statements altogether, can be made to work in spite of awkward coding. But when you progress to real calculations, the programmes become much longer, and awkward coding leads you to commit many more coding errors than clean coding. Furthermore, the worst of all, with awkward coding the coding errors become much harder to find. In this early stage of student exercise coding, the most frequent errors are violations of the language rules of FORTRAN and these are detected by the FORTRAN compiler itself (see Chapter VI). But in more advanced coding, the trivial errors which arise from violation of the grammar of FORTRAN are corrected quickly enough, and are rare anyway. The dangerous errors arise from incorrect relations between different FORTRAN statements, for example, from finishing a loop too late by one step, or too early by one step.

The reason for the awkwardness of the coding in the example above is the location of the command HEIGHT=HEIGHT+1.5 at the *beginning* of the loop. This command should be placed at the *end* of the loop. Let us suppose that the first statement of the desired calculation with the current value of HEIGHT is WIDTH=3.1*HEIGHT. Then the loop can be, and should be, recoded as follows:

```
1000 HEIGHT=7.39
1500 WIDTH=3.1*HEIGHT
     ...(OTHER FORTRAN STATEMENTS USING THE CURRENT VALUE OF HEIGHT)
2000 HEIGHT=HEIGHT+1.5
3000 IF(HEIGHT.LT.97.8) GO TO 1500
     STOP
```

During the execution phase, the effect of this programme is exactly the same as before. But the coding is now *clean:* The value of HEIGHT set before entering the loop is the first value of HEIGHT actually used in the loop, and the condition (HEIGHT.LT.97.8) states correctly the limitation on the values of HEIGHT which we wish to employ inside the loop.

Note that the only statement which *requires* a statement number in the above programme is statement number 1500, for this is the *only* statement to which an unconditional control transfer is made. The other statement numbers have been assigned for convenience in discussing the programme.

Note also that all our statement numbers are four-digit integers, that they are widely spaced numerically, and that they form a strictly increasing sequence of numbers. None of this is *necessary*, but these are all aspects of *clean coding*. A very common programming error is to assign duplicate statement numbers, i.e., to assign the same statement number to two or more distinct FORTRAN statements. Keeping all statement numbers in increasing numerical order minimizes the chance of making that particular error. Keeping the statement numbers well separated from each other is desirable to allow insertion of additional statement numbers in between, as required. For example, when we found out that we needed a numbered statement between statements number 1000 and 2000 of the earlier programme, there were lots of numbers left available for use in between. By assigning the statement number 1500 to this extra statement, as we did, we have left ourselves lots of leeway for inserting additional numbered statements on either side of statement 1500.

E. Loops and Flow Charts

The following features of finite loops are universal: There is a loop *variable* whose value decides whether we continue the loop or exit from the loop. This loop variable is *preset* before the loop itself is entered. Within the loop, the loop variable is *incremented* and *tested*.

In our example, the loop variable has the identifier name HEIGHT. It is preset by statement number 1000. The loop itself extends from statement 1500 to statement 3000, inclusive. The loop variable is incremented by statement number 2000, and is tested by statement number 3000.

It is very helpful to look at the flow of control in a programme by means of a *flow diagram, or flow chart*. This is a chart containing rectangles and other simple geometrical figures, together with directed lines (lines with arrows) between these figures. Within each figure we indicate some connected set of operations, which form part of the programme. Unconditional jump statements (GO TO) are represented by directed lines, conditional jump statements (IF) are represented by ovals containing the condition (wflf) to be tested, with a pair of directed lines emerging, one labelled "T" for .TRUE., the other labelled "F" for .FALSE.; and so on. As an *example of a flow chart*, we show below a flow chart for the loop which we have just been discussing.

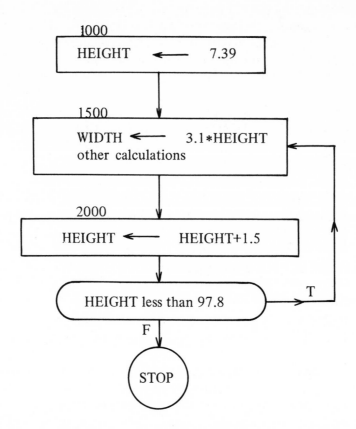

Note that the number on the upper left of each "box" is the statement number for the corresponding statement in the FORTRAN programme. The "loop" in this programme is obvious geometrically, just by looking at the picture, whereas it requires some analysis to "see" the loop directly from the FORTRAN commands.

Example: *Cumulative Investment:* A man has a principal sum P, equal to $500, to invest each year. He invests it at an interest rate of R percent, say 8 percent. If he follows this investment plan for 30 years, what is the total value T of his investment at the end of that time?

Solution: We refer back to the first example given in Chapter I. If an investment P accrues at R percent, for Y years, the value V at the end of that time is $V=P(1 + 0.01R)^Y$.

Here we have a number of such investments. The investment made at the beginning of the 30th year accumulates interest for only 1 year, i.e., Y=1 for this case; the investment made at the beginning of the 29th year accumulates interest for exactly 2 years, i.e., Y=2 for that case; finally the investment made at the very beginning accumulates interest for the full 30 years, i.e., Y=30 for this case. We must compute all the separate values, and add them up to give a total T. We shall do so by means of a loop on the number of years Y during which each investment draws interest.(*)

In coding a loop, it is best to work "from the inside out": that is, we start with the computations which must be done every time we go around the loop. In our case, these are:

1.   we must compute the value V of the investment after Y years
2.   we must add this value to the total T

(*)   This addition can be done more efficiently by using the mathematical solution for the sum of a geometric progression. But we want to illustrate coding of a loop, not give a lesson in mathematics.

Having decided this, we must then arrange for the loop to start off with correct values, and to end at the right point. The values we wish to start with are P=500.0, R=8.0, Y=1.0, and an initial total T=0.0. The loop should stop after Y has reached 30 years, that is, after Y=30 and before Y=31. In order to avoid possible trouble from roundoff errors (see the discussion in Section B), we shall test whether Y exceeds 30.5. If it does, we want to go out of the loop. The flow diagram and FORTRAN code follow:

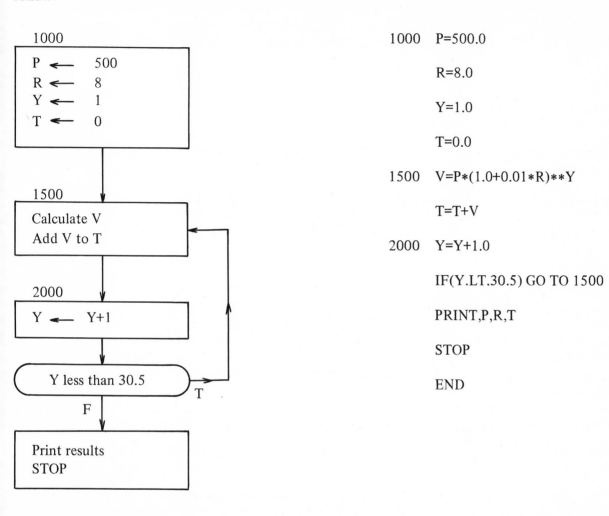

```
1000    P=500.0

        R=8.0

        Y=1.0

        T=0.0

1500    V=P*(1.0+0.01*R)**Y

        T=T+V

2000    Y=Y+1.0

        IF(Y.LT.30.5) GO TO 1500

        PRINT,P,R,T

        STOP

        END
```

F. The Two-Way Branch

Example: The two-way branch: **Very** frequently we wish to perform one set of calculations if a certain condition is satisfied, and another set of calculations altogether if that condition is violated. As an example, consider the solution of the quadratic equation $ax^2+bx+c=0$. This has real roots if and only if the discriminant $D=b^2-4ac$ is non-negative. Suppose that the coefficients a, b, and c are already stored in the machine, in memory locations A, B, and C respectively. We wish to compute the discriminant, and test it. If the discriminant is non-negative, we compute the two real roots; if the discriminant is negative, we compute the real and imaginary parts of the two complex conjugate roots. The formula which we use for the roots is:

First root $= x_1 + iy_1 = (-b + D^{1/2})/(2a)$

Second root $= x_2 + iy_2 = (-b-D^{1/2})/(2a)$

If D is greater than or equal to zero, $D^{\frac{1}{2}}$ is a real number; both roots are purely real, i.e., $y_1 = y_2 = 0$, and x_1, x_2 are given directly by the formulas.

On the other hand, if D is negative, $D^{\frac{1}{2}}$ is pure imaginary; we write

$$D^{\frac{1}{2}} = i(-D)^{\frac{1}{2}} \text{ for negative D}$$

where i is the imaginary unit (square root of -1) and $(-D)^{\frac{1}{2}}$ is a positive real number, since -D is positive. Separating out the real and imaginary parts in the formulas for the two roots, we obtain:

First root: $\quad x_1 = -b/(2a) \qquad y_1 = (-D)^{\frac{1}{2}}/(2a)$

$\qquad\qquad\qquad\qquad\qquad\qquad\qquad\qquad\qquad$ Negative D

Second root: $\quad x_2 = -b/(2a) \qquad y_2 = -(-D)^{\frac{1}{2}}/(2a)$

Thus we must perform two quite different sets of computations, depending upon whether D is negative, or D is greater than or equal to zero.

Rather than writing down a programme immediately, let us first show what we want by means of a *flow diagram.* We must compute D, test its sign, and then go into one of two branches of the programme; the two branches must then rejoin for further computations. The flow chart is:

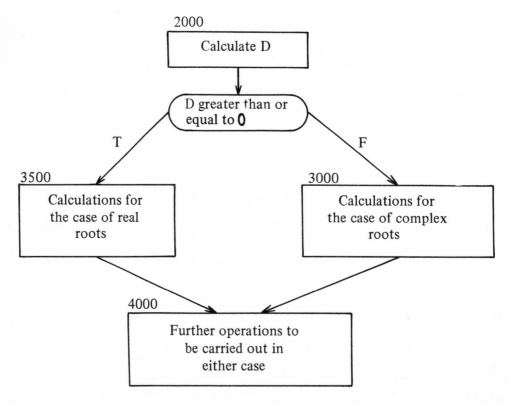

The flow chart shows clearly what is meant by a "two-way branch". We have inserted statement numbers in this flow chart, to correspond to the programme now to be written down; in practice, the statement numbers would be inserted by the programmer one by one, as he actually writes the programme and assigns these numbers. Unlike the earlier flow chart, this chart does not contain a loop, and of course neither does the programme written by use of this chart.

A clean way of programming this two-way branch is:

```
2000 DSCRM=B**2-4.0*A*C
C     NOW TEST THE DISCRIMINANT
2500 IF (DSCRM.GE.0.0) GO TO 3500
C     THE SECTION WHICH FOLLOWS HANDLES COMPLEX ROOTS
3000 X1=-B/(2.0*A)
     X2=X1
     ROOTI=(-DSCRM)**0.5
     Y1=ROOTI/(2.0*A)
     Y2=-Y1
     GO TO 4000
C     THE SECTION WHICH FOLLOWS HANDLES REAL ROOTS
3500 ROOT=DSCRM**0.5
     X1=(-B+ROOT)/(2.0*A)
     X2=(-B-ROOT)/(2.0*A)
3700 Y1=0.0
     Y2=0.0
C     PATHS REJOIN HERE
4000 ... (NEXT FORTRAN STATEMENT, TO BE EXECUTED IN EITHER CASE)
```

Explanation of example: Statement number 2000 evaluates the discriminant. We use the identifier name DSCRM rather than just D, to help the memory. It is surprising how easily the meanings of simple letters, such as D, are forgotten by the programmer himself, from one week to the next. Furthermore, with simple letters, one runs a big chance of using the same identifier name for two different quantities in the calculation; this type of programming error is among the hardest to detect.

The statement following after statement number 2000 is a *comment*.

DEF: A card containing the letter C in column 1 is a *comment card*. Comments are not translated into machine language by FORTRAN but are merely reproduced in the printed listing of the source programme (see phase 2 in Chapter I).

Comments are inserted to remind yourself, and explain to others reading the programme, just what it is you meant to do. Comments are most desirable, and experienced coders insert large numbers of comments into all their programmes. A programme without comments, or with only a few comments, is exceedingly hard to read, as well as to correct. Unless one knows, from the comments, what the commands were meant to do, it is difficult indeed to tell whether they actually carry out the programmer's intention.

As explained by this comment, the next statement, numbered 2500, serves to test the discriminant.

If the condition (DSCRM.GE.0.0) is .TRUE., we obey the command GO TO 3500, that is, we jump forward to statement 3500. This is the first statement of the ".TRUE. branch" of our two-way branch. In our case, .TRUE. means that the discriminant is non-negative, so that the two roots of the quadratic are real. Since both formulas involve the square root of the discriminant, we evaluate this square root once and for all in statement 3500. This has the effect of *saving computer time* in the execution phase: evaluating a square root is a lengthy process, and we want to do it as rarely as possible. The four statements immediately following statement 3500 serve to evaluate the real parts, X1 and X2, and the imaginary parts, Y1 and Y2, of the two roots of the quadratic. The identifier names X1, X2, Y1, and Y2, are all grammatically correct real number identifiers. For purely real roots, the imaginary parts Y1 and Y2 are naturally equal to zero. Note that we include a decimal point in writing the zero, i.e., we write Y1=0.0 rather than Y1=0; the character string 0.0 denotes the *real number* zero (since the character string contains a decimal point), whereas the single character 0 denotes the *integer* zero. The statement Y1=0 would actually give the desired result; but machine time would be wasted by converting the integer zero to the real number zero, before storing that real number into memory location Y1. Having calculated everything that needs to be calculated in the case of real roots, we now reach statement number 4000, at which the two branches rejoin.

Let us now see what happens *if the condition (DSCRM.GE.0.0) is .FALSE.* In that case, the command GO TO 3500 is *skipped,* and the next command obeyed in execution is command number 3000. This is the first statement of the ".FALSE. branch" of our two-way branch. Note that the ".TRUE. branch" involves jumping forward in the programme, whereas the ".FALSE. branch" comes immediately after the logical IF statement. In our case, .FALSE. means that the discriminant is negative, so that the two roots of the quadratic are conjugate complex numbers. The real part of both roots equals -b/(2a), and this real part is computed and set first. Note that we save machine time by writing X2=X1, rather than X2=-B/(2.0*A). The command X2=X1 means that the machine makes the content of memory location X2 equal to whatever is contained in memory location X1 at this moment. The alternative form X2=−B/(2.0*A) would involve the machine in a completely unnecessary additional calculation, including one multiplication, one division, and the taking of a negative. Having evaluated the real parts X1 and X2, we now turn to the imaginary parts. Since DSCRM now contains a negative number, we cannot just take its square root (if we did attempt to do so, the FORTRAN master programme would stop execution of the programme, print out an error message, and go on to the next student job in the batch). However, (−DSCRM) is a wfae whose value is a positive number, and whose square root we may therefore take. We call this ROOTI to indicate that it denotes the imaginary part of the square root. We then compute Y1 and Y2, the latter again in such a way as to save machine time. Finally, having done all that needs to be done for complex roots, we jump straight to statement 4000, where the two branches rejoin. The unconditional transfer statement GO TO 4000 at this point is *necessary;* without it, the next statement obeyed would be statement number 3500, which would stop programme execution through the attempt to take the square root of a negative number! More generally, the last statement of the ".FALSE. branch" in a two-way branch must be a GO TO statement, to jump over the ".TRUE. branch".

Coding error in the example: Before you read on, try to find the coding error yourself!

Well, here it is: in the programme as written, we have failed to allow for the case a=0, when the quadratic equation $ax^2+bx+c=0$ degenerates to a linear equation bx+c=0. There are several divisions by 2a in the commands of the example, and these are divisions by zero in this nasty case. We therefore require a "pre-test" to check that the content of A is not zero. This can be programmed as follows:

```
1500 IF(A.NE.0.0) GO TO 2000
C      DEGENERATE CASE, LINEAR EQUATION
1600 X1=-C/B
     X2=X1
C      NOW GO TO THE POINT WHERE Y1 AND Y2 ARE SET EQUAL TO ZERO
     GO TO 3700
C      NORMAL CASE, QUADRATIC EQUATION, EVALUATE THE DISCRIMINANT
2000 DSCRM=B**2-4.0*A*C
     ... (FROM HERE ON, SAME AS BEFORE)
```

Note that we assigned the statement number 3700 to the statement Y1=0.0 before, with malice aforethought: any statement to which we wish to transfer control must carry a statement number. Note however that we could have supplied this statement number 3700 as an afterthought: there is lots of room between statement numbers 3500 and 4000, for just this purpose.

If we wish to distinguish the special case of repeated roots (discriminant = 0) from the case of two distinct real roots, we require still a third conditional transfer (logical IF) statement. Try to programme this yourself!

The FORTRAN statements IF and GO TO are logically entirely sufficient to organize all possible loops and other control transfers. Additional facilities for programme flow control and loop organization are available in FORTRAN and will be discussed in Chapter XI. For the time being, IF and GO TO are all you need to write programmes and have them work correctly on the machine.

DRILL EXERCISES FOR CHAPTER III

1. Construct well-formed logical expressions for the following conditions:

    a) A exceeds B, and either C is less than 3.0 or D equals 5.0 or both

    b) A lies between 2.0*B and 4.0*C, that is, A is greater than 2.0*B and less than 4.0*C

    c) X is greater than at least one of A, B, C

    d) X is greater than all of A, B, C

    e) X differs from A, and Y differs from all of B, C, D

    f) X lies between 1.5 and 2.3, and Y is either less than 1.5 or greater than 2.3

    g) either both X and Y are less than 1.5, or both exceed 2.3

2. State, in words, the meaning of the following wfle:

    a) (X.LE.Y).OR.(Y.LT.Z)

    b) (Z.GT.Y).AND.(X.GT.Z)

    c) (X.GE.2.0).AND.(X.LE.4.0).OR.(Y.GT.1.5).AND.(Y.LT.5.6)

    d) .NOT.((X.GE.2.0).AND.(X.LE.4.0))

    e) (X.LT.2.0).OR.(X.GT.4.0)

3. Correct the following statements for grammatical errors:

a) IF(A=B) GO TO 2300

b) IF A.GT.B GO TO 1525

c) IF(A.LE.B) GO TO C

d) IF(A EQ B) GO TO 3000

e) IF(A.GE.C.AND.(B.EQ.D) GO TO 1000

f) IF(PROGRAM.EQ.RUBBISH GO TO 2000

4. Write flow diagrams and short programme segments to do the following:

a) If F is positive, move the larger one of C and D to location BIG; if F is negative or zero, move the smaller one of C and D to location SMALL

b) If both A and B lie between 2.5 and 3.5 (exclusive of the endpoints of the interval), move D to location TEST; if A lies inside the interval, B outside, move C to TEST; if A lies outside the interval, B inside, move D to TEST; if both A and B lie outside the interval, move C to location TEST

c) When X is negative, Y is set equal to zero; when X is zero, Y is set equal to ½; when X is positive but less than 1.0, Y is set equal to X; and when X is larger than or equal to 1.0, Y is set equal to 1.0.

5. Which of the following statement numbers are valid?

```
COLUMNS:   12345678...

A)           1000HEIGHT=1.
B)           100 HEIGHT=1.
C)          14000 HEIGHT=1.
D)        100000 HEIGHT=1.
E)             1)  HEIGHT=1.
F)            10X HEIGHT=1.
G)          14000HEIGHT=1.
```

6. What is wrong with the following programme segments?

```
A)         A=1.0
    1000   IF(A.EQ.10.0) STOP
           A=A+1.0
           B=A**2
           GO TO 1000

B)         A=A+1.0
           GO TO 1100
           B=A**2
           C=(B+1.0)**0.5
    1100   D=A+B+C
```

7. We wish to programme a "three-way branch" to the following specifications: if A is negative, control is to be transferred to statement 1500; if A lies between zero and 1.0 (inclusive), control is to be transferred to statement 2000; and if A exceeds unity, control is to be transferred to statement number 2500. Can you write this three-way branch using

    a) three logical IF statements?

    b) two logical IF statements?

    c) one logical IF statement?

8. Same specifications as problem 7, except that for negative A, programme flow is to continue on after the last logical IF statement of the set of IF statements (that is, statement number 1500 is to come right after the set of IF statements). Answer the same questions a, b, c.

CHAPTER IV

FREE INPUT AND OUTPUT IN WATFOR

A. Free Output

So far, we know how to make the computer compute and go through loops. But the machine does not as yet print out any results! The standard FORTRAN IV commands for printing out results are among the most difficult FORTRAN commands to learn, and to use correctly. They will be described and discussed in Chapter XV. To make life easier for the beginner, WATFOR contains a much simpler command which will satisfy our needs for the time being.

DEF: A *simple list* consists of identifiers, separated by commas. There is *no* comma after the last item of the list.

DEF: The WATFOR statement "PRINT,*List*", where *"List"* is a simple list, causes the machine to print the current values of all the items in the *List,* in sequence. The first item of the *List* appears on a new line; thereafter, items appear next to each other in a line, a new line being started only when the current line has no more room.

Note: The list must *not* contain actual numbers, only identifier names which tell the machine from which memory locations to take the numbers to be printed. Thus the statement PRINT, HEIGHT, WIDTH is grammatically correct, and causes a line of output containing two numbers, the first of which is the current numerical value of HEIGHT, the second is the current numerical value of WIDTH. But the statement PRINT,6.89,20.67 is *grammatically wrong;* it will not be translated by the compiler, nor will it be obeyed during the execution phase.

The numbers printed out by WATFOR appear in "exponential form", which we shall now explain. The number 523.78 can also be written as 0.52378×10^3, since $1000 = 10 \times 10 \times 10 = 10^3$. In WATFOR output, this number would be printed as (*)

   0.5237800E 03

That is, the "mantissa" 0.5237800 is printed with exactly 7 decimal digits following the decimal point, and a zero just before the decimal point. The letter E indicates that an exponent of 10 follows. This exponent is printed as a two-digit number, with a blank space before it if the exponent is positive, a minus sign before it if the exponent is negative.

As an example of a number with a negative exponent of ten, consider the number 0.00052378. This can also be written as $0.52378 \times (1/1000) = 0.52378 \times (1/10)^3 = 0.52378 \times 10^{-3}$, using the convention that 10 raised to the power (-3) is the same thing as 1/10 raised to the power 3. In WATFOR output, this number would be printed as:

   0.5237800E-03

(*)   Note that a narrow printed symbol 0 is used for "zero", whereas a wide O is used for the letter "oh".

It should be apparent by now that the exponent of a number in exponential form is a good quick guide to the size of the number, and one should look at the exponent first of all. There is, let us face it, a good deal of difference between the numbers 523.78 and 0.00052378; but in exponential form, this difference appears as the difference between "E 03" and "E-03", only!

The exponential form of a number *may be,* but *need not be,* used in other statements of the programme. If the exponential form is used for constants within the programme, it is not necessary to write it in strictly the same form as is used in WATFOR free output. In particular, it is not necessary to start the mantissa with a zero before the decimal point, nor need the mantissa have exactly seven digits after the decimal point. For example, the number 0.0000005 could be written as 0.5E-6 or as 5.0E-7 or as 500.E-9, as well as in the standard WATFOR output form 0.5000000E-06. For elementary programming, it is best to avoid the exponential form for all except very large and very small numbers.

Beginning programmers tend to become confused about when output occurs as a result of a PRINT statement in the source language programme. Referring back to Chapter I, we recall that there are two distinct phases in the handling of a job:

1. The compile phase, during which the FORTRAN compiler is fully in charge; the compiler reads one source language card after another, and translates the contents of each card from source language (FORTRAN language) into machine language. At the same time, the compiler lists (prints out) the contents of each card onto the printed output page.

2. The execution phase, during which the translated ("object") programme is in charge, with the FORTRAN master programme merely exercising more or less paternal supervision.

A PRINT statement in the source language programme causes printed output in phase 2 above, the execution phase, *not* in phase 1. In fact, it is not the PRINT statement itself which causes the output; rather, the *translated version* of the FORTRAN language statement PRINT causes printed output during the execution phase.

Thus, on the final printed output from the run, the listing of the entire source language programme appears *first;* output *numbers,* arising from the translated PRINT statements during the execution phase, appear *afterwards.*

Another way of saying the same thing is this: The listing of the source programme (which comes first) is produced under control of the compiler; printed output numbers (which come later) are produced under control of the object programme. In order to create an object programme which causes printed output of numbers, it is necessary to insert PRINT statements into the source language programme; these PRINT statements are translated into machine language by the FORTRAN compiler; when these translated statements are reached during the execution of the object programme, they cause printout of numbers to occur.

B.   Free Input

Having discussed printing of output in its simplest form, we now turn our attention to *input* of numbers. If all numbers with which the machine calculates appear explicitly in assignment statements such as HEIGHT=5.89, then the object programme can be executed only once. If executed once more, the machine merely prints out *identical* output. Having gone to all the trouble of writing a programme, we want this programme to work with many different input data numbers, nor merely with one set of data. To permit this, the object programme is able to read *data cards* from the card reader attached to the computer, *during the execution phase.*

Punched cards contain 80 columns, each of which may contain a single character.

DEF: A *numerical data card* is a punched card containing one or more decimal numbers, with or without + and − signs, with blank spaces and/or commas separating any two numbers on the card. Numbers without explicit sign will be taken to be positive.

DEF: The WATFOR statement READ, *List* ,where *List* is a simple list, causes the machine to read input numbers from the available numerical data cards during the execution phase. As many items as there are items in the list are read from the numerical data cards, starting with the first card not previously read. The first number on that card is placed into the memory location associated with the first identifier in the list; the second number read is placed into the memory location associated with the second identifier in the list; and so on until we reach the end of the list.

Example: Consider a programme containing as the first two statements

    READ,HEIGHT,WEIGHT
    READ,DAMNED,DOG,PROF

and suppose that there are three numerical data cards, punched as follows:

    First card: 6.89, 10.6, 7.3
    Second card: 4.65, 7.01, 23.77, 12.7
    Third card: 2.12, 3.75

These cards appear in the card deck later on, *not* right after the cards with the READ statements (see Chapter V).

During the compilation phase, the two READ statements are translated into machine language. Then, later on, during the execution phase, execution of the (translated) first READ statement causes HEIGHT to assume the value 6.89 and WEIGHT to assume the value 10.6. These are the first two data numbers available. Execution of the (translated) second READ statement causes numbers to be read in from the *next* data card; thus DAMNED assumes the value 4.65, DOG assumes the value 7.01, and PROF assumes the value 23.77. Notice that the number 7.3, the last number on the first of the data cards, has been "lost": it was not needed for the first READ statement, and the second READ statement starts by reading a new card.

If another READ statement is encountered in execution, later on, the first number placed into memory by that READ statement will be the number 2.12, i.e., the first number appearing on the next data card.

Although each READ statement, in execution, causes reading to start from the beginning of a new data card, it is possible that the *List* contains more identifier names than there are numbers on that new data card. In that case, reading continues, card after card, number after number on each card, until the *List* is filled up with numbers. For example, suppose that the first two statements of the programme are:

    READ,A,B
    READ,C,D,E,F,G,H,P,Q,R,S,T

and suppose that the first four data cards read

First data card:	6.7, 4.5, 78.3
Second data card:	3.2, 3.4, 5.8, 4.7
Third data card:	6.1, 6.3, 6.8, 3.9, 9.1, 12.5
Fourth data card:	4.8, 5.73

Then the values of A and B in the machine are set to A=6.7 and B=4.5, from the first data card. The number 78.3 on that data card is "lost". The second READ statement causes input of numbers to start from the second data card, i.e., C is set equal to 3.2. Thereafter, reading of cards continues until the list is exhausted, i.e., we set, successively, D=3.4, E=5.8, F=4.7 (now we have exhausted data card 2), G=6.1, H=6.3, P=6.8, Q=3.9, R=9.1, S=12.5 (now we have exhausted data card number 3), T=4.8. The number 5.73 on the fourth data card is "lost".

Just as the printing from the PRINT statement, the reading arising from a READ statement occurs *during the execution of the object programme,* after the entire translation process has been finished. For this reason, the data cards which are to be read must appear in the card deck after the entire source language programme, and after the control card $ENTRY (or //DATA, as the case may be) which initiates execution of the object programme. This is discussed in more detail, and examples are given, in Chapter V.

C.   Free Input and Output for a Simple Programme

As an *example* of the use of free input and output, let us consider the programme of Chapter III, Section F, for computing the roots of a quadratic equation. We recall that we wrote a set of FORT-RAN statements to compute the discriminant and organize a two–way branch, depending upon whether this discriminant is negative (complex roots of the quadratic equation) or not (real roots of the quadratic equation).

We then found that we had made an error, by omitting to test for the special case A=0.0, in which the quadratic equation degenerates to a linear one.

When the two programme segments arising in this way are combined, we still do not have a complete programme: We must still organize *input of data,* namely the values of the coefficients A, B, and C, and *output of results,* that is, the values of the two roots x_1+iy_1 and x_2+iy_2.

All right, what do we have to do? Before starting the computation, we must read the input data. So the first statement of the programme is

1000 READ,A,B,C

The next statement *could* already be one of the "working" statements, doing the calculation. But this would be a grievous mistake!

The *first thing we must do is "echo-check" the input numbers,* that is, we must put a statement

PRINT,A,B,C

immediately after the READ statement. After translation of the programme from FORTRAN into machine language is finished, and execution of the object programme has started, the effect of these two statements in sequence is the following: Every time the machine reads in numerical values for the three numbers A, B, C, the machine immediately afterwards prints out, on the line printer, one line with the values of these three numbers. When we look at the printed output afterwards, we can tell immediately what numbers the machine was using for the subsequent calculation.

This is particularly important in the (very common) case that the calculation *fails,* i.e., something is wrong with the programme and we never get to the point at which we print out results of the calculation: unless we have an echo-check of the input numbers, we do not know which actual numbers caused failure of the calculation. Naturally, it is possible to look at the input data cards, to see what numbers were there. But, to an experienced programmer, that is a highly unsafe procedure: by looking at the data cards, we can tell what numbers we *wanted* to give the machine to work on; we have no real certainty that these were the numbers actually read by the machine; the cards might have been out of order; or the READ statement might not interpret the numbers in the way we want; etc. etc. etc. The only way to tell what numbers the machine used for the calculation is to force the machine to print out the numerical values actually stored in machine memory; i.e., to make an echo-check.

At the end of the calculation, we must arrange for output of results. Looking at the earlier programme, we see that all paths of control converge to statement number 4000, which we have not specified explicitly (just "next FORTRAN statement, to be executed in either case"). This is the natural place for the statements

```
4000 PRINT,X1,Y1,X2,Y2
     GO TO 1000
```

The first of these causes printout of the results of the calculation. The second causes us to go back to statement number 1000, *to read further data.* In this way, the programme "recycles"; in each "cycle", we read data numbers for A, B, C (the coefficients of the quadratic equation), we echo-check these numbers, we then compute the real and imaginary parts of the two roots of the quadratic, and print out results. This "recycling" continues until we run out of data.

Although this is a possible way of doing things, it has one disadvantage: the WATFOR master programme assumes that data will be available to the programme whenever a READ statement is encountered during the execution phase. If no more data are there, WATFOR assumes that this is the result of an error, and says so on the output page (see Chapter VI for a discussion of the printed output).

It is better to write the programme in such a way that error messages from the master programme occur only for real errors. We should therefore arrange our own *termination test* for the recycling. For example, we shall never wish to solve a quadratic equation with A=B=C=0; hence, we can use the fact that all coefficients are zero as an indication that we want the recycling to cease. The FORTRAN statement to achieve this can be placed immediately after the echo-check; it is

```
IF((A.EQ.0.0).AND.(B.EQ.0.0).AND.(C.EQ.0.0)) STOP
```

We are now in a position to give a complete flow diagram and FORTRAN code of the quadratic equation programme. Here they are:

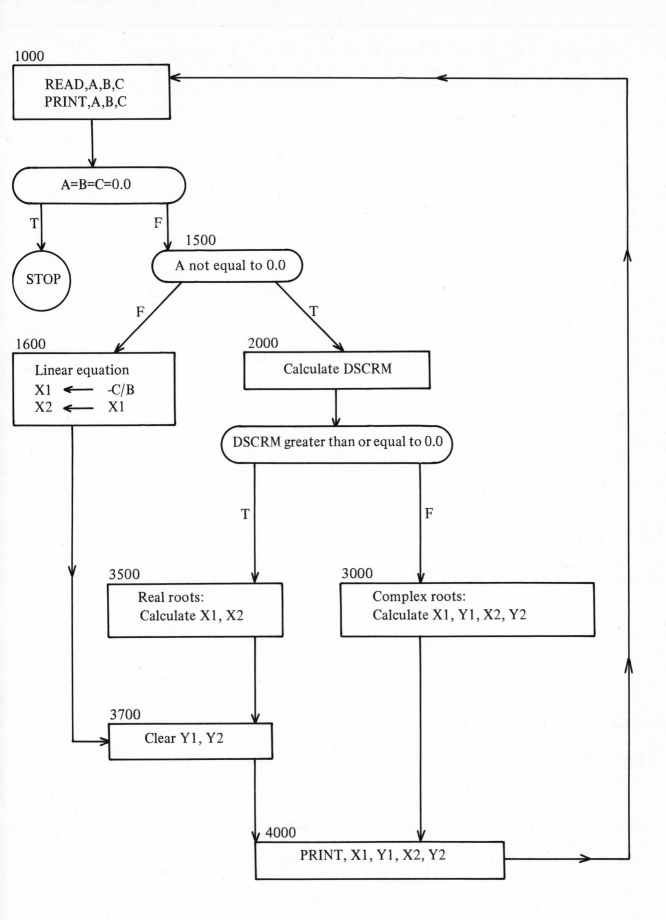

1000
READ,A,B,C
PRINT,A,B,C

A=B=C=0.0

T   F

STOP

1500
A not equal to 0.0

F   T

1600
Linear equation
X1 ← -C/B
X2 ← X1

2000
Calculate DSCRM

DSCRM greater than or equal to 0.0

T   F

3500
Real roots:
Calculate X1, X2

3000
Complex roots:
Calculate X1, Y1, X2, Y2

3700
Clear Y1, Y2

4000
PRINT, X1, Y1, X2, Y2

```
C          PROGRAMME TO FIND THE ROOTS OF A QUADRATIC EQUATION
C          INPUT DATA ARE THE COEFFICIENTS A,B,C, OF A*X**2+B*X+C=0
C          OUTPUT IS ECHO CHECK OF A,B,C, FOLLOWED BY X1,Y1,X2,Y2
C            WHERE X1 + I*Y1 = ROOT NUMBER 1
C                  X2 + I*Y2 = ROOT NUMBER 2
 1000 READ,A,B,C
      PRINT,A,B,C
      IF((A.EQ.0.0).AND.(B.EQ.0.0).AND.(C.EQ.0.0))STOP
C          NOT ALL COEFFICIENTS ARE ZERO. TEST FOR LINEAR CASE.
 1500 IF(A.NE.0.0) GO TO 2000
C          DEGENERATE CASE, LINEAR EQUATION
 1600 X1=-C/B
      X2=X1
C          NOW GO TO THE POINT AT WHICH Y1 AND Y2 ARE SET TO ZERO
      GO TO 3700
C          NORMAL CASE, QUADRATIC EQUATION, EVALUATE THE DISCRIMINANT
 2000 DSCRM=B**2-4.0*A*C
C          NOW TEST THE DISCRIMINANT
 2500 IF(DSCRM.GE.0.0) GO TO 3500
C          THE SECTION WHICH FOLLOWS HANDLES COMPLEX ROOTS
 3000 X1=-B/(2.0*A)
      X2=X1
      ROOTI=(-DSCRM)**0.5
      Y1=ROOTI/(2.0*A)
      Y2=-Y1
      GO TO 4000
C          THE SECTION WHICH FOLLOWS HANDLES REAL ROOTS
 3500 ROOT=DSCRM**0.5
      X1=(-B+ROOT)/(2.0*A)
      X2=(-B-ROOT)/(2.0*A)
 3700 Y1=0.0
      Y2=0.0
C          PATHS REJOIN HERE
 4000 PRINT,X1,Y1,X2,Y2
      GO TO 1000
```

DRILL EXERCISES FOR CHAPTER IV

1. Write in usual form the values represented by the FORTRAN constants below

    4.19E0   4.19E+3   4.19E-3   .419E-2   .00419E+6   9999.E-4

2. Write the following numbers in exponential form, suitable for data cards

    3.76×10^{15} -3.76×10^{15} 3.76×10^{-15} -3.76×10^{-15}

3. The following FORTRAN real numbers are intended to express the ordinary numbers given next to them. State which are correct, and correct the errors in the others:

a) 476E-5   .00476
b) .476E+1   47.6
c) .537E+3   -537
d) 436   436
e) 74.8E   74.8
f) 5.1E-5   .000051

4. In the programme of Section C, the output is misleading if the equation is actually a linear equation, i.e., if A=0. For then, we output two equal roots (both equal to-C/B), whereas in fact such an equation has only one root, not a repeated root. Modify the programme so that the output for this special case is just one real number, equal to the root-C/B.

5. In the programme of Section C, the third statement tests for A=B=C=0. Why are we *not* allowed to write

a) IF(A=B=C=0.0) STOP

b) IF(A.EQ.B.EQ.C.EQ.0.0) STOP

c) IF((A.EQ.B).AND.(C.EQ.0.0)) STOP

Would the following form of the condition work?

d) IF((A.EQ.B).AND.(B.EQ.C).AND.(C.EQ.0.0)) STOP

e) Can any parentheses be omitted in the preceding statement? In the statement actually appearing in the programme of Section C?

f) Explain why the warning, in Chapter III, against using the comparison operator .EQ. does *not* apply here.

6. a) Write a programme segment to read 5 numbers, 3 from the first data card and 2 from the second data card, and to print out all five numbers on one line.

b) Same as (a), but the numbers are to be printed in reverse order to the order in which they are read in.

CHAPTER V

THE INPUT CARD DECK. CONTROL CARDS.

A.   Punching a Fortran Card

Below, we show a typical FORTRAN card, with a FORTRAN statement punched onto the card.

The card has 80 columns; holes may be punched in any of 12 different positions within one column, i.e., in any of the 12 rows. The nomenclature of these 12 rows is somewhat peculiar: the top row is called the + row, the next row down is the − row (because a − sign appears as a single punched hole, in that row); the next row down is called row number 0, then comes row number 1, ..., until the bottom row, which is row number 9. A single numerical digit, say the digit 7, appears as a single punched hole in row number 7 (by this peculiar counting). Alphabetic characters are encoded as *two* punched holes in a single column. For example, the code for the letter A is (+,1), meaning that holes appear in the + row and in row number 1; the code for the letter B is (+,2), i.e., holes appear in the + row and in row number 2. Certain other FORTRAN symbols, such as *, are encoded on the card as three punched holes in one column.

Fortunately, it is not necessary to remember these codes. Most card punching machines not only punch the holes into the card, but they also "interpret" the information on the card: that is, typed characters appear near the top edge of the card, on top of any column in which something has been punched. This is shown also in the illustration.

FIGURE V.1.   A TYPICAL FORTRAN CARD

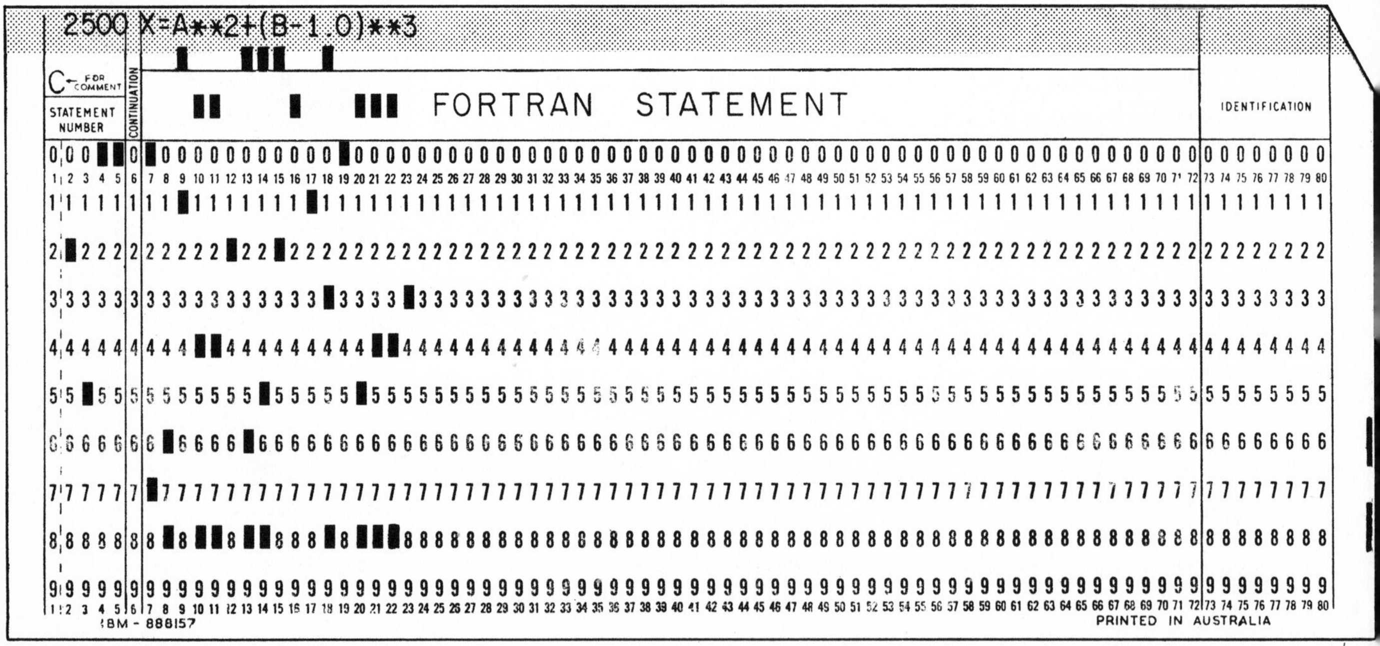

40

A warning is in order here: although all the permissible FORTRAN characters are represented by combinations of holes punched into the card, *not* all combinations of holes punched into a card are valid FORTRAN characters. In fact, if four or more holes are punched in one column of the card, the character is not a valid FORTRAN character; if three holes appear in one column, it may or may not be a valid FORTRAN character (it is certainly invalid if none of the three punches is in row number 8, by the peculiar counting explained above). An invalid character on a FORTRAN card is detected by WATFOR, and gives rise to the error message CC-2, see Appendix B. When you get such an error message on your output, you must look at the actual holes punched into the card in that column; it is *not,* repeat *not* sufficient to look at the interpretation on the top edge of the card: the interpretation is all right for valid characters, but an invalid character is either not interpreted at all, or is interpreted incorrectly.

The machine on which this punching is done is called an electric *key punch.* From the point of view of the user, it is very similar to an ordinary typewriter. There is a shift key, for "upper shift" characters. All numerals are "upper shift", all the characters of the ordinary alphabet A, B, ..., Z are "lower shift".

Once a blank card is in position, it moves one column to the left whenever a key on the typewriter keyboard is depressed. If the key in question is the long one at the bottom of the keyboard, nothing is punched into that column of the card, and nothing is typed into that column near the top edge of the card; we have produced a "blank column". Otherwise, one or more holes are punched into the column, and a symbol is typed near the top edge on top of that column, as a result of depressing the typewriter key once.

There is a key which can be pressed to "eject" a card, and bring the next card into position for being punched. This should be done whenever we have finished typing what we want on that card, or whenever we have made a mistake in typing.

In the latter case, there is a key for *copying* information just punched on one card, onto the next, blank card, column by column. This key should be used to copy, column by column, until we reach the incorrect column. The number of the "current" column can be seen in a little window, just above the card being copied. By copying the correctly punched columns, and altering only the incorrect punching, even a rather poor typist can produce correctly punched cards in a reasonable time.

The *standard layout* of a FORTRAN card is as follows:

1. Comment cards have a letter C punched into column 1, anything thereafter; the compiler merely lists the card, does not translate it.

2. Statement numbers, if any, appear normally in columns 2 to 5 of the card (for four-digit numbers). Five-digit statement numbers appear in columns 1 through 5.

3. Column 6 is normally left blank. If anything is punched into column 6, then the card in question is interpreted by the FORTRAN compiler as a "continuation card", i.e., as a continuation of the FORTRAN statement appearing on the immediately preceding card.

4. The FORTRAN statement itself starts in column 7 of the card, and goes on for as many columns as needed, until column 72 inclusive. If the statement is too long to fit into columns 7 through 72, inclusive, continuation cards must be used. Although any symbol (other than a blank) in column 6 suffices, it is conventional to put the numeral 1 in column 6 of the first continuation card, the numeral 2 in column 6 of the second continuation card, and so on.

5. Any identifier name must consist of immediately adjacent characters (up to 6 alphameric characters), i.e., there can not be interior blanks: BE WARY is not an identifier name, BEWARY is an identifier name. Identifier names must appear wholly on one card, i.e., it is *not* permissible to "break" an identifier name at column 72 on one card, and continue that name on the continuation card which follows (this last rule is specific to WATFOR).

6. Otherwise, blank columns on the cards do not matter, i.e., the statements A=B and A = B and A   =   B are equivalent.

7. Columns 73 through 80 of the card are not used by FORTRAN. In big programmes, these columns are often employed for *card identification,* i.e., an abbreviated version of the name of the programme, followed by the order number of the card within that programme. This is not essential for student programmes, which are short enough to put together into order by hand, after they are dropped on the floor. (Don't !)

There are different types of key punches. The most common is the IBM model 29; but the IBM model 26 is also used in many installations, and key punches are made by other manufacturers, also. There are differences between key punches, mostly minor. For example, the model 29 and model 26 key punches differ with respect to the keyboard positions, on the typewriter keyboard, of a few of the symbols used in FORTRAN, for example, the symbols for +, =, (, and). They also differ in the codes which are used to encode some of these characters as patterns of holes in the card.

B.   Input Deck Structure. Control Cards.

A complete input deck of cards suitable for running under FORTRAN control contains not only the FORTRAN language statements of the programme, and such data as the object programme may require in the execution phase, but also contains certain other cards, usually called *control cards.*

The *first card* of every input deck must be the *job card.* This card is required to be of a distinctive colour (e.g., red), to make it easy for the machine operator to tell that a new job starts with this card.

The first few columns of the card contain information to the effect that this *is* a job card. For WATFOR jobs, in many installations, these identifying characters are four in number, to wit: $JOB in columns 1 through 4 of the card. However, some installations use different identifying characters, for example, some installations use nine characters, to wit: //PROGRAM in columns 1 through 9 of the card. You shall need to know which it is at your own installation (see later, however).

After this identifying information, there are blank columns on the job card, until column 15, inclusive.

From here on, the pattern differs from installation to installation. The pattern suggested below is desirable, in that it makes it possible to supply students with *pre-punched job cards* containing all that information which is the same for all students in a given subject.

Starting in column 16, there appears the *subject number* of the course, for example, the number 10.001 to indicate the subject Mathematics 10.001.

If the key punch used is a model 26, the subject number is followed immediately (without intervening blanks) by a comma, followed in turn immediately by the characters KP=26; no spaces are allowed within this area.

42

Normally, pre-punched job cards with this much information already punched on them will be available to students in the key punch room.

In addition to this pre-punched information, certain other information must be punched onto the job card by the student himself. A typical prescription might be:

1. Starting in exactly column 30, punch your own last name. Do not punch first names or initials. Do not leave blank spaces inside your name.

2. Starting exactly in column 50, punch your student record number.

3. Starting exactly in column 60, punch the name of the tutor in your tutorial section.

This information is required, or is at least very desirable, to identify the student to whom the card deck belongs, so that the card deck can be returned to the student after the job has been run on the machine. Since the content of the job card also appears at the beginning of the printed output, the printed output can be identified easily, also. (See Chapter VI).

Both the input card deck and the printed output must be returned to the student: the printed output, to tell what went wrong with the job; and the input card deck, to allow correction of the errors, and subsequent re-running of the job.

Identifying information such as the name of the subject, the name and number of the student, and the name of the tutor, could in principle be on later cards in the card deck; but this would be inefficient: one would then have to "flip through the deck" of cards to read this identifying information The less flipping of cards is done, the better for all concerned. Among other things, bent cards can easily jam the card reader attached to the computer. *Cards should be handled with care and kept flat at all times. Bent or otherwise damaged cards should be copied on the key punch onto new, .clean cards, then thrown away.*

Following the job card, there is the FORTRAN language programme. Usually, a FORTRAN language programme starts with some comment cards, to tell what the programme is designed to do, what input data card it requires, and what the printed output means.

The last card of the FORTRAN programme must be a card with the word END *appearing starting in column 7.* This card informs the "translator" that translation of this programme may now cease (*).

The *next card* of the input card deck is another control card, which in standard WATFOR takes the form: $ENTRY in *columns 1 through 6* of the card. In certain other installations, that same control card has the form: //DATA in columns 1 through 6 of the card. Generally, control cards have their punchings starting in column 1 of the card; FORTRAN language statements (except for statement numbers and comment cards) start in column 7 of the card.

(*)   Two separate cards, an END card and a $ENTRY card, may seem to be redundant here, and so they are. However, in more advanced programming, the FORTRAN programme is broken up into a main programme followed by a number of subprogrammes. This is discussed in Chapter XIV. The last card of the main programme is an END card; the last card of every subprogramme is an END card; the $ENTRY card appears on the card deck after all the programmes and subprogrammes. The END card says that here is the end of the translation of one programme or subprogramme. The $ENTRY card says that here is the end of the entire translation operation.

Following the $ENTRY (or //DATA, as the case may be) control card, there are the *data cards,* as many as are needed by the programme during execution. If the programme does not contain any READ statement, then no data cards are needed. However, a $ENTRY card *must* be supplied even in that case.

In some, but not all, installations, there is a special control card at the very end, after the last data card (if any; after $ENTRY if there are no data cards at all). This *job termination card* is $IBSYS, in columns 1 through 6 of the card. In some installations, no such card is desired or even allowed; in other installations, a job termination card is mandatory. You must find out what the rules are in your own installation.

As a simple *example,* we give below the complete job deck for a programme which calculates the area of a triangle from its base and height. Input numbers for BASE and HEIGHT are read, the AREA is calculated, and BASE, HEIGHT, and AREA are printed out. We then return to read the next values of BASE and HEIGHT.

```
$JOB              10.001,KP=26  BROWN              68235179   JONES
C     THIS PROGRAMME COMPUTES THE AREA OF A TRIANGLE
C     INPUT DATA ARE BASE, HEIGHT
C     OUTPUT NUMBERS ARE BASE, HEIGHT, AREA
 1000 READ,BASE,HEIGHT
      AREA=0.5*BASE*HEIGHT
      PRINT,BASE,HEIGHT,AREA
      GO TO 1000
      END
$ENTRY
25.6   14.7
28.9   22.3
.148   .005
3.E-6  4.E-8
$IBSYS
```

Explanation of Example:

1. The information in columns 1 through 29 of the job card is pre-punched.

2. The student's name is BROWN. The letter B appears in column 30 of the card.

3. The student number is 68235179. The first numeral (the '6') appears in column 50 of the card.

4. The tutor's name is JONES. The first letter of that name (the J) appears in column 60 of the card.

5. In some installations, the symbols $JOB are replaced by something else, for example, by //PRO-GRAM.

6. In some installations, the card $ENTRY is written differently, for example, //DATA.

7. With the READ statement in the programme, the numbers used for BASE and HEIGHT are:

first cycle:	BASE=25.6	HEIGHT=14.7
second cycle:	=28.9	=22.3
third cycle:	=0.148	=0.005
last cycle:	=0.000003	=0.00000004

8. In some installations, the $IBSYS card is replaced by some other job termination card. In still other installations, no job termination card is used at all.

PROGRAMMING EXERCISES FOR CHAPTER V:

Note: These exercises should be run on the machine.

1. The above programme to compute the area of a triangle will print out an error message when there are no more data cards in the card reader. To avoid this, insert statements which have the effect to terminate execution when the numbers read in for BASE and HEIGHT are both less than or equal to zero. Alter the job card suitably to agree with your own name, etc.; alter all control cards, if necessary, to conform with standard practice at your computer installation. Then submit the job.

2. Complete the programme given at the end of Chapter IV by

   1. supplying the necessary control cards, and

   2. supplying some suitable data cards. Punch up the card deck, submit it for running, and check the printed output.

3. Supply control cards for the programme appearing at the end of Section E of Chapter III, and run the job on the computer.

4. Alter the programme of exercise 3 to *read in* a set of values for P and R (rather than supplying these values by assignment statements in the FORTRAN programme itself). Supply the necessary data, and run the job on the machine.

5. Alter the programme of exercise 4 to read in, in addition, the total time TIME for the investment plan, so that it need not be exactly 30 years. (Pay careful attention to the IF statement at the end of the loop!) Also alter the programme to recycle, i.e., to read in new data for P, R, and TIME after the end of every computation.

6. Alter the programme of exercise 5 to prevent error termination when there are no more data: use the condition P.LE.0.0 to terminate execution of the object programme. Supply the necessary data card after the real data, to force "normal" rather than "error" termination of the computation.

CHAPTER VI

THE PRINTED OUTPUT

A. Diagnostics

This Chapter contains the information you will require to interpret the printed output which results from the running of your programme.

The first line of the output page is a copy of the $JOB card of the input deck.

Thereafter, the printed output contains a listing of the FORTRAN language input cards of your input deck, one by one. Each card image is listed as a separate line.

The FORTRAN language statements, other than comments, are numbered consecutively by the compiler, and these consecutive numbers are listed on the extreme left of the printed page. Comment cards (starting with a "C" in column 1) are merely listed on the printed output, without being assigned running numbers. FORTRAN statements which require more than one card (i.e., for which there are continuation cards) are given only one running number, which appears to the left of the card image of the first card of that statement. The running numbers appear for convenience in later references; they do not supersede, or influence, the statement numbers which you may have assigned to some or all of the FORTRAN statements.

If the compiler detects any *language error* in a statement, *diagnostic messages* appear in the printed output immediately below the faulty statement.(*) For example, the following faulty statement has two adjacent plus signs, something which is explicitly forbidden by parentheses omission rule no. 4 of Chapter II. The statement was assigned statement number 3000 by the programmer, and turned out to be the fifth non-comment statement of the programme. The printed output for this statement reads:

```
        5              3000  Z=B++C
   ***ERROR***               SX-D
```

The first line lists the statement as it is, with the running statement number 5 assigned by the compiler, as well as the statement number 3000 assigned by the programmer. The next line tells the programmer that this statement is erroneous, and gives an *error code,* to wit SX-D, to tell the programmer the nature of the error. A complete list of all error codes appears in Appendix B. From this appendix, we see that error code SX-D stands for: "Missing Operand or Operator". The point is that the compiler expected an operand after the first + sign, and instead found another + sign. The statement Z=B+D+C, with the extra operand "D" after the first + sign, is a grammatically correct statement. The statement Z=B++C has one operand missing.

(*)   Diagnostic printout differs from compiler to compiler. We use the diagnostic printout produced by the WATFOR compiler.

This example shows that the diagnostic error message printed out by the compiler does not necessarily tell you what the error really was. For example, it is entirely possible that you *meant* to write Z=B+C, and your error consisted in punching an extra + sign onto the card. In that case, it is not true that there is either an operator or an operand missing; in fact, there is one operator too many!

The machine cannot and does not read your mind! The diagnostic error message tells you that an error has occurred, and gives at least one possibility for the nature of that error. But it is up to you to look at your own programme and determine what really went wrong; no one else can do it for you, and experience at doing this very thing is the main skill required for successful computer programming. Any fool can write a programme; but it takes a good programmer to "debug" the programme efficiently and completely.

It is possible for an error at one point to cause "spillover diagnostics" at some other point in the programme. We shall encounter such errors later on, for example in Chapter XIII. But even at this early stage, errors can occur which are *not* local to any one statement of the programme, but refer to the programme as a whole. Such errors can be detected, and a warning issued, only after the entire programme has been read. The most common error of this type is omission of a statement number from a statement to which an unconditional transfer is made. For example, our "two-way branch" in Chapter III contained a statement which would be listed as

7   2500 IF(DSCRM.GE.0.0) GO TO 3500

This command requires that some other statement in the programme be given the statement number 3500; for otherwise, the computer is not told where to transfer control if the discriminant DSCRM is greater than or equal to zero. In the actual programme in Chapter III, there was a statement with that number, which would be listed as:

14   3500   ROOT=DSCRM**0.5

Let us now suppose that, by mistake, the statement number has been omitted! The incorrect listed line is

14   ROOT=DSCRM**0.5

This omission can be detected by the compiler only after the entire programme has been read and translated; as long as there are more statements to follow, *any one of them might turn out to have the desired statement number 3500 (*)*.

The error message now appears at the end of the programme. It is

ERROR   ST-0   3500   USED IN LINE   7

We determine, from the list of error messages in Appendix B that ST-0 means "missing statement number". The remainder of the message tells us that the missing statement number is actually 3500, and that such a statement number was required by the statement occurring in line 7 of the listing of the programme.

(*)   During the translation process itself, statements are translated one by one. Transfer addresses of this sort are left open, and filled in by the compiler when it comes to translate the later card with the desired statement number. If, at the end of the translation process, there are still some open addresses left, then the compiler diagnoses an error in the programme.

Note that the statement on that line is *not* in error at all; the actual error occurs in line 14, where the desired statement number 3500 has been omitted. But the WATFOR compiler has no way of telling to which part of your programme you wished to transfer control! You, and only you, can determine that!

In spite of the best intentions of the people who write compilers, error messages are sometimes confusing to beginners. If you do not understand all the error messages, correct those errors which you can understand, and resubmit the programme. If the obscure error messages were caused by the errors which you have corrected, the obscure messages will not reappear in the new printed output. If they were real errors, they will reappear as errors, but likely in more understandable form. *Do not run to your tutor in panic as soon as you encounter an error message which you fail to understand.*

B.   Termination Messages

Let us return to discussion of the printed output from your programme under more normal (though perhaps less usual) conditions, when there are no grammatical errors. After listing the FORTRAN source language statements of your input card deck, the next item listed is the image of your $ENTRY card. At this stage, the translation phase is finished, and the execution phase starts. The subsequent output in the normal case, is controlled by the (translated) PRINT statements in your programme. When encountered during the execution phase, each (translated) PRINT statement causes a new line of output to appear on the printed output page.

The last item on the printed output is a *termination message,* which is printed out by the master programme when it resumes control. In the case of a *normal termination* the termination message occupies only one line, and reads:

COMPILE TIME=. . .SECONDS, EXECUTION TIME=. . .SECONDS,OBJECT
CODE=. . .BYTES, ARRAY AREA=. . .BYTES, UNUSED=. . .BYTES

where the . . . represent numbers. The first number gives the time used to translate (compile) the source language statements; the second number is the time spent executing the object programme; the remaining three numbers tell you about memory space in the machine; a "byte" represents the smallest effective unit of information storage in the machine (see Chapter VII; one "memory location" for number storage usually, but not always, requires four bytes of memory); the "object code" is the translated programme, including all the associated memory locations named by simple identifiers; the "array area" is the area in memory occupied by array storage (see Chapter XIII); this array area will be zero in the programmes you can write so far; "unused" is the remaining area in memory available for further object programme and/or storage of numbers. Since the compiler itself occupies a large area in machine memory, the sum of "object code", "array area", and "unused" memory is very much less than the total amount of memory area in the machine.

Error termination of execution occurs when you attempt to do an impossible calculation (e.g., dividing by zero) or when you attempt to execute an untranslatable (because grammatically incorrect) statement of your source programme. For example, the incorrect statement Z=B++C discussed at the beginning of this Chapter gives rise, in the execution phase, to the error message:

ERROR   KO-0
PROGRAMME WAS EXECUTING LINE 5 in ROUTINE M/PROG
WHEN TERMINATION OCCURRED

Looking at the list of error messages in the Appendix, we see that message KO-0 means "Job terminated in execution because of compile time error". The following line tells you which compile time error (there could have been several!) caused the disaster. LINE 5 refers to the running numbers assigned by the compiler to your input statements, and printed in the source programme listing to the extreme left of each statement. ROUTINE M/PROG means the "main programme", which is also the only programme at this early stage (see Chapter XIV for sub-programmes in the FORTRAN language). The error termination message is then followed by a normal termination message.

C.   A Sample Output

We conclude this Chapter by reproducing a copy of the printed output obtained from the input card deck at the end of Chapter V.

```
   $JOB              10.001,KP=26   BROWN                    68235179   JONES
      C       THIS PROGRAMME COMPUTES THE AREA OF A TRIANGLE
      C       INPUT DATA ARE BASE, HEIGHT
      C       OUTPUT NUMBERS ARE BASE, HEIGHT, AREA
1    1000 READ,BASE,HEIGHT
2         AREA=0.5*BASE*HEIGHT
3         PRINT,BASE,HEIGHT,AREA
4         GO TO 1000
5         END
   $ENTRY
0.2560000E 02   0.1469999E 02   0.1881600E 03
0.2889999E 02   0.2230000E 02   0.3222348E 03
0.1480000E 00   0.4999998E-02   0.3699997E-03
0.3000000E-05   0.3999999E-07   0.5999996E-13
***ERROR***      UN-0
             PROGRAMME WAS EXECUTING LINE     1 IN ROUTINE M/PROG WHEN
TERMINATION OCCURRED COMPILE TIME=0.81 SECONDS, EXECUTION TIME=0.69
SECOND, OBJECT CODE=336 BYTES,ARRAY AREA=0 BYTES
```

Discussion of this output:

1.   Note the running numbers 1,2,3,4,5 to the left of the FORTRAN language statements. Note also that comment cards are not given running numbers.

2.   The error message UN-0 means, according to Appendix B, "control card encountered on unit 1 during execution - probable cause - missing data or improper FORMAT statements". What has happened is that we have run out of data, and the READ statement in the programme caused the machine to attempt to read in the termination card $IBSYS as if it were a data card; it wasn't. The next line tells us that the statement being executed at that moment was the statement with running number 1, i.e., the READ statement. "M/PROG" means "main programme"; at this stage of your knowledge of FORTRAN, there are no other types of programmes.

3. Note that the first value of HEIGHT printed out is 0.1469999E 02 rather than 0.1470000E 02, the input number on the data card. The two numbers are the same to machine accuracy. The same remark applies to various other numbers in this printed output.

PROGRAMMING EXERCISES FOR PART A

Note: To complete any one of these exercises, it is *not* sufficient to make up a flow diagram and a written FORTRAN code. That is just the start. Thereafter, the programme has to be punched onto cards with all necessary control cards and data cards, the input card deck has to be submitted for running on the computer, and the printed output must be inspected for errors; the corrected programme must be resubmitted for running on the computer, and the output from that run must be checked again: this process of submitting the input card deck, and checking the output, must be continued until the programme is *debugged,* that is, until

1. No more language errors are flagged by the compiler, *and*

2. The output numbers are *correct*

Then, and only then, is the exercise completed.

1. The volume of a cylinder is $V=\pi r^2 h$ where r is the radius, h is the height. Read r and h as data, find V, print out r, h, and V. (*Hint:* Look at the programme at the end of Chapter V).

2. Alter the above programme as follows: Test whether *both* r and h are zero; if so, terminate execution of the programme by means of a STOP statement. This has the effect of avoiding an error message UN-0 at the end of the output, provided that the last two data numbers read are both zeros.

3. Print a table of values, from 1 to 25, and their squares. *Hints:* No data need be read in; the programme should be written as a loop: the loop variable is initialized by VALUE=1.0; it is incremented, at the end of the loop, by VALUE=VALUE+1.0; the new value is tested by IF(VALUE.LE.25.0) GO TO . . . where . . . is the statement number of the first statement inside the loop. Where should the statement STOP appear?

4. Same as 3, but the table should contain not only values and squares, but also cubes, fourth powers and fifth powers. The table should have five columns, the values appearing in column 1, the squares in column 2, the cubes in column 3, the fourth powers in column 4, and the fifth powers in column 5. *Hint:* Compute and print one line of the table at a time. Use statements such as SQUARE=VALUE**2, CUBE=SQUARE*VALUE, FOURTH=CUBE*VALUE, etc., then print out one line. Do *not* use a statement such as VALUE=VALUE**2, since this has the effect of overwriting the content of the storage location VALUE, thereby upsetting the operation of the loop.

5. A man takes a job for 40 days. His pay for the first day is $0.01. His pay for the second day is double that, or $0.02. For the third day, $0.04, for the fourth day, $0.08, and so on, each day double the pay of the day before. The programme should generate a table with three columns: the number of the day in column 1, the day's pay in column 2, and the total pay so far in column 3.

6. Write a programme to read four numbers A,B,C,D from a data card, find the biggest of the four, store that in location BIG, and print out all five numbers. Can you do it in seven FORTRAN statements?

7. Read the coefficients A, B, C, D, E, F in the pair of linear equations A*X+B*Y=E   C*X+D*Y=F, and echo check; then determine X and Y, and print them out. *Hint:* Watch out for the degenerate case where DET=A*D-B*C vanishes; in this programme, stop the computation when this happens.

8. A loan of $2000 is to be repaid at the rate of $80 per month. The rate of interest is 1 percent (0.01) per month, on the unpaid balance. The programme should generate a four column table showing, for each month,

   1. The number of the payment,
   2. the old balance,
   3. the amount of interest due,
   4. the amount by which this payment has reduced the principal.

   Hint: The new balance is obtained by subtracting item 4. from item 2. Output should stop when the new balance turns negative (for then the loan has been repaid in full).

9. Improve the programme of problem 8, by reading input data (rather than assuming fixed values of $2000, $80, and 0.01). Let the programme recycle until the value of DEBT read in is zero.   The numbers read in are DEBT, PAYMNT, and RATE, respectively.

10. Write a programme to do a payroll. The input is WAGE (the hourly wage), HOURS (number of hours worked), SURATE (superannuation rate), TXRATE (tax rate), SVRATE (rate of savings); these are on one card per employee, the rates as decimal fractions (not percentages). The output should be an echo-check of the input, followed by: gross pay, superannuation deduction, tax deduction, savings deduction, and take home pay. The programme should recycle until we read a card with a value of zero for WAGE.

11. Improve the programme of problem 7 as follows: In the normal case, the print-out includes the value of DET, i.e., the numbers printed out are, first, the echo check, then a line containing DET,X, and Y. If DET.EQ.0.0 determine whether these equations have any solution at all; if not, print out the value of DET only, nothing else, on the second line of the print-out. If a solution does exist, it is not unique. In that case, print out the value of DET, followed by the value of X *on the assumption* that Y=1.0. Thus, the second line of the print-out contains 3 numbers (DET,X,Y) in the normal case; and either 2 numbers or 1 number in the abnormal case DET.EQ.0.0.

12. Write a programme to evaluate the square root of a number X by the following iterative scheme: Let Q be a guess at the value of the square root; then the following mathematical formula provides an improved guess:

$$p = \tfrac{1}{2}(q + \frac{x}{q})$$

The programme should start by reading a number into location X; test whether X is positive, negative, or zero (go to read the next X if X is negative); for positive X, use Q=0.5*(1.0+X) as the initial guess, and keep on improving the guess until the result stabilizes to 6 significant figures. Print out the value of X, the value of the square root so found, and the value of the square root obtained from the well-formed arithmetic expression X**0.5, for a comparison. *Hint:* For code-checking purposes, it is most desirable to print out intermediate results at the end of each iteration; the PRINT statement for this can be removed from the programme after the bugs have been removed.

PART B

In this, second part of the book, we present a detailed introduction to, and explanation of, the entire FORTRAN IV language. There are various "dialects" of FORTRAN IV. These dialects differ from each other only in minor details, details which are learned easily when required, but which would tend to confuse a beginning programmer. The particular dialect of FORTRAN IV presented in the body of the book is IBM G-level FORTRAN IV, the language implemented in the student compiler WATFOR for the IBM/360.

A discussion of the various dialects of FORTRAN IV, and the differences between them, can be found in Appendix D.

CHAPTER VII

ORGANIZATION OF STORAGE. REPRESENTATION OF NUMBERS AND CHARACTERS

Compiler source languages, such as FORTRAN, enable the programmer to get results out of the machine without knowing everything that goes on inside the machine. However, it is much easier to understand *why* FORTRAN has certain language rules, and it is much easier to remember these rules, if one knows at least a little bit about what really happens inside the machine. In this Chapter, we explain how numbers and characters are stored in the memory of an IBM 360 computer. You may find it advisable to read this Chapter rather quickly, *without* attempting to understand and remember everything in it. When reading the later Chapters, you may then refer back to Chapter VII at appropriate points, to refresh your memory.

The elementary unit of memory is one "binary digit" of information. A binary digit can take one of two values only: 0 or 1. In the machine, each binary digit of information is represented by one tiny, doughnut shaped piece of magnetic material, called a "magnetic core". This ring can be magnetized in one of two ways: clockwise around the ring, or counterclockwise around the ring. One of these magnetizations represents the binary digit 0, the other magnetization represents the binary digit 1.

Electric wires pass through the hole of each ring, and by means of electric signals in these wires it is possible to

1. read the stored information, i.e., determine whether it is 0 or 1

2. set the magnetization to a desired value, either 0 or 1

The first of these, reading out the information, does not destroy the information, i.e., the ring remains magnetized in whatever direction it was magnetized before. But the second process, storing information into this ring, means magnetizing the ring afresh. This necessarily destroys the information stored there previously.

Binary numbers are represented by sequences of binary digits, for example, 1011 is a sequence of four binary digits. The binary number represented in this way is written in decimal form as $1 \times 2^3 + 0 \times 2^2 + 1 \times 2^1 + 1 \times 2^0 = 1 \times 8 + 0 \times 4 + 1 \times 2 + 1 \times 1 = 8 + 2 + 1 = 11$.
(*Note:* the *decimal* number 11 means $1 \times 10 + 1$; the *binary* number 11 means $1 \times 2 + 1$).

Binary numbers are inconvenient and lengthy to write down, and give rise to frequent mistakes. We shall write binary numbers in an alternative form, as *hexadecimal* numbers, written with *hexadecimal digits*. Each hexadecimal digit is equivalent to *four* binary digits next to each other. There are only 16 different possible sequences of four binary digits, from 0000 all the way to 1111. In the Table below, we show these 16 different sequences in column 1. Column 2 gives a decimal number equivalent of this binary number. Column 3 gives the hexadecimal digit used to represent this pattern of four binary digits. We shall write hexadecimal digits in italics, to distinguish them from ordinary decimal digits and letters of the alphabet.

TABLE VIII. 1

THE HEXADECIMAL DIGITS.

Patterns of four binary digits	Equivalent decimal number	Hexadecimal digit
0000	0	0
0001	1	1
0010	2	2
0011	3	3
0100	4	4
0101	5	5
0110	6	6
0111	7	7
1000	8	8
1001	9	9
1010	10	A
1011	11	B
1100	12	C
1101	13	D
1110	14	E
1111	15	F

Note that we ran out of the usual digits after the digit 9; we had to use something else to represent the remaining binary digit patterns, so we used the letters A through F. The italics are to remind us that these are hexadecimal digits (equivalent to groups of four binary digits), not ordinary letters of the alphabet. The hexadecimal digit F, for example, means the pattern of binary digits 1111. It must not be confused with the alphabetic character F.

It is conventional to abbreviate the words "binary digit" to "bit", that is, we say that each hexadecimal digit represents four bits.

This hexadecimal form can be used, for example, to write down patterns of 8 bits at a time. The 8-bit pattern 10111001 is broken up into two groups of 4 bits each, namely 1011 1001. The first group is represented by the hexadecimal digit B, the second by the hexadecimal digit 9. The entire 8-bit pattern can therefore be written in the hexadecimal form B9.

Groups of 8 bits at a time are in fact the practical unit of organized memory in an IBM/360 machine. Such 8-bit groups are called "bytes" and each byte in the machine has its own "address", and can be referred to straightforwardly in a machine-language programme. On the other hand, to refer to a single bit of information, it is necessary to first "fetch" the byte which contains this bit, and then carry out further operations to separate this one bit from the other 7 bits within the byte.

Since there are 8 bits of information within one byte, there are altogether $2^8 = 256$ different choices for one byte. In hexadecimal code, these choices range through *00, 01, . . ., 0E, 0F, 10, 11, . . ., 1E, 1F, 21, 22, . . ., FE, FF;* 256 choices in all.

Some, but not all, of these choices are used within the machine to represent characters which appear on FORTRAN input cards. There are only 49 (not 256) possible characters in FORTRAN input, and these 49 characters fall into three classes:

   i)   alphabetic characters, including the symbol $ (27 characters)

   ii)   numeric characters, i.e., the decimal digits (10 characters)

   iii) "special" characters, which are: the blank, +, -, /, =, .(period),), *, ,(comma), (, '(apostrophe), &(ampersand) (12 characters)

Each of these 49 FORTRAN input characters is represented by a particular pattern of 8 bits (by one particular byte) within the machine memory. The actual bytes used to represent these FORTRAN characters will not be needed here. Since the blank (nothing at all punched onto the column of the card) is sometimes not counted as a "character", one may say that FORTRAN input uses a 48-character set. The blank character is important in practice, however, since it serves as a "delimiter", telling the compiler when some character string has come to an end.

In most cases (for the main exception, see Chapter XV, A-type format) an input character on the card, other than one of the 48 characters or a blank, is simply considered an error, and is described as an "illegal character". Such "illegal characters" give rise to diagnostic error messages in the listing of the input programme.

If we attempted to use single bytes to store *numbers,* to be used in calculations, we would be very limited indeed in what we could calculate. There are only 256 different choices for a byte. These can be used to represent the integers 0 to 255, for example; but how would we then store negative numbers, or numbers bigger than 256?

The only way out of this dilemma is to use groups of several adjoining bytes to represent a single number. The choice employed most frequently is a group of 4 adjoining bytes in machine memory, i.e., 32 bits of information. This is the usual size of a "memory location" in the machine. The "address" of any memory location is the address of the first byte within the group of bytes. Not all memory locations are four bytes long, but in simple FORTRAN programmes most of them are. Special type declarations (see Chapter IX) are required to specify any length other than four bytes.

Four-byte integers are stored in the machine as patterns of 4 bytes, or 32 bits, adjacent to each other. The first bit is the *sign bit,* with 0 indicating a positive number, and 1 indicating a negative number. The other 31 bits contain the value of the integer, in coded form.
With 31 bits, we have $2^{31} = 2147483648$ different choices, and we can therefore represent integers from 0 up to $2^{31}-1 = 2147483647$, with either sign. This suffices for most practical purposes, although it is sometimes insufficient for special applications, e.g., the study of very large integers in the branch of mathematics known as the theory of numbers.

Actually, for many applications, this range of possible values is excessive, and wastes valuable memory space. *Two-byte integers* are stored in the machine as patterns of 2 bytes, or 16 bits, adjacent to each other. The first bit is the sign bit, again, and the remaining 15 bits contain the value of the integer in coded form. With 15 bits, we have 2^{15} = 32768 different possibilities, and we can therefore represent integers from 0 up to 2^{15}-1 = 32767, with either sign. This is usually enough for counting times around a loop, and other forms of indexing required in computer programmes.

Integers, or whole numbers, do not require a decimal point; we may think, if we wish, of each integer as having a decimal point at its extreme right; for this reason, integers are sometimes called "fixed-point numbers" in the machine, to distinguish them from rational numbers which are called "floating-point numbers".

In the IBM/360, rational numbers are written in the "normalized form"

$$r = f \times (16)^{k-64} \qquad \text{where} \qquad \begin{aligned} 1/16 &\leq |f| < 1 \\ 0 &\leq k \leq 127 \quad (k = \text{integer}) \end{aligned} \qquad (7.1)$$

k-64 is called the "exponent", and f is called the "fractional part" or "mantissa". As an example, consider the number 25.0. We cannot write it as $(25/16) \times 16^1$ since f = 25/16 would exceed unity. Hence we write

$$25.0 = \left(\frac{25}{256}\right) \times 16^2 \quad \text{i.e., } f = 25/256 \text{ and } k = 66 \text{ (so that } k-64=2)$$

Since k can range from 0 to 127 the magnitudes of floating point numbers can range from $(16)^{-64}$ to $(16)^{+63}$, or roughly 10^{-78} to 10^{+75}. This is sufficient for most applications.

Four-byte real numbers are stored in the machine as patterns of 4 bytes, or 32 bits, adjacent to each other. The first bit is the sign bit, indicating the sign of the number. The remaining 7 bits of the first byte represent the integer k in (7.1). With 7 bits available, there are 2^7 = 128 choices for k, which we take to represent the range k=0 to k=127. The remaining three bytes, or 24 bits, are used to store the absolute value of the fractional part f of (7.1), in coded form.

The limitation to only 24 bits of information for the fractional part f implies a very severe limit for the *precision* with which we can handle such numbers. In fact, two rational numbers which differ from each other by less than 2 parts in 10^7 are usually represented by exactly the same 4-byte pattern in the machine! A precision of 2 parts in 10^7 may appear quite adequate at first sight; however, the rounding-off errors during the computations carried on in the machine tend to accumulate, and it is not at all unusual to find that the final answer has less than 2 significant digits!

To avoid this problem, we can also store *eight-byte real numbers,* sometimes called "double precision floating point numbers". These are stored in the machine as patterns of 8 bytes, or 64 bits, adjacent to each other. The first byte contains the sign bit and the 7 bits representing the integer k, just as before. But now we have 7 bytes, or 56 bits, of information left for the mantissa f. This gives a precision of roughly 1 part in 10^{16} for the fraction f. This is sufficient for most practical computations, even after one allows for the inevitable loss of precision by accumulation of round-off errors.

A *complex number* is of the form x+iy, where x and y are real numbers, and i stands for the square root of -1. An *eight-byte complex number* is stored in the machine as a pattern of 8 adjacent bytes; the first 4 bytes represent the real number x in four-byte real number form, and the other 4 bytes represent the real number y (the imaginary part) in four-byte real number form. The precision of an 8-byte complex number is therefore the same as that of a 4-byte real number; both the real part x and the imaginary part y have a precision of roughly 2 parts in 10^7.

To get higher precision, we use *sixteen-byte complex numbers*, which are stored in the machine as patterns of 16 adjacent bytes; the first 8 bytes represent the real part, x, in 8-byte real number form; the remaining 8 bytes represent the imaginary part, y, in 8-byte real number form. The precision of a 16-byte complex number is the same as that of an 8-byte real number; both the real part x and the imaginary part y have a precision of roughly 1 part in 10^{16}

In our discussion of flow control, in Chapter IV, we saw that well-formed logical expressions can assume only two different values., .TRUE. and .FALSE.; to store a "logical constant" therefore requires only a single binary digit of information: 0 can stand for .FALSE., and 1 can stand for .TRUE.

However, single bits cannot be handled easily within the framework of the IBM/360 order code; the smallest directly addressable unit is the byte, or 8-bit pattern. In FORTRAN, therefore, *logical constants* are stored at least as single bytes. This wastes 7 of the 8 bits of information in a byte, but simplifies the translation from source language to machine language; it also makes the object programme (translated programme) faster in execution. Only if very many logical quantities need to be stored, is it worth while to be more efficient in the use of storage for this type of information.

The alternative FORTRAN form uses *four* bytes of information to represent a single logical constant. In this case, we waste 31 out of 32 bits of information. The advantage is that storage of information in four-byte groups is fairly standard in FORTRAN, and this simplifies translation from source language to machine language. If only very few logical constants are used in a programme, we can afford to waste some memory space for the sake of convenience.

The last type of information storage of interest to us is actually the most general type, called a *character string*. This is a group of k adjacent bytes in the machine, where k ranges from 1 to 255. These bytes contain the coded "images" of various FORTRAN characters. For example, a "card image" is a character string of length k=80, one character for each column of the card.

OPTIONAL EXERCISES FOR CHAPTER VII.

1. Write the following binary numbers in (i) hexadecimal notation (ii) decimal form
   a) 01101001
   b) 11000011
   c) 110100110001

2. Convert the following hexadecimal numbers into decimal form
   a) *11*   d) *1AB*
   b) *100*   e) *AB1*
   c) *A00*

3. Convert the following decimal integers into four-byte machine integers, and write the four bytes in hexadecimal form:
   a) 1
   b) 12
   c) 240
   d) 1984

4. Given that the fractional part f of a four-byte real number is equal to the ratio $g/16^6$ where g is the 6-hexadecimal-digit-number stored in the last three of the four bytes, write the following sets of four bytes as equivalent common fractions:

a) *42190000* b) *40190000* c) *00190000*

CHAPTER VIII

FORTRAN CONSTANTS

In the source programme written in FORTRAN, numbers and non-numerical information appear in two forms: explicitly, as information to be converted directly into machine form, and implicitly, as the contents of certain named memory locations. For example, the arithmetic assignment statement

HEIGHT=HEIGHT+1.5

contains the explicit number 1.5, which must be added to the contents of the named memory location HEIGHT, and the result stored back into that location. Explicit information, be it numerical or logical or character string, is called "FORTRAN constants", whereas named memory locations are referred to as "FORTRAN variables". For both of these, the compiler must be told just what sort of information it is. Thus there are a number of conventions for FORTRAN constants, which are the subject of this Chapter; and there are specific "type declaration" statements for FORTRAN variables, which are taken up in Chapter IX.

From the machine point of view (but not from the programmer's point of view) the simplest type of constant is the *hexadecimal constant,* which describes precisely what is stored into the machine memory, without any conversion being necessary. In FORTRAN, the code for a hexadecimal constant is the letter Z, followed by any number of hexadecimal digits, two hexadecimal digits to one byte of information in the machine. For example, the hexadecimal constant Z000001A9 describes four adjacent bytes, containing in sequence: *00, 00, 01, A9.* For convenience, the leading zeros may be omitted, i.e., we may write Z1A9 instead. This form of constant can be used (within FORTRAN) only for data initialization (see Chapter IX, in particular the discussion of the DATA statement, and Chapter XV, Section E.)

For all other FORTRAN constants, conversion operations are required; that is, the FORTRAN constant as it appears in the programme is not the same as the pattern of binary digits which is stored into machine memory. The appearance of the FORTRAN constant is used by the compiler to decide, not only what the constant is numerically, but also how it should be converted into internal machine form.

DEF: A *FORTRAN integer constant* is an ordinary integer with decimal digits written next to each other, *without a decimal point,* preceded by either a blank, a +, or a -; a blank in front has the same meaning as a + sign.

When such a character string is read by the FORTRAN compiler, it is converted automatically from decimal form to binary form, and is stored into the machine as a four-byte integer. If the value of the decimal number exceeds the maximum allowable value $2^{31}-1 = 2147483647$, an error is diagnosed.

For instance, the decimal integer 425 is equal to 256+10x16+9, and therefore appears inside the machine as the four-byte integer with hexadecimal code *000001A9*. This kind of conversion is carried out automatically by the compiler, and there is no need to learn how to carry out such conversions yourself. Let the machine do it!

DEF: A *FORTRAN 4-byte real constant* appears in one of two forms:

i)   an ordinary decimal number of from *1 to 7 decimal digits, with a decimal point,* preceded by either a blank, a +, or a - sign;

ii)   an ordinary decimal number of from 1 to 7 decimal digits, with or without a decimal point, *followed by the letter E,* followed by a decimal exponent in the range -75 to +75 inclusive; the whole is preceded by either a blank, a +, or a - sign.

In the first form, (i), the presence of the decimal point signals to the compiler that the number is to be converted to floating point real number form; in form (ii), also called the exponential form or "E-Format", the letter E is used as a signal that conversion to floating point form is required, and that an exponent still follows. Thus the explicit appearance of the decimal point within the mantissa is not required in the exponential form, though it is permitted. The restriction to no more than 7 decimal digits reflects the fact that 4-byte floating numbers have a precision of no more than 7 significant decimal digits.

Example: The FORTRAN constants +0., -999.9999, 0.0, 5764.1, 7.0E+0, 7.0E0, 9761.25E+1, 7.E3, 7.0E3, 7.0E03, 7.0E+03, 700.0E1, .7E4, are all grammatically correct FORTRAN 4-byte real constants. The first 4 are written in ordinary decimal form (with between 1 and 7 decimal digits and an explicit decimal point), the remaining ones are written in E-format. The last 6 constants are all equal to the decimal number 7000.0.

The constants 0 and 7000 are *not* real constants, since they are *integer* constants;

3,471.2   is invalid because it contains an embedded comma;

1.E   is invalid because no exponent follows the letter E; write 1.E0!

1.2E+113   is invalid because the exponent has three digits;

23.5E+97   is invalid because the decimal exponent, 97, exceeds the maximum allowed value of 75.

DEF: A *FORTRAN 8-byte real constant* appears in one of two forms:

i)   an ordinary decimal number of from *8 to 16 decimal digits, with a decimal point,* preceded by either a blank, a +, or a - sign; or

ii)   an ordinary decimal number of from 1 to 16 decimal digits, with or without a decimal point, *followed by the letter D,* followed by a decimal exponent in the range -75 to +75 inclusive; the whole is preceded by either a blank, a + sign, or a - sign.

In the first form, conversion to floating point form is indicated by the presence of the decimal point, and the 8-byte length is indicated by the large number (8 to 16) of decimal digits; in the second form, both conversion to floating point form and the 8-byte length are indicated by the presence of the letter D. Form (ii) is often called the "D-Format".

Examples: 21.98753829457169, 1.0000000, 7.D3, 7D3, 7.0D3, 7.0D03, 7D+03, .7D4, 700.D1 are all grammatically correct FORTRAN 8-byte real constants. The last 7 of them are all equal to 7000.0000 (but *not* to 7000.000, since the latter would be interpreted by FORTRAN as a 4-byte real constant).

DEF: A *FORTRAN 8-byte complex constant* is a pair of FORTRAN 4-byte real constants, separated by one comma, and enclosed within parentheses.

DEF: A *FORTRAN 16-byte complex constant* is a pair of FORTRAN 8-byte real constants, separated by one comma, and enclosed within parentheses.

Examples: (21.4,-6E-8) is a FORTRAN 8-byte complex constant;
                (21.400000,-6D-8) is a FORTRAN 16-byte complex constant.

In each case, the first member of the pair represents the real part, the second member of the pair represents the imaginary part, of the complex number.

Note that both members of the pair must have the same number of bytes; the character string (21.4,-6D-8) is *invalid* because the real part is a 4-byte real constant, whereas the imaginary part is an 8-byte real constant. In the machine, complex numbers are stored either in 8-byte form (4 bytes for the real part, 4 bytes for the imaginary part) or in 16-byte form (8 bytes for the real part, 8 bytes for the imaginary part). Mixed forms are not permitted.

DEF: A *FORTRAN logical constant* can assume only one of two values, these being written as .TRUE. and .FALSE.; the periods before and after the letters are necessary; in certain cases, to be described later, .TRUE. may be abbreviated by the single letter T (without periods), and .FALSE. may be abbreviated by the single letter F (without periods).

When encountered in the source programme, a FORTRAN logical constant is translated automatically to *four-byte logical* form.

DEF: A *FORTRAN character string constant,* or *literal constant,* appears in one of two alternative forms:

i)   An integer between 1 and 255, followed by the letter H, followed by the precise number of characters indicated by the integer; blanks are counted as characters here; or

ii)   Between 1 and 255 characters, immediately preceded by an apostrophe ' and immediately followed by an apostrophe '; in this form the particular character "apostrophe" either must not appear at all within the character string, or if it is desired, it must appear in coded form namely two adjacent apostrophes: ''.

Example: The character string DON'T can be written as 5HDON'T or as 'DON''T'.

DRILL EXERCISES FOR CHAPTER VIII

1. State which of the following are valid integer constants, and correct the invalid ones.

    a) 0

    b) 91

    c) 0.

    d) 5,396

    e) -173

    f) -2147483647

    g) 27.

    h) 3145903612

2. State which of the following are valid 4-byte real constants, and correct the invalid ones.

    a) +0.

    b) -0

    c) -99.99999

    d) 3,471.1

    e) 3.E

    f) 47.8E90

    g) 7.9D2

    h) 19762.38E+1

    i) 1.0000000

    j) 0.

    k) 0.0

3. State which of the following are valid 8-byte real constants, and correct the invalid ones.

    a) +0.

    b) -0D0

    c) 00000001.

    d) 1.0000000

    e) 1.D0

    f) 1D0

    g) 5.9D81

    h) 35.78354219

    i) 6.3D03

    j) 6.3D3

    k) 6.3D+3

4. State which of the following are valid 8-byte complex constants, and correct the invalid ones.

    a) (4.7,-2.36)

    b) (292604,1.653)

    c) (4.E3,4E3)

    d) (4.12,.412E+1)

    e) (3576.34512,5672.143)

    f) (3.1,0.)

    g) (4.7,0)

5. State which of the following are valid 16-byte complex constants, and correct the invalid ones.

    a) (.47D0,-2.36D0)

    b) (292604.543,1.653D2)

    c) (4.D3,4D3)

    d) (4.12,4.12D0)

    e) (3576.34512,5672.143)

    f) (3.1D2,0.)

    g) (3.1D2,0)

    h) (3.1D2,0.0)

    i) (3.1D2,0.D0)

    j) (3.1D2,0D)

    k) (3.1D2,0D0)

6. State which of the following are valid character string (literal) constants, and correct the invalid ones.

a) DON'T

b) 'DON'T, PLEASE

c) 'DON'T, PLEASE'

d) 'DON''T, PLEASE'

e) 'PLEASE DON''T'

f) 12HDON'T, PLEASE

g) 12HPLEASE DON'T

h) 12HPLEASE DON''T

CHAPTER IX

FORTRAN VARIABLES. TYPE DECLARATIONS. INITIALIZATION.

A. Predefined Type Convention

As mentioned at the beginning of Chapter VIII, a FORTRAN source programme contains numbers and non-numerical information in two main forms: as explicit information, or FORTRAN constants; and as the contents of named memory locations, or FORTRAN variables. In Chapter VIII, we gave the conventions FORTRAN uses to recognize the various types of FORTRAN constants; in this Chapter, we define the rules FORTRAN uses to recognize different types of FORTRAN variables. We also show how one may set some or all of the named variables to desired initial values at the start of the execution phase.

The *identifier name* serves two separate functions:

i)   it tells the location in memory of the named memory location (to be more precise, of the first byte of whatever number of bytes are required for this type of variable); and

ii) it tells the type of storage involved, e.g., 2-byte integer, 16-byte complex, etc.

We are now concerned with the second of these two functions.

The statements which tell the compiler how to interpret various identifier names are called *type declaration statements*. Unlike most of the statements encountered so far (assignment statements, GO TO, IF, READ, PRINT), type declaration statements are *not* translated directly into machine language; rather, type declaration statements tell the compiler just how to translate *other* statements, namely statements in which certain variable identifier names appear.

Statements which are instructions to the compiler, but are not themselves translated into machine language by the compiler, are called *"non-executable statements"*. This horrible bit of jargon means that, since these statements are never translated into machine language, they do not give rise to (translated) machine commands which are obeyed, or "executed", during the execution phase. Type declaration statements are non-executable statements; we shall encounter other non-executable statements later on.

There is a *hierarchy of type declaration statements* in FORTRAN. The lowest member of this hierarchy is not a statement at all, being merely the type convention *assumed,* or "predefined", by FORTRAN in the absence of other information. Next in the hierarchy comes the *implicit* type declaration, and highest of all is the *explicit* type declaration. In case of conflict, the type declaration of superior hierarchical rank determines the type FORTRAN associates with any variable identifier name.

DEF: The lowest rank of the hierarchy is the *predefined* type convention, which types variable identifier names by the *first letter* of the name.   *Variables whose names start with one of the letters I, J, K, L, M, N are taken to be 4-byte integers; all other variable names are taken to be 4-byte real numbers.*

Note that the predefined convention associates *every* identifier name with a memory location of length 4 bytes; the initial letter of the name merely tells whether these four bytes are to be interpreted by the machine as a 4-byte integer or as a 4-byte floating-point number.

B.   Implied Conversion

Once a variable name has been associated with a certain type of variable, only a number of that type can be stored into the corresponding memory location.   This rule can give rise to *implied conversions.*

For example, an implied conversion occurs in the assignment statement

AWFUL=23

for the following reason: The FORTRAN constant 23 is interpreted as an integer number (4-byte integer form within the machine), because no decimal point has been written.   The variable name AWFUL is the name of a 4-byte real number, since it starts with the letter A.   Thus, on the face of it, the above statement is contradictory.

What FORTRAN does with such a statement is this: The integer constant 23 (in 4-byte integer form within the machine) is fetched; it is then *converted* to 4-byte real number form; and this converted number is stored into memory location AWFUL.

This process is called *implied conversion* since the conversion operation is not programmed explicitly as such, but is implied by the number types appearing to the right and to the left of the equal sign in the assignment statement.

Whereas the above statement implies a conversion operation, the statement

AWFUL=23.0

implies no conversion at all: the real number 23.0 is already in 4-byte floating point number form inside the machine (since a decimal point has been included); thus this pattern of binary digits is fetched, and then stored directly into memory location AWFUL.

Since conversion takes machine time, implied conversions should be avoided.   Nothing of value is obtained by writing AWFUL=23 rather than AWFUL=23.0 — the same number is stored into location AWFUL eventually!   But with AWFUL=23 we have used machine time unnecessarily.

An even stronger reason for avoiding implied conversions is the possibility of *truncation of the number.*   For example, the statement

IDIOT=23.9

presents the machine with a difficulty: a memory location named IDIOT (name starting with the letter I) must contain an integer, yet the number 23.9 is not an integer. Naturally, any sensible person would replace 23.9 by the nearest integer, i.e., by the integer 24. However, FORTRAN does *not* do this; rather, it simply ignores everything after the decimal point, and *truncates* 23.9 to the integer 23. Since this is very rarely what the programmer really wants, implied conversion from real number form to integer form should be avoided.

C. Implicit Type Declaration

The second member of the hierarchy of type declarations is the *implicit type declaration*. The purpose of the implicit type declaration is to *alter* the predefined type convention, to some other convention desired by the programmer; but variable names are still assigned types according to the *first letter* of the variable identifier name. There can be *only one* implicit type declaration statement in any one FORTRAN programme or sub-programme (see Chapter XIV for sub-programmes). In a main programme, the implicit type declaration must be the *very first statement* of the programme (comments excluded); in a subprogramme, the implicit type declaration must be the second statement of the sub-programme.

The implicit type declaration statement contains *type codes* and *lists of initials*. We start by defining these two terms.

DEF: There are exactly 12 type codes, namely INTEGER, INTEGER*4, INTEGER*2, REAL, REAL*4, REAL*8, COMPLEX, COMPLEX*8, COMPLEX*16, LOGICAL, LOGICAL*4, and LOGICAL*1. Type codes containing a number declare the desired number of bytes, e.g., REAL*8 declares an 8-byte real variable; type codes in which this specification is omitted are equivalent to the type code appearing immediately after them, in the list above; i.e., INTEGER is equivalent to INTEGER*4, REAL is equivalent to REAL*4, COMPLEX is equivalent to COMPLEX*8, and LOGICAL is equivalent to LOGICAL*4.

DEF: An *initial* is a single alphabetic character; a *range of initials* is a set of alphabetically adjacent characters, abbreviated by writing only the first and last initial, separated by a minus sign.

Example: B is an initial; B-F is a range of initials, equivalent to the set of initials: B, C, D, E, F.

DEF: A *list of initials* consists of one or more initials and/or ranges of initials, separated by commas, and enclosed in parentheses.

Example: (B-F, H, U-W) is a list of initials; an equivalent list would be (B, C, D, E, F, H, U, V, W).

DEF: The *implicit type declaration* statement must be the first statement of a main programme, the second statement of a subprogramme (not counting comments); it starts with the word IMPLICIT followed by at least one blank, followed by a list of type codes and associated lists of initials, with a comma preceding all but the first type code. The effect of this statement is to declare all variables starting with one of the initials in the lists of initials, to be of the type declared by the associated type code. The various lists of initials must not overlap, i.e., no letter may appear in more than one such list.

Examples: 1) IMPLICIT REAL*4(A-H,O-Z,$), INTEGER*4(I-N). This declares all variable names starting with I, J, K, L, M, or N to be 4-byte integers, and all other variables (named memory locations) to contain 4-byte real numbers. Note that this is identical with the pre-defined convention of FORTRAN; thus, if this typing convention is what we desire, there is no need for the type declaration statement at all.

2)   IMPLICIT REAL*8 (B-F, H, U-W), COMPLEX*16(X-Z),INTEGER*2(I-K), LOGICAL*1(P)
Here we have altered the pre-defined convention. Variable names starting with any of the letters B, C, D, E, F, H, U, V, W are declared to be 8-byte real variables (double precision floating point numbers); variable names starting with any of X, Y, Z are declared to be 16-byte complex variables (double precision complex numbers); variable names starting with any of I, J, K are declared to be 2-byte integer variables (rather than 4-byte integer variables in the pre-defined convention); and finally, variable names starting with the letter P are declared to be 1-byte logical variables. Note that not all initials are covered by that declaration statement. Initials which do not appear in the IMPLICIT statement lists of initials retain the type defined by the pre-defined convention. In our case, this leaves variable names starting with any of A, G, O, Q, R, S, T, $ as 4-byte real variables, and variable names starting with any of L, M, N as 4-byte integer variables.

Although this implicit type declaration statement is grammatically correct, it represents an example of *poor coding*. The programmer is most unlikely to succeed in remembering such a peculiar set of conventions for his variables. As soon as he names one or more of his variables incorrectly, i.e., with initial letters in disagreement with these conventions, the programme will fail to do what he wants; but this kind of failure is among the hardest to detect and correct. For example, suppose he names a variable ALPHA, wanting it to be a double-precision real variable (REAL*8 rather than REAL*4). It is rather unlikely that FORTRAN will diagnose an error or give any indication of an error, since ALPHA is still a valid real variable identifier. However, the object programme will carry the variable ALPHA to a precision of only 1 part in 10^7, rather than the desired 1 part in 10^{16}; the errors arising from this are likely to be small, and correspondingly hard to detect; but they are still errors!

It is therefore most desirable to adopt *simple* type conventions, which are easily remembered. One possible choice is:

IMPLICIT COMPLEX*8(C), REAL*8(D), COMPLEX*16(Z), LOGICAL*1($)

This type convention has mnemonic value: 'C' reminds one of "complex", 'D' reminds one of "double precision"; in fact, just these two conventions are used for FORTRAN inbuilt functions (see Chapter XII); the FORTRAN convention for inbuilt double precision complex functions is the set of two starting letters 'CD', which is beyond the capability of the implicit type declaration statement; we therefore use the initial letter Z for double precision complex variables; finally, the initial 'alphabetic' character $ for logical variables is not likely to be confused with anything else.

Of course, the above is by no means always the best type declaration statement for all programmes; it depends very much on the particular programme! For example, a programme dealing exclusively with integers could well have the simple type declaration

IMPLICIT INTEGER(A-Z,$)

This declares *every* variable name to refer to a 4-byte integer. Conversely, if there is a great deal of calculation with double-precision real numbers, but no complex numbers are used in the calculation, we may use

IMPLICIT REAL*8(A-H,O-Z,$)

This differs from the pre-defined convention only through the fact that all real variable identifier names refer to 8-byte real variables, rather than 4-byte real variables. Since round-off errors arising from the use of single precision (4-byte) real numbers are intolerably large in most serious calculations, *it is highly advisable to use the above type convention in all serious FORTRAN programming of calculations not involving complex numbers.* The convention is easy to remember, since it agrees with the pre-defined convention in everything except precision of the variables. Use of 8-byte real variables through-out the calculation costs memory space, naturally; but with most of the larger models of the IBM/360, it costs very little machine time.

D.   The Data Statement

We now interrupt our discussion of type declaration statements, to insert a discussion of *variable initialization statements.* As we mentioned in Chapter II, the initial values of named variables, at the start of the execution phase, are in general unknown, just stuff left over from the preceding job in the batch. If one wants to assign some definite initial value to a named variable, this must be done explic-itly. One way, but a rather inefficient way, is the use of assignment statements, such as HEIGHT=5.89, at the start of the source programme. A more efficient method would be to write, at the beginning of the programme,

DATA HEIGHT/5.89/

This makes sure that the named memory location HEIGHT contains the number 5.89 *at the start of the execution phase.* If the value of HEIGHT is changed later on, say by an assignment statement such as HEIGHT=HEIGHT+1.5, the initial value is "forgotten" and never restored by the machine. Thus the DATA statement is most useful for variables whose values are not meant to change at all during the calculation.

More than one variable can be initialized in a single DATA statement. For example, suppose we wish to initialize HEIGHT, A, K, M, and S; this can be done by the single statement

DATA HEIGHT/5.89/,A/3.24/,K/-14/,M/245/,S/2.E-23/

giving the name of each variable, followed by its desired initial value enclosed by slashes: / . . ./ . Dif-ferent items of this list are separated by commas, but there is neither an initial comma, nor a final comma.

As an alternative, the lists of variable names and their initial values can be consolidated, as follows:

DATA HEIGHT,A,K,M,S/5.89,3.24,-14,245,2.E-23/

This statement is equivalent to the preceding one. However, the earlier statement is *cleaner coding,* since it shows directly the initial value assigned to every named variable in the list. The consolidated list form invites programming errors, i.e., getting items out of order, or omitting an item altogether.

In practice, a bit of common sense by the programmer goes a long way in deciding what DATA statements to write. To get a clean code, it is desirable to write separate DATA statements, or at least separate item lists within one DATA statement, for variables of different types. It is desirable to write consolidated lists only for those sets of items which naturally belong together; and to keep other items distinct. For example, suppose that we have the IMPLICIT type declaration

IMPLICIT COMPLEX*8(C), REAL*8(D), COMPLEX*16(Z), LOGICAL*1($)

at the beginning of the programme. We might then wish to initialize the values of PI and E, both in

69

single and double precision, to initialize the complex cube root of 1 to the value $-\frac{1}{2} + i\sqrt{3}/2$, again in both single and double precision, to declare I, J, and K to have initial values 1, 3, and 3 respectively, and to declare the logical variables $BILL and $JACK to be .TRUE. and .FALSE., respectively, at the start of the execution phase. The DATA statements to achieve this might read

```
DATA PI,E/3.141593,2.718282/
DATA DPI,DE/3.141592653589793,2.718281828459045/
DATA COMEGA/(-.5,.8660254)/,ZOMEGA/(-.5D0,.8660254038844385)/
DATA I,J,K/1,2*3/,$BILL,$JACK/T,F/
```

Notes:

1. All these could have been combined into a single DATA statement, with item lists separated by commas, as in the last DATA statement shown; but this would be of doubtful value: it is a good deal easier to correct an error in a short statement, than in an excessively long statement. In fact, when one corrects an error in a single very long statement, one is only too likely to introduce some new error purely through incorrect copying. Since errors *will* occur, the programme should be planned from the start so as to make correction of these errors easy!

2. Note the mnemonic names for PI, E, and OMEGA; the initials required for correct type identification are put in front of the mnemonic as required; that is, the name of the storage location which contains PI to double precision is DPI, the single precision complex value of OMEGA is stored in COMEGA, the double precision complex value is stored in ZOMEGA. After a while, the programmer gets accustomed to such conventions, and they become practically second nature. Good mnemonic names are an essential in clean programming.

3. The short-hand form 2*3 is permitted for successive equal constants, such as 3,3.

4. In DATA statements, the FORTRAN logical constants .TRUE. and .FALSE. may be abbreviated by the single letters T and F, respectively.

5. The constants supplied within the DATA statement must fit, in number and type, the variable names in the lists of variables. There is no implied conversion; rather, a constant of wrong type for the variable name in question is diagnosed as an error.

However, there is one exception to this: In the DATA statement, we are permitted to use the hexadecimal constant and literal constant forms, for any named memory location; the number of bytes so stored is determined by the the name of the named memory location, e.g., a 4-byte real variable is filled with 4 bytes of information, a 2-byte integer variable is filled with 2 bytes of information and so on.

In the hexadecimal form, the programmer specifies in full detail just what pattern of binary digits is to appear inside the machine, by use of the hexadecimal digits described in Chapter VII. Leading hexadecimal zeros may be omitted. If the number of bytes supplied exceeds the number of bytes that can be stored within the named location, the left-most bytes are dropped, one by one, until the correct number of bytes remain; these are then stored. No conversion of any sort is carried out in this form of data initialization.

As an example, and using the same type convention as before, consider the statement:

DATA L/Z1A9/,A/Z1A9/,DA/Z1A9/,$Q/Z1A9/

Since L is a variable of type INTEGER*4, it contains enough room for four bytes of information. Thus L is initialized by this data statement to the value 000001A9. Interpreted as an integer, this represents 1x256 + 10x16 +9 = 425. The variable A, of type REAL*4, is initialized to exactly the same pattern of binary digits, i.e., the four adjacent bytes named by the identifier A also contain the pattern 000001A9; however, this pattern of digits is now interpreted as quite a different number. According to Chapter VII, the first byte contains the sign bit and the integer k which is used in the exponent, k-64. Since this byte is 00, the sign is positive, and the value of k is also zero, leading to an exponent of exactly -64. The remaining three bytes are the mantissa, interpreted as a rational number. The implied value of A is therefore the rational number

$$+ \quad \frac{425}{(256)^3} \times (16)^{-64}$$

Since DA is of type REAL*8, it is filled with 8 bytes, namely 00000000000001A9. The interpretation of this pattern of digits by the machine is again a rational number, with the same sign and same exponent of 16, but a different mantissa, to wit,

$$+ \quad \frac{425}{(256)^7} \times (16)^{-64}$$

Finally, $Q has been declared as LOGICAL*1, and therefore can contain only 1 byte of information. Thus the leading "1" is dropped from "1A9", and the content of the single byte named $Q is made equal to A9. This is not a valid logical constant for FORTRAN, but no checking of this sort is carried out: the given pattern of hexadecimal digits is stored, willy-nilly.

It should be apparent by now that hexadecimal constants should not be used by beginning programmers.

In the literal form, or character string form, the conversion carried out by the machine occurs one character at a time: the literal character supplied by the programmer is converted to the associated bit pattern of a single byte in the machine, and that byte is stored. Unlike hexadecimal notation, where a single byte is represented by two hexadecimal digits, the literal notation assigns one entire byte to each character supplied by the programmer.

We are not concerned, in this book, with the internal form of character storage used by FORTRAN. However, for purposes of illustration, let us mention that the character "1" is stored as the byte F1, i.e., the 8 binary digits 11110001; the character "9" is stored as the byte F9, i.e., the 8 binary digits 11111001; the character "A" is stored as the byte C1, i.e., the 8 binary digits 11000001; and the blank character is stored as 40, i.e., the 8 binary digits 01000000. With this information in mind, consider the effect of the statement

DATA M/'1A9'/,$P/3H1A9/

Both constants are the same, namely the string of three characters 1A9. These are coded as 3 bytes inside the machine. Since M has been declared to be of type INTEGER*4, the storage location M must contain 4 bytes, not 3. Unlike hexadecimal form, the literal form supplies the missing part to the right (not to the left) and as coded blanks (not zeros). Thus, the content of the four bytes labelled by the identifier name M are F1, C1, F9, 40, respectively, these being the coded forms of the characters 1, A, 9, and blank.

Since $P has been declared to be of type LOGICAL*1, this memory location can contain only one byte-coded character. Unlike the hexadecimal form, in the literal form the right-most characters are dropped, one by one, until we get a character string of the desired length. Thus, the characters 9 and A are dropped in turn; the single character 1 is retained, and is stored into memory location $P in the coded form F1.

E.   The Explicit Type Declaration

Having discussed the predefined type convention, the implicit type declaration statement, and the use of the DATA statement for initialization of the values of named variables, we now turn to the third, and hierarchically superior, form of type declaration, the *explicit type declaration*. In the explicit type declaration, variables are typed, not by the first letter of their identifier name, but by the entire name. For example, the predefined type convention makes everything starting with I, J, K, L, M, or N into a 4-byte integer variable. Suppose we would like KLOT to be an 8-byte real variable identifier. We may then write the explicit type declaration

REAL*8 KLOT

This has the effect of declaring the particular variable name KLOT to be of type REAL*8, but other variable names starting with K remain of type INTEGER*4.

We give below, in small print, the detailed rules for the explicit type declaration statement. We use small print because *we advise against the use of explicit type declarations*. The IMPLICIT type declaration statement is sufficiently flexible for all reasonable programming; declaring a particular variable name to be of a type conflicting with the IMPLICIT type convention adopted, is practically an open invitation to commit programming errors. In the example above, why should we insist on the name KLOT for a variable of type REAL*8? Why not make it agree with a reasonable type convention, merely by calling it DKLOT? Coding mistakes come sufficiently easily and frequently to make special invitations quite unnecessary.

The explicit type declaration starts with a type code (see the definition of type codes earlier in this Chapter), followed by at least one blank, followed by a set of "explicit type list items" separated by commas.

DEF: An explicit type list item may take one of four forms (further forms will be introduced in Chapter XIII, for array variables):

  i)   NAME, this being a grammatically correct variable identifier name

  ii)   NAME*s where s is an integer constant, equal to 1, 2, 4, 8, or 16; s denotes the number of bytes of storage reserved for this variable. If a value of s appears next to a particular name, this overrides the value of s, if any, in the type code at the beginning of the declaration statement.

  iii) NAME/constant/ where constant stands for a FORTRAN constant of the correct type; this constant is used to set the initial value of the named variable, i.e., it serves the same function as the DATA statement.

  iv)   NAME*s/constant/

DEF: The explicit type declaration statement starts with a type code, followed by at least one blank; thereafter we have a list of items, as defined above, separated by commas. There is no comma before the list, and no comma at the end of the list.

Example: The explicit type declaration statement:

REAL*8 KLOT,ITEM*4,LADY/2.5D0/,LOUT*4/-3.1E2/

declares KLOT and LADY to be of type REAL*8, ITEM and LOUT to be of type REAL*4. For the latter two, the length code '8' of the declaration REAL*8 in front is overridden by the length code '4' attached to the name itself, i.e., ITEM*4 and LOUT*4. In addition to declaring these types, the variables LADY and LOUT are initialized to 2.5 and

-310., respectively.

Overriding the type specification in front, such as REAL*8, by explicit specification of the number of bytes next to the name, such as ITEM*4, is likely to lead to errors; we advise strongly against this.

In our view, explicit type declarations should be avoided altogether, but if used, at least variables of the same type should be declared together; thus the single declaration statement above should be split into two separate statements:

REAL*4 ITEM,LOUT/-3.1E2/
REAL*8 KLOT,LADY/2.5D0/

Insistence on clean, easily readable code is not an affectation or a frill; it is a necessity in computer programming.

In the explicit type statement, the type code REAL*8 can be replaced by a synonym called DOUBLE PRECISION. That is, the declaration statement

DOUBLE PRECISION KLOT,LADY/2.5D0/

is completely equivalent to

REAL*8 KLOT,LADY/2.5D0/

This is one of the examples of different "dialects" of FORTRAN: in some dialects of FORTRAN, the form DOUBLE PRECISION is the only one permitted; other dialects use such expressions as TYPE DOUBLE. The form of FORTRAN IV described in the body of this book recognizes DOUBLE PRECISION and REAL*8 as synonyms, but does not recognize TYPE DOUBLE at all. (*)

Note that DOUBLE PRECISION is a synonym for REAL*8 only within an explicit type declaration. It is not a synonym in an IMPLICIT type declaration, and should not be used for IMPLICIT type declarations.

F.   Type Character in WATFOR

Although standard FORTRAN, at present, allows only the type codes listed in Section C, it is likely that the FORTRAN language will be extended soon, to include a type declaration for character strings. The WATFOR compiler already includes such a type code.

DEF: The type code CHARACTER*s where s is an unsigned integer between 1 and 120, is a valid type code in WATFOR. It may be used in either the IMPLICIT or the explicit type declaration statements. With this type code, storage is set aside for a character string of length s.

Example: The implicit type declaration

IMPLICIT CHARACTER*25($)

(*)   In our view, a length specification in terms of numbers of bytes, such as REAL*4 or REAL*8, is more machine-dependent than a compiler language ought to be. Not all computer memories are organized by 8-bit groups called bytes. A more neutral term such as S for "single precision" and D for "double precision"would be preferable. That is, in our view, REAL*S and REAL*D would be preferable to REAL*4 and REAL*8. It may be hoped that future versions of FORTRAN IV will permit some such useage. In practice, there are only two options for the length code (number of bytes) in all of the types INTEGER, REAL, COMPLEX, and LOGICAL; thus length codes S and D would suffice. Only for the type CHARACTER do we need a numerical indication of the length; but since the number 24 in CHARACTER*24 is simply the number of characters contained in that area of storage, this is not a machine-dependent definition, and allows implementation of this type on any machine (including machines whose memories are not organized in 8-bit groups).

declares all variable names starting with the symbol $ to be character strings of length 25. In this way, we can set up "messages" of length 25 characters by DATA statements, e.g.,

```
DATA $MSSG1/'THIS IS A MESSAGE'/,$MSSG2/'ANOTHER MESSAGE'/
```

The character string stored into the 25-byte area named $MSSG1 is actually

```
THIS,IS,A,MESSAGE,,,,,,,,
```

where we have used ,to indicate a blank character. That is, sufficiently many blank characters are supplied *to the right* to make the total length of the message equal to 25 characters.

The same effect can be achieved by an *explicit* type declaration:

```
CHARACTER*25 $MSSG1/'THIS IS A MESSAGE'/,$MSSG2/'ANOTHER MESSAGE'/
```

Here is a case where the explicit type declaration may be preferable to the implicit one, particularly since the *length* of the messages can be varied from one message to the next, e.g.,

```
CHARACTER $MSSG1*17/'THIS IS A MESSAGE'/,$MSSG2*15/'ANOTHER MESSAG
   1E'/
```

This last statement is *not* equivalent to the earlier ones: now $MSSG1 occupies only 17 bytes of core storage, $MSSG2 only 15 bytes of core storage, whereas before these identifier names referred to areas of 25 bytes of core storage, each.

The great advantage of this type code in WATFOR is that it *allows free output of messages by means of PRINT statements*. It is very bad practice to print out numbers without any indication what these numbers mean. *Output numbers, be they echo-check or final results, should always be accompanied by messages telling what the output numbers mean*.

As an example, let us amend the simple programme of Chapter V to give messages for the output. We recall that we read in values of BASE and HEIGHT, compute AREA (the area of a right-angle triangle with that base and height), and print out these three numbers. So far, these have been just three numbers, no messages. Suppose we wish the output to appear in the form

FOR BASE AND HEIGHT OF . . . .   AREA OF TRIANGLE EQUALS   . . . .

where the dots denote the actual numerical values of BASE, HEIGHT, and AREA, respectively. To achieve this the modified programme reads:

```
$JOB              10.001,KP=26   BROWN                  68235179    JONES
C     THIS PROGRAMME COMPUTES THE AREA OF A TRIANGLE
C     INPUT DATA ARE BASE,HEIGHT
C     OUTPUT NUMBERS ARE BASE, HEIGHT, AREA
      CHARACTER*25 $MSSG1/'FOR BASE AND HEIGHT OF'/,$MSSG2/'AREA OF TRIA
     1NGLE EQUALS'/
 1000 READ,BASE,HEIGHT
      AREA=0.5*BASE*HEIGHT
      PRINT,$MSSG1,BASE,HEIGHT,$MSSG2,AREA
      GO TO 1000
      END
```

74

```
$ENTRY
 25.6 14.7
 28.9 22.3
 .148 .005
 3.E-6 4.E-8
$IBSYS
```

With this programme, the first line output in execution reads:

FOR BASE AND HEIGHT OF 0.2560000E 02 0.1470000E 02 AREA OF TRIANGLE EQUALS
0.1881600E 03

This form of output is much preferable to just three numbers on the line.

At the present time, the type CHARACTER exists only in WATFOR, not in standard G-level FORTRAN. In order to minimize incompatibility with other versions of FORTRAN, we shall *not*, in the next few Chapters, include this form of message output in our explicit examples. That is, our worked-out examples will be restricted to purely numerical output, no messages, until we get to Chapter XV (FORMAT-controlled output). But the programming exercises done by students should contain messages, in a form similar to the above, for *all* output numbers. If and when standard FORTRAN is augmented to include the type CHARACTER, this book will be modified accordingly.

DRILL EXERCISES FOR CHAPTER IX

1. We want variable names starting with A, B, ..., H to be double precision real, starting with O, P, Q, ...,Z to be double precision complex variables, and names starting with $ to be logical variables. Write an appropriate type declaration statement. Where should this statement be placed in the programme?

2. With the above type convention, we want to initialize ALPHA, BETA, GAMMA, and DELTA to unity, OMEGA to $-\frac{1}{2}+i\frac{1}{2}\sqrt{3}$, ZI to square root of -1, and $TEST to .TRUE. Write FORTRAN statements to achieve this.

3. Assuming the pre-defined type convention, which of the following statements involve implied conversions? Which of these conversions, if any, give results different from the usual "rounding" of numbers?

    a) HEIGHT=2.76
    b) HEIGHT=314
    c) IDIOT=314
    d) IDIOT=2.76

4. Assuming the type declaration of exercise 1 to be in effect, write a type declaration suitable to make PRICE a double precision real variable and BESSEL a double precision complex variable.

5. Write type declaration statements to make all variable names starting with letters between A and T, inclusive, the names of 4-byte integer variables, and to make names starting with U, V, W, X, Y, or Z the names of logical variables. However, the particular variable names FRED, NURK, NING, and NONG are to be the names of double precision real variables, initialized to unity, unity, zero, and unity, respectively.

CHAPTER X

FORTRAN ARITHMETIC.   MIXED MODE CONVENTIONS

A.   Integer Arithmetic

Chapters VII, VIII, and IX have dealt with information storage in the machine, and the FORTRAN conventions and declaration statements required to assure the desired storage of information. The present Chapter is concerned with the *use* of this information, i.e., with calculations performed by the use of the stored information.

The basic arithmetic operations carried out by the machine are addition, subtraction, multiplication, and division; these are indicated in FORTRAN by the special characters +, -, *, and /, respectively. However, it is important to understand what the machine actually does when these operations are specified by the programmer; particularly since what the machine does is sometimes not what a beginning programmer would expect it to do!

The two main forms of arithmetic in the machine are *integer arithmetic* and *floating point arithmetic*. Although the FORTRAN symbol "+" is the same for integer addition and floating point addition, the machine orders are different, and do different things. The FORTRAN compiler looks at the *types* of variables (or constants) to be added, and translates the symbol "+" accordingly. Thus, the FORTRAN statement I=J+3 gives rise to an integer addition of the integer 3 and the integer contained in storage location J; whereas the FORTRAN statement A=B+3.0 gives rise to a floating point addition of the floating point number 3.0 and the floating point number contained in storage location B.

We first discuss *integer arithmetic*. This is *exact* for addition, subtraction and multiplication. The only thing which can go wrong in these operations is that the result may *overflow* the maximum size of integers permitted in the machine. We recall, from Chapter VII, that integers in the machine must not exceed $2^{31}-1=2147483647$ in absolute value. Thus the integer 1000000 is within the permitted range, and so is the integer 2000000; but their product is too large to fit into a 4-byte integer storage location, and gives rise to *integer arithmetic overflow*. Some versions of WATFOR ignore this error; other versions terminate execution of the object programme, with the error message KO-5, meaning "too many fixed-point overflows" (in practice, one is too many; but see Chapter XIV, D, example 1).

In integer arithmetic, *division* is not always possible; e.g., there is no integer quotient of 7 by 4. The FORTRAN convention for integer division is *not* the integer nearest to the true answer (i.e., 2 for 7/4), but rather is the *integral part* of the true quotient, i.e., 1 is the integral part of 1.75. For negative numbers, we truncate irrespective of sign, i.e., the division (-7)/4 gives rise to the answer -1 in the machine.

Arithmetic operations necessary to evaluate a well formed arithmetic expression are carried out *before* storage of the answer into some memory location. Thus, the assignment statement

A=3/4

does *not* imply that the integers 3 and 4 are converted to real number form, their quotient computed as a real number, and the real number stored into location named A. Far from it! There is an implied conversion here, but the conversion is done *after* evaluation of the arithmetic expressions; thus, what the machine does is to perform an *integer division* of the integer 3 by the integer 4, obtaining the result 0 as the integral part of 0.75; the integer 0 is then converted to the floating point number 0.0, and this number is stored into memory location A. Thus, the FORTRAN statements A=3/4 and A=0.0 are *equivalent;* both give the answer 0.0 for A! This peculiarity of FORTRAN gives rise to many coding errors by beginners. But there is nothing which can be done about it, other than learning to live with it. All dialects of FORTRAN agree in this feature, and so many FORTRAN-coded programmes make use of it deliberately, that changing this convention is out of the question by now.

Since integer arithmetic is exact (i.e., there is no round-off error), there is no danger in using the comparison operators .EQ. and .NE. to compare integer results. For example, suppose we wish to produce a table of the squares, cubes, and fourth powers of the odd integers between 1 and 99. Letting I be the identifier name of the integer, we want I to range over the values I=1,3,5,7, . . . , 97,99. We can write a loop to do this, by setting I=1 initially, advancing I by 2 units each time, and stopping after I has reached the exact value 101. The flow diagram is given below, and next to it we give the FORTRAN code for the programme.

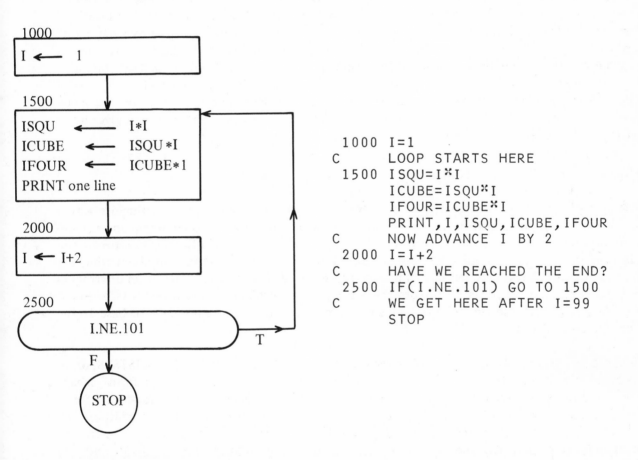

```
1000  I=1
C       LOOP STARTS HERE
1500  ISQU=I*I
       ICUBE=ISQU*I
       IFOUR=ICUBE*I
       PRINT,I,ISQU,ICUBE,IFOUR
C       NOW ADVANCE I BY 2
2000  I=I+2
C       HAVE WE REACHED THE END?
2500  IF(I.NE.101) GO TO 1500
C       WE GET HERE AFTER I=99
       STOP
```

Unlike floating point arithmetic, the exact nature of integer arithmetic means that if the number 101 is reached at all, it is reached exactly; that is, I eventually becomes equal to exactly 101, not perhaps 100.99997. Thus, the comparison statement IF(I.NE.101) will give the desired result; when I has reached 101 the well-formed logical expression I.NE.101 assumes the value .FALSE.; at this stage, we *skip* the command GO TO 1500, and jump straight to the following command, to wit, STOP.

Although this programme would work, it is another example of *poor coding*. The condition which we want to impose for going around the loop once more is not really (I.NE.101) but rather (I.LE.99). Thus, the cleanly coded programme reads

```
 1000  I=1
C       LOOP STARTS HERE
 1500  ISQU=I*I
       ICUBE=ISQU*I
       IFOUR=ICUBE*I
       PRINT,I,ISQU,ICUBE,IFOUR
C       NOW ADVANCE I BY 2
 2000  I=I+2
C       HAVE WE REACHED THE END?
 2500  IF(I.LE.99) GO TO 1500
C       WE GET HERE AFTER I=99
       STOP
```

Note: We have coded IFOUR=ICUBE*I, rather than IFOUR=I**4. Mathematically, the two are equivalent. But within the machine, evaluating the fourth power of the number stored in location I can not be done as a single multiplication. The least that is required is to multiply I by itself, to get the square of I, and then to multiply that result by itself; altogether two multiplications, the first of which merely produces a number we have had to compute anyway, namely ISQU! Thus the statement IFOUR=I**4 is wasteful of machine time, and should be replaced either by IFOUR=ISQU*ISQU or be IFOUR=ICUBE*I, either of which requires only a single multiplication. This is one of many instances where the FORTRAN language can be used in alternative ways, some of which give rise to more efficient object code than others.

B.   Floating Point Arithmetic.   Truncation and Rounding.

Having discussed integer arithmetic, we now turn to the second main type of arithmetic within the machine, *floating point arithmetic*. In this form of arithmetic, division presents no special problem, and arithmetic overflow is rare, since the absolute values of numbers in floating point form can go as high as 10^{75}. But the results are now not exact, and something must be said about rounding errors, about the difference between rounding and truncation, and about the propagation of errors in an extended computation. We shall discuss these things using ordinary decimal numbers, with exponents to base 10, even though the machine stores binary numbers with exponents to base 16, the principles are quite the same.

Suppose we wish to add the two single-precision real numbers 12.36483 and 0.04351878, or, in "normalized" exponential form, 0.1236483E+2 and 0.4351878E-1; the "normalized form" means that the mantissa lies between 0.1 and 1 in absolute value (in the machine, with hexadecimal form, the normalized mantissa lies between 1/16 and 1 in absolute value). To carry out the addition, the machine looks at the two numbers, decides which one has the bigger exponent, and then rearranges the other number to have the same exponent. In this case, the number 0.4351878E-1 would be rewritten as 0.0004351878E+2, no longer normalized. In this form, the mantissa has too many digits. The machine keeps 8 digits, i.e., the standard 7 digits plus one "guard digit", and then performs the addition

        0.1236483E+2
   +   0.00043518E+2   (the "8" is the guard digit)

   = 0.12408348E+2,   rounded up to 0.1240835E+2

The result of this addition is *rounded,* that is, the number which eventually emerges has a mantissa with last digit equal to 5 (rounded result of 48) rather than 4.

On the other hand, in the addition of two *double-precision* (8-byte) floating point numbers, there is no guard digit, and *no rounding occurs. No rounding occurs in multiplication or division* of either single-precision or double-precision floating point numbers. The results in all these cases are obtained by *truncation* rather than by *rounding.*

The insistence on the difference between truncation and rounding in floating point arithmetic operations may strike the reader as a technical quibble of no real significance; after all, one might be tempted to say, what difference does it all make? The error, if any, occurs down in the last digit of a number which already has at least 7 significant decimal digits, or 16 significant decimal digits for the double-precision case. Who cares?

The answer is, you had better care! True enough, in any one operation, the error produced by not rounding is quite small. But if you wished to carry out only one operation, why go to the trouble of programming an electronic computer? The whole purpose of the computer is to carry out a *large number* of arithmetic operations; what is a small error in any one operation, can easily become a large error in the final result!

Let us make a quick estimate: at the rate of 6 micro-seconds = 6×10^{-6} seconds per floating point addition in an IBM 360/50, we can perform 10^7 additions in 1 minute=60 seconds. If we add numbers of the same sign and of the same general order of magnitude, then the error per addition is of the order of 1 part in 10^7. *If all these errors reinforce each other,* then the total error after 1 minute of computation is 10^7 times the error per addition, i.e., *we have no significant digits at all after 1 minute of computation.* Now do you see why you should care?!

Here is where rounding really helps: the error made in any one addition is not decreased very much by rounding, as opposed to truncation; the error is perhaps halved, but that by itself would not help much. What *does* help is that rounding makes the errors *random in sign:* there will be, on an average, as many errors tending to make the answers larger, as errors tending to make the answers smaller.

The effect of this on the overall error is dramatic. It is the difference between a sober man, always going in one direction, and a drunken man who is as likely to step forward as backward. After 10^7 steps, the sober man is 10^7 steps away from his starting point; but the drunken man is as likely to be to the left of the starting point, as to the right; his distance from the starting point is not likely to be anywhere near 10^7 steps. In fact, a good estimate of his likely distance from the starting point is the *square root* of the number of steps, i.e., his likely distance from the starting point is only about $(10^7)^{1/2} \cong 3 \times 10^3$ steps, in one or the other direction!

Thus, with rounding, an error of one part in 10^7 per addition produces, in all likelihood, only about 3000 times that error after 10^7 additions; the result, after our 1 minute of computation, has an error of perhaps 3000 parts in 10^7, or 1 part in $10^7/3000 = 3300$, roughly. Thus, instead of having no significant digits left at all, we still have a bit better than 3 significant digits for our answer.

Two things should be apparent at this stage:

1. that "guard digit" in floating point addition and subtraction of single precision numbers is absolutely necessary to get any reasonable answers at all, and

2. the absence of the guard digit for addition and subtraction of double precision numbers is most unfortunate. It looks very good to say that double precision numbers have 16 significant decimal digits; but after 1 minute of operation on the machine, the elementary error of 1 part in 10^{16} per addition has been incurred some 10^7 times, and the resulting true precision is only 10^7 parts in 10^{16}, or 1 part in 10^9. Still bearable perhaps, but by no means as good as it could be, and ought to be. (*)

What makes things even worse is the possibility of *error propagation,* and even *error multiplication,* during the course of a numerical computation. In many calculations, results obtained at an early stage are used in later work, and thus the errors made in the early stages get propagated into the later calculations; in unfortunate (but sadly enough, all too common) cases, these early errors are effectively multiplied in their influence on the final results. The study of error propagation and error multiplication is a branch of the mathematical discipline called *numerical analysis.* We cannot go into this area here; we merely wanted to show that error analysis is important, and must not be neglected when planning an electronic machine computation. There is nothing easier than to spend hours of machine time in order to get an answer of no significance at all!

C. Mixed Mode Arithmetic

Having discussed integer arithmetic and floating point arithmetic within the machine, let us now turn to the conventions FORTRAN uses to decide what sort of arithmetic to perform in order to evaluate a well-formed arithmetic expression. If all quantities appearing within that expression, be they FORTRAN constants or FORTRAN variables, are of the same type, then there is no problem: the expression is translated from FORTRAN source language to machine language by using the type of arithmetic appropriate to this type of variable; e.g., if all constants and variables which appear in the expression are of type REAL*8, then the additions, multiplications, etc. are all translated into machine operations on double precision floating point numbers. If the constants and variables are all of type COMPLEX*8, the arithmetic operations are translated by FORTRAN into the proper operations for complex numbers with single precision real and imaginary parts; in this case, translation is not directly from the FORTRAN source symbol "+" to a single machine operation; rather, the "+" now means *two* successive single precision floating point additions, namely we must add the two real parts, and then we must add the two imaginary parts. But this sort of translation is no trouble.

Trouble does arise when the constants and variables in an arithmetic expression are not all of the same type. In early versions of FORTRAN, such a situation was declared to be a grammatical error, and the programme was diagnosed as being faulty, the fault in question being called "mixed mode" (the word "mode" is sometimes used for what we call "type" here). This, however, proved intolerable to many users; for example, the simple assignment statement

X=3*Y+4

was declared a failure, the compiler insisting on

(*)   The absence of rounding in multiplication and division is less serious in practice, since it turns out that additions and subtractions are far more common in most programmes, than multiplications and divisions.

X=3.0*Y+4.0

instead! Yet, any reasonable person reading the first statement would know precisely what the programmer meant!

To overcome this, FORTRAN now has a *hierarchy of number types,* given below:

INTEGER*2   INTEGER*4   REAL*4   REAL*8   COMPLEX*8   COMPLEX*16

DEF: A well-formed arithmetic expression containing FORTRAN constants or variables of different types is said to be a *mixed expression.* When the compiler encounters a mixed expression, it determines the "dominant type" of the expression, then converts all quantities into that dominant type, and does arithmetic of the kind appropriate for this dominant type. With one exception, the *dominant type* is simply the type of highest hierarchical rank occurring within the mixed expression; the exceptional case is one in which quantities of type REAL*8 and COMPLEX*8 both occur in the mixed expression: in that case the dominant type is declared to be COMPLEX*16 (so as not to lose the precision of the numbers in REAL*8 type).

With this rule, the assignment statement X=3*Y+4 is now grammatically acceptable. If Y is of type REAL*4, the integers 3 and 4 are converted to type REAL*4, and the evaluation of the expression proceeds using single-precision floating point arithmetic for "+" and "*". If Y has been declared to be of type REAL*8, the integers 3 and 4 are converted to *that* type, and the evaluation of the expression proceeds using double-precision floating point arithmetic for "+" and "*".

Note: Although FORTRAN now accepts mixed expressions, and handles them in a commonsense fashion, *mixed expressions should be avoided* since they contain implied conversions, which require machine time. The expression X=3.0*Y+4.0 takes less machine time to evaluate than X=3*Y+4, since the latter expression requires the computer to convert the integers 3 and 4 to real number form, before the actual evaluation can start.

A further form of "mixing" occurs in an assignment statement if the wfae to the right of the = sign has a dominant type different from the type associated with the variable identifier name to the left of the equal sign. Using the predefined convention for typing, let us consider the assignment statement

I=3*Y+4

There are two kinds of "mixing" here: the wfae 3*Y+4 is a mixed expression, of dominant type REAL*4, since Y is of type REAL*4 in the predefined type convention. The wfae is therefore evaluated in single-precision floating point arithmetic; if the current value of Y is 1.6, say, the value of the arithmetic expression to the right of the = sign is the single-precision real number 8.800000. Now, however, we are to store this result into memory location "I", which must contain a number of type INTEGER*4 in the predefined type convention. What FORTRAN does in such a case is to truncate (*not* round) the number to integral form, i.e., the fractional part is dropped altogether, and the value stored into memory location I is the integer 8 (*not* 9). (*)

(*)   Note that the <u>sequence</u> of conversions matters for the final result. If all numbers had been truncated to integers from the start, Y would have been truncated from 1.6 to 1, and I=3*Y+4 would have resulted in the value 7 for I, rather than the actual value, 8. Remember that the evaluation of the wfae in an assignment statement is carried out as the first step; the type of the result of that operation is the "dominant type" defined above; only afterwards does the machine take cognizance of the number type associated with the memory location into which the result is to be stored.

D. Raising A Number To Some Power

Besides the elementary arithmetic operations "+", "-", "*", and "/", the FORTRAN language also contains the arithmetic operator "**" which means "raising to a power", i.e., I**K is an arithmetic expression whose value is the integer I raised to the integer power K. Unlike the arithmetic operations discussed so far, this operation is not a simple machine operation in most machines. Thus FORTRAN, when encountering the symbol **, must translate this into a little machine programme, or "subroutine", to be carried out at this point. The nature of the machine programme depends strongly on the *type of the exponent.*

If the *exponent* is of type INTEGER, the number is raised to the desired power by successive multiplications. For example, we can obtain A**4 by two successive multiplications: first we multiply A by itself, say B=A*A, then we multiply that value by itself: B*B. Since there is no difficulty organising such multiplications, FORTRAN imposes no restriction on the type of number which can be raised to an integer power: in A**K, assuming that K is of type INTEGER, A may be of type INTEGER*2, INTEGER*4, REAL*4, REAL*8, COMPLEX*8, or COMPLEX*16. The result of the operation is of the same type as A.

If the *exponent* is of type REAL*4 or REAL*8, the procedure used to obtain A**B, say, is quite different. The machine finds the *logarithm* of A, multiplies this logarithm by B, and finds the anti-logarithm of the result. Obviously, this procedure takes much longer than the previous one. Thus, *if the exponent is actually an integer, be sure to write it that way.*

Example: Consider the two wfae A**4 and A**4.0; mathematically, there is no difference, but computationally, the difference is enormous: A**4 is evaluated by two successive multiplications (see above), whereas A**4.0 is evaluated by finding the logarithm of A, multiplying that by 4.0, and then finding the antilogarithm of the result. Not only does this take much longer, but the result is likely to have larger rounding errors!

Complex number exponents are not permitted in FORTRAN. This rule is not just a caprice; rather, it stems from the fact that A**Z with Z complex cannot be defined uniquely, in general.(*)

Certain special cases lead to trouble even for integer or real number exponents:

1.   zero to the power zero is undefined

2.   zero to a negative power is undefined

3.   for real exponent B and negative A, A**B is undefined since we can not take the logarithm of the negative number A.

These troubles will usually show up only during the execution phase, when the time comes to actually carry out the computation. They give rise to execution time error messages, and termination of programme execution. It is up to the programmer to prevent this from happening, by suitable tests on A and B in A**B.

(*)   There is some ambiguity also for real number exponents, but this causes no trouble in A**B as long as the value of A is positive: the logarithm of A is then well-defined and the procedure used leads to a unique result called the "principal value". For complex exponents, the principal value is harder to define, and is often not what we really want, anyway.

E.   Logical Assignment Statements.   Boolean Algebra

The rules given so far define what the FORTRAN-translated programme will do with any grammatically correct arithmetic assignment statement. However, there are other forms of "arithmetic" in the machine, besides ordinary arithmetic operations on integers, real numbers, and complex numbers. There are operations possible on *logical variables,* which form the mathematical subject called Boolean algebra, and there are operations possible on *character strings.*

The operations on logical variables start from the logical assignment statement:

DEF: A *logical assignment statement* has the form *NAME=wfle* where *NAME* is a grammatically correct variable identifier name which has previously been declared to be of type LOGICAL, LOGICAL∗1, or LOGICAL∗4; and where *wfle* is any well-formed *logical* expression, constructed according to the rules of Chapter III augmented by the two additional rules:

10)   .TRUE. and .FALSE. are wfle

11)   Any grammatically correct variable name which has previously been declared to be of type LOGICAL, LOGICAL∗1, or LOGICAL∗4 is a wfle.

Examples: Suppose that we have the type convention IMPLICIT LOGICAL($), declaring all variable names starting with $ to be of type LOGICAL.

1. $AEQB=A.EQ.B is a logical assignment statement; it assigns the value .TRUE. to $AEQB iff (if and only if) the numbers stored in A and B are equal;

2. $NEG=.NOT.$AEQB is a logical assignment statement; it assigns the value .TRUE. to $NEG iff $AEQB has the value .FALSE.;

3. $COMP=$AEQB.OR.(TRUMAN.GT.HITLER) is a logical assignment statement; it assigns the value .TRUE. to $COMP iff at least one of $AEQB or TRUMAN.GT.HITLER has the value .TRUE.;

4. $ALW=$AEQB.AND.$NEG is a logical assignment statement; if preceded by statements of examples 1 and 2 above, $ALW always has the value .FALSE. (why?).

There are some obvious *rules and restrictions* to which logical expressions are subject. These are not likely to cause trouble, but we state them here for the sake of completeness.

1.   The "relational operators" .EQ., .GE., .GT., .LE., .LT., .NE. are used to compare the numerical values of two well-formed *arithmetic* expressions. The dominant type of these expressions *must not* be COMPLEX∗8 or COMPLEX∗16 (this is obviously necessary for comparisons such as .GT., but is a FORTRAN rule also for .EQ. and .NE.). The operands *must not* be logical expressions.

2.   If the two arithmetic expressions above have different dominant type, the value of lower type is converted to the higher type (in the hierarchy of types), before the comparison is carried out.

3.   The "logical operators" .AND., .OR., and .NOT. must have as their operands two (for .AND. and .OR.) or one (for .NOT.) well-formed *logical* expressions; the operands of logical operators *must not* be arithmetic expressions.

4. Two logical operators may appear in immediate sequence if and only if the second logical operator is .NOT.

5. All logical expressions are evaluated in the dominant type LOGICAL∗4. If the variable identifier name of the variable on the left of the = sign in a logical assignment statement is declared to be of type LOGICAL∗1, the answer of the evaluation is truncated to type LOGICAL∗1 before being stored. No error is possible in this conversion.

Evaluation of well-formed logical expressions, using the logical operators .NOT., .AND., and .OR., is sometimes referred to as Boolean algebra, after the English mathematician George Boole. The rules of Boolean algebra are similar to, but not quite the same as, the rules of ordinary arithmetic, if we agree to represent .TRUE. by 1 and .FALSE. by 0. In that case, .AND. becomes the same as ordinary multiplication: for example, the fact that 0∗1 turns out to be 0 is related to the fact that .FALSE..AND..TRUE. turns out to be .FALSE. But .OR. is *not* quite the same as usual addition:

.FALSE..OR..FALSE.	gives	.FALSE.	0+0 gives 0
.FALSE..OR..TRUE.	gives	.TRUE.	0+1 gives 1
.TRUE..OR..FALSE.	gives	.TRUE.	1+0 gives 1
.TRUE..OR..TRUE.	gives	.TRUE.	1+1 gives 1 (in Boolean algebra!)

The last line indicates the striking difference between Boolean rules and the rules of ordinary arithmetic.

While FORTRAN in its present form can be used to programme Boolean algebra directly, operations on *character strings* (e.g., putting a set of names in alphabetical order) can be done, within FORTRAN, only by special tricks; these are explained in Chapter XV. It is to be hoped that future versions of FORTRAN will allow easier manipulation of character strings, and this is indeed likely. The WATFOR type code CHARACTER∗*s* is a first, most welcome, step in this direction.

DRILL EXERCISES FOR CHAPTER X

1. Assuming the numerical values I=2, J=2, K=7, and L=-3, evaluate the following expressions:
   a) I∗(J-K)/(7+L)
   b) (I∗(J-K)/7+L)
   c) I∗((J-K)/(7+L))
   d) (I∗(J-K))/(7+L)

2. With I, J, K, L as before, and A=-2.0, B=3.0, state the dominant type of each of the following expressions, and determine its value; state which involve implied conversions:
   a) I∗A/J+L
   b) I∗K/J+L
   c) I∗K/J+B
   d) A∗∗J+B∗∗K
   e) B∗∗A+I∗∗J
   f) J∗∗A+K∗∗B

3. With I=72000 and J=200000 what are the values of
   a) I+J
   b) J-I
   c) I∗J
   d) I/J
   e) J/I
   f) I∗∗2
   g) J∗∗2

4. With IMPLICIT LOGICAL($) and $A=.TRUE., $B=.FALSE., state the values of

   a) $A+$B   d) .NOT.$B.AND.$A

   b) $A.OR..NOT.$B   e) $A.NE.$B

   c) $B.OR.$A   f) $A.EQ..NOT.$B

5. Detect the errors in the following programme segments:

a)
```
        DATA A,B,C/-1.0,0.0,1.0/
1000    I=1
1100    Y=(I-5)**A
        YNOT=(I-6)**B
        YOYO=(I-7)**C
        I=I+1
        IF(I.LE.8) GO TO 1100
        STOP
```

b)
```
        IMPLICIT LOGICAL($)
        X=5.0
        $AB=X.GT.$X
        $CD=$CD**2
        $CDC=X.EQ.X
        $EF=.NOT.$CDC
```

PROGRAMMING EXERCISES FOR CHAPTER X

These exercises should not merely be coded, but run on the machine. No exercise is complete until the programme has been debugged by use of actual machine output.

1. Produce a table of square roots of the integers 1 through 25; the table should contain, on each line, the value of the integer I, the value of its square root as a single-precision real number, and as a double-precision real number.

2. Produce a table of square roots, cube roots and fourth roots of the integers from 1 to 25, inclusive. Each line of the table should contain the value of the integer I, the value of its square, cube, and fourth roots as single-precision numbers. (*Note:* Why does CUBRT=I**(1/3) give the wrong answer?)

3. Same as problem 2, but the answers to double precision.

4. Alter programmes 2 and 3 in such a way that they read, as data, three integers M1, M2, and M3 such that the range of I for the table is from an initial value M1 up to a final value no larger than M2, in steps of M3. Make these programmes "recycling", i.e., after computations have finished with one set of data M1, M2, M3, control is returned to the READ statement to read the next set of data.

5. Correct the above programmes in two respects: (1) after each READ operation, perform an "echo check", that is, print onto the output page the values which you have just read in, so that you know by looking at the output what the current values of M1, M2, and M3 are; and (2) perform tests on the values of M1, M2, and M3 to make sure they are reasonable: M1 had better be positive, same for M2 and M3; M2 should be bigger than M1; if the data are unsatisfac-

tory, *do not* stop the computation; rather, transfer control to the READ statement, to read the next set of data: maybe those will be all right!

6. Find all prime integers between 3 and 100 and print them out one by one. *Hints:* 1) It suffices to test the *odd* integers. 2) To test any odd integer I, divide it by all odd integers J from J=3 to J=I-2, in each case seeing whether the division "goes". The wfae I-(I/J)*J gives the value zero if and only if J divides I exactly (why?). If none of these divisions "goes", I is a prime and should be printed out.

7. Use the power series $\sin(x) = x - x^3/3! + x^5/5! - x^7/7! + \ldots$ to find the sine function of a number read in from a data card; stop computation and print out the answer when you have five-figure accuracy.
   Hints: The loop is on the number N of the term in the series. We precede the loop with TERM=X, SUM=TERM, and N=1. This sets up the initial value of N, of TERM, and of SUM The first statement within the loop is N=N+1, advancing the number of the term computed. The new term is obtained from the old one by the assignment statement:

   TERM= TERM*X**2/((2*N-2)*(2*N-1))

   (check this for the first three terms!). We update SUM by SUM=SUM+TERM. We then test the ratio TERM/SUM. If it is more than +1.E-5, or less than -1.E-5, we go back to continue the loop. If neither condition holds, the new term has made only an insignificant contribution to the SUM, and further terms of the power series would make even smaller contributions (this is not true of all power series, unfortunately, but it is true of this one). We therefore have five-place accuracy at this moment, and can terminate the loop. Note that the termination condition on this loop is a condition on currently computed numbers, *not* a condition on the value of the loop variable N.

8. Same as exercise 7, but obtain the $\sin(x)$ to 12-figure accuracy.

9. Same as exercise 7, but let X be a complex number. Note: You can check your numerical results against simple tables of trigonometric and hyperbolic sines and cosines, by using the identity:

   $\sin(x+iy) = \sin(x) \cosh(y) + i \cos(x) \sinh(y)$

10. Same as exercise 9, but obtain the value to 12-figure accuracy.

11-14.
   Same as exercises 7 through 10, but for the series:

   $J(x) = 1 - (x/2)^2/(1!)^2 + (x/2)^4/(2!)^2 - (x/2)^6/(3!)^2 + (x/2)^8/(4!)^2 - \ldots$

   (Note: This series represents the "Bessel function" $J_0(x)$, which can be found in many standard tables.)

CHAPTER XI

PROGRAMME FLOW CONTROL, CONTINUED

A. The Arithmetic IF

In Chapter III, we presented the flow control statements GO TO and the logical IF statement, as well as the termination statement STOP. These suffice in principle for all flow control decisions which can occur in computer programmes. In Chapter X, for example, we showed how these statements can be used to arrange a loop on the integer variable I, starting with I=1, advancing I by 2 units every time, and terminating after I=99 has been used.

In order to simplify FORTRAN programming, a number of additional flow control statements have been made part of the FORTRAN language. This Chapter is devoted to their definition and discussion.

Quite frequently, we want to look at the value of an arithmetic expression, and do different things depending upon whether this value is less than, equal to, or greater than zero. For the sake of illustration, suppose that the "less than zero" branch of the programme starts at statement number 1010, the "equals zero" branch starts at statement number 1020, and the "greater than zero" branch starts at statement number 1030; then the desired comparison can be programmed as a series of two logical IF statements in sequence:

```
      IF(N.EQ.0) GO TO 1020
      IF(N.GT.0) GO TO 1030
C     WE REACH THE NEXT STATEMENT IF AND ONLY IF N IS NEGATIVE
 1010 ...
```

For the sake of convenience, however, FORTRAN provides a *single* statement, called the *arithmetic IF statement*, which has exactly the same effect:

DEF: The *arithmetic IF statement* has the form IF*(wfae)* n_1, n_2, n_3 where *wfae* is any well-formed arithmetic expression of dominant type INTEGER*2, INTEGER*4, REAL*4, or REAL*8 (but *not* of complex type), and n_1, n_2, n_3 are the statement numbers of executable statements in the programme. Control is transferred to statement n_1 iff (if and only if) the value of the *wfae* is negative; to statement n_2 iff the value is zero; and to statement n_3 iff the value is positive.

Example: The set of two logical IF statements given above is equivalent to:

IF(N) 1010,1020,1030

Note: The first executable statement following an arithmetic IF statement must have a statement number; otherwise, it can never be reached during execution of the (translated) programme: the arithmetic IF results in a transfer of control to *some* numbered statement, no matter which of the three conditions is satisfied.

Note: The cautions in Chapter III against the use of the logical IF(A.EQ.0.0) and IF(A.NE.0.0) for REAL (rather than INTEGER) quantities apply equally strongly to the arithmetic IF statement. *The wfae in the arithmetic IF statement should be of dominant type INTEGER*2 or INTEGER*4; type REAL should be avoided, since it is likely to give rise to errors arising from the approximate nature of floating point arithmetic.*

Note: It is not necessary that the three statement numbers n_1, n_2, n_3 are all different from each other. However, if two of them coincide, the arithmetic IF becomes logically equivalent to a single logical IF statement, and it is cleaner coding to use the latter statement in such a case. For example, the statement

        IF(N) 1040,1040,1050

is logically completely equivalent to

        IF(N.GT.0) GO TO 1050
    1040   . . .

and this latter form is cleaner coding.

B.   The Computed GO TO

In Chapter III, we showed how a two-way branch may be coded by use of the logical IF statement and the GO TO statement. One often encounters situations demanding a 3-way, 4-way, . . .branching of control. These can also be coded by use of logical IF statements. Suppose that we have an *indicator variable* named I, for example; and suppose we wish to transfer control to statement number 1100 iff I equals 1, to statement number 1200 iff I equals 2, to statement number 1300 iff I equals 3, and to statement number 1000 if I is not equal to any of 1, 2, 3. This can be programmed by three successive logical IF statements as follows:

        IF(I.EQ.1) GO TO 1100
        IF(I.EQ.2) GO TO 1200
        IF(I.EQ.3) GO TO 1300
    1000   . . .

For convenience, the same branching can be achieved by a single *computed GO TO* statement, namely

        GO TO (1100,1200,1300),I
    1000   . . .

There is no *logical* difference between the three statements above and the single computed GO TO statement; it is merely a question of convenience in programming, with a slight saving of machine time in execution.

DEF: The *computed GO TO* statement has the general form GO TO $(n_1, n_2, . . ., n_k)$, *NAME* where $n_1, n_2, . . ., n_k$ is a list of statement numbers of executable statements in the programme, separated by commas and enclosed within parentheses; this is followed by a comma (note!), followed by a variable identifier name *NAME* which must be the name of an INTEGER variable, which is *not* an array variable (see Chapter XIII). Control is transferred to statement number n_1 iff the value of *NAME* is 1, to n_2 iff the value is 2, . . ., to n_k iff the value is k; and to the first executable statement following the computed GO TO if the value of *NAME* is not equal to any of 1, 2, 3, . . ., k.

In addition to the computed GO TO, the FORTRAN language also contains an alternative method of programming a multi-way branch, called the ASSIGN and assigned GO TO statements.

DEF: The assigned GO TO statement has the form

GO TO M, $(s_1, s_2, s_3, . . ., s_n)$

where M is a variable identifier name of type INTEGER*4, and $s_1, s_2, . . ., s_n$ are integer constants each of which is the statement number of an executable statement in the same programme (or subprogramme). When this statement is encountered during execution of the object programme, control is transferred to a statement with one of the statement numbers in the list; the statement number selected depends on the current assignment of the selector variable M.

DEF: To assign a statement number s to a selector variable M, the following form is used: ASSIGN s TO M. Here s is the statement number of an executable statement appearing in the bracketed list of an assigned GO TO statement using M as a selector variable; and M is a variable identifier name of type INTEGER*4.

Note: The numerical value given to the selector variable M as the result of an ASSIGN statement is not the constant s; rather, it is the machine address at which the translated statement with statement number s appears in the object code stored in the machine. Thus, the statement ASSIGN 158 TO MARKER has a completely different effect from the statement MARKER=158. A variable name which is used as a selector variable must not be set by anything except an ASSIGN statement; in particular, such a variable name must not appear to the left of the = sign in an arithmetic assignment statement.

Note: The ASSIGN and assigned GO TO represent merely an alternative, and inferior, way of achieving the same purpose as the computed GO TO statement. The assigned GO TO and ASSIGN statement should not be used.

C. The DO Statement

In Chapter X, Section A, we showed how the logical IF can be used, together with the GO TO, to arrange a loop on an integer variable. In the example given there, the integer variable had variable name I. This variable is called the *loop variable*. The *initial value* of I was 1, the *termination test value* of I was 99 (i.e. the loop was considered to be finished when the next value of I to be used would exceed 99), and the *loop increment* was 2, i.e., I was increased by 2 units each time around the loop.

In order to simplify reading, we reproduce here the part of the coding which organizes the loop; the FORTRAN statements in the interior of the loop are of no interest to us here, so we replace them by rows of dots. The full coding appears at the end of Section A of Chapter X.

```
 1000  I=1
C       LOOP STARTS HERE
 1500  ...
        ...
        ...
C       NOW ADVANCE I BY 2
 2000  I=I+2
C       HAVE WE REACHED THE END?
 2500  IF(I.LE.99) GO TO 1500
C       WE GET HERE WHEN THE NEXT VALUE OF I EXCEEDS 99
        ...
```

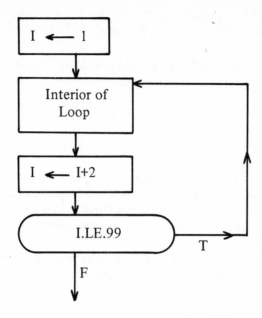

Loops of this sort arise frequently in programming, and therefore the FORTRAN language contains a special statement for setting up and controlling such loops. This statement is called the DO statement. With the DO statement, the above loop would be written as follows

```
1000 DO 2500 I=1,99,2
       . . .
       . . .
       . . .
 2500 CONTINUE
C     WE GET HERE WHEN THE NEXT VALUE OF I EXCEEDS 99
```

We *note* that the FORTRAN DO statement contains the following information

1. The *end of the range* of the loop, i.e., the statement number of the last statement within the loop; in the above case, statement number 2500,

2. The *name of the loop variable,* in our case, I,

3. The *initial value* of the loop variable, in our case, 1,

4. The *termination test value* of the loop variable, in our case, 99,

5. The *loop increment,* in our case, 2.

Furthermore, the last statement of the loop is the dummy statement CONTINUE. This does not by itself give rise to any calculations, but serves as a convenient "no action" statement to which the final statement number 2500 of the loop can be assigned. The last statement of a FORTRAN DO loop *need not* be a CONTINUE statement; in fact, it may be any executable statement other than one of: GO TO, PAUSE, STOP, arithmetic IF, another DO, and RETURN. However, *it is clean coding to terminate every* DO *loop with a separate* CONTINUE *statement.* This defines clearly the range of each DO loop, and also gives notice that at this point some DO loop has come to the end of its range.

DEF: The DO statement has the general form DO n $I=m_1,m_2,m_3$. n is the statement number of an executable statement in the programme; this becomes the last statement within the range of the loop. I is a variable identifier name of a variable of type INTEGER: this must be a simple variable name (no subscripts allowed). m_1, m_2, and m_3 are each either an unsigned *integer constant,* or the *name of an integer variable.* None of them may be negative or zero. The value of m_1 is the initial value of I, m_2 is the termination test value of I, and m_3 is the loop increment. If $m_3=1$, i.e., the loop variable is increased by 1 each time around the loop, the last comma together with the value of m_3 may be omitted, i.e.,

DO n $I=m_1,m_2$ is equivalent to DO n $I=m_1,m_2,$ 1

Certain *restrictions* apply to FORTRAN DO loops; these will be stated later.

DEF: The dummy statement CONTINUE does not give rise to any calculation at execution time. If supplied with a statement number n, however, this statement can be used as the last statement of a DO loop.

It is important to pay detailed attention to the standard form of the DO statement, in particular the places where commas do, and do not, appear. There are *no commas* before or after the statement number; *blanks* at these points are desirable (and with some FORTRAN compilers, even necessary). The name of the loop variable is followed by an equal sign = (again no commas), but there *are* commas between m_1 and m_2, and between m_2 and m_3. These rules are not easy to get used to, but any violation of these rules results in a grammatically incorrect FORTRAN statement. Thus, the rules must be learned and obeyed.

It is also important to remember which quantities must be constants, which must be variable names, and which may be either. The statement number n must be a number, not a variable name. The loop variable must be a variable name, not a number. The quantities m_1, m_2, and m_3 may be either.

We now turn our attention to the restrictions on the use of the FORTRAN DO loop. The first restriction is that all of m_1, m_2, and m_3 *must be positive.* We must not start with a negative (or zero) value of the loop variable; the termination test value must not be negative (or zero); and the loop increment must not be negative or zero. Only the last of these three conditions applies also to the explicitly coded version of the loop, given at the beginning of this Section: In Statement 2000 I=I+2 the increment need not equal 2, but it must be a positive integer, otherwise the coding will fail. On the other hand, statement 1000 I=1 could have the "1" replaced by any integer, including negative or zero values. Similarly, statement 2500 IF(I.LE.99) GO TO 1500 could have the "99" replaced by any integer, positive, negative, or zero. Thus, here is an example of a restriction on the FORTRAN DO loop which can be overcome by "hand-coding" the loop (i.e. by replacing the FORTRAN DO statement by logically equivalent coding, using the logical IF and the GO TO).

The *second restriction* on DO loops in FORTRAN *forbids jumping into the range of the loop from outside.* For example, the following coding is *forbidden:*

```
1000 DO 2500 I=1,99,2
1500 ISQU=I*I
     ICUBE=ISQU*I
     IFOUR=ICUBE*I
     PRINT,I,ISQU,ICUBE,IFOUR
2500 CONTINUE
     I=150
     GO TO 1500
```

The last statement, GO TO 1500, is a transfer of control *from* outside the range of the DO loop, *to* a statement within the range of the DO loop. This is called "jumping into the range of the loop from outside", and is prohibited. Note that the "range of the loop" in this example includes all statements between statements 1500 and 2500, inclusive; but the DO statement itself, statement number 1000 above, is *not* counted as part of the range for the purpose of this rule. For example, the statement GO TO 1000 in place of GO TO 1500 in the above programme would be grammatically correct FORTRAN. (Can you explain why it would produce a never-ending loop?)

The *third restriction* on DO loops in FORTRAN *forbids redefining the loop variable* (I in our example) *within the range of the loop.* That is, the loop variable I must not appear to the left of an arithmetic assignment statement or in the list of a READ statement within the range of the loop. For example, the statement I=I+5 *must not* appear anywhere within the range of the DO loop. The idea behind this restriction is that the information contained in the DO statement, and *only* that information, is to be used for determining how the loop variable advances during execution of the loop. A statement such as I=I+5 within the range of the loop would, in effect, advance I an additional 5 units every time we go around the loop. If the programmer wants to achieve this, he should write the original DO statement as DO 2500 I=1,99,7 rather than DO 2500 I=1,99,2 with an additional I=I+5 within the range of the loop.

The *fourth restriction* on DO loops in FORTRAN applies if one or more of the loop control numbers m_1, m_2, m_3 are given as variable names, rather than as FORTRAN constants. In that case, these variable names must not appear to the left of arithmetic assignment statements within the range of the loop. The reason for the restriction is the same as before.

Besides these restrictions, certain *cautions* are necessary:

The *first caution* concerns the possibility that the termination test value m_2 is less than the initial value m_1. Let us first look at the explicitly coded loop at the beginning of this section. Suppose the statement 1000 I=1 were replaced by 1000 I=155; this makes the initial value equal to 155, whereas the termination test value (appearing in the condition of statement number 2500) remains equal to 99. It is easy to see that, in this case, the loop will be traversed once and only once. In effect, we do not find out that I=155 exceeds the termination test value, 99; rather, we increment I by 2, getting a new value equal 155+2=157, and we test that new value against 99. Since 157 exceeds 99, we jump out of the loop; but we have already traversed the loop once. *The FORTRAN DO loop does exactly the same thing: if m_1 exceeds m_2, the loop is traversed exactly once.*

The caution is important, since many beginning programmers assume that m_1 greater than m_2 means that the loop will be skipped altogether. This is *not true* for DO loops in FORTRAN. If one wants to achieve this, a test must be inserted explicitly into the programme, as follows:

```
       IF(M1.GT.M2) GO TO 3000
1000 DO 2500 I=M1,M2,M3
      ...
      ...
2500 CONTINUE
3000 ... (NEXT STATEMENT AFTER CONCLUSION OF THE LOOP)
```

With this coding, the loop is executed once if M1=M2, and not at all if M1.GT.M2.

The *second caution* concerns the value of the loop variable (I in our case) after the loop has run to completion. Beginning programmers take it for granted that, at the end, this will be equal to the last value of I actually used in the loop. This is not necessarily true for DO loops in FORTRAN. On the contrary, if the loop runs to a normal completion, the content of memory location I *need not equal* the last value of the loop variable I within the loop. *After normal completion of a* FORTRAN DO *loop the value of the loop variable is undefined.*

Of course, a FORTRAN DO loop need not run to a normal completion; we are free to test, within the range of the loop, some condition or other (perhaps one not directly involving the loop variable at all, but rather a condition on numbers computed within the loop), and to *jump out of the loop prematurely.* For example, in evaluating a power series, term by term, we may set up a DO loop to compute the sum of the first 1000 terms, say; but within the range of the loop, we insert a test to see whether the term presently being added into the series makes any difference to the result, to the accuracy we desire; and we jump out of the loop if the desired accuracy has been achieved, probably long before a full 1000 terms have been computed. In such a case, but *only* in such a case, the content of memory location I (the name of the loop variable) is actually equal to the last value of I used in the loop.

In addition to these restrictions and cautions, we observe that the quantities m_1, m_2 and m_3 in the FORTRAN DO loop must be integer constants or simple integer variable names. They *must not* be more complicated well-formed arithmetic expressions of dominant type INTEGER. For example, the statement DO 2500 I=1,K+2 is grammatically incorrect FORTRAN, since K+2 is not a simple variable name. One must replace this by two statements:

```
KPLUS2=K+2
DO 2500 I=1,KPLUS2
```

On the whole, we see that we have paid heavily indeed for the convenience of the DO statement. The explicitly coded loop shown at the beginning of this section does everything the DO loop does, is *not* particularly hard to write, and is not subject to so many irksome restrictions. Quite frequently, the explicitly coded loop is preferable to the FORTRAN DO loop.

D. Examples of DO Loops

As a first example of the use of a DO loop, let us compute the sum of the squares of all odd integers between 1 and 99. Since we are doing integer arithmetic exclusively in this programme, we start with the type declaration

```
IMPLICIT INTEGER*4(A-Z,$)
```

93

which declares *all* variable names to be of type INTEGER*4. We use INTEGER*4 rather than INTEGER*2, because 2-byte integers cannot exceed $2^{15}-1=32767$ in absolute value; the term 99^2 of the desired sum is already close to 10000, so we are in danger of arithmetic overflow if we use INTEGER*2.

In preparing the flow diagram, it is best to start *from the inside out,* that is, we ask ourselves first of all what is the typical thing which we must do inside the loop? If I is the loop variable (which will be an odd integer between 1 and 99) we must find its square, and add it into the already existing sum of squares. Thus the innermost statement of the loop is

SUM=SUM+I**2

Next, we ask ourselves what we must do to *initiate* the loop, how we are to *terminate* the loop, what we must do *after completion* of the loop. To take these in order:

1. To initiate the loop, we must set I equal to its initial value 1, and we must set SUM equal to zero; if we omitted this precaution, the final content of memory location SUM would not be the sum of squares which we *want* to have there; rather, it would be that *plus* whatever junk was in memory location SUM before we entered the loop!

2. We wish to terminate the loop after we have added in the term $(99)^2$, i.e., as soon as the *next* value of the loop index I would exceed 99.

3. The only thing we need to do after completion of the loop is to print out the result, i.e., the content of memory location SUM. Still, we wouldn't want to forget *that!*

With this in mind, we are ready to put down the flow diagram for the loop, in explicitly coded form, and next to it, the FORTRAN programme:

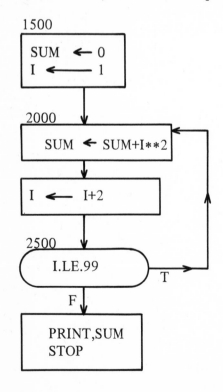

```
        IMPLICIT INTEGER*4(A-Z,$)
1500    SUM=0
        I=1
C       LOOP STARTS HERE
2000    SUM=SUM+I**2
        I=I+2
2500    IF(I.LE.99) GO TO 2000
C       LOOP IS ALL FINISHED
        PRINT,SUM
        STOP
```

Now let us code the same loop, using the DO statement. We require a symbol on the flow diagram to indicate a loop controlled by a DO statement; for this, we take a "squashed hexagon" containing, within it, the statement number n of the final statement of the loop, the name of the loop variable, and the values of M1, M2, and M3 in the DO statement.

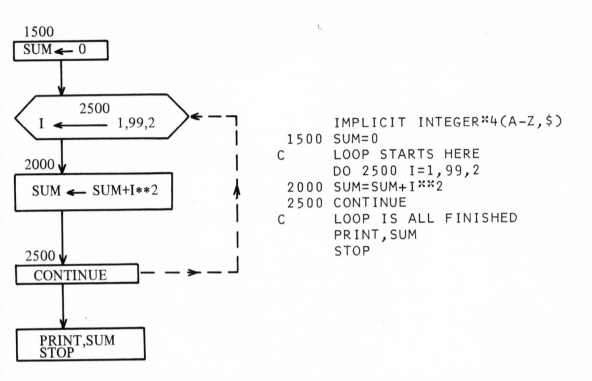

```
      IMPLICIT INTEGER*4(A-Z,$)
1500  SUM=0
C     LOOP STARTS HERE
      DO 2500 I=1,99,2
2000  SUM=SUM+I**2
2500  CONTINUE
C     LOOP IS ALL FINISHED
      PRINT,SUM
      STOP
```

Note: The CONTINUE statement could have been avoided in this loop, merely by giving the statement number 2500 to the statement SUM=SUM+I**2. This would agree with the rules for the DO statement, i.e., SUM=SUM+I**2 is an executable statement and is not a statement of one of the forbidden types for final statements of a DO loop. However, it is clean coding practice to end every DO loop with an explicit CONTINUE statement carrying the statement number used in the DO statement. This defines the extent of every DO loop cleanly, and also calls to the attention of whoever reads the programme listing that here is a point at which some DO loop has come to the end of its range. This is particularly desirable if there are several DO loops in the programme.

Example: We now give an example of loops within loops, also called *nested loops.* In the preceding example, we evaluated the sum of the squares of certain odd integers. Suppose we wish to evaluate the sum of the cubes, fourth powers, and fifth powers as well, and do it all within the same programme. One way to achieve this (though not the best way from the point of view of machine time) is to start from the programme we already have, and write another loop *around* that one, the outer loop being a loop on the power K of the integers; that is, the loop variable K will range over the values 2 (for squares), 3 (for cubes), 4 (for fourth powers), and 5 (for fifth powers).

The innermost statement, which controls the actual calculation is now

SUM=SUM+I**K

that is, we take the K-th power of the integer I, where K is going to range over the values K=2,3,4,5.

Since the variable K is incremented by 1 every time around the K-loop, the increment M3 need not be specified in the corresponding DO statement.

Below, we give the flow diagram for that programme, and next to it, the FORTRAN code. Note the position, within the flow diagram and within the programme, of the statement SUM=0; what would be the result if we had put this statement as the *first* executable statement of the programme, i.e., immediately after the implicit type declaration statement? Do you see how easy it is to make coding errors?

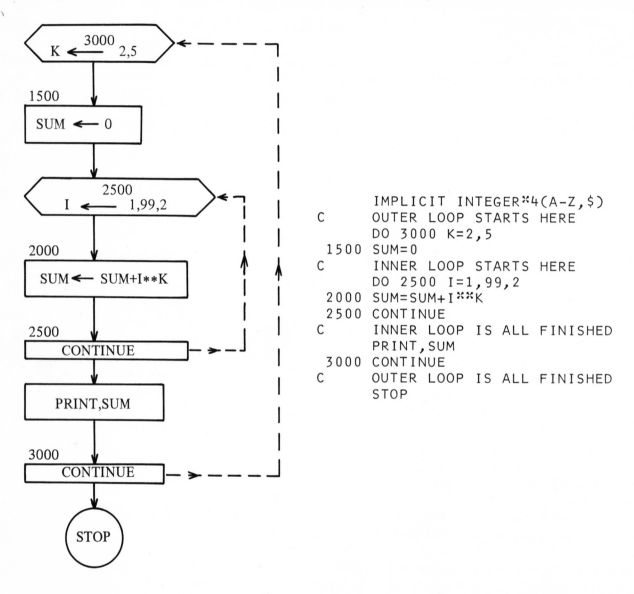

```
        IMPLICIT INTEGER*4(A-Z,$)
C       OUTER LOOP STARTS HERE
        DO 3000 K=2,5
  1500  SUM=0
C       INNER LOOP STARTS HERE
        DO 2500 I=1,99,2
  2000  SUM=SUM+I**K
  2500  CONTINUE
C       INNER LOOP IS ALL FINISHED
        PRINT,SUM
  3000  CONTINUE
C       OUTER LOOP IS ALL FINISHED
        STOP
```

Coding error in above example: All right, where is it? Think a bit before reading on!

Bet you didn't find it! It has nothing to do with the formal properties of the coding, but is concerned with the size of numbers in the machine! If we take the sum of the fifth powers of integers from 1 to 99, in steps of 2, the largest number we encounter is $(99)^5$ which is not far below $(100)^5 = (10)^{10}$. This is larger than $2^{31} - 1 = 2147483647$, approximately 2×10^9. Thus we are getting into arithmetic overflow in this programme; the sum of the fourth powers barely avoids overflowing, and the sum of the fifth powers actually overflows.

To avoid this trouble, and still get answers which are accurate, it is necessary to compute the sum as a double-precision real number. We shall not need single-precision real numbers at all, hence a useful type declaration is now IMPLICIT REAL*8(A-H,O-Z,$), which agrees with the pre-defined type for integers, and differs from the pre-defined type for real numbers only by going to double precision. The corrected programme reads:

```
        IMPLICIT REAL*8(A-H,O-Z,$)
C       OUTER LOOP STARTS HERE
        DO 3000 K=2,5
 1500   SUM=0.0
C       INNER LOOP STARTS HERE
        DO 2500 I=1,99,2
        EYE=I
 2000   SUM=SUM+EYE**K
 2500   CONTINUE
C       INNER LOOP IS ALL FINISHED
        PRINT,SUM
 3000   CONTINUE
C       OUTER LOOP IS ALL FINISHED
        STOP
```

The statement EYE=I converts the integer I to double-precision floating form and stores it into memory location EYE. This does not cause any numerical error, and neither does raising the content of EYE to the K-th power. Rounding errors arise in performing the addition "+" in SUM+EYE**K; however, double-precision real numbers have a precision of roughly 1 part in 10^{16} whereas the sum of the fifth powers is a bit less than 10^{11} and is an integer, hence needs to be known only to a precision of 1 part in 10^{11}; thus the rounding errors arising from the addition are not going to cause a significant error in the final answer. Note that this would *not* have been true had we used 4-byte real numbers for EYE and SUM: there is no danger of arithmetic overflow, in either case, but the precision of 4-byte floating point numbers is only a few parts in 10^7, whereas we want our final answer for SUM to be good to at least 1 part in 10^{11}.

This example therefore illustrates not merely the mechanics of coding nested DO loops, but the much more important fact that *no amount of staring at the source programme can guarantee that that programme will work correctly when actually put on the computer.* One can find coding errors by looking at the source programme, but one is most unlikely to find *all* the coding errors, and it is impossible to guarantee that one has found all the coding errors. There is only one way to debug programmes: on the computer, using test output from actual runs.

There is another lesson to be learned here: a programmer wishing to debug this programme expeditiously is very likely to replace the statement DO 2500 I=1,99,2 by a "test version" DO 2500 I=1,7,2, making the loop variable I take the values I=1,3,5,7 only. The idea is that the resulting numbers are easy to calculate by hand, and check against the machine output; if these numbers are all right, then nothing much can go wrong when M2=7 is increased to M2=99; after all, the logic of the programme is completely unaltered by this! "Nothing much can go wrong" indeed!! The only thing wrong is the answer! With I=1,3,5,7 only, there is no danger whatever of arithmetic overflow, and the first version (all integers) of the programme will *work*.

Thus, not only is it impossible to debug a programme completely by staring at the source listing; even a series of machine test runs may not be enough to ensure that the final run, with the parameters we actually want, will really work!

There is still another lesson: one and the same FORTRAN-coded programme may work on one machine, and fail to work on another machine! On the CDC 3600 machine, for example, one memory location contains 48 bits (rather than 32), and thus integers can go up to $2^{47}-1$ in absolute value, without overflowing. Hence the first version of the programme, in purely integer arithmetic, would *work* on a CDC 3600. Conversely, if this programme had been debugged on a CDC 3600, and was then transferred to an IBM/360, a working, debugged code would suddenly fail. The logic of a programme is not enough: a programme is not an exercise in logic, it is a series of instructions to an electronic machine; and what the programme does depends on the machine, sometimes in quite subtle ways.

E. The Pause Statement

In Chapter III, Section A, we introduced the STOP statement, which terminates execution of the object programme.

Sometimes it is desirable to interrupt the computation to permit the machine operator to take some action (e.g., insert one of several prepared sets of data cards into the card reader; which set depends on the results printed out so far). For this purpose, a STOP statement is unsuitable, since it stops computation altogether.

DEF: The three forms of the PAUSE statement are:

1. PAUSE
2. PAUSE *n* where *n* is an unsigned integer constant of no more than 5 digits
3. PAUSE *'message'* where *'message'* is a character string enclosed within apostrophes.

This statement, when encountered in the execution phase, causes the machine to display the word PAUSE followed by the value of *n*, or by the *message*, in a form visible to the machine operator (for example, as typed output on the on-line typewriter attached to the machine). The machine then waits until the operator presses the "start" button. When this happens, execution of the object programme is resumed, starting with the FORTRAN command immediately following the PAUSE statement.

Special Note on WATFOR: In the WATFOR implementation of FORTRAN IV, the machine is not permitted to pause during the running of student jobs. The WATFOR PAUSE statement is equivalent to the CONTINUE statement: the machine does not pause, and nothing is displayed to the operator.

General Note on PAUSE: Most large installations discourage the use of the PAUSE statement, because it is claimed that this wastes machine time: the machine stands idle while the operator does something or other. Even if the operator acts very rapidly, a large number of computations could have been carried out in the time that the machine stood idle.

With "multi-programming" coming to the fore, the PAUSE statement is likely to come into its own again: when a PAUSE statement is encountered, the machine, rather than stopping altogether to await operator action, may instead start to work on someone else's problem; it will then resume work on the original problem as soon as the operator signifies that everything is once more ready for action.

As far as any one programmer is concerned, PAUSE does what it is claimed to do; but the machine is not in fact prevented from carrying out useful computations while waiting for the operator to act.

DRILL EXERCISES FOR CHAPTER XI

1. Write a programme segment for "flexible input": each input card contains two numbers: a (real number) value, followed by an INDEX which is either 1, 2, or 3. The number is to be stored into location A1 if INDEX.EQ.1, into location A2 if INDEX.EQ.2, into location A3 if INDEX.EQ.3, and into location DIRT if INDEX is none of the above. Use the computed GO TO statement.

2. Correct the following statements for FORTRAN language errors, if necessary:

   a) DO 2354,I=1,K
   b) DO 3400 I=1,K+3
   c) DO 3400 J=2,L,A
   d) DO TILL 3400 J=2,KTH34
   e) DO 3400 FOR I=1,99,2
   f) DO 3400 I=1,99,2,
   g) DO 3400 P=1,MAXI
   h) DO 3400 J=I,J,K

3. Same as problem 1 (flexible input), but assume that INDEX will *always* have one of the values 1,2,3; and use an arithmetic IF statement to organize the branching.

4. In each of the following programme segments there is at least one error. Identify as many errors as you can.

```
A)          DO 1000 I=1,10,-1
            A=A+I**2
      2000  I=I+1
      1000  CONTINUE
            IF(I.EQ.5) GO TO 2000


B)          DO 1000 I=10,19
            A=I1+2*I*A
      1000  DO 2000 J=1,10
      2000  B=B+J*A


C)          DO 1000 I=1,J,I
      3000  B=C+I*D
            CONTINUE
      1000  IF(J.EQ.10) GO TO 2000
            K=I+6
      2000  I=J-5
            GO TO 3000
```

5. Which of the following PAUSE statements are valid?

   a) PAUSE+1
   b) PAUSE OPERATOR I HATE YOU
   c) PAUSE

d)   PAUSE 100001

e)   PAUSE 'OPERATOR, PLEASE FIX MY PROGRAMME'

PROGRAMMING EXERCISES FOR CHAPTER XI

1. to 7.

Rewrite the first seven programming exercises of Chapter X, using the DO statement to control the loops. Make sure that the new codes actually work, by running them on the machine. Problems 6 and 7 are particularly important; the first illustrates nested DO loops, the second illustrates jumping out of a DO loop before its nominal completion.

8.   The squares on a chessboard are designated by a row number I (which may be any one of 1,2,3,..., 8) and a column number J (which may be any one of 1,2,3,...,8). A knight's move goes from (I,J) to (IPRIME,JPRIME) where IPRIME=I+K JPRIME=I+L and *either* $K=\pm 2$ and $L=\pm 1$ *or* $K=\pm 1$ and and $L=\pm 2$; all combinations of plus and minus signs are permitted, as long as (IPRIME,JPRIME) turn out to fall on the chess board. Write a programme to read the input number I,J, and count the number of permissible knight's moves from this position.

CHAPTER XII

BUILT-IN FUNCTIONS AND ARITHMETIC STATEMENT FUNCTIONS.

A.   Built-In Functions

FORTRAN has "built-in" mathematical function evaluation programmes. These contain the commands necessary to make the machine compute, starting from a number in some storage location, the desired function of that number. For example, the FORTRAN statement

Y=3.0+2.0*SIN(X)

results in the following action: the machine fetches the real number (we are using the predefined type convention) contained in memory location named X, and the machine then transfers control to that region of memory which contains the commands required for evaluating the sine function. These commands are obeyed, and the result appears in the arithmetic register, ready to be used further. Control reverts to the programme. The number so obtained is multiplied by 2.0, the number 3.0 is added to it, and the final result is stored into the memory location named Y.

There is no strictly *logical* necessity for this. In principle, you yourself could write a set of orders to evaluate the sine function. Indeed, if you have been diligent in carrying out the exercises, you have done just that, already! However, to do this for every common mathematical function occurring in the programme would be tedious, highly inefficient, and would put an intolerable burden on the ordinary programmer. Hence every efficient master programme, such as FORTRAN, must supply standard mathematical function evaluation routines.

DEF: If *W* is any well-formed arithmetic expression (wfae) and if *FNAME* is one of the reserved words standing for a function name in FORTRAN, then*(FNAME(W))* is also a wfae, whose value is that particular function of the value of *W*. Function evaluation takes precedence over all other arithmetic operations, i.e., in the hierarchy of arithmetic operations given in Chapter II, function evaluation has the highest hierarchical rank, rank 4.

Note: Because of the high hierarchical rank of function evaluation, the parentheses around *FNAME(W)* can usually be omitted.

Before giving a list of the FORTRAN standard function names, it is necessary to say something about the *type* of the argument of the function, and the type of the function value. What the programmer would like is one function name for a given mathematical function; when he writes SIN(X), the machine should decide what the type of X is, and evaluate either the sine of a 4-byte real number, or the sine of a 16-byte complex number, as the case may be; naturally, the value of SIN(X) should have the same type as X itself.

Unfortunately, while some computer languages have this feature, the present version of FORTRAN does *not* have it. The function name is used by FORTRAN to recognize, not only what the function is, but also the type of the function argument, and the type of the result. Thus FORTRAN uses *different* names for one and the same mathematical function, if the argument on the function has different type, and/or if the result of the function evaluation has different type.

For example, the mathematical sine function has four different names in FORTRAN. If X and Y are of type REAL*4, we use the form

    Y=SIN(X)

On the other hand, if DX and DY are both of type REAL*8, we must use

    DY=DSIN(DX)

If CX and CY are both of type COMPLEX*8, we must use

    CY=CSIN(CX)

Finally, if both ZX and ZY are of type COMPLEX*16, we must use

    ZY=CDSIN(ZX)

Thus, the four different names of the sine function are SIN, DSIN, CSIN, and CDSIN. These names are mnemonic, in the sense that the initial letter D in DSIN stands for "double precision", the initial letter C in CSIN stands for "complex", and the two initial letters CD in CDSIN stand for "complex double precision".

Some compilers, in particular most student compilers, check that the argument of the function has the right type for the function name; such compilers diagnose an error in a statement such as

    Y=DSIN(X)

if X has not been declared to be of type REAL*8.(*) Some production versions of FORTRAN, however, do not carry out such checks, and the resulting errors are incredibly hard to detect, since they are usually very small errors.

As a result of this multiplicity of names for the same mathematical function, conversion of a FORTRAN programme from single-precision to double-precision arithmetic is not a simple matter. The statement IMPLICIT REAL*8(A-H,O-Z,$) has the effect of changing the predefined convention from REAL*4 to REAL*8, for all real variable identifier names. But this is not enough: in addition, all FORTRAN *constants* appearing in the programme must be rewritten as REAL*8 constants (D-format instead of E-format); and all FORTRAN *built-in function names* must be altered, throughout the programme.

We now give a TABLE OF FUNCTION NAMES. This Table is divided into three sections: (1) Functions of one variable; (2) Functions of exactly two variables; and (3) Functions of two or more variables. Discussion of this Table follows immediately after the Table itself.

(*)   If DX is of type REAL*8, the statement Y=DSIN(DX) is <u>not</u> in error; it merely <u>implies a conversion</u> of the double-precision result DSIN(DX) to single precision form, before this result is stored away in the four-byte memory location reserved for the single-precision variable Y.

TABLE XII. 1   NAMES OF FORTRAN BUILT-IN FUNCTIONS

1.   Functions of one variable.   FNAME(X)

Definition of Function	FORTRAN name	Type of the argument	Type of the function value	In-line(I) or Out-of-line(O)
Exponential e^x	EXP	REAL*4	REAL*4	O
	DEXP	REAL*8	REAL*8	O
	CEXP	COMPLEX*8	COMPLEX*8	O
	CDEXP	COMPLEX*16	COMPLEX*16	O
Natural logarithm $\log_e(x)$	ALOG	REAL*4	REAL*4	O
	DLOG	REAL*8	REAL*8	O
	CLOG	COMPLEX*8	COMPLEX*8	O
	CDLOG	COMPLEX*16	COMPLEX*16	O
Common logarithm $\log_{10}(x)$	ALOG10	REAL*4	REAL*4	O
	DLOG10	REAL*8	REAL*8	O
Arc sine arc sin(x)	ARSIN	REAL*4	REAL*4	O
	DARSIN	REAL*8	REAL*8	O
Arc cosine arc cos(x)	ARCOS	REAL*4	REAL*4	O
	DARCOS	REAL*8	REAL*8	O
Arc tangent arctan(x)	ATAN	REAL*4	REAL*4	O
	DATAN	REAL*8	REAL*8	O
Trigonometric sine sin(x)	SIN	REAL*4	REAL*4	O
	DSIN	REAL*8	REAL*8	O
	CSIN	COMPLEX*8	COMPLEX*8	O
	CDSIN	COMPLEX*16	COMPLEX*16	O
Trigonometric cosine cos(x)	COS	REAL*4	REAL*4	O
	DCOS	REAL*8	REAL*8	O
	CCOS	COMPLEX*8	COMPLEX*8	O
	CDCOS	COMPLEX*16	COMPLEX*16	O
Trigonometric tangent tan(x)	TAN	REAL*4	REAL*4	O
	DTAN	REAL*8	REAL*8	O
Trigonometric co-tangent cot(x)	COTAN	REAL*4	REAL*4	O
	DCOTAN	REAL*8	REAL*8	O

TABLE XII. 1   (Cont'd).

Definition of Function	FORTRAN name	Type of the argument	Type of the function value	In-line(I) or Out-of-line(O)
Square root $(x)^{1/2}$	SQRT	REAL*4	REAL*4	O
	DSQRT	REAL*8	REAL*8	O
	CSQRT	COMPLEX*8	COMPLEX*8	O
	CDSQRT	COMPLEX*16	COMPLEX*16	O
Hyperbolic tangent $\tanh(x)$	TANH	REAL*4	REAL*4	O
	DTANH	REAL*8	REAL*8	O
Hyperbolic sine $\sinh(x)$	SINH	REAL*4	REAL*4	O
	DSINH	REAL*8	REAL*8	O
Hyperbolic cosine $\cosh(x)$	COSH	REAL*4	REAL*4	O
	DCOSH	REAL*8	REAL*8	O
Error function $\text{erf}(x)=$ $=(2/\pi^{1/2})x\int_0^x e^{-u^2}du$	ERF	REAL*4	REAL*4	O
	DERF	REAL*8	REAL*8	O
Complemented error function $\text{erfc}(x)=1-\text{erf}(x)$	ERFC	REAL*4	REAL*4	O
	DERFC	REAL*8	REAL*8	O
Gamma function $\int_0^\infty u^{x-1}e^{-u}du$	GAMMA	REAL*4	REAL*4	O
	DGAMMA	REAL*8	REAL*8	O
Natural log of the gamma function	ALGAMA	REAL*4	REAL*4	O
	DLGAMA	REAL*8	REAL*8	O
Absolute value $\lvert x \rvert$	IABS	INTEGER*4	INTEGER*4	I
	ABS	REAL*4	REAL*4	I
	DABS	REAL*8	REAL*8	I
$\lvert z \rvert =(x^2+y^2)^{1/2}\ldots$	CABS	COMPLEX*8	REAL*4	O
where $z=x+iy$	CDABS	COMPLEX*16	REAL*8	O
Conjugate complex of a complex number	CONJG	COMPLEX*8	COMPLEX*8	I
	DCONJG	COMPLEX*16	COMPLEX*16	I
Convert from integer to real	FLOAT	INTEGER*4	REAL*4	I
	DFLOAT	INTEGER*4	REAL*8	I
Convert from real to integer	IFIX	REAL*4	INTEGER*4	I
	HFIX	REAL*4	INTEGER*2	I

TABLE XII. 1   (Cont'd).

Definition of Function	FORTRAN name	Type of the argument	Type of the function value	In-line(I) or Out-of-line(O)
Truncation: sign(x)x largest integer less than $|x|$	INT	REAL*4	INTEGER*4	I
	AINT	REAL*4	REAL*4	I
	IDINT	REAL*8	INTEGER*4	I
Most significant part of a REAL*8 number	SNGL	REAL*8	REAL*4	I
Extend REAL*4 to REAL*8 by adding zero digits	DBLE	REAL*4	REAL*8	I
Real part of a complex number	REAL	COMPLEX*8	REAL*4	I
Imaginary part of a complex number	AIMAG	COMPLEX*8	REAL*4	I

2.   Functions of exactly two variables: FNAME(A,B).

Phase angle $\arctan(a/b)=p$ $\sin(p)=a/r$ $\cos(p)=b/r$ $r=(a^2+b^2)^{1/2}$	ATAN2	REAL*4	REAL*4	O
	DATAN2	REAL*8	REAL*8	O
Transfer of sign $|a| \times sign(b)$	SIGN	REAL*4	REAL*4	I
	ISIGN	INTEGER*4	INTEGER*4	I
	DSIGN	REAL*8	REAL*8	I
Positive difference $a - min(a,b)$	DIM	REAL*4	REAL*4	I
	IDIM	INTEGER*4	INTEGER*4	I
Modular arithmetic $a(mod\ b) = a-kb$ where k = largest integer $\leq |a/b|$	MOD	INTEGER*4	INTEGER*4	I
	AMOD	REAL*4	REAL*4	I
	DMOD	REAL*8	REAL*8	I
Express two real arguments as a complex number: $z=a+ib$	CMPLX	REAL*4	COMPLEX*8	I
	DCMPLX	REAL*8	COMPLEX*16	I

TABLE XII. 1   (Cont'd).

Definition of Function	FORTRAN name	Type of the argument	Type of the function value	In-line(I) or Out-of-line(O)
	3. Functions of two or more variables:	FNAME(A,B,C, . . .).		
Largest value among the arguments	AMAX0	INTEGER*4	REAL*4	O
	AMAX1	REAL*4	REAL*4	O
	MAX0	INTEGER*4	INTEGER*4	O
	MAX1	REAL*4	INTEGER*4	O
	DMAX1	REAL*8	REAL*8	O
Smallest value among the arguments	AMIN0	INTEGER*4	REAL*4	O
	AMIN1	REAL*4	REAL*4	O
	MIN0	INTEGER*4	INTEGER*4	O
	MIN1	REAL*4	INTEGER*4	O
	DMIN1	REAL*8	REAL*8	O

Let us now discuss some of the features of this Table. First of all, you may note certain *standard conventions for the function names:*

1. Function names starting with I, J, K, L, M, or N have function *values* of type INTEGER*4;

2. Function names starting with H have function *values* of type INTEGER*2 ("half-word integer");

3. Function names starting with C, but not CD, have function *values* of type COMPLEX*8 (exceptions: CABS, COS, COSH, COTAN);

4. Function names starting with D have function *values* of type REAL*8 (exceptions: DIM, DCONJG, DCMPLX);

5. Function names starting with the two letters CD have function *values* of type COMPLEX*16 (exception: CDABS);

6. All other starting letters indicate that the function value is of type REAL*4;

7. If the usual mathematical name of a real variable function has the wrong starting letter, the starting letter A is supplied: ALOG, ALGAMA, AIMAG; similarly, if the usual mathematical name of an integer-valued function has the wrong starting letter, the starting letter I is supplied: IABS, IFIX, ISIGN;

8. In the extensive set of function names for maximum and minimum, the final character of the name is 0 if the *arguments* are integers, the final character is 1 if the *arguments* are real numbers; the initial letters follow the standard conventions for indicating the type of the function *value;*

106

thus, AMAX0(I,J,K) implies a conversion: we find the largest one of the three integers I, J, and K, and convert that value to type REAL*4.

Although we have called these operators "mathematical functions", this name is really appropriate only for some of them; in Table XII. 1, part 1, the functions after the dashed line are used to carry out *conversions* from one type of number storage in the machine, to some other type; the functions CMPLX and DCMPLX have the same purpose.

The words "in-line" and "out-of-line" require explanation: the calculation of sin(x), for example, requires quite a few commands; it would be highly inefficient to put all these commands into the object (translated) programme whenever the source programme calls for evaluating the sine of some quantity. To avoid this inefficiency, the sine function is handled "out of line": the relevant commands are kept in a separate section of the machine memory, and control is transferred to that section whenever the sine of a quantity is required. On the other hand, taking the absolute value of a real number merely requires making the sign digit (the first binary digit of the storage location) equal to 0, no matter what it was before; it would be silly to transfer control to a special region of memory just to do *that*. Therefore, the relevant machine command is inserted into the object programme at every appropriate place, and we say that the function ABS(X) is "in-line".

The function SQRT(X) and other functions for taking a square root are *not* equivalent to X**0.5 in what they do. X**0.5 uses the logarithm of X, and can not be used at all if the argument is a complex number. The function SQRT(X) uses an iterative procedure for finding the square root, in fact the same procedure which appeared as an exercise in Chapter VI. This procedure is faster and more accurate than the use of logarithms (remember, the machine does not have a *table* of logarithms; it *computes* the logarithm every time it is needed); the procedure also works well if the number is complex.

Many functions are available only for real number arguments, for example, the inverse trigonometric functions, the hyperbolic functions, etc. In some cases, one can get around this quite simply, by using other functions. For example, the hyperbolic sine of a high-precision complex number Z1 can be obtained by the statement

Z2=0.5D0*(CDEXP(Z1)-CDEXP(-Z1))

Note the use of 0.5D0 rather than just 0.5; we want to avoid implied conversion to double precision, including a possible loss of precision.

Although the above statement would *work,* it would be quite inefficient, since we have to compute *two* complex exponential functions. To save machine time, it would be much better to write *two* statements:

ZE=CDEXP(Z1)
Z2=0.5D0*(ZE-1.0D0/ZE)

The second of these statements is mathematically equivalent to, but faster in operation than,

Z2=(ZE-1/ZE)/2

which latter statement has two implied conversions from integer to COMPLEX*16.

For other functions, where such straightforward alternatives are not available, the programmer must write his own function generating routines. The FORTRAN methods for doing so are discussed in Chapter XIV.

There are two separate inverse tangent functions, ATAN(X) and ATAN2(A,B). These are defined differently, and give (in general) different results. ATAN(X) is the principal branch of the ordinary inverse tangent function; the value of ATAN(X) lies between $-\frac{1}{2}\pi$ and $+\frac{1}{2}\pi$. The function of two variables ATAN2(A, B) is defined to be that angle p (in radians) with the properties:

$$\sin(p) = a/r \qquad \cos(p) = b/r \qquad \text{where} \qquad r = (a^2+b^2)^{\frac{1}{2}}$$

Thus the value of ATAN2(A,B) ranges from $-\pi$ to $+\pi$. If XR and XI represent the real and imaginary parts, respectively, of a complex number, then the phase angle of that complex number is *not* always equal to P=ATAN(XI/XR); it *is* always equal to P=ATAN2(XI,XR).

All trigonometric functions assume that the argument is in *radians,* not degrees; similarly, all inverse trigonometric functions give the value of the function in *radians.*

Special Note on WATFOR:

The handling of built-in functions in WATFOR is slightly different from standard FORTRAN IV.

1. WATFOR handles *all* built-in functions "out-of-line"; this makes little difference to the programmer;

2. WATFOR does not have "reserved words", and therefore does *not* do automatic typing of the names of double-precision, complex, and complex double precision functions.

If such functions are required by the programmer, *they must be typed by him.* The following cards, inserted at the start of a WATFOR programme, can be used to accomplish this typing:

```
IMPLICIT REAL*8(D), COMPLEX*8(C)
COMPLEX*16 DCONJG,DCMPLX,CDEXP,CDLOG,CDSIN,CDCOS,CDSQRT
REAL*4 CABS,COS,COTAN,COSH,DIM
REAL*8 CDABS
INTEGER*2 HFIX
```

We observe that the first of these declaration statements makes *all* names starting with the letter D into names of double precision real variables, and *all* names starting with the letter C into names of single precision complex variables. This is a good general convention for clean programming, in most cases.

The above five cards are not always necessary, in fact, they would rarely all be needed. For example, if we require no complex arithmetic at all, and do not use 2-byte integers, then the *only* additional declarations needed in WATFOR, compared to standard FORTRAN, are

```
IMPLICIT REAL*8(D)
REAL*4 DIM
```

The other exceptions to this rule, namely the function names DCONJG and DCMPLX, would never appear in such a programme, anyway.

It is at least possible that this profusion of different function names for one and the same mathematical function will not be retained in the FORTRAN language indefinitely. There is no *logical* reason for it: the compiler must recognize, in any case, the type of the function argument: the compiler can then select, automatically, the appropriate function generating routine for an argument of that type. This makes it a bit harder to write the compiler, but it makes it a lot easier for the ordinary programmer, and would be a most desirable change in the FORTRAN language of the future.

B. Arithmetic Statement Functions

Although the use of simple subterfuges for functions which are not built-in FORTRAN functions, of the sort mentioned before, is logically all that is required, it can become very inconvenient in practice. For this, as well as certain other purposes, it is possible within FORTRAN to define your own short-hand notation through so called *arithmetic statement functions.*

For example, suppose we have a programme which requires a good deal of complex arithmetic, in single-precision. We therefore write an IMPLICIT type definition, followed by a set of arithmetic statement functions:

```
IMPLICIT COMPLEX*8(C)
CTAN(CA)=CSIN(CA)/CCOS(CA)
CCOTAN(CA)=CCOS(CA)/CSIN(CA)
CSINH(CB)=(0.5,0.0)*(CEXP(CB) - (1.0,0.0)/CEXP(CB))
CCOSH(CC)=(0.5,0.0)*(CEXP(CC) + (1.0,0.0)/CEXP(CC))
CTANH(CD)=CSINH(CD)/CCOSH(CD)
CCOTH(CD)=CCOSH(CD)/CSINH(CD)
PHASE(CA)=ATAN2(AIMAG(CA),REAL(CA))
```

These statements become *prototype* statement for the remainder of that particular programme. That is, when the compiler encounters, later on in the programme, a statement such as

```
CU=CTAN(CV)*CSINH(CW)
```

the compiler recognizes the names CTAN and CSINH as names of previously defined arithmetic statement functions, and translates the statement accordingly. To be precise, the statement just written would be compiled just as if it had been written out "in longhand":

```
CU=(CSIN(CV)/CCOS(CV))*(0.5,0.0)*(CEXP(CW)-(1.0,0.0)/CEXP(CW))
```

The arguments CA, CB, ... which appear in the definition of the arithmetic statement functions are *dummy arguments,* which are replaced by whatever arguments appear later on in the programme. The *type* of the number computed by an arithmetic statement function is related to the name by the usual typing conventions, predefined, implicit, or explicit (the last of these should be avoided).

To continue our example, we can now write the remainder of our programme *as if* CTAN, CCOTAN, CSINH, CCOSH, CTANH, CCOTH, and PHASE were built-in FORTRAN functions. The names will be recognized, and treated correctly, everywhere in this programme. It is apparent that this is likely to reduce programming errors; just compare the two statements above!

DEF: The *definition of an arithmetic statement function* must appear before the first executable statement of the programme. The definition has the form

$$NAME\,(A,\,B\,\ldots,\,E)=wfae$$

where *NAME* is a grammatically correct identifier name, and $A, B, \ldots, E$ are distinct (within this definition) non-array variables, which are the *dummy arguments* of the function; the well-formed arithmetic expression on the right of the =sign *must not* contain array variables; it may contain other arithmetic statement functions, but if so, their definitions must appear earlier in the programme; it may contain built-in functions. There must be at least one dummy argument. The wfae on the right may contain identifier names other than the dummy arguments $A, B, \ldots, E$; if so, these other quantities are treated as actual variables, not as dummy variables, when the function is used. The types of $NAME, A, B, \ldots, E$ are related to the identifier names in the usual way.

DEF: After an arithmetic statement function $NAME(A, B, \ldots, E)$ has been defined, the definition of a well-formed arithmetic expression in the rest of the programme is extended as follows: Let $AP, BP, \ldots, EP$ be any well-formed arithmetic expressions, with AP of dominant type equal to the type of the dummy argument A, BP of dominant type equal to the type of the dummy argument B, etc. Then $(NAME(AP, BP, \ldots, EP))$ is itself a well-formed arithmetic expression, whose value is obtained by substituting the values of AP for A, BP for B, $\ldots$, EP for E, in the definition of the function $NAME$.

Special Note for WATFOR: In WATFOR, arithmetic statement function definitions are allowed to contain array variables. It is *not* advisable to make use of this freedom, since WATFOR programmes written in this way would not work with other FORTRAN compilers.

At first sight, it may seem that arithmetic statement functions are all that is ever needed. We can use arithmetic statement functions defined earlier, within the definition of new arithmetic statement functions, and hence can build up more and more complicated functions.

However, the restriction that the definition of the function must be in the form of one arithmetic statement, turns out to be excessively severe! To illustrate this, suppose that we wish to define, as a standard function, the Bessel function which appeared as an exercise in Chapter X, see programming exercises X.11 through X.14. This function was defined through its power series; to compute the value of the power series, we must write a loop (*not* a single arithmetic statement!), and we must terminate that loop when the next term becomes small enough; i.e., we do not know beforehand just how many terms of the series we shall need: it depends on the value of x. None of this can be done within the framework of single arithmetic statements. Even worse: most power series, this one included, become practically useless when the variable x gets large; this has nothing to do with the mathematical concept of convergence of the series: the power series for the Bessel function, given in problem X.11, converges for all x. But for large x, we require a huge number of terms before we can ignore the remainder of the series; and even worse, the terms have alternating + and - signs. Thus, we lose numerical precision by subtracting large quantities from each other, to get a small difference. For large values of x, the power series should not be used at all; alternative methods exist in that region. Thus, a reasonable Bessel function definition must involve quite different procedures for large x and for small x.

In the first version of FORTRAN these problems were not recognized fully; it became apparent quite quickly, however, that arithmetic statement functions are simply not good enough. FORTRAN II therefore made it possible to write FUNCTION subprogrammes, which do not suffer from these restrictions. These are discussed in Chapter XIV. From the practical point of view, everything that can be done with arithmetic statement functions, can be done as well or better by FUNCTION subprogrammes.

DRILL EXERCISES FOR CHAPTER XII.

1. Write arithmetic expressions, using built-in functions, for the following mathematical expressions (use PSI for ψ, and ALPHA for α); assume all quantities are of type REAL*4.

   a) $A \sin \psi - B$

   b) $A \sin(\psi - \alpha)$

   c) $\sin \sqrt{\log_e(u^2 - v^3)}$

   d) $\cot(e^u + \sqrt{v})$

   e) $\tanh(\arctan(u) + \arccos(v))$

   f) $A \sin y$ where y is the largest of u, v, and w

2. Write similar expressions, plus the required type declaration statements, if all quantities in problem 1 are double precision real numbers (type REAL*8).

3. Using built-in functions plus arithmetic statement functions, where required, write arithmetic expressions for problem 1, parts (a) through (d), assuming all quantities are of type COMPLEX*8. Why are 1(e) and 1(f) impossible?

4. Same as 3, but with double-precision complex numbers, type COMPLEX*16.

5. The following programme segments, each of which uses built-in functions or arithmetic statement functions or both, all contain errors. See how many errors you can detect.

   a)
   ```
   I=1
   ISQ(I)=I**2
   M=ISQ(I)
   PRINT,M
   ```

   b)
   ```
   EXPSQ(X)=CDEXP(-(X**2))
   X=10.0D0
   Z=EXPSQ*SIN(X)
   ```

   c)
   ```
   FUNC(X)=EXP(ATAN(SQRT((X+(1./X)**2)/2.)))
   X=1.0
   Z=FUNC(X)
   ZZ=FUNC(5.0)
   ```

CHAPTER XIII

ARRAYS

A. Vector Arrays.   Definition and Initialization

Very frequently, we have to deal with lists of similar items, for example, marks obtained by a student in different subjects. If a student takes physics, chemistry, mathematics, and biology, we could give different names to the marks, e.g., MARKPH, MARKCH, MARKMA, MARKBI.

In many applications, however, it is simpler and more convenient to refer to the four subjects by numbers from 1 to 4, say 1 for physics, 2 for chemistry, 3 for mathematics, and 4 for biology; and to use a single variable name MARK for all four marks. The first mark is then referred to as MARK(1), the second mark as MARK(2), the third mark as MARK(3), and the fourth mark as MARK(4). In the machine, these four numbers appear in adjacent storage locations, the first storage location (the one to which the name MARK "points") contains MARK(1), the next storage location contains MARK(2), and so on. We refer to this ordered set of numbers as a *linear array* or *vector array*, of *dimension* 4.

There are three methods of setting aside vector array storage within FORTRAN, two of which will be given now, the third in Chapter XIV (in connection with the COMMON statement). The first is the DIMENSION statement. For example, to set aside four adjacent storage locations for the vector array MARK, we write the specification statement

DIMENSION MARK(4)

In this form, the *type* of the variable is deduced from the initial letter of the variable name, in conjunction with the predetermined type convention modified, if desired, by an IMPLICIT statement at the beginning of the programme. In our case, the initial letter M of MARK decides that MARK is of type INTEGER*4; thus FORTRAN sets aside four storage locations of four bytes each, a total of 16 bytes of storage for the array; furthermore, whenever MARK(3), say, appears somewhere in the programme, it is taken to be of type INTEGER*4.

The DIMENSION statement is non-executable; it instructs the compiler how to translate certain other statements in the source programme, but does not itself get translated into the object programme. We defer the formal definition of the DIMENSION statement till later, after we have discussed arrays other than vector arrays.

The second method to declare a vector array is through an explicit type specification statement, for example:

INTEGER*4 MARK(4)

This serves the double function of (i) declaring this variable to be of type INTEGER*4, and (ii)

declaring it to be a vector variable, with four components to the vector. In fact, the explicit type declaration can be used to serve still a third function, namely of setting initial values (at the start of the execution phase) for some or all of the vector components; the form:

INTEGER*4 MARK(4)/3*100,98/

declares that, at the start of the execution phase, the initial values are MARK(1)=100,MARK(2)=100, MARK(3)=100, MARK(4)=98.

The reasons we gave in Chapter IX for avoiding explicit type declarations apply less strongly here, since a single explicit type declaration can take the place of two separate statements (a DIMENSION and a DATA statement). However, when the explicit type declaration is used in this way, the first letter of the array name should always be in accordance with the convention (pre-defined or IMPLICIT, as the case may be) adopted for variable names in the rest of the programme.

The DATA statement, discussed in Chapter IX, may be used to set initial values of the elements of an array at the start of the execution phase, provided that a DIMENSION statement defining the array has come before the DATA statement. For example, the sequence of statements (assuming predefined type convention)

DIMENSION MARK(4),VEC(3)
DATA MARK/3*100,98/,VEC/1.9,2*0.0/

has the effect of declaring MARK to be a vector array of dimension 4, type INTEGER*4, and initial components MARK(1)=100, MARK(2)=100, MARK(3)=100, MARK(4)=98; and of declaring VEC to be a vector array of dimension 3, type REAL*4, and initial components VEC(1)=1.9, VEC(2)=0.0, and VEC(3)=0.0.

B.   Vector Arrays.   Subscripts, Use Within a Programme

Having dicussed how one *declares* a vector array, we go on to show how one may *use* the components of a vector array.

DEF: A *subscript* is any well-formed arithmetic expression of dominant type INTEGER or REAL; the *value* of the subscript is always of type INTEGER*4; if the wfae is of type REAL, the value of the subscript is obtained by the usual truncation method (see Chapter X); *the value of the subscript must not be zero or negative.*

DEF: To refer to a particular component of a declared vector array with name *NAME,* we use the form *NAME(sub)* where *sub* is any valid subscript. Once *NAME* has been declared as the name of a vector array, *NAME(sub)* is itself a well-formed arithmetic expression, and may be used in the construction of more complicated wfae. *NAME(sub)* is also the name of a storage location in the machine, and may be used to the left of the = sign in an assignment statement.

Example: Assume that the programme starts with the declaration statements

DIMENSION MARK(4),VEC(3),SCRMBL(125)
DATA MARK/3*100,98/,VEC/1.9,2*0.0/

Then MARK(3) represents the third element of the vector array MARK; this has the initial value 100.

MARK(3) is also a valid *subscript,* since (at least initially) its value is a positive integer.

SCRMBL(100) is the 100-th element of the vector array SCRMBL; its value is not preset by the DATA statement, but can be set within the programme by an assignment statement, for example,

SCRMBL(100)=3.0*VEC(1)

This has the effect of making SCRMBL(100) contain the number 3.0*1.9=5.7.

SCRMBL(MARK(3)) is an element of the vector array SCRMBL, with subscript equal to MARK(3), i.e., to 100. Thus, initially at least, SCRMBL(MARK(3)) is the same as SCRMBL(100). If MARK(3) is itself altered by an assignment statement, SCRMBL(MARK(3)) will then refer to a different element of the vector array SCRMBL.

Note: MARK(5) should not be used in the programme, since the array MARK has been declared to be of dimension 4; i.e., only 4 storage locations have been reserved for this array. If we ask for MARK(5), we are looking at the next storage location after those four, and this storage location has nothing to do with the array MARK.

Student compilers, such as WATFOR, check for this sort of thing during programme execution, and print out an error message: SS-1 'Subscript out of Range'. But working compilers do not normally check for this in execution, since such checks take machine time themselves. In working compilers, unlike student compilers, the machine time taken by the object programme in execution is the most important consideration.

With a compiler which does not check for subscript overflow, the actual occurrence of subscript overflow gives rise to particularly nasty and elusive bugs. An assignment statement, such as MARK(5)=0, then is actually executed, and results in the clearing of some other storage location, which may be needed elsewhere in the programme to mean something or other which should most definitely not be zero. In aggravated instances of this, whole big areas of memory may be filled with completely erroneous information, and some of these memory areas may have held machine orders, rather than stored numbers. When we then get to the point where we wish to execute these machine orders, we find that they have been destroyed and some meaningless junk sits in their place. The machine encounters a meaningless order, and promptly stops programme execution. We get a message from the monitor system, informing us that a meaningless order has been encountered in a certain location in core memory. But that is actually very little information to go on: what we need to know is not the location of the memory area which has been destroyed, but the location of the machine order which was responsible for the destruction. The absence of this information is what makes this type of bug so terribly elusive.

If checking for subscript overflow is done at all, it must be done in execution, not during compilation. A statement such as MARK(5)=0 could indeed be caught during compilation. But this is not the most likely form of this nasty bug. The most likely form is a statement such as MARK(J)=0, which is perfectly all right if the value of J is one of 1,2,3, or 4; but which wreaks havoc if there is a loop on J in which J goes from 1500 to 10000! This can be caught only in execution, not in compilation; but checking for errors in execution takes machine time, unnecessary machine time if the programme is actually correct.

Subscript overflow is among the nastiest of all bugs, for another reason: during the process of debugging the programme (see Chapter XVI) we are likely to use only a small part of the array storage which has been reserved; if the programme is to handle vectors of dimension 1000, we are likely to use much smaller vectors for checking purposes, vectors with perhaps 3 or 4 components only. Subscript overflow does not then occur. But when we use the "debugged" programme for actual production running, we want the large vectors, and subscript overflow may promptly set in.

Little can be done against this sort of bug: all we can do is to warn you to be on the lookout for subscript overflow, at all times, both while writing a programme and while debugging it.

C.   Vector Arrays.   Input and Output in WATFOR.   Implied DO Loops.

We must still discuss how we read in, and print out, the elements of some vector array. For example, suppose that the programme contains the declaration

DIMENSION SAMPLE(25)

and we wish to read in 25 numbers, one for each component of this vector array.

One method to achieve this is to organize a DO loop:

```
      DO 1000 J=1,25
      READ,SAMPLE(J)
 1000 CONTINUE
```

This piece of WATFOR coding (WATFOR, not standard FORTRAN, because we are using the "free" form of input) results, during the execution phase, in the following action: We read one number from the first data card, and store that number into location SAMPLE(1); we then read one number from the next data card, and store that number into location SAMPLE(2); and so on, until we get to the 25th data card, and store the number contained on that card into location SAMPLE(25). 25 separate data cards are required here; execution of each READ statement in WATFOR free input causes reading of a new card. Because of the DO loop, we execute the single READ statement 25 separate times, and we therefore need 25 separate cards to read.

We can shorten the coding, and avoid the need for so many separate data cards, by using the *implied DO loop:*

READ,(SAMPLE(J),J=1,25)

This statement is completely equivalent to the following (we have used dots to indicate some of the list items):

READ,SAMPLE(1),SAMPLE(2),SAMPLE(3), . . . ,SAMPLE(25)

Thus the 25 items to be read have been written as a single composite list item, enclosed in parentheses: (SAMPLE(J),J=1,25).

DEF: Let *NAME* be the declared name of a vector array. Then the statement

READ,$(NAME(I),I=m_1,m_2,m_3)$

results in reading in exactly the same set of numbers as the DO loop

$$DO\ 1000\ I=m_1,m_2,m_3$$
$$READ,NAME(I)$$
1000 CONTINUE

However, in WATFOR free input, the former statement allows more than one input number to appear on any one data card; the DO loop requires as many separate data cards as numbers to be read.

We observe that the first number read is stored into the memory location called $NAME(m_1)$. The second number read is stored into location $NAME(m_1+m_3)$; the third number read is stored into location $NAME(m_1+2*m_3)$; and so on, until the index I of the next component to be read would exceed the termination test quantity m_2. The rules for I, m_1, m_2, and m_3 are as for DO loops.

A second, even shorter, method can be employed if and only if we want to read in the *entire* array, i.e., as many numbers as the declared dimension of the vector array with name *NAME*.

DEF: Let *NAME* be the name of an array, declared as such earlier in the programme. Then the statement

READ,*NAME*

causes, in the execution phase, reading of exactly as many data numbers as there are storage locations set aside for this array in the machine. These data numbers are stored into consecutive storage locations in the machine, until the entire storage set aside for the array has been filled up with data numbers.

Note: With this form of the definition, the definition also applies to reading of matrix arrays (see later).

In our earlier example, the dimension for the vector array SAMPLE was given as 25, and we wished to read in all 25 components of that vector. Thus, the READ statement could be written most simply as

READ,SAMPLE

with the same effect as

READ,(SAMPLE(J),J=1,25)

However, if we desire to read only 10 components, say, of SAMPLE, we *must not* use READ,SAMPLE with just 10 data numbers supplied: this will be diagnosed as an error, and execution of the programme terminated; with READ,SAMPLE the machine expects to read 25 numbers, no more or less, and diagnoses an error if 25 numbers are not made available to it. We can read the first 10 components of SAMPLE by means of the statement

READ,(SAMPLE(J),J=1,10)

Both types of composite list items, i.e., the implied DO loop and the array name by itself, can be used with WATFOR PRINT statements as well as with READ statements:

DEF: Let *NAME* be the declared name of a vector array. Then the statement

    PRINT,*(NAME(I),I=m₁,m₂,m₃)*

results in output, onto a printed page, of exactly the same set of numbers as would be output by the DO loop

    DO 1000 $I=m_1,m_2,m_3$
    PRINT,*NAME(I)*
 1000 CONTINUE

However, the former statement results in output of as many numbers per line of print-out as can fit onto one printed line; whereas the DO loop results in one new line for each number.

DEF: Let *NAME* be the name of an array, declared as such earlier in the programme. Then the statement

    PRINT,*NAME*

causes, in the execution phase, print-out of exactly as many machine numbers as there are storage locations set aside for the array in the machine. The contents of successive storage locations in the machine are printed out, as many numbers to a line as will fit onto a line, until the whole array has been printed out.

D.   Examples Of The Use Of Vector Arrays

As our first example, let us write a programme to read sets of 25 data numbers and find their mean, their sum of squares, and their root-mean-square deviation.

As usual, we start by observing that we shall need to organize a loop, and we proceed to code this loop "from the inside out". Let us use I as the name of the loop variable, and let the i'th data item be stored in the vector array component SAMPLE(I). I shall have to range from 1 to 25. Within the loop, we shall need to accumulate the sum of the numbers, and the sum of their squares. Thus the innermost statements of the loop will be

    SUM=SUM+SAMPLE(I)
    SUMSQU=SUMSQU+SAMPLE(I)**2

Having decided this, we next ask what we must do (1) before entering the loop, and (2) after leaving the loop.

Before entering the loop, we must clear (set to zero) the values of SUM and SUMSQU (otherwise SUM will not be the sum we want, but that sum *plus* some unknown junk initially in storage location SUM, left over from the previous student programme in the batch); we must also read in the 25 data numbers, and echo-check them.

After leaving the loop, we must use the value of SUM to compute the average AVE=SUM/25.0; and we must use SUM and SUMSQU to compute the value of the root-mean-square deviation(*).

(*)   Note that for simple expressions like the above, the FORTRAN statement is practically as easy to read as conventional mathematical notation.

DEV=SQRT(SUMSQU/25.0 - AVE**2)

Having computed these answers, we must print them out. Finally, we transfer control back to the beginning of the programme, to allow read-in of more sets of data numbers.

We now give a flow diagram of the code, and next to it, the FORTRAN programme.

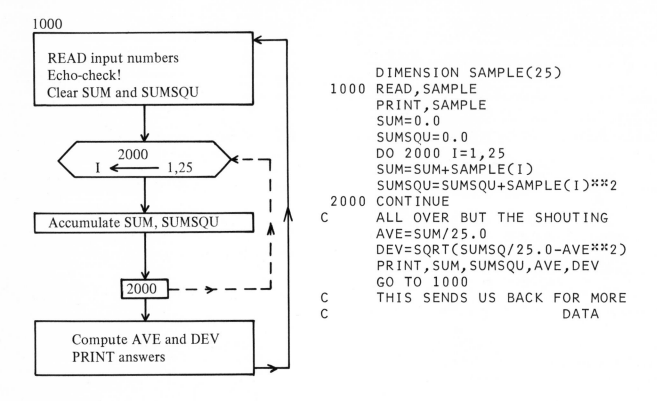

```
                    DIMENSION SAMPLE(25)
              1000  READ,SAMPLE
                    PRINT,SAMPLE
                    SUM=0.0
                    SUMSQU=0.0
                    DO 2000 I=1,25
                    SUM=SUM+SAMPLE(I)
                    SUMSQU=SUMSQU+SAMPLE(I)**2
              2000  CONTINUE
              C     ALL OVER BUT THE SHOUTING
                    AVE=SUM/25.0
                    DEV=SQRT(SUMSQ/25.0-AVE**2)
                    PRINT,SUM,SUMSQU,AVE,DEV
                    GO TO 1000
              C     THIS SENDS US BACK FOR MORE
              C                         DATA
```

Coding error in the example: All right, where is it?

Here it is: in the computation of the mean square deviation DEV, we omitted the final letter U in SUMSQU on the right side of the = sign! Since the name SUMSQ, without a final U, is a valid variable identifier name, no error is diagnosed by FORTRAN during the compile phase. During the execution phase, the error may or may not be detected, depending upon the version of FORTRAN used. In most versions, the likely form in which the error will appear in the printed output is a warning that the programmer has attempted to take the square root of a negative number! Why? Well, SUMSQ contains some junk or other, quite likely zero or a negative number. We subtract SUM**2, which is intrinsically positive, and attempt to take the square root of the difference.

Special student versions of FORTRAN such as WATFOR are much kinder to the programmer; the execution time error message given to the programmer by WATFOR is:

ERROR   UV-0   SUMSQ
     PROGRAMME WAS EXECUTING LINE 10 IN ROUTINE M/PROG WHEN TERMINATION
                                                          OCCURRED

Looking through Appendix B, we see that the code UV-0 means "undefined variable - simple variable". Next to it is the name of the variable; and the line below informs us which statement of the source programme was the culprit.

Note re diagnostics: A particularly frequent coding error is *omission of the DIMENSION statement* for an array. How is this omission diagnosed by FORTRAN? This may be surprising, but the most likely diagnostic messages are:

SR-0 'MISSING SUBPROGRAMME'
SF-1 'PREVIOUSLY REFERENCED STATEMENT NUMBER ON STATEMENT FUNCTION'
SF-2 'STATEMENT FUNCTION IS THE OBJECT OF A LOGICAL IF STATEMENT'
SF-3 'RECURSIVE STATEMENT FUNCTION, NAME APPEARS ON BOTH SIDES OF ='
FN-4 'SUBSCRIPTS ON RIGHT HAND SIDE OF STATEMENT FUNCTION'

These diagnostic messages all refer to statement functions or missing subprogrammes. The reason is this: When the FORTRAN compiler encounters the character string SAMPLE(I), say, in the source programme, the compiler first looks whether there is a DIMENSION statement for SAMPLE. If not, FORTRAN looks whether an arithmetic statement function with name SAMPLE has been defined for this programme, or whether perhaps the statement now being translated can be interpreted as the definition of such an arithmetic statement function. A perfectly innocuous assignment statement such as

SAMPLE(I)=SAMPLE(I)+1.0

is interpreted, in the absence of a DIMENSION statement for SAMPLE, as an attempt to define SAMPLE(I) as an arithmetic statement function with dummy variable I. As such, it is an invalid definition, since the function to be defined appears also to the right of the = sign, as part of the definition. Thus we generate diagnostic message SF-3.

On the other hand, consider the statement SUM=SUM+SAMPLE(I). Here SAMPLE(I), in the absence of the DIMENSION statement, cannot be interpreted as an arithmetic statement function definition; for that, SAMPLE(I) would have to appear to the *left* of the = sign. On the other hand, SAMPLE could still be the name of a built-in function, or of a FUNCTION subprogramme written by the programmer, and included later on in the input deck (see Chapter XIV). So the compiler makes *that* assumption, sits back and waits. Only after all source statements have been translated, and it is time to execute the object programme, will the compiler notice that something is amiss: in fact, there is no built-in function by name SAMPLE, and there is no FUNCTION subprogramme for a function of name SAMPLE supplied by the programmer. At this moment, and only at this moment, the compiler finds that the programme cannot be executed. Thus, at this point, we get the diagnostic message SR-0 'MISSING SUBPROGRAMME'.

Modification of Example: Suppose we do not wish to have the programme restricted to computing the averages and standard deviations for exactly 25 samples. Rather, we would like to use the same programme for different numbers of samples. What must we do to change the programme?

Clearly, the innermost part of the loop (accumulation of SUM and SUMSQU) is unchanged. But the DO loop does not range from 1 to 25, necessarily, rather it ranges from 1 to some number K which we must tell to the machine, and which represents the number of data numbers to be averaged.

The main change is therefore that we must READ the number K of data; and arrange everything else to go from 1 to K, not necessarily from 1 to 25. The DIMENSION statement, on the other hand must specify a definite constant dimension for the vector array SAMPLE.(*) Thus we must decide, ahead of time, that we shall never wish to average more than, say, 125 numbers with this programme (or whatever is a reasonable upper limit for our purposes); we then declare SAMPLE to be an array with 125 (or whatever it is) components.

The new READ statement can *not* be READ,K,SAMPLE; this statement would result in reading in one integer constant, to be stored into location K, followed by exactly 125 numbers, to be stored into SAMPLE(1), SAMPLE(2), SAMPLE(3), ..., SAMPLE(125). This is *not* what we want to happen; we want to read exactly K sample numbers, no more.

The correct READ statements are

READ,K
READ,(SAMPLE(I),I=1,K)

the second of which uses the number previously read in, and stored into location K, as the terminating condition for the implied DO loop. It is permissible to combine these two READ statements into one:

READ,K,(SAMPLE(I),I=1,K)

It is essential, however, that K is read in, and set, before we get to the implied DO loop; otherwise, the machine would have no way of knowing what value of K to use. Thus

READ,(SAMPLE(I),I=1,K),K   is *wrong*.

There is very little change in the flow diagram, so we do not reproduce that, and merely give the FORTRAN programme:

```
      DIMENSION SAMPLE(125)
1000  READ,K,(SAMPLE(I),I=1,K)
      PRINT,K,(SAMPLE(I),I=1,K)
      SUM=0.0
      SUMSQU=0.0
      DO 2000 I=1,K
      SUM=SUM+SAMPLE(I)
      SUMSQU=SUMSQU+SAMPLE(I)**2
2000  CONTINUE
C     ALL OVER BUT THE SHOUTING
      AVE=SUM/K
      DEV=SQRT(SUMSQU/K-AVE**2)
      PRINT,SUM,SUMSQU,AVE,DEV
      GO TO 1000
C     THIS SENDS US BACK FOR MORE DATA, STARTING WITH A NEW K
```

Discussion of modified code: Both the READ statement and the echo-checking PRINT statement have implied DO loops, going up to K. In the PRINT statement, but *not* in the READ statement, we could have written the list in opposite order; i.e., the statement

(*)   This restriction applies to arrays appearing in main programmes, and is relaxed for array declarations in sub-programmes, see Chapter XIV.

```
PRINT,(SAMPLE(I),I=1,K),K
```

would *not* be actually wrong. Why??

Though not wrong, this would be poor coding: in all echo-checking, the numbers should be printed out *in the same sequence* in which they are read in. Otherwise, it is all too easy to get confused when making up data cards for the programme.

Note that we have corrected the error in the computation of DEV. We have also divided by K, rather than by 25, in the computations of AVE and DEV. Division by K contains an implied conversion from the integer K to the 4-byte floating point form of this number; in this case, the machine time taken is insignificant, since this conversion occurs after we have already gone through the loop, not within the loop. We would have to convert K to floating point form once, in any case; here it happens twice - hardly worth the trouble to alter the programme.

However, one change in this programme is most desirable! Note that we read in a number K, which may be anything at all, and then store further numbers into SAMPLE(1), SAMPLE(2), . . ., SAMPLE(K). What if K exceeds 125??! Well, WATFOR would warn us that a subscript has exceeded range, and terminate the computation; but other versions of FORTRAN would not do so; the storing would proceed, thereby probably overwriting and destroying information of vital importance for successful running of the programme. It is most desirable to check that K is within range, and stop computation if it is not. Thus, the first few statements of the corrected programme might be

```
1000 READ,K
     IF(K.LE.125) GO TO 1200
     PRINT,K
     STOP
1200 READ,(SAMPLE(I),I=1,K)
     PRINT,K,(SAMPLE(I),I=1,K)
     . . .
```

In this version, we read K first, check it, and only if it is less than or equal to 125, do we go on to read the sample numbers themselves. Otherwise, we print out the offending value of K, and stop execution altogether! A message should be printed in that case, see Chapter IX, Section F or Chapter XV, Section C.

In machine programming, it is necessary, at all stages, to pay careful attention to the universal law: "If anything can go wrong, it will!"

All right, what else can go wrong here? Well what about round-off errors? Let us make some estimates: the individual numbers stored in locations SAMPLE(1), SAMPLE(2), . . ., SAMPLE(K) have a precision of roughly 1 part in 10^7. If we add about 100 of those, the cumulative round-off error in SUM and SUMSQU is of the order of $(100)^{1/2}=10$ times that, i.e. 1 part in 10^6 (remember that guard digit for floating point addition of low-precision floating point numbers? If you have forgotten, read Chapter X again.) The fractional error in AVE is of the same order (since both the number, and its error, are divided by K in going from SUM to AVE, the fractional error does not change). The error in DEV could be larger, since we may lose significant figures as a result of the subtraction in the argument of the SQRT function. But it is unlikely that we are going to lose more than 2 significant figures here, so DEV will still have a precision of at least 1 part in 10^4, which should be more than ample, for most practical purposes. *It is always necessary to estimate precision, at least roughly, and to go to double-precision arithmetic if single-precision is insufficient.*

E. Matrix Arrays

In addition to vector arrays, which are indexed by a single subscript, FORTRAN also allows the use of *matrix arrays,* which are indexed by two or more (up to seven) subscripts. For example, suppose we have 50 students in a class, each one of whom takes 4 subjects. It is then natural to allocate the storage location MARK(45,3), say, to the mark of student no. 45 on subject number 3. If we write the marks for each student in a horizontal line, each student in a line to himself, we have a table with 50 rows (one row for each student) and 4 columns (one for each subject). Such a table is called a *matrix array.* The total number of entries in this table is 50x4 = 200. Thus, to store such a matrix array, we must set aside 200 adjacent storage locations, one location for each entry in the table. The table entry in row I and column J, say, is referred to as MARK(I,J); this represents the mark of student number I in subject number J; I may be any one of 1,2,3,..., 50; and J may be any one of 1,2,3,4.

To set aside this amount of storage, and to declare MARK to be the name of a matrix array of size 50-by-4, we can use either of the declaration statements

DIMENSION MARK(50,4)

or

INTEGER MARK(50,4)

where the latter form, the "explicit" type + array declaration, also declares the type of the numbers stored within the array.

It is sometimes important to know just how FORTRAN arranges the storage of such matrix arrays. The most reasonable, commonsense method would be to store the numbers in the same sequence in which an ordinary person would read such a table, that is reading from left to right, line after line. *This is not the method used in FORTRAN matrix storage.*

Rather, FORTRAN arranges storage column by column. The entire first *column* of the matrix is stored first; next in core memory comes the entire second column of the matrix; then the entire third column, and so on. In the figure below, we show, schematically, the sequence of storage locations for the matrix array, with consecutive *order numbers* 1,2,3, ..., 200, and the matrix element stored in each memory location:

Order Number	Matrix Element
1	MARK(1,1)
2	MARK(2,1)
3	MARK(3,1)
..	. . .
50	MARK(50,1)
51	MARK(1,2)
52	MARK(2,2)
53	MARK(3,2)
...	. . .
100	MARK(50,2)
101	MARK(1,3)
102	MARK(2,3)
...	. . .

Order Number (cont'd)	Matrix Element (cont'd)
150	MARK(50,3)
151	MARK(1,4)
152	MARK(2,4)
153	MARK(3,4)
...	...
200	MARK(50,4)

We can represent the relationship between the order number in storage, and the subscripts I and J of the matrix element MARK(I,J), by a simple *formula,* namely

Order number for storage of MARK(I,J) = I + 50*(J-1)

More generally, the number 50 would be replaced by the *first* number in the DIMENSION statement defining the matrix array; i.e., the number 50 is taken from DIMENSION MARK(50,4).

Note that exactly this formula is computed by the FORTRAN-compiled object programme every time we wish to refer to MARK(I,J). This computation takes machine time, and in some programmes considerable machine time can be saved (particularly in the execution of loops) by making use of this knowledge. Let us give a simple *example:* Suppose we wish to find the average mark of all students in all subjects, i.e., just the one grand total average. To do this, we add up the entire table of marks, and divide by 200, the number of entries in the table. This can be coded as nested DO loops:

```
      SUM=0.0
      DO 1200 I=1,50
      DO 1100 J=1,4
      SUM=SUM+MARK(I,J)
 1100 CONTINUE
 1200 CONTINUE
      AVE=SUM/200
```

Now, first of all, it was stupid to accumulate a floating-point variable SUM, rather than a fixed-point (integer) variable MSUM, say. The statement

SUM=SUM+MARK(I,J)

carries an implied conversion of MARK(I,J) from integer to floating-point form, and we have to do this every single time. The following programme is faster in execution:(*)

```
      MSUM=0
      DO 1200 I=1,50
      DO 1100 J=1,4
      MSUM=MSUM+MARK(I,J)
 1100 CONTINUE
 1200 CONTINUE
      AVE=FLOAT(MSUM)/200.0
```

(*)   Explain why it would be disastrous to write AVE=FLOAT(MSUM/200)

But even this programme suffers, from the point of view of execution time, from the need to carry out the address computation I+50*(J-1) every single time we traverse the loop. This is foolish, since all we want to do is to add up the contents of 200 adjacent storage locations. We really want to think of it, for this purpose, as vector storage of a vector of dimension 200, not as matrix storage of a 50×4 matrix array. On the other hand, for other purposes it may be most convenient to think of the set of 200 storage locations as a matrix array, not as a vector array. How can we do both simultaneously?

F.   The Equivalence Statement

FORTRAN allows us to do so, by use of the EQUIVALENCE declaration statement. In our example, we may write:

```
DIMENSION MARK(50,4),MARKVC(200)
EQUIVALENCE (MARK(1,1),MARKVC(1))
```

The DIMENSION statement by itself would set aside 200 storage locations for the matrix array MARK, and another 200 storage locations for the vector array MARKVC. However, the EQUIVALENCE statement declares that MARK(1,1), i e., the first location of the matrix array MARK, and MARKVC(1), i.e., the first storage location of the vector array MARKVC, are to be the *same* storage location in the machine.

We have therefore declared *synonyms,* different names for the same actual storage location. Not only have we done so for MARK(1,1) and MARKVC(1), but the remaining 199 storage locations of these two arrays carry synonyms as well. To be precise, let

K=I+50*(J-1)

be the "order number" of MARK(I,J) discussed before. Then

MARK(I,J) is synonymous with MARKVC(K)

Either "name" refers to the same actual storage location in the machine. Note that the relationship between K and (I,J) contains the number 50, which appears in the dimension statement DIMENSION MARK(50,4). If the first dimension of the matrix array is not 50 but some other number, that other number also replaces "50" in the formula for the "order number" K.

The previous set of orders can now be written, equivalently but much more efficiently in terms of machine time, as

```
      DIMENSION MARK(50,4),MARKVC(200)
      EQUIVALENCE (MARK(1,1),MARKVC(1))
      MSUM=0
      DO 1200 K=1,200
      MSUM=MSUM+MARKVC(K)
 1200 CONTINUE
      AVE=FLOAT(MSUM)/200.0
```

In this case, since we want the sum of all the marks, the precise correspondence between K and (I,J) is actually irrelevant; but of course, it is important in other situations.

DEF: The EQUIVALENCE statement has the form EQUIVALENCE *(A,B,C,...), (D,E,F,...)* where *A,B,...* are names for storage locations in the machine. These may be simple storage locations or storage locations within arrays. If the latter, the subscripts must be given as integer constants. The subscripts must not be variables themselves. The effect of the EQUIVALENCE statement is to declare *A,B,C,...* to be synonyms for the same storage location in the machine; to declare *D,E,F,...* to be synonyms for the same storage location in the machine; and so on. If any of these are storage locations within arrays, the whole array is placed into machine storage correspondingly.(*)

EQUIVALENCE statements are used mainly by more advanced programmers, and present dangerous traps for beginners. Nonetheless, careful use of such declarations can enable one to avoid some of the inefficiencies of FORTRAN-compiled programmes; one may force the compiler, so to speak, to produce an efficient object programme. We shall see another example of this a bit further on.

G. Input and Output of Matrix Arrays

One inconvenience arising from FORTRAN array storage is in input and output of the elements of a matrix array. The statement

    PRINT,MARK

does indeed result in printing out *all* elements of the 50 x 4 matrix array MARK. *But* the *sequence* in which they are printed out is the FORTRAN sequence, *not* the natural sequence. As a result, this form of print-out is seldom convenient.

To print the array MARK in easily readable form, we have to resort to DO loops and implied DO loops; that is, we want MARK printed out row after row; there is a DO loop on the row number I, and an implied DO loop on the column index J=1,2,3,4, within each row:

    DO 1200 I=1,50
    PRINT,(MARK(I,J),J=1,4)
1200 CONTINUE

In execution, the PRINT statement is encountered 50 times. The first time, it prints out a line containing MARK(1,1), MARK(1,2), MARK(1,3), and MARK(1,4). The second time, it prints out a line containing MARK(2,1), MARK(2,2), MARK(2,3), and MARK(2,4). This goes on, until the 50th time, when we print out a line containing MARK(50,1), MARK(50,2), MARK(50,3), and MARK(50,4).

It is possible to have implied DO loops within implied DO loops; if we do not care about having the separate rows of the matrix appear on separate lines, we can write the single PRINT statement

    PRINT,((MARK(I,J),J=1,4),I=1,50)

(*) FORTRAN allows, within equivalence statements only, a different designation of storage locations within a matrix array; the normal form is MARK(3,2), say, and EQUIVALENCE (MARK(3,2),B) means that the variable named B occupies the same storage location as element MARK(3,2) of the matrix array MARK. The special form replaces the two subscripts (3,2) by the order number K=3+50*(2-1)=53; hence we may write EQUIVALENCE (MARK(53), B) to get the same effect. This method is highly efficient in producing coding errors, and should be avoided.

This double implied DO loop is equivalent, as far as what numbers are going to be printed out and in which order, to the preceding set of three statements. Note that the inner parentheses enclose the inner implied DO loop (MARK(I,J),J=1,4), whereas the outer parentheses enclose the outer implied DO loop, varying I from 1 to 50. However, in this form, the PRINT statement will not start a new line of print for each new row I of the matrix. Rather, we continue printing out matrix elements next to each other on one line, until we come to the end of a line on the printer (i.e., the next matrix element to be printed would no longer fit onto the line); then, and only then, do we skip to the next line.(*)

Although the output obtained from the set of three statements given above is reasonable, it is hard to keep track which row we are reading. It would be better to have the rows *numbered* in the output. Nothing easier! We have a loop on the row number, I, anyway; so let us just print out the value of I, each time round the loop:

```
      DO 1200 I=1,50
      PRINT,I,(MARK(I,J),J=1,4)
 1200 CONTINUE
```

Similar considerations apply to input. The *input* statement READ,MARK would read in 50*4=200 input numbers, and store them into the matrix array MARK *in standard FORTRAN sequence.* Thus we would have to prepare the input numbers in this sequence, and mistakes are extremely likely.

If we really know that we want to read in the entire array, i.e., the marks of exactly 50 students, the read-in sequence given below suffices:

```
     DO 100 I=1,50
     READ,(MARK(I,J),J=1,4)
 100 CONTINUE
```

This assumes that each data card has the four marks of a student, one card per student; and it assumes that there are exactly 50 such cards.

However, we may wish for more flexibility; indeed, this is usually true. Suppose we have fewer than 50 students in the class, but still one card per student. We want to keep reading student results, advancing the row index I each time, until we come to a card telling us that we have finished the reading operation. For example, since negative marks are not given to students, a card with the mark -1 for the first subject can be used to indicate that we have come to the end. At this point we wish to set the value of NSTUDT, the total number of students; and we wish to fill the rest of the matrix array MARK with zeros. We assume that NSTUDT will never be as high as 50.

The reading loop can be basically the same as above. But, after each reading operation, we check whether the value of MARK(I,1) which has just been read in is negative. If not, we continue with the loop. If MARK(I,1) *is* negative, this means we have just read the card with -1 as the mark for the first subject, i.e., the termination card. At this point, we jump out of the DO loop. With a premature jump out of the DO loop, the loop variable I retains the value it last had inside the loop (compare the rules for DO loops in Chapter XI); this last value of I is one more than the number of students in the class (the one extra "student" is the one with a mark of -1 on his first subject). Therefore, we can use the statement

    NSTUDT=I-1

(*)   This is true for the "free" output statement PRINT. It is <u>not</u> true for format controlled output, as described in Chapter XV.

to set the correct value for NSTUDT, the number of students in the class, as soon as we jump out of the DO loop. We should also clear the rest of the matrix array MARK to zeros, for safety, at this point.

Notice that we do not expect the DO loop on the variable I to come to a "normal" termination. By assumption, there are less than 50 students in the class; even if there are exactly 49 students in the class, the non-existent "student" with a mark of -1 will correspond to I=50, and the logical IF statement in the code below will send us out of the DO loop before we get quite to the end of it (i.e., before we reach the CONTINUE statement of that DO loop with I equal to 50). If we actually get to a normal termination of the DO loop, it means that something is wrong with our input data: either there are really 50 or more students in the class, or we have forgotten to place a termination card with a first mark of -1 at the appropriate point, within the set of data cards. In either case, the input data are faulty, and no computation should be carried out. Thus, if the DO loop for the card reading runs to a normal completion, something is wrong, and we must stop the computation. (We should really issue a message at this point, before stopping, to inform the person reading the printed output just why the run has been stopped. This can be done either by the technique discussed in Chapter IX, Section F, which is at the moment restricted to WATFOR, or by normal FORTRAN output under FORMAT control, which will be discussed in Chapter XV. Thus, we do not show this part of the coding in the actual example, below; but it should be supplied in one form or another, in any realistic programme).

Having discussed what we mean to do, we now give the FORTRAN coding:

```
      DIMENSION MARK(50,4)
      DO 1200 I=1,50
      READ,(MARK(I,J),J=1,4)
      IF(MARK(I,1).LT.0) GO TO 1250
 1200 CONTINUE
C     WE SHOULD NEVER GET TO THIS POINT. STOP IF WE DO.
      STOP
C     WE JUMP TO THE POINT BELOW ON READING A NEGATIVE MARK.
 1250 NSTUDT=I-1
C     NOW CLEAR THE REST OF THE ARRAY MARK TO ZEROS.
      DO 1270 K=I,50
      DO 1260 J=1,4
      MARK(K,J)=0
 1260 CONTINUE
 1270 CONTINUE
C     READING OPERATION IS COMPLETE AT THIS POINT.
```

This type of coding is a good deal easier for the poor devil who has to make up the data cards, than asking for the number NSTUDT in advance; let the machine do the counting! Naturally, we shall want to echo-check the input at this stage, to see how many students' cards were read in, and what the marks were. A possible echo-checking sequence is

```
 1300 PRINT,NSTUDT
      DO 1350 I=1,NSTUDT
      PRINT,I,(MARK(I,J),J=1,4)
 1350 CONTINUE
```

Now suppose that we wish to compute the class average mark for the class, in each of the four subjects. Thus we need to compute the sum of all the marks in a subject, then divide by the number of students, and print out the result; and we want to do this in turn for each of the four subjects. The flow diagram for this operation is given below, and next to it the coding. Note that the *outer* loop is now on the subject number J=1,2,3,4; the *inner* loop is on the student number I=1,2,3,..., NSTUDT.

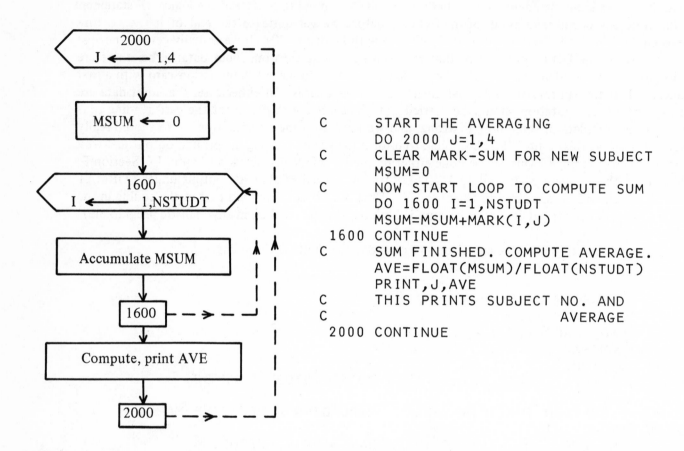

```
C          START THE AVERAGING
           DO 2000 J=1,4
C          CLEAR MARK-SUM FOR NEW SUBJECT
           MSUM=0
C          NOW START LOOP TO COMPUTE SUM
           DO 1600 I=1,NSTUDT
           MSUM=MSUM+MARK(I,J)
  1600 CONTINUE
C          SUM FINISHED. COMPUTE AVERAGE.
           AVE=FLOAT(MSUM)/FLOAT(NSTUDT)
           PRINT,J,AVE
C          THIS PRINTS SUBJECT NO. AND
C                              AVERAGE
  2000 CONTINUE
```

Note the statement used to compute the average. Why would it have been quite wrong to use AVE=FLOAT(MSUM/NSTUDT)?

If we put together the programme segments we have written so far, we obtain a complete programme for reading in student data cards, 4 marks for each student, computing the number of students in each class, and the class average in each of the 4 subjects. This code reads:

```
           DIMENSION MARK(50,4)
C          READING SEQUENCE
  1000 DO 1200 I=1,50
           READ,(MARK(I,J),J=1,4)
C          DO WE HAVE A NEGATIVE MARK?
           IF(MARK(I,1).LT.0) GO TO 1250
C          NO. CONTINUE READING DATA CARDS.
  1200 CONTINUE
```

128

```
C          WE SHOULD NEVER GET TO THIS POINT. STOP IF WE DO.
           STOP
C          WE JUMP TO THE POINT BELOW ON READING A NEGATIVE MARK.
 1250 NSTUDT=I-1
C          NOW CLEAR THE REST OF THE ARRAY MARK TO ZEROS.
           DO 1270 K=I,50
           DO 1260 J=1,4
           MARK(K,J)=0
 1260 CONTINUE
 1270 CONTINUE
C          READING IS COMPLETE AT THIS POINT. START ECHO CHECK.
 1300 PRINT,NSTUDT
           DO 1350 I=1,NSTUDT
           PRINT,I,(MARK(I,J),J=1,4)
 1350 CONTINUE
C          ECHO CHECK COMPLETE. START THE AVERAGING
           DO 2000 J=1,4
C          CLEAR THE MARK-SUM FOR EACH NEW SUBJECT J
           MSUM=0
C          NOW START INNER LOOP TO COMPUTE MARK-SUM.
           DO 1600 I=1,NSTUDT
           MSUM=MSUM+MARK(I,J)
 1600 CONTINUE
C          MARK-SUM FINISHED. COMPUTE AND PRINT CLASS AVERAGE IN
C                                    SUBJECT NO. J
           AVE=FLOAT(MSUM)/FLOAT(NSTUDT)
           PRINT,J,AVE
C          THIS PRINTS SUBJECT NUMBER, FOLLOWED BY CLASS AVERAGE.
 2000 CONTINUE
C          LOOP ON SUBJECT NUMBER J IS FINISHED. GO BACK TO READ NEXT
C                                    CLASS.
           GO TO 1000
```

Note: This coding is still a bit awkward, in the read-in sequence. We need a nested loop on K and J, K=I,I+1, I+2, ..., 50 and J=1,2,3,4, to clear the rest of the matrix. There are two ways to avoid this awkwardness.

1.   Don't bother to clear at all - we never use these matrix elements anyway!

2.   Clear the *whole* matrix *before* we read in anything.

The first of these choices is *poor coding*. We avoid a clearing operation because the numbers in question will not be used. True; but later on we may wish to alter the code, add more operations, etc. and presto, we may find that we have assumed, silently, that the rest of the matrix *is* cleared to zeros - and the extended code will fail!

So we had better do the clearing, but we can certainly do it before reading in anything; and, at that point, we can be more efficient about it than a nested loop would be; we again use the trick of introducing a vector array MARKVC of dimension 200, occupying the same storage locations as the matrix array MARK. If we clear MARKVC, by a single loop, MARK is cleared automatically, since these are the same storage locations in the machine!

```
      DIMENSION MARK(50,4),MARKVC(200)
      EQUIVALENCE (MARK(1,1),MARKVC(1))
C     CLEAR STORAGE BEFORE READING STARTS
1000  DO 1100 K=1,200
      MARKVC(K)=0
1100  CONTINUE
C     NOW START READING STUDENT DATA CARDS
      DO 1200 I=1,50
      READ,(MARK(I,J),J=1,4)
C     DO WE HAVE A NEGATIVE MARK?
      IF(MARK(I,1).LT.0) GO TO 1250
C     NO. CONTINUE READING DATA CARDS.
1200  CONTINUE
C     WE SHOULD NEVER GET HERE. STOP IF WE DO.
      STOP
C     WE JUMP TO THE POINT BELOW ON READING A NEGATIVE MARK
1250  NSTUDT=I-1
C     CLEAR THE ONE NEGATIVE MARK WHICH HAS BEEN READ IN.
      MARK(I,1)=0
C     READING IS COMPLETE AT THIS POINT. START ECHO CHECK.
1300  PRINT,NSTUDT
      .... (SAME FROM HERE ON)
```

It may be asked why we used an explicit loop to clear the array MARKVC, rather than simply a DATA statement DATA MARKVC/200*0/. The DATA statement clears the array to zero at the beginning of the execution phase, but not thereafter. In the programme itself, we want to be able to "recycle", i.e., there is a statement GO TO 1000 at the very end of the programme, sending us back to the starting point to read further data cards. The DATA statement would have cleared MARKVC only once, at the very beginning, and MARKVC would not be cleared again thereafter. The loop, as actually written, clears MARKVC every time we recycle back to statement 1000.

H. Multi-Dimensional Arrays

We must say something about arrays with more than two dimensions. As an example, suppose that we have a very large group of students, which are divided into parallel classes, in each of their four subjects. We may then refer to each mark by three subscripts: MARK(I,J,K) where:

I = number of the class, say I=1,2,3,4,5 for 5 parallel classes
J = running number of the student, within that class, J=1,2,3,..., NSTUDT
K = number of the subject, K=1,2,3,4

If we have to carry all this information in the machine simultaneously, and if the number of students in any one class can go up to 50, we would have to allow storage for 5*50*4=1000 separate marks. The DIMENSION statement to do this would read

DIMENSION MARK(5,50,4)

It may be hard to visualize such a three-index array, and actually there is no need to do so. We know what the three indices I,J,K mean, and as far as the machine is concerned, the array is just a set of 1000 adjacent storage locations. What we do need to know is the method used in FORTRAN to arrange this storage. That is, we need to know the "order number" of the element MARK(I,J,K,) This is given by an extension of the rule for two-dimensional matrix arrays, as follows:

Order number for storage of MARK(I,J,K)=I+5*(J-1) + 5*50*(K-1)

where the "5" and the "50" are the first and second entry, respectively, in the dimension statement for MARK. A pictorial way of saying this is the following: as we walk along the machine storage, storage location after storage location, the first index I varies most rapidly; it changes all the time; the second index, J, varies more slowly; it changes only every 5th storage location; and the third index, K, varies most slowly of all; it changes only every 250th storage location.

DEF: FORTRAN allows arrays with up to seven separate subscripts. The declaration statement for a k-dimensional array is

DIMENSION NAME (m1,m2,m3, . . . ,mk)

where NAME is a grammatically correct identifier name, whose first letter determines the type of the numbers in the array (including the number of bytes per storage location) in accordance with the predefined and/or IMPLICIT type convention; and where m1, m2, etc. are positive integer constants.

In the programme, the general element of the array is referred to as

NAME(I1,I2,I3, . . . ,IK)

where I1 = 1, 2, 3, . . . , m1
      I2 = 1, 2, 3, . . . , m2
      . . .
      IK = 1, 2, 3, . . . , mk

The storage is arranged according to the rule:

Order number of NAME(I1, I2, I3, . . . , IK) =
I1 + m1*(I2-1) + m1*m2*(I3-1)+ m1*m2*m3*(I4-1) + . . . + m1*m2*m3* . . . *mj*(IK-1)

where j in mj is equal to j=k-1. Index I1 varies most rapidly, I2 less rapidly, I3 even less rapidly, . . ., and IK most slowly of all, as we walk along the storage locations of the array.

Multi-dimensional arrays take lots of room in storage, and the computation of the order number in the machine (which is required to get at any one element of the array in storage) takes appreciable time.

I.   Further Examples

It is best to avoid the use of multi-dimensional arrays, especially in those portions of a programme which take the most time in execution (innermost loops). This can often be achieved with a bit of thought, and suitable arrangement of the flow of the programme. As an *example*, consider the averaging of marks programme given before: suppose the students are really in five parallel classes, rather than all in one class; does this mean we *must* use a three-dimensional array MARK(I,J,K) with dimensions DIMENSION MARK(5,50,4)?

Not at all! After all, the student cards contain data for one student at a time. If we can arrange to have the programme process the data on each card, immediately after reading the card, we do not even need a *two*-dimensional array for MARK! Let us see what we need to do. If we want to process the cards as they come in, we must accumulate the sum of marks for every one of the four subjects, simultaneously. So we shall want to arrange storage for four different mark-sums, with a dimension statement DIMENSION MSUM(4); the innermost statements will be a loop accumulating these four sums:

```
       DO 1600 J=1,4
       MSUM(J)=MSUM(J)+MARK(J)
 1600  CONTINUE
```

where MARK(J) is the mark of the current student on subject number J. Also for echo-checking, we must print out the student mark cards as we read each one. We must check for the famous student with a negative mark on the first subject, to tell us when we have come to the end of one class; at this point we want to compute the class averages. If, at the very end, we want grand total averages as well, we had better accumulate, at this point, a total mark-sum for each subject, as well as a total for the number of students in all classes. We also need an indication when we have come to the very end; we may use the convention: MARK(1)=-1 and MARK(2)=0 to indicate the end of a class; but MARK(1)=-1 and MARK(2)=-1 to indicate the end of the last class; in this way, we are not restricted to precisely five parallel classes of students. We test for MARK(1).LT.0; if this is true, we print out totals and averages for that class; having done so, we test for MARK(2).LT.0; if false, we read the data cards for the next class, but if true, we compute and print grand totals and grand total averages. A flow diagram and the code follows:

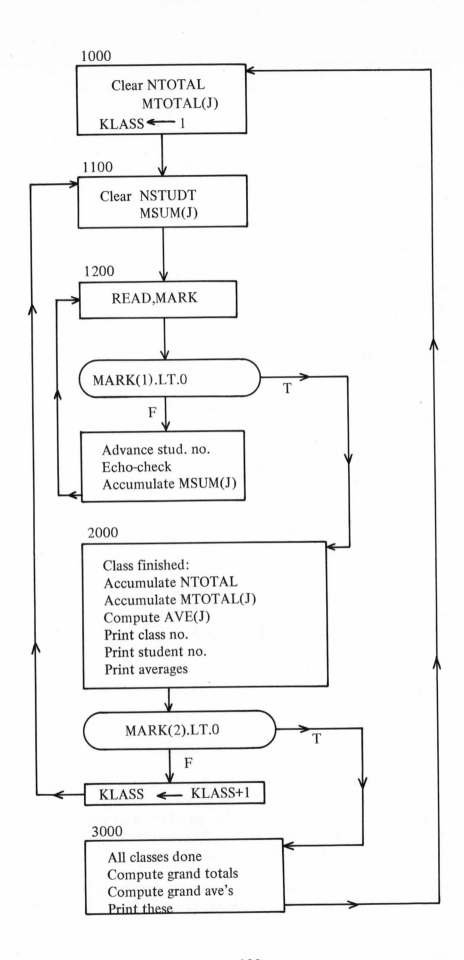

```
      DIMENSION MSUM(4),MARK(4),MTOTAL(4),AVE(4)
C     CLEAR GRAND TOTALS ETC.
 1000 NTOTAL=0
      KLASS=1
      DO 1050 J=1,4
      MTOTAL(J)=0
 1050 CONTINUE
C     PREPARE TO READ IN ONE CLASS
 1100 NSTUDT=0
      DO 1150 J=1,4
      MSUM(J)=0
 1150 CONTINUE
C     NOW READ IN ONE STUDENT
 1200 READ,MARK
      IF(MARK(1).LT.0) GO TO 2000
      NSTUDT=NSTUDT+1
C     ECHO-CHECK
      PRINT,KLASS,NSTUDT,MARK
      DO 1250 J=1,4
      MSUM(J)=MSUM(J)+MARK(J)
 1250 CONTINUE
      GO TO 1200
C     CLASS IS FINISHED. COMPUTE CLASS AVERS.
 2000 NTOTAL=NTOTAL+NSTUDT
      DO 2050 J=1,4
      MTOTAL(J)=MTOTAL(J)+MSUM(J)
      AVE(J)=FLOAT(MSUM(J))/FLOAT(NSTUDT)
 2050 CONTINUE
      PRINT,KLASS,NSTUDT,AVE
C     IS THIS THE LAST CLASS?
      IF(MARK(2).LT.0) GO TO 3000
C     NO.ADVANCE KLASS. READ NEXT CLASS.
      KLASS=KLASS+1
      GO TO 1100
C     LAST CLASS FINISHED. GRAND TOTALS.
 3000 DO 3050 J=1,4
      AVE(J)=FLOAT(MTOTAL(J))/FLOAT(NTOTAL)
 3050 CONTINUE
      PRINT,KLASS,NTOTAL,AVE
      GO TO 1000
C     START ALL OVER AGAIN.
```

Notice how much more general, simpler, and less demanding on storage this programme is, than the ones written before. Instead of matrix arrays, or even three-dimensional arrays, we now have only 4 vector arrays, each of dimension 4, i.e., 16 storage locations in all for array storage! Furthermore, we have gotten rid of side conditions such as no more than 49 students in a class, no more than 5 classes, etc. A bit of thought can go a long way in machine programming.

As another *example,* also illustrating the need for thought, let us consider the story of the aircraft company engineer who needed to find the determinant of a certain matrix (note: if you haven't heard f determinants, you can nonetheless appreciate the story; but you may wish to skip the material after he story). The definition of the determinant involves a sum over permutations, with various products nd plus or minus signs - never mind. The engineer wrote a FORTRAN programme to compute the eterminant from the definition. Since he was a careful man, he wrote the programme for an N-by-N natrix, and he checked the programme by letting it compute determinants of 2-by-2, 3-by-3, and -by-4 matrices; all of these came out like a charm. So, convinced that the programme was working properly, he input the matrix elements of his actual, 30-by-30 matrix, and watched while the machine ot to work. An hour later, he was still watching. A day later, the Section Head was watching, too.)n the third day, they called in a consultant, who had bad news for them.

The number of permutations of N things is $N!=1*2*3*4*...*N$. For N=30, this number is $2.65*10^{32}$, roughly. Assuming that the machine can calculate one term of the determinant in 10^{-5} seconds (this may be optimistic; there are 29 multiplications to be done, for each such term), it would ake a mere $2.65*10^{27}$ seconds to do the job. This is roughly 10^{20} years!

Furthermore, having kept the machine occupied with the computation for all this time, and assuming that the Universe would not have run down by then, what would be the precision of the answer? That's simple: *zero* significant figures.

So perhaps that is not the way to compute determinants!

To do it better, we make use of the fact that we may subtract a constant multiple of any one row, from any other row, without changing the value of the determinant. Let us subtract a FACTOR times row i, from row k, by means of the inner loop:

```
      DO 1200 J=1,N
      A(K,J)=A(K,J)-FACTOR*A(I,J)
 1200 CONTINUE
```

This operation on the *matrix* A does not change the value of the *determinant* of A.

For any given I and K, we can choose the value of the FACTOR so that the new element A(K,I), the one in column J=I, vanishes. All we need is to put, *before* this loop,

```
      FACTOR=A(K,I)/A(I,I)
```

and we can do this provided A(I,I) is not equal to zero. We shall assume this for now, and we shall leave the question of "pivoting" the matrix for the end of this Chapter.

If we let I=1 and K=2, then at the end of this operation the new element A(2,1) will equal zero. If we do it with I=1 and K=3, we alter the third row so that the new element A(3,1) is zero. Continue with I=1 and K=4, 5, 6, . . . ,N, in turn. At the end, the *entire first column* of the new matrix will vanish, except for A(1,1) which is unchanged.

Now let I=2 and K=3, 4, 5, . . . , N, in turn, each time performing this same operation. At the end of this set of steps, the matrix elements in column 2 situated *below* A(2,2) are all zero, that is, the matrix elements A(3,2), A(4,2), A(5,2), . . . ,A(N,2). Note also that the first column is *unaffected* since A(2,1) is zero already.

We continue with I=3 and K=4, 5, 6, . . ., N. At the end, the third column is zero below the diagonal element A(3,3); columns 2 and 1 are unaffected.

Keeping on like that, we eventually transform the matrix A into "superdiagonal form", that is, all elements below the main diagonal are zero: A(K,L)=0 if K.GT.L. In this form, however, the determinant is easy to evaluate: it equals the product of the diagonal elements! We can evaluate the product in stages, by starting with DET=1.0 and then multiplying DET by each new diagonal element after we complete a step of the process.

The flow diagram and code are given below:

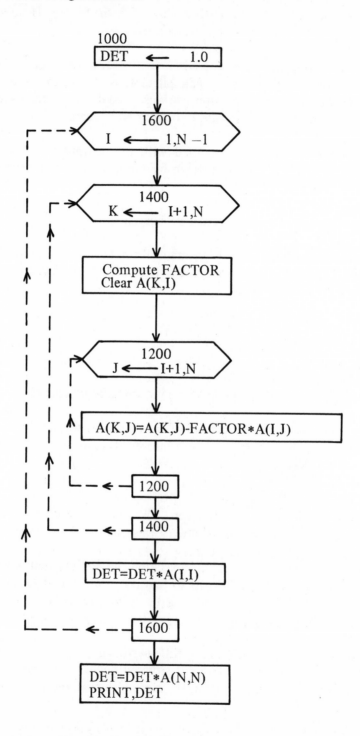

```
      DIMENSION A(30,30)
C     ASSUME MATRIX STORED ALREADY
 1000 DET=1.0
      NMIN1=N-1
C     NOTE DO LOOP NEEDS SINGLE VARIABLE
      DO 1600 I=1,NMIN1
      IPLUS1=I+1
C     SAME REASON.
      DO 1400 K=IPLUS1,N
      FACTOR=A(K,I)/A(I,I)
      A(K,I)=0.0
C     THIS IS THE NEW VALUE NOW.
C     J.LE.I NOT NEEDED IN LOOP BELOW.
      DO 1200 J=IPLUS1,N
      A(K,J)=A(K,J)-FACTOR*A(I,J)
 1200 CONTINUE
C     ROW K FINISHED
 1400 CONTINUE
C     STEP NUMBER I FINISHED
      DET=DET*A(I,I)
 1600 CONTINUE
      DET=DET*A(N,N)
C     WHOLE OPERATION FINISHED
      PRINT,DET
```

Comments:

(1)   We had to compute NMIN1=N-1 explicitly because of the rules for FORTRAN DO loops: The statement DO 1600 I=1,N-1 is grammatically incorrect within FORTRAN, since the termination test quantity of the DO loop must be either an integer constant or a single (non-array) integer variable name. It must not be an arithmetic expression such as N-1. For the same reason, we had to compute IPLUS1=I+1.

(2)   The loop on J can go from IPLUS1 up to N, rather than having to go from 1 up to N. For J=1,2,3, . . . , I-1, we would be subtracting zero from A(K,J). And for J=I, we have already set the new matrix element A(K,I) equal to zero, before starting the DO loop.

(3)   A bit of thought, aided by writing down a few simple cases like N=2, N=3, and N=4, will show that the innermost statement of all these loops is reached exactly $N(N-\frac{1}{2})(N-1)/3$ times; i.e., once for N=2, 5 times for N=3, 14 times for N=4, 30 times for N=5, and so on. In particular, for N=30 the innermost statement is reached 8555 times. Each time, we require one multiplication and one subtraction. Even on a not too modern machine, this should take less than 10^{-4} seconds per step, and there are less than 10000 steps. Hence the total calculation now takes less than 1 second of machine time! Rather less than 10^{20} years!

J.   More Advanced Programming Consideration

Considerable time can be saved in execution if the FORTRAN address computations are bypassed. This makes the code more messy, but faster. In the innermost loop (which matters most for timing considerations), FORTRAN computes the "order number" for A(K,J) and for A(I,J), each time round the loop. This means two unnecessary multiplications. Actually, when J increases in steps of 1, these two order numbers both increase in steps of 30, for DIMEN-SION A(30,30). Furthermore, the two order numbers always differ by the same amount, namely I-K. The initial order number for A(K,J) is L1=K+30*(IPLUS-1)=K+30*I; the final order number is that of A(K,N), namely L2=K+30*NMIN1. We now write down the code based on these considerations:

```
       DIMENSION A(30,30),AVEC(900)
       EQUIVALENCE (A(1,1),AVEC(1))
C      ASSUME MATRIX STORED ALREADY
 1000  DET=1.0
       NMIN1=N-1
       DO 1600 I=1,NMIN1
       IPLUS1=I+1
       DO 1400 K=IPLUS1,N
       FACTOR=A(K,I)/A(I,I)
       A(K,I)=0.0
C      NOW SET UP FAST ADDRESS COMPUTATIONS
       L1=K+30*I
C      THIS IS ORDER NUMBER OF A(K,IPLUS1)
       L2=K+30*(N-1)
C      THIS IS ORDER NUMBER OF A(K,N)
       IMNSK=I-K
C      THIS IS DISPLACEMENT FROM A(K,J) TO A(I,J), FOR ALL J
       DO 1200 L=L1,L2,30
       AVEC(L)=AVEC(L)-FACTOR*AVEC(L+IMNSK)
 1200  CONTINUE
 1400  CONTINUE
       DET=DET*A(I,I)
 1600  CONTINUE
       DET=DET*A(N,N)
       PRINT,DET
```

Unlike the code written before, this version is nearly as fast as one could obtain by writing in assembly language (see Chapter XVII). FORTRAN DO loops on a single variable, using vector rather than matrix arrays, are pretty well optimized from the point of view of machine time, for most FORTRAN compilers.

Thus, by using our knowledge of the way FORTRAN stores matrices, we have gained the advantage of coding in FORTRAN (which can be translated into any machine language nowadays) without the disadvantage of wasting time by inefficient use of the machine.

Conversely, the fact that a large number of programmers have already produced codes with just such tricks in them, implies that the FORTRAN language cannot be altered at this stage, with respect to the way matrix storage is arranged, without making a large number of working programmes obsolete.

Now let us turn to the problem, mentioned earlier, of possible zero elements A(I,I) during this process. In computing FACTOR, we divide by A(I,I), thus zero values for this quantity cannot be tolerated.

To get around this difficulty, we make use of the fact that the rows of a matrix may be interchanged without altering the absolute value of the determinant of this matrix. In fact, if any two rows of a matrix are interchanged with each other, the determinant of the new matrix is the negative of the determinant of the old matrix.

138

Suppose, for example, that at a certain stage in the elimination process, we find that A(I,I) is zero; but A(I+1,I) is not zero. We can then <u>interchange</u> these two rows, so that the new value of A(I,I) (which equals the old A(I+1,I)) is no longer zero, and proceed merrily on our way.

For reasons of numerical accuracy, it is better to look down through the entire column I below the element A(I,I), determine which element A(IPRIME,I) in that column has the largest <u>absolute value</u>, and interchange rows I and IPRIME. This should be done even if A(I,I) is not equal to zero: the process requires little new coding, and improves the final accuracy of the value of the determinant. This procedure is called <u>pivoting.</u>

We shall give the determinant evaluation programme, with pivoting, for the first form of the programme, i.e., without introduction of a vector array AVEC.

Looking back at the earlier flow diagram, the determination of the pivot index IPRIME, and interchange of rows of the matrix when IPRIME.GT.I, must be done for each new I, i.e., within the DO loop on I, but before entering the DO loop on K. You should check that the following coding achieves the desired purpose:

```
      DIMENSION A(30,30)
C     ASSUME MATRIX STORED ALREADY
 1000 DET=1.0
      NMIN1=N-1
      DO 1600 I=1,NMIN1
      IPLUS1=I+1
C     NOW SET UP THE SEARCH FOR THE LARGEST ELEMENT BELOW A(I,I)
      ATOP=ABS(A(I,I))
      IPRIME=I
C     START THE ACTUAL SEARCH
      DO 1100 IP=IPLUS1,N
      IF(ABS(A(IP,I)).LE.ATOP) GO TO 1100
C     WE HAVE FOUND A BIGGER ELEMENT. REMEMBER IT.
      ATOP=ABS(A(IP,I))
      IPRIME=IP
 1100 CONTINUE
C     SEARCH FINISHED. IPRIME IS THE PIVOT ROW. IS IPRIME.EQ.I ?
      IF(IPRIME.EQ.I) GO TO 1150
C     NO. IT IS NOT. INTERCHANGE ROWS I AND IPRIME.
C     NO NEED TO INTERCHANGE COLUMNS 1 THROUGH I-1. THEY ARE ZERO.
      DO 1120 J=I,N
      TEMP=A(IPRIME,J)
      A(IPRIME,J)=A(I,J)
      A(I,J)=TEMP
 1120 CONTINUE
C     PIVOTING FINISHED. NOW PROCEED AS BEFORE.
 1150 DO 1400 K=IPLUS1,N
      FACTOR=A(K,I)/A(I,I)
      A(K,I)=0.0
      DO 1200 J=IPLUS1,N
      A(K,J)=A(K,J)-FACTOR*A(I,J)
 1200 CONTINUE
 1400 CONTINUE
```

139

```
C      STEPNUMBER I FINISHED.
       DET=DET*A(I,I)
       IF(IPRIME.NE.I) DET=-DET
 1600 CONTINUE
C      NOW MULTIPLY BY THE LAST DIAGONAL ELEMENT
 1700 DET=DET*A(N,N)
C      WHOLE OPERATION FINISHED.
 1800 PRINT,DET
```

This programme is more accurate numerically than the ones given before, and division by zero is now most unlikely: it requires that, at some stage, all matrix elements $A(I,I)$, $A(I+1,I)$, $A(I+2,I)$, ..., $A(N,I)$ are simultaneously exactly zero in the machine; because of round-off errors, this is quite unlikely to happen even if the matrix is really singular. We can guard against this eventuality, unlikely though it be, by a simple test: Just after statement 1100 of this programme, we can test whether ATOP is zero:

```
C      THE FOLLOWING STATEMENTS COME RIGHT AFTER STATEMENT 1100
       IF(ATOP.GT.0.0) GO TO 1110
C      IF WE GET TO THIS POINT, ATOP.EQ.0.0 AND THE DETERMINANT=0
       DET=0.0
       GO TO 1800
C      THE PIVOT ELEMENT IS NOT ZERO. CARRY ON WITH ZEST.
 1110 IF(IPRIME.EQ.I) GO TO 1150
       ...
```

With this modification, division by zero is excluded absolutely.

Though more accurate and foolproof, this programme is slow in execution for two reasons:

1.   The actual interchange of two rows, i.e. the DO loop DO 1120 in the programme, takes appreciable machine time;

2.   We have not made any use of the possibility of speeding up the programme by introduction of an equivalent vector array AVEC .

We shall deal with the first of these questions in the text, and leave the second as an advanced exercise. The material which follows below is quite tricky to understand, and belongs to rather more advanced coding than most of this book. If you find difficulty understanding it, just skip it for now; but you may find it most useful when, later on, you have to deal with large matrices in real programmes.

In order to avoid interchanging pairs of rows, we shall interchange the row subscripts instead. At any stage of the calculation, let the vector elements IPER(1), IPER(2), IPER(3), ..., IPER(N) be a permutation of the numbers 1, 2, 3, ..., N, i.e., the same numbers in some altered sequence. Suppose that we refer to a matrix element A(IPER(I),J) in the machine: then we pick up the same actual number as if we had carried out a permutation of the rows first, and then asked for element number A(I,J). (*)

We therefore define a vector array IPER with up to 30 elements. Initially, IPER(1)=1, IPER(2)=2, ..., IPER(N)=N. If, later on, we need to interchange two rows of the matrix, we shall instead interchange the corresponding elements of the vector array IPER.

We shall have to distinguish, however, between the index I as an indication of the i'th step of the elimination

(*)   Some care is in order here, to distinguish between a permutation and its inverse. The process as programmed below takes care of this.

140

process, and as a row index. So far, at the i'th step of the elimination process, we have concerned ourselves with rows number I, I+1, I+2, . . . , N. Henceforth, this means that at the i'th step of the elimination process, we shall be concerned with rows number IPER(I), IPER(I+1), IPER(I+2), . . . , IPER(N), instead. The columns are not permuted, however!

We now give the altered code; if you have understood the discussion to this point, you should check through the code to see that it does what we want to do.

```
      DIMENSION A(30,30),IPER(30)
C     ASSUME MATRIX STORED ALREADY
 1000 DET=1.0
      NMIN1=N-1
C     SET INITIAL VALUES OF IPER
      DO 1010 I=1,N
      IPER(I)=I
 1010 CONTINUE
C     NOW DO STEP NUMBER I OF THE ELIMINATION
      DO 1600 I=1,NMIN1
      IPLUS1=I+1
C     NOW SET UP THE SEARCH FOR THE LARGEST ELEMENT IN RELEVANT
C          COLUMN OF THE PERMUTED MATRIX
      II=IPER(I)
      ATOP=ABS(A(II,I))
      IPRIME=I
C     NOTICE IPRIME IS I, NOT II. THIS FIXES INVERSE PERMUTATION
C          TROUBLE.
C     START THE ACTUAL SEARCH
      DO 1100 IP=IPLUS1,N
      IIP=IPER(IP)
      IF(ABS(A(IIP,I)).LE.ATOP) GO TO 1100
C     WE HAVE FOUND A BIGGER ELEMENT. REMEMBER IT.
      ATOP=ABS(A(IIP,I))
      IPRIME=IP
 1100 CONTINUE
C     SEARCH FOR PIVOT ROW FINISHED. IS THE MATRIX SINGULAR?
      IF(ATOP.GT.0.0) GO TO 1110
C     IF WE GET TO THIS POINT, ATOP.EQ.0.0 AND THE DETERMINANT
C          VANISHES
      DET=0.0
      GO TO 1800
C     THE PIVOT ELEMENT IS NOT ZERO. CARRY ON WITH ZEST.
 1110 IF(IPRIME.EQ.I) GO TO 1150
C     THE ORDER IS WRONG. INTERCHANGE ROW POINTERS.
      ITEMP=IPER(IPRIME)
      IPER(IPRIME)=IPER(I)
      IPER(I)=ITEMP
C     NOTE THE ABSENCE OF A DO LOOP ON J. THIS SPEEDS IT UP.
C     PIVOTING FINISHED. NOW PROCEED.
 1150 DO 1400 K=IPLUS1,N
      KK=IPER(K)
```

```
      II=IPER(I)
      FACTOR=A(KK,I)/A(II,I)
      A(KK,I)=0.0
      DO 1200 J=IPLUS1,N
      A(KK,J)=A(KK,J)-FACTOR*A(II,J)
 1200 CONTINUE
 1400 CONTINUE
C     STEP NUMBER I FINISHED.
      DET=DET*A(II,I)
      IF(IPRIME.NE.I) DET=-DET
 1600 CONTINUE
C     NOW MULTIPLY BY THE LAST DIAGONAL ELEMENT OF THE PERMUTED
C           MATRIX
 1700 NN=IPER(N)
      DET=DET*A(NN,N)
C     WHOLE OPERATION FINISHED.
 1800 PRINT,DET
```

This form of the programme is faster, but still not as fast as it might be, since we have a lot of order numbers to compute. We should still introduce an equivalent vector array AVEC, as before, and fix up the address computations properly. This will be given as an exercise at the end; it is quite an advanced exercise, and should not be attempted by beginning programmers.

The considerations given in this Section, and the coding based on these considerations, are typical of more advanced programming. One has to worry, at all stages, not only about whether the programme does logically what needs to be done, but also:

1. Is the programme likely to run into failure conditions (division by zero in our example)?

2. Is the numerical accuracy as high as possible? (This was our reason for doing the pivoting operation even for A(I,I).NE.0.0).

3. Having taken care of (1) and (2), is the resulting programme as fast as possible, or are we performing unnecessary operations?

4. Are we using machine storage space as efficiently as possible?

In our example above, considerations (1), (2), and (3) all arose, but (4) did not. Furthermore, we did not have to worry about conflicting requirements. In most advanced programming, all four questions arise, and requirements(2), (3), and (4) often conflict with each other: a fast programme requires, frequently, more machine storage space for the speeding up; if we are short of storage space in the machine, we may have to write a programme which is slower in execution than we would like. Similarly, high numerical accuracy frequently conflicts with both storage space and time requirements: for example, double precision arithmetic, which is more accurate numerically, is somewhat slower in execution, and requires twice as much storage space for the array elements. Thus, advanced programming involves careful and delicate balancing of mutually conflicting requirements, and wholesale use of tricks like the vector array IPER in our example. This book is not meant as an advanced programming manual. But it would be wrong to leave the impression that there is nothing more to programming than an understanding of the language, and skill in eliminating outright programming bugs.

DRILL EXERCISES FOR CHAPTER XIII

1. Given the declaration statements:

DIMENSION K(5),A(6)
DATA A/2., 3., -1., -3., 4., 5./,K/5,3,6,4,1/

142

find the numerical values of

a)   A(K(5))   e)   K(A(K(1)))

b)   A(K(K(2)))   f)   K(K(A(5)))

c)   A(A(2))   g)   SQRT(A(K(1)))

d)   K(A(1))   h)   A(K(4))**2

2.   Write FORTRAN statements to do the following:

a)   The vector array A has 15 components; permute them cyclically, i.e., A_2 is to contain the value formerly stored in A_1, A_3 the value formerly stored in A_2, ..., A_{15} the value formerly stored in A_{14}, and A_1 the value formerly stored in A_{15}.

b)   In a list of N values, B_1, B_2, ..., B_N with N odd, interchange the value of the last item with the value in the middle of the list

c)   In a list of N values, C_1, C_2, ..., C_N with N even, interchange C_1 and C_2, interchange C_3 and C_4, ...; interchange C_{N-1} and C_N.

3.   Declare the array KOOKOO to be 8-by-8, and write commands to ensure that the value of KOOKOO(I,J) is I+J if I is even and J is odd, I-J if I is odd and J even, and zero otherwise.

4.   Let A and B be vector arrays, with 15 components each; let C be a simple (non-array) variable name. Write FORTRAN programme segments for the following operations:

a)   Multiplication of a vector by a scalar: put C times A into B

b)   Add the two vectors, placing the vector sum into array A

c)   Subtract vector B from vector A, placing the vector difference into array B

d)   Find the scalar product of A and B, and place it in location C

e)   Find the length of the vector A and place it in location C

5.   Repeated product: store in ANSWER the value of the product: $(1+X_1)(1+X_2)(1+X_3)...(1+X_n)$

6.   Reverse the order of the elements B_j for j=1,2,..., m; i.e., interchange B_1 and B_m, interchange B_2 and B_{m-1}, etc.

7.   A checkerboard is described by an 8-by-8 array KB(I,J), as follows: the value of KB(I,J) is +1 if a white "piece" is in position I,J; it is +2 if a white "king" is in that position; it is -1 if a black piece is in that position; it is -2 if a black king is in that position; and it is zero if the position is unoccupied.

a)   Write a programme to count white pieces and white kings, the counts to be placed into KWP and KWK, respectively.

b)   Same for black pieces and kings, into storage locations KBP and KBK.

c)   Count the number of white kings on the main diagonal (I=J) of the board.

d)   Count the number of black pieces below the main diagonal (I.GT.J).

e)   Count the number of white pieces which are *not* on the main diagonal.

f)   A white piece in position I,J is required to "jump" under the following conditions:

  a)   a black piece or king is in position I-1,J-1 and there is an empty square at I-2,J-2; and/or

  b)   a black piece or king is in position I-1, J+1 and there is an empty square in position I-2, J+2.

  Write a programme to count the number of white pieces which are required to jump.

8.   Write suitable DIMENSION and EQUIVALENCE statements for the verbal specifications given below:

a)   Array A is 9-by-9 and the vector V, with 9 components, coincides with the first column of array A.

b)   Same as above, but V coincides with the *last* column of A.

c)   V is to appear in storage *immediately following* the last element of A.

d)   An array CARDS has 4 rows, each of length 13. The last three columns of the array are to have the names QUEENS, QINGS, and ACES, respectively.

9.   Given the programme segment

DIMENSION A(10,4)
DATA A/10*1.0,10*2,0,10*3.0,10*4.0/

what are the numerical values of the following at the start of the execution phase?

a)   A(3,1)   d)   A(8,3)
b)   A(7,2)   e)   A(10,1)
c)   A(7,3)

10.   Find the errors or redundancies in the following DIMENSION statements:

a)   DIMENSION A(1000,1000,2000)
b)   DIMENSION ARRAY(4,2,3,2,2,5,2,2),
c)   DIMENSION VECTORA1(3,3,1)

PROGRAMMING EXERCISES FOR CHAPTER XIII

1.   A vector array A has 10 elements. Read, from data cards, the components of the vector; echo-check; then rearrange the elements in non-decreasing order, i.e., in such a way that A_{i+1} is greater

than or equal to A_i for i=1,2, . . . , 9. Use the following method of sorting, called "ripplesort": On the first run through, compare A_{i+1} with A_i and interchange the two values if the condition above is violated; do this for i=1, 2, . . . , 9. On the second run through, repeat for i=1, 2, . . . , 8; on the third run through, repeat for i=1, 2, . . . , 7; keep going until *either* no more interchanges are required (*note:* you must arrange to keep track of whether any interchanges were required during a run), *or* until the range of i required for the run is i=1 only (i.e., we compare only A_2 with A_1). Then print out the vector elements in their new order.

2. Same as above, but use a different method of sorting: on the first run, compare A_i with A_{10} and interchange if the condition A(10).GE.A(I) is violated; do this for i=1, 2, . . . , 9; on the second run, compare A_i with A_9, for i=1, 2, . . . , 8; keep going till you are sure the array A is properly ordered.

3. Same as 1, except that we read in not only the vector A but also two numbers N and M, with N.LT.M and both N and M in the range 1 to 10; the sorting is to be done, not for the whole vector A, but only for components N through M, inclusive, of this vector. Other vector components are to remain unsorted.

4. Read in two 3-by-3 matrices A and B, find their matrix product and store it in matrix array C; print out A, B, and C. The matrix product is defined by

    $$C_{ij} = A_{i1}B_{1j} + A_{i2}B_{2j} + A_{i3}B_{3j}$$

5. Read in a 3-by-3 matrix G and find its 16th power, efficiently!

6. Read in a 3-by-3 matrix A and find the exponential exp(A) from the power series, stopping when four-figure accuracy has been achieved.

7. Read in a 3-by-3 matrix A and find the exponential exp(A) by evaluating $(1+(1/N)A)^N$ for N=2, 4, 8, 16, . . . , until the results coincide to four figure accuracy. Compare your results with those of problem 6.

8. (More advanced exercise) Speed up the determinant evaluation programme at the very end of this Chapter, by introducing an equivalent vector array AVEC and avoiding unnecessary address computations.

CHAPTER XIV

SUBPROGRAMMES

A. Introduction

At the end of Chapter XII, we introduced arithmetic statement functions, as a convenient short-hand in case the desired function was not one of the FORTRAN built-in functions. However, we also remarked that arithmetic statement functions are severely restricted, and there are many things which we would like to do but cannot do within the framework of arithmetic statement functions. The FUNCTION subprogramme is not so restricted.

There are often good reasons for breaking up one big programme into a "main programme" plus a series of "subprogrammes". Any one coding error in a big programme requires re-compilation of the entire programme; by contrast, after the programme has been broken up into smaller "pieces", the pieces can be debugged one by one; a coding error found in one piece, or subprogramme, requires re-compilation of only that one subprogramme.

The things which we may wish to do by means of subprogrammes are quite varied, and correspondingly the FORTRAN language provisions for the writing and use of subprogrammes are manifold. In this Chapter, we proceed from the simplest type of subprogramme, the FUNCTION subprogramme, to more complicated matters.

As a first example, consider the "unit step function" defined by

f(x) = 0 for negative x
f(x) = ½ for x=0
f(x) = 1 for positive x

We would most naturally use an arithmetic IF statement:

```
      IF(X) 1100, 1200, 1300
C     NEGATIVE X
 1100 USTEP=0.0
      GO TO 2000
C     ZERO X
 1200 USTEP=0.5
      GO TO 2000
C     POSITIVE X
 1300 USTEP=1.0
 2000 ....   (whatever we want to do next)
```

146

We would have to insert this set of statements (with suitably altered arguments and statement numbers) *every time* we wished to use the function USTEP. We could *not* write, within the main programme, statements such as

Y=3.0*USTEP(A)
Z=3.0*USTEP(B)-USTEP(C)

The FUNCTION subprogramme, on the other hand, allows us to do just that. A separate area in machine memory is set aside for the *translated* subprogramme to evaluate USTEP. The arithmetic statements above are then translated in terms of "calls" on this special area of machine memory.

To *define* the subprogramme USTEP, we need to tell the compiler a number of things:

1. Here comes a subprogramme, rather than part of the main programme.

2. What is the "calling name" of the function?

3. How many arguments does it have, of what types?

4. What is the type of the function value?

5. How should the machine compute the function value?

6. When should control be returned to the calling programme?

7. When have we come to the end of the source language cards defining this particular subprogramme?

In FORTRAN, these things are told to the compiler in certain standard ways. As an example, we give below the *defining programme* for the function USTEP.

```
      FUNCTION USTEP(X)
      IF(X) 1100, 1200, 1300
C     NEGATIVE X
 1100 USTEP=0.0
      GO TO 2000
C     ZERO X
 1200 USTEP=0.5
      GO TO 2000
C     POSITIVE X
 1300 USTEP=1.0
C     CALCULATION FINISHED. NOW BEAT IT.
 2000 RETURN
C     DEFINING PROGRAMME FOR USTEP FINISHED. TELL THE COMPILER.
      END
```

Comparison of these FORTRAN statements with the sequence of statements written earlier shows what additional statements are required to produce a FUNCTION subprogramme, rather than merely a programme segment of the main programme.

1. The statement FUNCTION USTEP(X) tells FORTRAN that it should start to translate a subprogramme, of function evaluation type, with function name USTEP; this function has only one

147

argument, with dummy argument name X. Using the predefined type convention, in the absence of any other type declaration, FORTRAN furthermore decides that both the argument X, and the function value USTEP, are of type REAL*4.

2.   The subsequent statements, down to 1300 inclusive, are the "meat" of the function definition for USTEP. They are to be translated and the resulting object programme stored in a separate section of machine memory, to be "called" whenever any other programme or subprogramme requires evaluation of USTEP.

3.   The statement RETURN is translated into machine language as follows: "When execution reaches this point, transfer control back to that area in machine memory from which USTEP was invoked." Thus RETURN is an executable statement, similar in its function to GO TO. But whereas a GO TO statement transfers control from one point in a programme, to another point in the same programme, the RETURN statement transfers control away from the subprogramme altogether, back to the calling programme. (Note that execution of the RETURN statement requires the machine to *remember,* during execution of USTEP, just *where* control should be returned to at the end. This sort of thing is called "linking", and is one of the things FORTRAN must arrange.)

4.   The last statement, END, tells the FORTRAN compiler that it has come to the end of the source language cards for subprogramme USTEP. Whatever cards come afterwards have nothing to do with defining the FUNCTION USTEP(X). The END statement is not itself translated into machine language (it is a "non-executable statement"); it merely tells the compiler how to translate other statements.

The concepts of programmes and subprogrammes, calls and returns of control, etc., are rather intricate; they should be understood to make effective use of this programming tool, and to appreciate the various FORTRAN rules connected with subprogrammes. As an aid to the beginner, we give below a schematic flow diagram of what happens in the machine, in *execution time,* when we reach the source language statement

Y=3.0*USTEP(A)

of the *main* programme. In execution time, the main programme occupies a certain part of memory; the subprogramme USTEP occupies a separate and distinct area of memory. The flow diagram below illustrates the fact that, within the area occupied by the subprogramme USTEP, memory locations are set aside for XA (the address used to pick up the argument), for X (the argument), for USTEP (the function value), and for RA (the return address)(*); the subprogramme also has an entry point, which is the location in core memory of the first machine order of the subprogramme.

(*)   In most modern machines, the return address is stored in an "index register", rather than in the more usual part of memory; but if different subprogrammes use the same index registers (as in fact they do), entry addresses and return addresses must be stored in core memory as well, to avoid overwriting. The gain from the use of index registers is sometimes strictly negative!

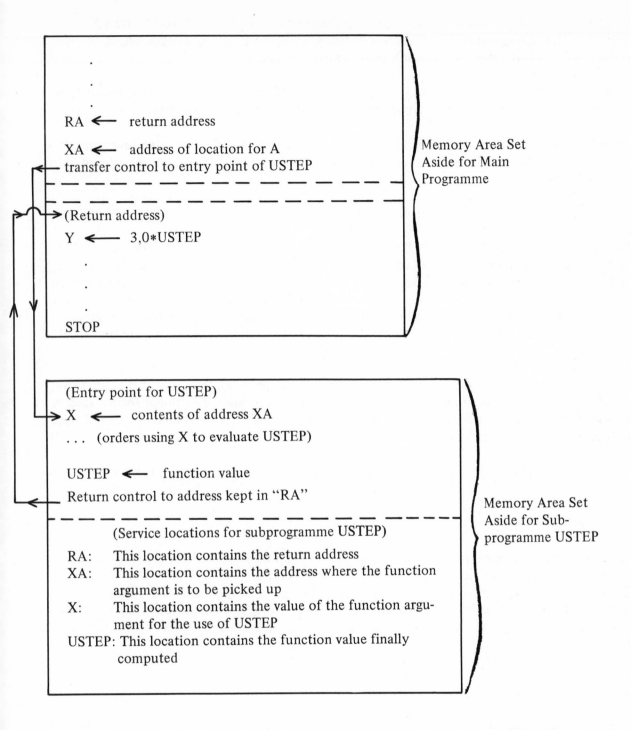

RA ← return address

XA ← address of location for A
transfer control to entry point of USTEP

(Return address)
Y ← 3,0*USTEP

STOP

Memory Area Set
Aside for Main
Programme

(Entry point for USTEP)
X ← contents of address XA
... (orders using X to evaluate USTEP)

USTEP ← function value
Return control to address kept in "RA"

(Service locations for subprogramme USTEP)
RA: This location contains the return address
XA: This location contains the address where the function
        argument is to be picked up
X: This location contains the value of the function argu-
        ment for the use of USTEP
USTEP: This location contains the function value finally
        computed

Memory Area Set
Aside for Sub-
programme USTEP

We see that we require a number of "red tape" commands, to do the "linking" between the main programme and the subprogramme:

1. The return address must be stored for later use by the subprogramme.

2. The address where A can be found must be given to the subprogramme.

3. Control is transferred to the subprogramme.

4. The first thing the subprogramme does is pick up the value of the argument from address XA, and store this value into a local service address called X. Whenever "X" is written within the subprogramme, this is the memory location from which X is taken.

5. The final function value is stored into a location USTEP (in practice, this is an "arithmetic register" rather than a core memory location, but this is not important in principle).

6. Control is transferred back to the main programme, which now uses the computed function value to evaluate the arithmetic formula: that is, the value is multiplied by 3.0, and this is stored into memory location Y.

7. The main programme proceeds to calculate as if nothing had happened.

The argument name X in FUNCTION USTEP(X) is called a "dummy argument". The actual value used for X may be A, or B, or some wfae - what actually happens is that the argument of the function, stored into some memory location such as A or B, is made available to the function subprogramme by transmitting the address XA to the subprogramme. The subprogramme picks up whatever number is at that address, and stores that number into its own "local" memory location called X. Thereafter, whenever evaluation of USTEP requires the use of the number X, this number is taken from the "local" storage location X.

If the argument of USTEP is itself a well-formed arithmetic expression, the value of the expression is evaluated by the main programme first; this value is stored into some convenient service storage location within the machine area occupied by the main programme; and the address of *that* storage location is given to the subprogramme as "XA".

This procedure makes it possible to evaluate functions of functions; for example, we are allowed to write

    Y=USTEP(USTEP(A))

The execution of this command proceeds in two steps. In the first step, we transmit to the subprogramme USTEP the address of A, and let the subprogramme evaluate the function value USTEP(A). This function value is then stored into some convenient storage location, call it B for now, and the address of B is transmitted to USTEP. We call USTEP once more, to evaluate USTEP(B); and this value is stored into location Y. The commands actually executed are equivalent to the set of two FORTRAN statements:

    B=USTEP(A)
    Y=USTEP(B)

While functions of functions are quite permissible, so-called "recursive functions" are *not* allowed in FORTRAN. That is, we cannot, *within* the subprogramme USTEP, call on the subprogramme USTEP itself. The reason for this restriction is the linking process used in FORTRAN. As soon as USTEP is called, a return address is put into the storage location RA, and thereby the earlier content of RA is overwritten. Thus, if USTEP were to call on itself, it would "forget" where the ultimate return of control is to go to; we'd get into a never-ending loop, with USTEP continuing to call on itself and "biting its own tail", so to speak. If recursive functions are wanted, the "linking" process becomes a good deal more complicated.

At this stage, you may well ask: "Why all this complication?" Looking at the flow diagram, just what have we gained by all this "linking", setting addresses, transfers of control, and so on? Why not simply put the orders required to evaluate USTEP into the main programme itself, and forget all this mess?

The truth is, we have gained nothing as long as the function is used only *once* by the main programme. In such a case, and this is the case illustrated in the flow diagram, it would have been better not to write a function subprogramme at all.

The advantage of subprogrammes becomes apparent only when they are used several times over in the main programme. For example, consider the set of statements:

B=USTEP(A)
Y=USTEP(B)
Z=V*USTEP(W)
T=B*USTEP(Z) - Y*USTEP(R)

Here we have five references to the function USTEP. With a function subprogramme FUNCTION USTEP(X) in memory, available for use, this means five "linking" operations and that is all. But if we do *not* have such a function subprogramme, we must write out, in full detail, the set of operations required to compute USTEP, *five times over*. This would be wasteful of machine memory space, wasteful of the programmer's time and effort, and highly productive of coding errors. Subprogrammes are not a "frill" purely for use by advanced programmers. On the contrary, subprogrammes are absolutely essential as a programming tool, and their use must be understood.

An additional advantage of subprogrammes is that they can be compiled and debugged one by one; a coding error in a subprogramme requires recompilation of only that subprogramme, not of the entire programme.(*) In Chapter I, we pointed out that there are two separate phases: a *compilation phase,* in which the source language programme is translated into machine language, and the machine language "object programme" is stored into machine memory; and an *execution phase,* in which the "object programme" is obeyed, or executed, by the machine. Most working compilers (but not many student compilers) allow the programmer an option of asking that each object programme or subprogramme be not only stored into machine memory, but also be punched out by the machine onto punched cards, in such a form that these punched cards can be used in a later run to avoid the need to re-translate the programme or subprogramme. Such decks of cards are called "relocatable object decks". If we find a coding error in one subprogramme, we can submit, for our next machine run, the corrected source language deck for that one subprogramme, together with the relocatable object decks for the main programme and for all the other subprogrammes. This often saves a good deal of machine time by avoiding unnecessary re-translation of working programmes and subprogrammes; equally important, relocatable object decks are usually considerably shorter than the source language decks for the same subprogrammes; this means read-in of fewer cards, hence, with fewer possibilities for errors in reading the cards, or for getting cards chewed up by the card reader.

B.   FORTRAN Language Rules for Writing Function Subprogrammes.

⏂ Having discussed the meaning of FUNCTION subprogrammes, we now present the formal rules of the FORTRAN language for *writing* FUNCTION subprogrammes (this section), and for *using* FUNCTION subprogrammes (Section C); illustrative examples are given in Section D.

(*)   This does not apply to student compilers such as WATFOR, which require that the entire programme, subprogrammes and all, be translated every time.

DEF: A FUNCTION subprogramme is generated by the FORTRAN compiler in response to a series of FORTRAN language statements, the first of which is a FUNCTION statement, the last of which is an END statement.   The statements between the FUNCTION and END statements may be any FORTRAN statements *other than*

    1.   another FUNCTION statement
    2.   another END statement
    3.   a SUBROUTINE statement
    4.   a BLOCK DATA statement

The statements between the FUNCTION and END statements must contain at least one RETURN statement.

DEF: Every FUNCTION subprogramme has a *function name* and a *list of dummy arguments* on which the function value depends. The function name is unique (no other function can be named by the same name), but the dummy argument names are replaced, in execution, by actual arguments as defined in Section C. Dummy argument names are purely "local" within the function subprogramme; the same names can be used in other programmes or subprogrammes to mean quite different things, without trouble.

DEF: The *preferred form* of the FUNCTION statement is

    FUNCTION *NAME(ARG1,ARG2, . . . , ARGN)*

where *NAME, ARG1, ARG2, . . . , ARGN* are grammatically correct FORTRAN identifier names (up to 6 alphameric characters, the first of which is alphabetic). *NAME* is the *function name* assigned to the function; *ARG1* is the dummy name of the first argument of the function; *ARG2* is the dummy name of the second argument of the function; etc.   There must be at least one dummy argument.

DEF: In this form of the FUNCTION statement, the *type* of the *function value* is determined by the first letter of the function name *NAME,* either by the pre-defined type convention, or by an IMPLICIT type declaration statement within the FUNCTION subprogramme itself; in the latter case, the IMPLICIT type declaration statement must follow *immediately after* the FUNCTION statement. The type of the function value *must not* be declared by means of an explicit type declaration within the FUNCTION subprogramme.

DEF: The *dummy argument names ARG1, ARG2, ...* may represent any of:

1.   A simple (non-array) variable, of type given by pre-defined type convention, implicit or explicit type declaration statements within the FUNCTION subprogramme;

2.   The name of an array; if so, a DIMENSION statement for an array of this dummy name must appear within the FUNCTION subprogramme; unlike DIMENSION statements within main programmes, in which the dimensions must be positive integer *constants,* the dimensions here may be integer *dummy variables,* provided dummy variables with just such dummy names are contained in the argument list (see Section D for explanation and use of this feature, called "adjustable dimensions"). The *type* of the array is determined from the array name by the pre-defined type convention, or by IMPLICIT or explicit type declaration statements appearing within the FUNCTION subprogramme.

3.   The name of another subprogramme.

Note: The dummy arguments *must not* be FORTRAN *constants;* actual arguments may be constants (see Section C), but dummy arguments must be identifier names. Dummy arguments are in effect replaced, at execution time, by actual arguments.

The second form of the FUNCTION statement (which is not recommended) allows explicit typing of the function name within the FUNCTION statement itself. Thus, if we want to type the function name CTANH to be of type COMPLEX*8, we are allowed to write a FUNCTION statement of form

COMPLEX FUNCTION CTANH*8(CZ)

Note: The type code is broken up here; COMPLEX appears before the word FUNCTION, but the length code (8 for an 8-byte complex number) appears adjacent to the function name, as CTANH*8. The alternative form:

FUNCTION CTANH(CZ)
IMPLICIT COMPLEX*8(C)

is cleaner coding. It is always preferable. In practice, CZ would have to be typed anyway, so there is no gain whatever in using the second form of the FUNCTION statement.

DEF: The statement RETURN, appearing anywhere within the FUNCTION subprogramme, has the effect (in execution) of returning control to the superior programme which invoked the FUNCTION subprogramme. At least one RETURN statement must appear within each FUNCTION subprogramme. Every possible path of control within the FUNCTION subprogramme must lead, eventually, either to a RETURN statement or to a STOP statement.

DEF: Every FUNCTION subprogramme must contain at least one statement which has the effect of assigning a numerical value to the *function name NAME;* the usual form of this is an arithmetic assignment statement:

NAME=wfae

where *NAME* is the function name declared in the FUNCTION statement, and *wfae* is any well-formed arithmetic expression.

The way in which a subprogramme handles its arguments depends on the nature of these arguments. If the dummy argument *ARG1,* say, represents a simple (non-array) variable, then a storage location by that name is set aside within the subprogramme area of machine memory; the numerical value of the actual argument is stored into that dummy location, and afterwards used by the subprogramme (see the illustration in Section A). This is called "reference by value".

If the dummy argument represents the name of an array, however, such a procedure would be wasteful of valuable machine storage space. We would be forced to set aside, within the area of machine memory occupied by the subprogramme, enough storage locations to store the entire array, even though that array is already stored somewhere else in memory, in association with the calling programme. Such duplication can be afforded for non-array variables, but not for arrays.

Thus, when the dummy argument represents the name of an array, only the *starting address of the actual array* is transmitted to the subprogramme. Whenever the subprogramme needs to refer to some element of that array, it uses this starting address as a base address for computing the address of the actual array element. This procedure is called "reference by name" (although "reference by address" would be better nomenclature).

Reference by name (by address) is used also if the dummy argument represents the name of another subprogramme; in that case, the entry address of that other subprogramme is the address transmitted to the FUNCTION subprogramme.

During execution of the FUNCTION subprogramme, one or more of the arguments may themselves be altered by the subprogramme; for example, if *ARG1* represents the name of a matrix array, and the purpose of the function is to evaluate the determinant of this matrix, it is entirely possible that the matrix is altered during computation of the determinant. We have seen this at the end of Chapter XIII, and we shall have more to say about this in Section D of this Chapter. If this is the case, the actual arguments of the FUNCTION are altered as a result of execution of the FUNCTION subprogramme. Since this is likely to be overlooked by the programmer in writing other parts of the programme, this practice is dangerous and should be avoided. Such coding errors are among the easiest to make, and the hardest to find: the subprogramme by itself works fine, and the superior programme making use of the subprogramme also looks fine, and compiles without trouble - but the subprogramme destroys information on which the superior programme depends later on!

It should be noted that dummy arguments which are altered within the subprogramme result in alteration of the actual arguments even if reference is "by value"; although the storage location used during computation by the subprogramme is a "local" storage location, the final content of this "local" storage is transferred to the "external" storage location just before control is returned (i.e., such transfers are made as part of the execution of the RETURN statement).

If the programmer desires that a dummy argument *ARG* representing a simple variable should be referenced "by name" rather than "by value", he can achieve this by placing the dummy argument name between slashes, i.e., */ARG/,* within the argument list of the FUNCTION statement. There is no *logical* reason for wishing to do this; but there can be a good *practical* reason: machine time! The process of transferring the actual value of X, say, to a dummy location named X within the subprogramme area of memory, requires machine time. If the subprogramme is itself quite short, and is invoked many times over, machine time may be gained by insisting on reference "by name" rather than "by value". On the other hand, if X is used many times within the subprogramme, reference "by name" is not used. In that, probably more common, case reference "by value" is faster in execution.

C. FORTRAN Language Rules for Using Function Subprogrammes

In Section B, we gave the FORTRAN language rules for defining a FUNCTION subprogramme. In this Section, we present the FORTRAN language rules involved in making use of a FUNCTION subprogramme, within some superior programme or subprogramme. Note that there can be quite a hierarchy of programmes, subprogrammes, sub-sub-programmes, etc. There is one "main programme", which may make use of any number of subprogrammes. Any one of those, in turn, may make use of still other subprogrammes, and so on. Furthermore, any one subprogramme may be called by programmes at any of these levels. For example, once we have defined the FUNCTION CTANH(CZ) for evaluating the hyperbolic tangent of a complex number, the main programme may make use of this function; if the main programme makes use of some other subprogramme as well, then this other subprogramme may *also* make use of the function CTANH. The FORTRAN master programme takes care that all these "calls" are organized properly and do not conflict with each other.

In making a "call" on a function, we use the *function name* precisely as it appears in the FUNCTION statement defining the function; but the *dummy arguments* are now replaced by *actual arguments*. We first describe the nature of these actual arguments.

DEF: The actual arguments $A1$, $A2$, ..., AN appearing in the superior programme which invokes a FUNCTION subprogramme, must agree in number, order, and type with the dummy arguments $ARG1$, $ARG2$, ..., $ARGN$ which appear in the FUNCTION definition.

1. If a dummy argument ARG represents a simple (non-array) variable of a certain type, then the actual argument A may be any well-formed expression of the same dominant type; in particular, A may be a FORTRAN constant of the right type.

2. If the dummy argument ARG represents the name of an array, then the actual argument A corresponding to it must also be the name of an array, of the same type and the same number of dimensions as ARG; if the DIMENSION statement for ARG within the FUNCTION subprogramme involved integer constants, then the DIMENSION statement for A within the superior programme must involve exactly the same constants.

3. If the dummy argument ARG represents the name of a subprogramme, then the actual argument A must also be the name of a subprogramme; this fact must be made known to the compiler by including a special declaration statement

EXTERNAL A

within the *superior* programme, somewhere prior to the statement invoking the subprogramme.

Having described the nature of actual arguments, we now show how FUNCTION subprogrammes are invoked.

DEF: Let $NAME$ be the function name of a FUNCTION subprogramme, with dummy arguments $ARG1$, $ARG2$, ..., $ARGN$. Let $A1$, $A2$, ..., AN be actual arguments as defined above. Then

NAME(A1,A2, ..., AN)

appearing within any other programme or subprogramme is a well-formed expression, whose value is obtained by substituting, in the definition of the function $NAME$, the value of $A1$ for $ARG1$, the value of $A2$ for $ARG2$, ..., the value of AN for $ARGN$. Each occurrence of this particular well-formed expression results in a "call" on the function subprogramme, for actual evaluation of the function.

Note: If the actual argument A, corresponding to a dummy argument ARG representing a simple (non-array) variable, is a well-formed expression more complicated than just a simple identifier name, then the well-formed expression is evaluated *first*, and the value placed into a temporary storage location, before the FUNCTION subprogramme is invoked. It is either the content (value) or the address of this temporary storage which is transmitted to the subprogramme (and conceivably altered by the subprogramme) when the subprogramme is invoked. A temporary storage location is used also if the actual argument is a FORTRAN *constant* to prevent all possibility of a subprogramme destroying the value of a constant used by the superior programme.

Note: The superior programme must see to it that the function name $NAME$ is recognizably of the same *type* as the type declared for this function name within the FUNCTION $NAME$ subprogramme. Thus, if FUNCTION CTANH(CZ) contains the type declaration statement

IMPLICIT COMPLEX*8(C)

then the superior programme calling on this function must contain either this same type declaration or an explicit type declaration

COMPLEX*8 CTANH

Otherwise, we have incompatibility between assumptions made within the subprogramme, and assumptions made by the superior programme. The master and the servant no longer speak the same language, and as a result the servant does not do what the master wants done.

Exactly the same remark applies to type declarations for actual arguments, to correspond to the declared types (within the subprogramme) of the dummy arguments.

Type incompatibilities are among the most frequent coding errors, and enormous care is required to keep track of the type declarations. It is precisely for this reason that IMPLICIT type declaration statements are so very much preferable to explicit type declarations: after a while, each programmer gets used to his own IMPLICIT type conventions, and they become second nature to him. By contrast, nothing is easier to forget than an explicit type declaration statement; either to forget to insert it, or to forget its existence once it has been inserted.

D. Examples of Function Subprogrammes

EXAMPLE 1:

As our first non-trivial example of a FUNCTION subprogramme, let us write a subprogramme to evaluate the inverse hyperbolic sine function, for which the mathematical formula reads:

$$\text{arc sinh } x = \log_e \left[x + (x^2+1)^{1/2} \right]$$

To keep things simple, let us suppose that both the function argument X and the function value, which we shall call ARSINH, are of type REAL*4.

Nothing simpler than to write this FUNCTION subprogramme! All we need to do is to code up the formula; so here is the defining programme:

```
FUNCTION ARSINH(X)
ARSINH=ALOG(X+SQRT(X**2+1.0))
RETURN
END
```

In fact, this is so simple that it could be handled as an arithmetic statement function, see the end of Chapter XII.

All right: *where is the mistake in the above programme?*

To recognize the mistake, it is necessary to keep in mind that a machine keeps numbers to limited accuracy only. Let us look what happens when x is negative and fairly large, say x=-100. We then take the square root of $x^2+1=10001$, which is, to seven significant figures, equal to 100.0050. This gets added to x=-100, so that the argument of the logarithm is equal to 0.0050, with *only two significant figures!* We have managed to lose no less than 5 out of our initial 7 significant figures, through this process. This gets even worse when x becomes more negative; for x=-5000, for example, there are no significant figures left at all!

156

The way to get around this difficulty is to use the fact that the hyperbolic sine as well as its inverse function are *odd* functions, i.e.,

arc sinh (-x) = - arc sinh x

Let y be the absolute value of x. We can evaluate the formula for w=arc sinh y. If x is positive, y=x, and w is our anwer. If x is negative, we just change the sign. The FORTRAN built-in function SIGN(W,X) has just this effect (see Chapter XII). Hence our corrected programme reads:

```
FUNCTION ARSINH(X)
Y=ABS(X)
W=ALOG(Y+SQRT(Y**2+1.0))
ARSINH=SIGN(W,X)
RETURN
END
```

This is a bit more complicated, but has the virtue that it works.

But does it? In all cases? What can still go wrong? Did you spot it?
Let us suppose that x is positive but either very small compared to 1, or very large compared to 1.

If x is *very small* compared to unity, we still lose accuracy: for example, suppose that $x=10^{-5}$. Then $x^2=10^{-10}$ and $x^2+1=y^2+1$ *equals* 1.000000 to machine accuracy! The argument of the logarithm is 1.000010 to machine accuracy, and the value of the logarithm is based on the excess of this over unity, i.e., it is based on a number with only 2 effective significant figures.

To overcome this, we must test whether y is small; if so, we use an approximate formula which preserves numerical accuracy. A simple choice is given by the first two terms of the power series:

arc sinh $y = y - y^3/6 + \ldots$

If y is less than 0.01, the error made by stopping after these two terms is less than 1 part in 10^8, i.e., less than single-precision accuracy in the machine.

Another sort of trouble can occur if x, and hence y, is *very large*. Let us take the case $y=10^{40}$; then $y^2=10^{80}$ exceeds the maximum size allowed for a floating point number in the machine. A "floating point overflow" is diagnosed, and the programme is thrown off the machine. However, this overflow refers to an intermediate result of the computation, not to the number which we really want. To better than machine accuracy, y^2+1 is the same as y^2 in this case, and the result we want is equal to $\log_e(2y)$, perfectly within the permissible size of numbers in the machine.

To fix this, we note that, for large enough y, the square root of y^2+1 is the same as y, in the machine. This is true for Y.GT.1.E4 for single precision numbers (since then y^2 exceeds 10^8). Hence we test for this, and evaluate the abbreviated formula

arc sinh $y = \log_e(2y) = \log_e(y) + \log_e(2)$ for $y > 10^4$ (REAL*4)

The second form, the sum of two logarithms, is preferable to the first form: for really large y, just below the upper limit for machine numbers, 2y will be out of range and hence cause arithmetic overflow; whereas $\log_e(y)+\log_e(2)$ involves numbers of all of which are within the allowable range.

We can now write down the FUNCTION subprogramme based on all these considerations. Before doing so, however, let us consider what we must do to *test* the resulting subprogramme. No subprogramme is finished until it has been tested thoroughly. In the present case, the simplest way to test the subprogramme is to make use of the fact that we are computing an inverse function, for which the direct function is available as a standard FORTRAN built-in function called SINH(X). Hence, if we take a number x, compute Y=ARSINH(X) and then Z=SINH(Y), the value of Z should equal the value x. This gives the following testing main programme:

```
C       TEST OF THE FUNCTION SUBPROGRAMME ARSINH
 1000 READ,X
      Y=ARSINH(X)
      Z=SINH(Y)
      PRINT,X,Y,Z
      GO TO 1000
      END
```

Having written this testing programme, we must decide, next, what data numbers to supply for the test. One procedure would be to use randomly chosen numbers, but this is quite dangerous, since we might not strike those particular numbers at which trouble is most likely to occur. The most reasonable test numbers are very small numbers, of either sign, very large numbers, again of either sign, the number 0, and numbers in the immediate neighbourhood of the "crossover" number 10^4 in the subprogramme.

We now show the complete input deck for this test run, under WATFOR control.

```
$JOB              10.001,KP=26   BROWN              68235179   JONES
C       TEST OF THE FUNCTION SUBPROGRAMME ARSINH
 1000 READ,X
      Y=ARSINH(X)
      Z=SINH(Y)
      PRINT,X,Y,Z
      GO TO 1000
      END
      FUNCTION ARSINH(X)
      DATA ALOG2/0.693147/
      Y=ABS(X)
      IF(Y.GT.1.0E4) GO TO 1500
      IF(Y.LT.0.01) GO TO 1300
C       Y BETWEEN 0.01 AND 10**4. USE THE FULL FORMULA.
      W=ALOG(Y+SQRT(Y**2+1.0))
      GO TO 2000
C       Y LESS THAN 0.01. USE THE FIRST TWO TERMS OF THE POWER
C               SERIES.
 1300 W=Y-Y**3/6.0
      GO TO 2000
C       Y GREATER THAN 10**4. USE THE ABBREVIATED FORMULA.
 1500 W=ALOG(Y)+ALOG2
C       PATHS REJOIN...
 2000 ARSINH=SIGN(W,X)
      RETURN
      END
$ENTRY
```

```
 0.
 0.009999
 0.0100
 0.100001E-1
 9.999996E+3
-9.999996E+3
 1.0E+4
 1.000005E+4
 1.E+75
-1.E+75
 1.E-74
-1.E-74
$IBSYS
```

Notes:

1.   The main programme and all the subprogrammes appear between the $JOB and $ENTRY control cards (or their equivalents in other installations). An END card appears after the main programme, and after each subprogramme. This END card indicates to the compiler that this particular programme or subprogramme has come to an end; the $ENTRY control card (or its equivalent such as //DATA) indicates to the master programme that the entire translation process is finished, and the translated (object) programme is ready for execution.

2.   The cards appearing at the end are data cards. Each card contains only one number, since the statement READ,X in the main programme reads from a new data card, each time it is reached in execution.

3.   The control cards are not the same in all installations. In some installations, $JOB is replaced by //PROGRAM; $ENTRY is replaced by //DATA; still other choices are possible. In some installations, a deck termination card, e.g., a card containing $IBSYS in columns 1 through 6, is required at the very end of the deck. It is necessary to know the rules for each particular installation. Fortunately, the total number of control cards in WATFOR runs is small (either 2 or 3 cards, depending on the installation).

4.   The use of the DATA statement to set $\log_e(2)$ speeds up the programme in execution, compared to using ALOG(2.0) in statement 1500. No need to ask the machine to evaluate the logarithm of 2, *every time* this subprogramme is invoked.

5.   If this programme is run under WATFOR, the data number 1.E-74 causes diagnosis of an execution time error KO-4 'Too many exponent underflows'. The reason for this is as follows. With Y equal to 1.E-74, the programme flow within FUNCTION ARSINH(X) leads to statement number 1300:

1300 W=Y−Y**3/6.0

The computation of Y**3, for Y equal to 10^{-74}, gives rise to the number 10^{-222}. This number is too small to be represented by a standard floating point number within the machine, and can only be represented by the number zero. Such a situation is called "exponent underflow". Actually exponent underflow is *not an error:* replacement of the number 10^{-222} by the number 0.0 is exactly what we *want* to happen.

Nonetheless, the IBM operating system OS/360 considers exponent underflow as an error, and interrupts the computation when this "error" occurs. WATFOR itself operates under OS/360, and thus WATFOR also considers exponent underflow as an error. If nothing is done about it, WATFOR stops the computation when the first such "error" occurs, and gives the error message KO-4.

Exponent underflow is not the only possible cause of a programme interruption. There are *five types of arithmetic error which cause interruption of programme execution.* They are:

1. Fixed-point Arithmetic Overflow (See Chapter X,A); this interruption occurs in some versions of WATFOR, but not in all versions.

2. Exponent Overflow: the result of a computation with floating point numbers has produced a floating point number too large for the machine to handle, i.e., larger than 16^{63} in absolute value (see Chapter VII).

3. Exponent Underflow (see the discussion above).

4. Fixed-point Division by Zero.

5. Floating-point Division by Zero.

With the exception of exponent underflow, all these are real errors, likely to lead to wrong results in the end.

Nonetheless, it is not always best to stop computation completely when such an error occurs. In a production run, where large amounts of machine time may be wasted on wrong numbers, computation should indeed be stopped immediately, once it is known that at least one computed number is really wrong. But in a code-checking run, the amount of machine time is small, and by letting the machine run on a bit longer it may be possible to catch one or two other programme bugs in the same test run. For this reason, we would like to be able to let the run continue, merely printing out a message that an arithmetic error has occurred at this point in the programme.

Furthermore, one of these "errors", the exponent underflow, is usually not an error at all; no run, code checking or production, ought to be stopped for a mere exponent underflow. It is even debatable whether an error message should be printed out whenever an exponent underflow occurs. Under IBM FORTRAN, a valid production programme may give rise to hundreds of pages of output containing one exponent underflow interrupt message after another, all these messages being quite useless since the results are correct. This can get particularly annoying when there is a limit on the number of output pages, and this limit is exceeded because of these "error" messages, so that the desired, correct result is never printed out at all!

It is necessary, therefore, to arrange a more flexible way of handling programme interruptions due to arithmetic errors. In WATFOR, this is achieved by combination of three standard subprogrammes, called TRAPS, OVERFL, and DVCHK.

The subprogramme TRAPS allows the programmer to alter the number of arithmetic interrupts permitted before WATFOR terminates execution of the object programme. For example, the statement

CALL TRAPS(25,85,45,55,781)

in the source programme has the following effect at execution time: from then on (or until another CALL TRAPS is encountered which resets some or all of these numbers) WATFOR permits up to 25 interrupts of type 1 (fixed-point overflows, see the list of types a bit earlier), up to 85 interrupts of type 2, up to 45 interrupts of type 3, up to 55 interrupts of type 4, and up to 781 interrupts of type 5. Thus, for example, we are allowed up to 781 floating-point divisions by zero, before WATFOR terminates execution with an error message KO-2 (it is unfortunate, but true, that the numbering of the KO error messages does not agree with the sequence of arguments in the call to TRAPS).

By making the numbers in the call to TRAPS very large, we can effectively inhibit one or more types of interrupt altogether. For example, if we wish to inhibit exponent underflow interrupts, but want to retain the other interrupts, an appropriate statement is:

CALL TRAPS(1,1,2000000000,1,1)

This permits up to 2000000000 exponent underflows before WATFOR terminates execution; this many underflows cannot possibly occur during a run, because of time limitations.

In the argument list of TRAPS, minus signs are ignored (i.e., the absolute value is used) and 0 is replaced by 1; for example,

CALL TRAPS(-2,0,1,-1,5)

is equivalent in its action to

CALL TRAPS(2,1,1,1,5)

Inhibiting WATFOR from terminating execution is not enough. When 5 floating point divisions by zero are permitted (as in the above call to TRAPS), the first 4 invalid divisions are not diagnosed at all, and the fifth invalid division causes termination of execution. This is inadequate for code-testing: we need warning that an incorrect division has occurred, even if we do not want to terminate execution at that point.

To get such warnings, we may use standard subprogrammes called OVERFL (for testing arithmetic overflows) and DVCHK (for testing the divide check indicator which is put "on" as a result of an attempt to divide by zero). These subprogrammes and their use are described in Appendix D, Section 1. We recommend placing statements CALL DVCHK(J) and CALL OVERFL(J), together with print out statements whenever J turns out to indicate that an incorrect arithmetic operation has occurred, into the source programme at quite frequent intervals (perhaps every 50-100 statements).

A call to TRAPS should be used at the very beginning to prevent termination of execution. In this way, we obtain the maximum possible information from every code-testing run. Later on, after the code has been debugged, it may be better to alter the initial call to TRAPS, so that execution of a production run is allowed to continue for exponent underflow interrupts, but for no other arithmetic failure interrupts. If that is done, the calls to DVCHK and OVERFL should be removed from the programme, since they are then meaningless: the first arithmetic failure which occurs terminates execution immediately, with a message produced by the WATFOR master programme; the next CALL DVCHK or CALL OVERFL statement is never even reached.

EXAMPLE 2:

As our *second example* of a FUNCTION subprogramme, we shall write a subprogramme to evaluate the *determinant of a matrix,* using the methods described at the end of Chapter XIII.

Rather than plunging straight into programming, let us do a bit of preliminary planning first, by looking at the two programmes given at the end of Section I of Chapter XIII, and seeing what would be required to make them into FUNCTION subprogrammes.

First of all, what are the *arguments* of our FUNCTION DETER, whose function value is the determinant of a matrix? In the programmes given earlier, we needed a name for the matrix array (it was called A and assigned DIMENSION A(30,30)), and we needed to specify the actual size of the matrix, i.e., the value of N for an N-by-N matrix A, stored within this set of memory locations. N could be any number between 2 and 30. (*Why* would the programmes in Chapter XIII fail for N=1?) We conclude that the dummy arguments of FUNCTION DETER(A,N) should be the dummy array name A and the dummy array size N.

However, what about the *dimension* assigned to the array? If we place the dimension statement DIMENSION A(30,30) into the subprogramme, then this subprogramme works correctly for matrices with only that particular dimension assignment within the superior programme. This is a severe, and unacceptable, restriction. We want to be able to handle matrices of any dimension MDIM, as well as of any actual order N. (*)

We get around this difficulty by making use of the FORTRAN feature of "adjustable dimensions" in subprogrammes. Let us make FUNCTION DETER(A,N,MDIM) depend upon *three* dummy arguments, the third of which is the dimension MDIM of the array A declared within the *superior programme.* The dimension statement in the subprogramme may now be: DIMENSION A(MDIM,MDIM). This conveys sufficient information to the compiler to allow pick-up of an arbitrary matrix element A(I,J) at execution time.

With this in mind, let us rewrite the first determinant evaluation programme of Chapter XIII as a FUNCTION subprogramme. We omit the PRINT,DET statement, since FUNCTION subprogrammes should not print out results (other than indications of errors); printing of results should be done by the superior programme. Instead of printing out a number, we store that number into location DETER, and transfer control back to the calling programme:

```
      FUNCTION DETER(A,N,MDIM)
C     EVALUATION OF DETERMINANT OF MATRIX A, N-BY-N,
C        OF DIMENSION A(MDIM,MDIM)
      DIMENSION A(MDIM,MDIM)
 1000 DET=1.0
      NMIN1=N-1
      DO 1600 I=1,NMIN1
      IPLUS1=I+1
      DO 1400 K=IPLUS1,N
      FACTOR=A(K,I)/A(I,I)
      A(K,I)=0.0
      DO 1200 J=IPLUS1,N
```

(*)   We remind the reader of the difference between these two concepts. The dimension of the array A(MDIM,MDIM) defines the total amount of storage set aside for this array (to wit: MDIM**2 storage locations), as well as the way in which the general matrix element A(I,J) is stored within that area: its "order number" is equal to I+(J-1)*MDIM. If we store an N-by-N matrix, with N less than MDIM, within that array, some of the locations set aside in core storage are not actually used.

```
      A(K,J)=A(K,J)-FACTOR*A(I,J)
1200 CONTINUE
1400 CONTINUE
      DET=DET*A(I,I)
1600 CONTINUE
      DET=DET*A(N,N)
C     OPERATION FINISHED. PUT RESULT INTO DETER.
      DETER=DET
C     BEAT IT.
      RETURN
      END
```

Apart from the absence of pivoting (see Section J of Chapter XIII), this subprogramme would work. However, it has several faults:

1. Any reasonable person would specify a value of N, the actual size of the matrix, less than or equal to the value of MDIM, the dimension declared for the matrix. True: but can we rely upon the fact that all users are reasonable persons, and what is much more, reasonable persons *who never make mistakes?* In fact this subprogramme will fail if N.GT.MDIM, since we then drag supposed matrix elements out of peculiar storage locations having nothing to do with the array A. Thus, we should include a test for *reasonableness of parameter values.*

2. The inner loop of the programme is slow in execution, because of the address computations needed to find the addresses of A(K,J) and A(I,J). We did give a more efficient version, in Section J of Chapter XIII. However, this more efficient version involved an EQUIVALENCE statement

    EQUIVALENCE (A(1,1),AVEC(1))

    This *cannot be done* in this way within a FUNCTION subprogramme: during the "linking" process, what is transmitted to the subprogramme is the *starting address* of the actual array corresponding to the dummy argument A of the FUNCTION subprogramme. On the other hand, the statement DIMENSION AVEC(900) within the FUNCTION subprogramme sets aside a storage area of 900 storage locations within the local area occupied by the subprogramme. The starting address of AVEC, i.e., the address of AVEC(1), is in a fixed position in memory, whereas the starting address of A, i.e., the address of A(1,1), needs to be different, in general, every time the subprogramme is invoked to evaluate the determinant of some new matrix. A fixed address can not be "equivalent" to an address which changes from one time to the next.

3. As written above, the subprogramme *destroys* the matrix A while evaluating the determinant of A. This is a poor way of doing things, since we are likely to forget this little fact when programming the superior programme which uses FUNCTION DETER.

It is clear that criticisms (2) and (3), taken together, indicate that a local vector array storage area AVEC should be reserved within the subprogramme. The external matrix A should be *transferred* to this local area, and only the elements of AVEC, not the elements of A, should be altered by the subprogramme.

This procedure carries a penalty, however; if we assign DIMENSION AVEC(900), for example, there are enough storage locations to store matrices of size up to 30-by-30, no more. We shall have to test that the actual matrix size, N, does not exceed this limit.

We have two reasonable choices about the way in which we fill the vector array AVEC with matrix elements from the external matrix A. We may use the dimension MDIM of the external matrix A to define the order number of A(I,J) within AVEC to be

NORDER=I+(J-1)*MDIM

or we may ignore MDIM for this purpose, and "pack AVEC tightly" by using

NORDER=I+(J-1)*N

i.e., we use the actual matrix size N instead of the dimension of the matrix, MDIM. Both choices avoid duplication of order numbers of different actual matrix elements A(I,J).

Clearly, the second choice is preferable, to keep down storage requirements.

It is convenient to define an arithmetic statement function NORDER(I,J) within the subprogramme, this being the order number of A(I,J) within the vector array AVEC.

The subprogramme follows; compare with the version in Section J of Chapter XIII, to see the differences. Explain why each difference is *necessary*. In particular, just why would the statement DET=DET*A(I,I), just after statement 1400 of the earlier version, *fail* within our subprogramme?(*)

```
      FUNCTION DETER(A,N,MDIM)
C     EVALUATION OF DETERMINANT OF MATRIX A, N-BY-N, DIMENSION
C          MDIM-BY-MDIM
      DIMENSION A(MDIM,MDIM),AVEC(900)
C     DEFINE AN ARITHMETIC STATEMENT FUNCTION FOR ADDRESS
C          COMPUTATION
C     THIS WILL BE THE ORDER NUMBER WITHIN AVEC, LOCAL
C          STORAGE, OF A(I,J)
      NORDER(I,J)=I+(J-1)*KK
      KK=N
C     NOW TEST THE PARAMETERS. DETER=0.0. FOR CRAZY PARAMETERS.
 1000 IF(N.GT.MDIM) GO TO 1010
      IF(N.LE.30) GO TO 1020
C     CRAZY PARAMETERS.
 1010 DETER=0.0
      RETURN
C     PARAMETERS ARE O.K. PROCEED TO TRANSFER THE MATRIX TO
C          LOCAL STORAGE
 1020 DO 1030 I=1,N
      DO 1029 J=1,N
      L=NORDER(I,J)
      AVEC(L)=A(I,J)
 1029 CONTINUE
 1030 CONTINUE
```

(*)   Until you have a clear answer to this question in your own mind, you have not yet understood the subprogramme.

```
C       MATRIX PUSHED INTO AVEC. NOW START DETERMINANT EVALUATION.
        DET=1.0
        NMIN1=N-1
        DO 1600 I=1,NMIN1
        IPLUS1=I+1
        DO 1400 K=IPLUS1,N
        KI=NORDER(K,I)
C       THIS IS ADDRESS, WITHIN AVEC, OF A(K,I)
        II=NORDER(I,I)
C       THIS IS ADDRESS, WITHIN AVEC, OF A(I,I)
        FACTOR=AVEC(KI)/AVEC(II)
        AVEC(KI)=0.0
        L1=NORDER(K,IPLUS1)
C       THIS IS ADDRESS, WITHIN AVEC, OF A(K,IPLUS1)
        L2=NORDER(K,N)
C       THIS IS ADDRESS, WITHIN AVEC, OF A(K,N)
        IMNSK=I-K
C       THIS IS THE DISPLACEMENT FROM A(K,J) TO A(I,J), FOR ALL J,
C           WITHIN AVEC
        DO 1200 L=L1,L2,N
C       NOTE THE THIRD VARIABLE OF THE DO STATEMENT. WHY IS IT
C           N, NOT MDIM?
        AVEC(L)=AVEC(L)-FACTOR*AVEC(L+IMNSK)
 1200   CONTINUE
 1400   CONTINUE
        III=NORDER(I,I)
        DET=DET*AVEC(III)
C       EXPLAIN THIS CODING!
 1600   CONTINUE
        NNN=NORDER(N,N)
        DET=DET*AVEC(NNN)
C       DETERMINANT EVALUATION FINISHED
        DETER=DET
        RETURN
        END
```

EXAMPLE 3:

As our *third example* of a FUNCTION subprogramme, let us write a subprogramme to evaluate the integral of an arbitrary function FUN(X) from X=A to X=B, using *Simpson's rule of numerical quadrature* with N intervals. We recall that Simpson's rule for 6 intervals, say, reads

$$\int_a^b f(x)\,dx \simeq \frac{h}{3}\left[f(a) + 4f(x_1) + 2f(x_2) + 4f(x_3) + 2f(x_4) + 4f(x_5) + f(b)\right]$$

where h=(b-a)/n is the interval size, and x_k=a+kh, k=1,2, . . . , n-1; in our example above, n is equal to 6.

There are a number of ways of doing this task, and it pays to do a bit of preliminary planning, before starting the coding. One might be tempted to define vector storage for the function values, the k-th component of the vector being equal to $f(x_k)$. This, however, would be sheer waste of valuable storage space! We do not need to remember the function values throughout the subprogramme: all we want is the sum which appears on the right side of the formula above; once a function value has been used and added into the sum, the function value can be "forgotten".

We note that there are different coefficients for different terms of the sum: the end values, $f(a)$ and $f(b)$, appear as they are; function values at "odd" points, like $f(x_1)$, $f(x_3)$, $f(x_5)$, are multiplied by 4; and function values at interior "even" points, like $f(x_2)$ and $f(x_4)$, are multiplied by 2. It is tempting to accumulate the sum as it is written; however, this means large numbers of multiplications by 2 and by 4. These take machine time. It is much more efficient to accumulate three different sums: an ENDSUM which is just $f(a)+f(b)$, an ODDSUM which is the sum of function values at odd points, and an EVNSUM which is the sum of function values at interior even points. These can be combined with the correct coefficients at the very end.

How do we arrange for an "arbitrary" integrand function FUN(X)? Nothing easier - we merely use the function name FUN as a *dummy argument* for our FUNCTION SIMPSN(FUN,A,B,N). The *actual argument* supplied by the superior programme which invokes FUNCTION SIMPSN then defines *which* function we wish to integrate. For example, if we wish to integrate the exponential function, between x=1 and x=2, the statement invoking FUNCTION SIMPSN would read

GRAL=SIMPSN(EXP,1.0,2.0,20)

where EXP is the name of the function to be integrated; this actual argument replaces the dummy argument FUN within FUNCTION SIMPSN(FUN,A,B,N). In this particular case, the function EXP is a standard built-in FORTRAN function. If we wish to integrate some non-standard function, for example $\exp(-x^3)$, we must supply a FUNCTION routine for that function, with some suitable name, and we must supply that name to FUNCTION SIMPSN at the point where FUNCTION SIMPSN is invoked. For example, we may supply the FUNCTION subprogramme

```
FUNCTION CRAZY(X)
CRAZY=EXP(-X**3)
RETURN
END
```

The superior programme to integrate this function from x=1 to x=2, with 20 intervals for Simpson's rule, would then read:

```
C     SUPERIOR PROGRAMME FOR USING SIMPSON'S RULE SUBPROGRAMME.
      EXTERNAL CRAZY
         .
         .
         .
 1500 GRAL=SIMPSN(CRAZY,1.0,2.0,20)
         .
         .
```

The statement EXTERNAL CRAZY is necessary to let the FORTRAN compiler know that the actual argument CRAZY in statement number 1500 is the name of a subprogramme, not the name of a variable or array. The "linking" operation is different in the two cases, and the compiler has no other way of knowing which is meant.

Note that we can use FUNCTION SIMPSN many times over, with different functions to be integrated, different ranges of integration, and different numbers of intervals for Simpson's rule. Once this FUNCTION subprogramme is written, it becomes part of the "accumulated wisdom" of our subprogramme library; we need not remember what is in it, all we need to remember is how to invoke it, i.e., the set of arguments which must be supplied when the subprogramme is invoked, including the precise number of arguments, their order, and the type of each argument. It is a good idea to put this information right into the FORTRAN source deck for FUNCTION SIMPSN, as *comment cards* immediately following the FUNCTION statement; in this way, the really important information about this subprogramme is "documented" right along with the subprogramme itself. "Documentation" of "software"(*) is most important - without proper documentation, the best standard programmes are useless to man or beast. To attempt to figure out, from a reading of the source language statements of the programme, what arguments the programme needs and what are the restrictions on these arguments, is *more* difficult than rewriting the whole programme from scratch, usually.

We now give a flow diagram and FORTRAN code for FUNCTION SIMPSN. In studying this coding, pay particular attention to the "two-way switch" within the DO loop: the "switch variable" J is continually altered from J=1 (meaning an odd point) to J=2 (meaning an even point). This is faster than testing the loop variable I itself for evenness, since the FORTRAN built-in function MOD(I,2) implies a *division* of I by 2, which is a slow operation.

Note also that we ensure that the actual number of intervals used, M, is an even number, by the statement M=(N/2)*2 at the very beginning. Also, we test that M is at least equal to two, otherwise we return zero as the answer. Such tests are most desirable in standard subprogrammes: never assume that the person using the subprogramme (for example, yourself) is above making mistakes in supplying actual arguments to replace the dummy arguments.

(*)   The word "software" is computer jargon for the standard programmes associated with a computing machine, as opposed to "hardware" which is the electronic circuitry etc. of the machine.

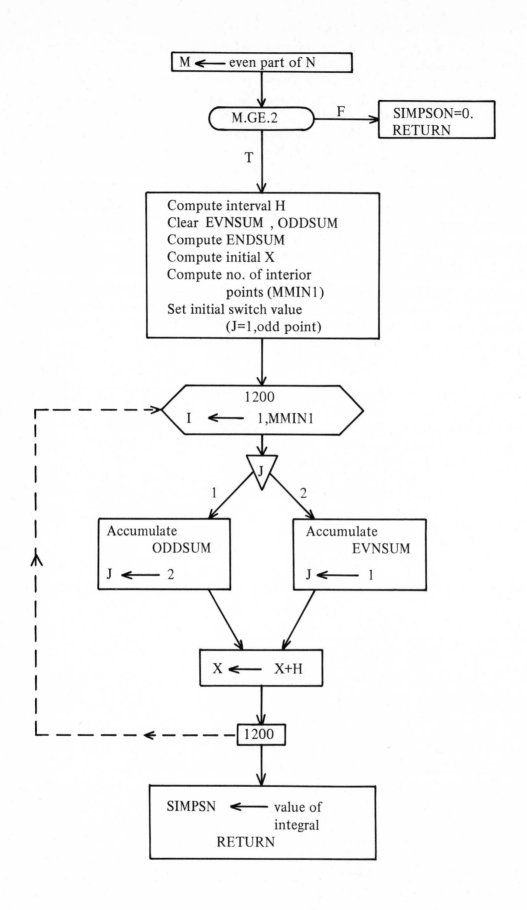

168

```
      FUNCTION SIMPSN(FUN,A,B,N)
C     SIMPSON'S RULE INTEGRAL
C     FUN=FUNCTION NAME
C     A =INITIAL VALUE OF X
C     B =FINAL VALUE OF X
C     N =NUMBER OF INTERVALS, EVEN
C     EVALUATE INTEGRAL OF FUN(X) FROM
C     X=A TO X=B, USING N INTERVALS
C
C     ENSURE EVEN NO. OF INTERVALS. GE.2
C
 1000 M=(N/2)*2
      IF (M.GE.2) GO TO 1050
C     CRAZY ENTRY. RETURN ZERO VALUE.
      SIMPSN=0.0
      RETURN
C     ENTRY O.K. SET UP STUFF
 1050 H=(B-A)/FLOAT(M)
      EVNSUM=0.0
      ODDSUM=0.0
      ENDSUM=FUN(A)+FUN(B)
      X=A+H
      MMIN1=M-1
      J=1
C     THIS J IS A SWITCH. J=1 MEANS AN ODD POINT, J=2 AN EVEN POINT
C     NOW START THE LOOP
      DO 1200 I=1,MMIN1
      GO TO (1101,1102),J
C     I IS AN ODD POINT
 1101 ODDSUM=ODDSUM+FUN(X)
      J=2
      GO TO 1150
C     I IS AN EVEN POINT
 1102 EVNSUM=EVNSUM+FUN(X)
      J=1
C     PATHS REJOIN
 1150 X=X+H
 1200 CONTINUE
C     ALL OVER BUT THE SHOUTING
      SIMPSN=(H/3.)*(ENDSUM+4.0*ODDSUM+2.0*EVNSUM)
 1300 RETURN
      END
```

Note that we did *not* test for B.GT.A: there is no reason to do so, since inspection of the sub-programme shows that we generate the correct value of the integral from x=a to x=b even if b is less than a (the interval size H is then negative, as it should be).

Round-off errors should be considered: they become serious if the number of intervals, N, starts to exceed 1000, say, but are tolerable otherwise. A nasty roundoff error can arise from the statement X=X+H within the loop; after many steps, the resultant value of X may differ appreciably from what we want. The alternative statement X=A+H*FLOAT(I) at the *beginning* of the loop, *before* the computed GO TO, would give better accuracy, but is much slower in execution. (Why would this statement have to be modified if it were to replace the present statement 1150, in that position, and how would it have to be modified?

Drill Exercises for Sections A through D.

1. Draw flow charts and write FUNCTION subprogrammes for the following functions:

    a. ZIGZAG(X) is equal to $|X|$ if X lies in the range $-1.0 < X < +1.0$. For other values of X, ZIGZAG(X) is defined by the condition that it is a periodic function of x with period 2, i.e., for all values of x, ZIGZAG(X) is equal to ZIGZAG(X-2.) and to ZIGZAG(X+2.).

    b) SQWAVE(X) is defined to be 0 if x is an integer. It is +1 if x lies between 2n and 2n+1 where n is some integer; it is -1 if x lies between 2m+1 and 2m+2 where m is some integer. (This is the "square wave" function.)

    c) Given a complex number C, KWAD(C) is 1 if C lies in the first quadrant (i.e., C=x+iy with both x and y positive), 2 if it lies in the second quadrant, 3 if in the third quadrant, 4 if in the fourth quadrant, and 0 if C lies on either the real of the imaginary axis (i.e., if at least one of x and y are 0).

    d) SMALL returns the smallest value within a vector array of variable dimension MDIM and size N.

    e) TRACE returns the sum of the diagonal values of a matrix array with variable dimension MDIM-by-MDIM and variable size N-by-N.

    f) Let WTNESS be a vector variable of type LOGICAL, with variable dimension MDIM and variable size N. We want FUNCTION VERDCT to be .TRUE. if a clear majority of the N "witnesses" testify to .TRUE., i.e., if the *number* of .TRUE. values within the set of variables WTNESS(1), WTNESS(2), . . . , WTNESS(N) exceeds N/2; otherwise VERDCT is to be .FALSE. (Note that the FUNCTION name VERDCT must itself be typed.)

2. Given the following superior programme and FUNCTION subprogramme, what numerical values will be printed out when the PRINT statement in the superior programme is reached in execution?

```
C     SUPERIOR PROGRAMME
      A=1.0
      B=2.0
      C=3.0
      SUM=ADD(A,B,C)
      PRINT,SUM,A,B,C
      STOP
      END
      FUNCTION ADD(X,Y,Z)
      ADD=X+Y+Z
      X=X+1.0
```

```
      Y=Y+1.0
      Z=Z+1.0
      RETURN
      END
```

Programming Exercises for Sections A through D.

1. Modify *and test* the function evaluation programme for the inverse hyperbolic sine function for double precision real number argument X and function value DRSINH(X).

2. Write *and test* a function evaluation programme for the inverse hyperbolic tangent function, with formula arc tanh x = ½ $\log_e[(1+x)/(1-x)]$. Assume that the argument and function values are
    a) REAL*4   b) REAL*8
    Pay particular attention to numerical accuracy, limitations on argument values, etc.

3. The greatest common divisor of two integers I and J can be found systematically by the method known as "Euclid's algorithm". (If you do not know this method, look it up in a textbook of college algebra). Write *and test* FUNCTION IDIV(I,J) whose value is the greatest common divisor of I and J.

The following programming exercises are more advanced.

4. Modify the determinant evaluation subprogramme to include pivoting, as discussed in Section J of Chapter XIII.

5. Do exercises 1 and 2 above for numbers of type COMPLEX*16 (this should be attempted only if you are familiar with functions of complex variables.)

E.   The Subroutine Subprogramme.

Not everything which we wish to do by means of subprogrammes can be reduced to evaluation of some function value. For example, we may wish to *transpose a matrix,* i.e., interchange the values of the matrix elements A(I,J) and A(J,I), for all I and J. This is quite sensibly the task of a subprogramme, but it is not usual to consider this subprogramme as the evaluation of a function. Again, given a vector array LIST, we may wish to *order* that LIST in increasing order, i.e., rearrange the components of this vector array, so that LIST(I).LE.LIST(I+1), for all I.

For such purposes, the FORTRAN language provides a second type of subprogramme, called the SUBROUTINE subprogramme. As an example, we show below a SUBROUTINE, called by the subroutine name TRANSP, for transposing an N-by-N matrix A with DIMENSION A(MDIM, MDIM), the actual dimension being given in the superior programme.

```
      SUBROUTINE TRANSP(A,N,MDIM)
C     PRODUCE THE TRANSPOSE OF THE MATRIX A, SIZE N-BY-N,
C      DIMENSION MDIM-BY-MDIM
      DIMENSION A(MDIM,MDIM)
C     START THE LOOPS ON I, FROM 1 TO N, AND ON J, FROM I+1 TO N
C     NO NEED FOR J=I, SINCE A(I,I) DOES NOT REQUIRE EXCHANGING
```

```
C          J MUST BE .GT.I, OTHERWISE WE DO THE INTERCHANGE TWICE OVER!
           DO 1400 I=1,N
           IPLUS1=I+1
           DO 1300 J=IPLUS1,N
C          FIRST SAVE A(I,J) IN A TEMPORARY LOCATION
           TEMP=A(I,J)
C          NOW SHUFFLE THEM
           A(I,J)=A(J,I)
           A(J,I)=TEMP
  1300 CONTINUE
  1400 CONTINUE
           RETURN
           END
```

In order to *use* this subprogramme, the superior programme might contain statements such as:

```
C          SUPERIOR PROGRAMME TO USE ABOVE SUBPROGRAMME.
           DIMENSION B(20,20),C(10,10)
           ...
           CALL TRANSP(B,12,20)
           ...
           CALL TRANSP(C,7,10)
           ...
```

The two "CALL" statements result in "calls" on the subprogramme. At the first call, the subprogramme is "linked in" with the starting address of matrix array B, and is told that B is actually a 12-by-12 matrix, dimensioned as a 20-by-20 matrix array. The subprogramme is executed, resulting in transposition of the matrix B. Control is then returned to the superior programme. Later on, a second "call" occurs on the subprogramme. This time, the subprogramme is told to transpose the matrix C; it is told that C is a 7-by-7 matrix, which has been dimensioned in the superior programme as a 10-by-10 matrix array.

We see that there is very little difference between SUBROUTINE and FUNCTION subprogrammes. The main differences are:

1. The *name* of a SUBROUTINE does not represent some sort of function value; rather, it is just a "name to remember by". Thus, there is no *type* information to be associated with the name of a SUBROUTINE, whereas the name of a FUNCTION gives information about the type of the function value.

2. The method of *invoking* a SUBROUTINE subprogramme differs from that of invoking a FUNCTION subprogramme. A FUNCTION subprogramme is invoked by using the name of the function within a well-formed expression. A SUBROUTINE subprogramme is invoked by using the name of the subroutine within a CALL statement.

In addition to these major differences, there are minor differences concerning the possible dummy arguments and actual arguments of these two kinds of subprogrammes; generally, the SUBROUTINE subprogramme has more flexibility in these things than the FUNCTION subprogramme. Since the additional features are used mainly in more advanced programming, we shall refer to them here only briefly.

We now give the formal FORTRAN language definitions for *writing* SUBROUTINE subprogrammes, and for *using* SUBROUTINE subprogrammes. These correspond to sections B and C of the discussion of FUNCTION subprogrammes, and comparison should be made with those sections.

DEF: A SUBROUTINE subprogramme is generated by the FORTRAN compiler in response to a series of FORTRAN statements, the first of which is a SUBROUTINE statement, the last of which is an END statement. The statements in between may be any FORTRAN statements *other than*

1.   another SUBROUTINE statement

2.   another END statement

3.   a FUNCTION statement

4.   a BLOCK DATA statement

The statements in between must contain at least one RETURN statement.

DEF: Every SUBROUTINE subprogramme has a *subroutine name* and a *list of dummy arguments.* The subroutine name is unique. The dummy arguments are replaced, in execution, by actual arguments.

DEF: The form of the SUBROUTINE statement is

SUBROUTINE *NAME(ARG1, ARG2, ARG3, . . . , ARGN)*

where *NAME, ARG1, . . . , ARGN* are either grammatically correct FORTRAN identifier names, or single asterisks *. *NAME* is the subroutine name assigned to this subroutine. *ARG1* is the dummy name of the first argument, . . . , *ARGN* is the dummy name of the N'th argument. There may be any number of arguments, including no arguments at all (note the difference!).

DEF: The *dummy argument names,* if grammatically correct FORTRAN identifier names, represent any of the argument types of a FUNCTION subprogramme (see section B). A dummy argument * represents a "special return point" for use by the RETURN I statement (see later, in small print).

DEF: The statement RETURN, appearing anywhere within the SUBROUTINE subprogramme, has the effect (in execution) of returning control to the superior programme which invoked the subroutine, at the point immediately following the CALL statement which did the invoking.

DEF: The statement RETURN *I*, where *I* is an integer constant or a variable of type INTEGER*4, appearing anywhere within the SUBROUTINE subprogramme, has the effect (in execution) of returning control to the superior programme which invoked the subroutine, at the "special return point" corresponding (as an actual argument) to the *I*'th asterisk among the dummy arguments (see later).

DEF: Every possible path of control within the SUBROUTINE subprogramme must lead eventually to a RETURN statement, to a RETURN *I* statement, or to a STOP statement.

DEF: Statements of form *NAME=wfae,* where *NAME* is the subroutine name appearing in the SUBROUTINE statement, are *expressly forbidden.*

We now turn to the FORTRAN language definitions for *using* a SUBROUTINE subprogramme. These definitions should be compared with the definitions of section C for FUNCTION subprogrammes.

DEF: The actual arguments *A1, A2, . . . , AN* appearing in the superior programme which invokes a SUBROUTINE subprogramme, must agree in number, order, and type with the dummy arguments *ARG1, ARG2, . . . , ARGN* which appear in the SUBROUTINE definition. For dummy arguments which are grammatically correct FORTRAN identifier names, the rules for actual arguments are the same as in Section C. For each dummy argument *, the corresponding actual argument must be of the form &n, where *n* is an integer constant (not a variable) which represents a *statement number* actually occurring in the calling programme. This is the statement number of a "special return point".

DEF: Let *NAME* be the subroutine name of a SUBROUTINE subprogramme, with dummy arguments *ARG1, . . . , ARGN.* Let *A1, . . ., AN* be actual arguments as defined above. Then the FORTRAN statement

   CALL *NAME(A1, A2, . . . , AN)*

appearing within any *other* programme or subprogramme results in a "call" on the SUBROUTINE of that name. The SUBROUTINE subprogramme thus invoked uses *A1* as the actual argument in place of the dummy argument *ARG1;* it uses *A2* as the actual argument in place of the dummy argument *ARG2;* and so on. If the actual argument corresponding to the first dummy argument * is, let us say, &1200, and if the actual argument corresponding to the second dummy argument* is, let us say, &2500, then the effect of a RETURN statement in the subprogramme is to return control to the superior programme at a point immediately following the CALL statement invoking the subprogramme; the effect of a statement RETURN 1 is to return control to the superior programme *at its statement number* 1200; the effect of a statement RETURN 2 is to return control to the superior programme *at its statement number* 2500. (See later in small print).

DEF: *No* numerical value is available to the calling programme in a location called *NAME*, where *NAME* is the subprogramme name; on the contrary, the identifier *NAME must not* be used as a variable name within the superior programme.

Note: The handling of dummy variables, including "reference by value" and "reference by name" are the same as in FUNCTION subprogrammes.

Note: Just as with FUNCTION subprogrammes, the superior programme must see to it that the actual arguments *A1, . . . , AN* are recognizably of the same types as declared within the SUBROUTINE subprogramme for the corresponding dummy arguments.

Note: The restrictions on the use of the subroutine name *NAME* all reflect the fact that the subroutine name is purely a "name to remember by", not the name of an actual variable in the machine.

The main new item in these definitions is the possibility of "special return points", that is

(i)   the occurrence of asterisks * as possible dummy arguments,
(ii) the possibility of writing RETURN I within the subroutine, rather than just RETURN; and
(iii) the occurrence of statement numbers n as actual arguments in the superior programme, in the special form &n.

These all work together in organising the "linking" of the return address. The easiest way to understand this is in terms of what happens inside the machine. We refer back to the flow diagram at the end of Section A. We recall that there was then a special service location, called RA, set aside within the memory area occupied by the subprogramme. The first step of "linking" is to place the return address into location RA, for later use.

174

If a SUBROUTINE subprogramme has, let us say, two asterisks among its dummy arguments, then there are three special service locations set aside within the memory area occupied by the subprogramme. These are called RA, RA1, and RA2, respectively. RA, "the" return address, is the place we return to when encountering a simple RETURN statement within the subroutine. RA1, the "first special return point", is the place in memory we return to when encountering a statement RETURN 1 within the subroutine. RA2, the "second special return point", is the place in memory we return to when encountering a statement RETURN 2 within the subroutine.

At the time the linking is done, that is, when the CALL NAME statement is executed, these return addresses are all set. RA is loaded with the address of the machine order, within the superior programme, immediately following the CALL statement. RA1 is loaded with the address of the machine order, within the superior programme, numbered by the statement number appearing as the actual argument in place of the first * dummy argument. RA2 is loaded with the address of the machine order, within the superior programme, numbered by the statement number appearing as the actual argument in place of the second * dummy argument.

The effect of all this is that we can "pick our return point". We need not return control exactly to the same point of the superior programme at which the subroutine was invoked. Rather, we are allowed to return control to any numbered FORTRAN statement within the superior programme.

The most common application of this special feature is for failure return. If the subroutine finds that something is wrong, it can signal this to the superior programme by returning control, not in the ordinary way, but to a special return point.

This feature of FORTRAN is in the nature of a "frill". There are other ways of signalling failure to the calling programme, some of them superior to the use of special return points. One such way, sense lights, is discussed in Section F below.

Drill Exercises for Section E.

3. A matrix of size N-by-N, dimension MDIM-by-MDIM, is to be replaced by its Hermitean conjugate, obtained as follows: we transpose the matrix, and take the complex conjugate of every matrix element of the new matrix.

4. Write a set of matrix operation subroutines, called MATADD, MATSUB, and MATMPY, for addition, subtraction, and multiplication of two matrices A and B, to get a new matrix C. All matrices are N-by-N and dimensioned as MDIM-by-MDIM. The rules for matrix addition (subtraction) are addition (subtraction) of corresponding elements, one by one. The rule for matrix multiplication is

$$C(I,J) = \sum_{K=1}^{N} A(I,K)*B(K,J)$$

where the symbol $\sum$ means "sum over values of K between K=1 and K=N, inclusive".

5. Write a combined matrix operation routine called SUBROUTINE MATOP(A,B,C,N,MDIM,OPER) which adds A and B if OPER is MATADD, which subtracts B from A if OPER is MATSUB, and which multiplies A by B if OPER is MATMPY; in each case, the result matrix is stored in array C. Is the statement EXTERNAL MATADD, MATSUB, MATMPY needed in the defining programme for the subroutine? In the superior programme invoking this subroutine? Explain.

6. The subroutine PUTIN inserts the argument value X into the K'th position of a vector array VEC, which has N positions filled and has dimension MDIM. The K'th vector element is pushed into position VEC(K+1), the (K+1)'th element is pushed into position VEC(K+2), and so on. Also,

the argument value N is increased by 1. We go to an error return point if N+1 exceeds MDIM or if K exceeds N+1 and in either case we perform no other operations.

7. The subroutine REMOVE removes the K'th element of the vector array VEC, which has N positions filled initially and has dimension MDIM. The later elements of the vector are "pushed down", i.e., VEC(K+1) is placed into VEC(K), VEC(K+2) is placed into VEC(K+1), and so on. N is altered to N-1. We go to a special failure return point if K exceeds N or N exceeds MDIM.

Programming Exercises for Section E.

6. Write a testing main programme for SUBROUTINE MATOP, exercise 5 above, and use this testing programme.

7. Same for the subroutines PUTIN and REMOVE.

8. Write and test a subroutine SORT which does, as a subprogramme, what programming exercise 3 of Chapter XIII did as a main programme, i.e., sort the vector elements between I and J of the vector A, of actual size N and dimension MDIM, in non-decreasing order. We go to one failure return point if N exceeds MDIM, to a second failure return point if J exceeds N, to a third failure return point if I exceeds J, and to a fourth failure return point if I is zero or negative. Write a main programme to test the subroutine, including testing of all the failure exists.

9. Write and test a SUBROUTINE EXPON(A,N,MDIM) which replaces the matrix A, of size N-by-N and dimension MDIM-by-MDIM, by its exponential, computed from the power series. The calculation of the sum of the series should be terminated when all matrix elements have stabilized to four significant figures, or after 50 terms have been computed, without stability being reached. In the latter case, we are to go to a failure return point. Hint: use the subroutines MATMPY and MATADD.

10. Write an *efficient* subprogramme to find the K'th power of a matrix A, where K is an integral power of 2. Use the method of successive squaring, L times if K.EQ.2**L.

11. Use this subroutine to write an alternative version of subroutine EXPON (problem 9), by evaluating $(1+(1/K)A)^K$ for K=2,4,8,16, ... until the matrices stabilize to four significant figures. Compare the results with those of problem 9.

12. Assuming that the input matrices for problems 9, 10, and 11 are of type REAL*4, explain why it is nevertheless desirable to do the internal calculations in double precision. Revise the programmes of problems 9 through 11 to achieve this, and compare the numerical results.

F. Communication between Subprogrammes. I. Sense Lights.

With a large programme, containing a main programme and a number of subprogrammes, communication between these can become quite a problem. So far, the only method of communication of information has been through the list of arguments: The superior programme communicates the values of the actual arguments to the subprogramme when the subprogramme is invoked; the subprogramme may then alter any or all of these numbers, and the altered values are transmitted back to the superior programme at the time control reverts to the superior programme.

This method is all right for small jobs. But when we get to really large jobs, these lists of arguments can become quite unwieldy. It then becomes easy to get arguments out of order, or to omit arguments altogether, with disastrous results.

FORTRAN provides two additional mechanisms for communication between subprogrammes, namely "sense lights" and COMMON regions of core memory. In this section, we discuss sense lights.

In earlier machines, the sense lights were actual lights on the panel of the machine, which could be watched by the machine operator. During normal operation, all sense lights were off. In case of some failure, detected by the programme during execution (for example: failure of an iteration to converge), one of the four sense lights could be turned on; the operator was told to watch out for sense lights turning on, and to stop computation if any sense light stayed on for more than a few seconds.

This is no longer true. Nowadays, the four sense lights, so-called, are simply four bytes of storage in the machine, within the storage area occupied by the standard FORTRAN subroutines SLITE and SLITET; a sense light is "off" if the byte in question is all zeros; the sense light is "on" if the byte in question is not all zeros.

The standard subroutines SLITE and SLITET are invoked by CALL statements as follows:

CALL SLITE(0) has the effect of turning all four sense lights "off".

CALL SLITE(*I*) has the effect of turning sense light number *I* "on"; the value of *I* must be one of 1, 2, 3, or 4.

CALL SLITET(*I,J*) has the effect of *testing* the status of sense light number *I*, where *I* must have one of the values 1, 2, 3, or 4. If sense light *I* is "on", *J* is made equal to 1; if sense light *I* is "off", *J* is made equal to 2; in either case, sense light *I* is left in the "off" position after the test. It is conventional to follow this statement with a computed GO TO (see Chapter XI, Section B) using *J* as the index variable.

As an example of the use of sense lights, let us consider the following problem: Many mathematical functions have restricted domains, i.e., not all argument values X are permitted. For example, the inverse hyperbolic tangent function is defined if x lies between -1 and +1, not otherwise. Suppose we wish to write a FUNCTION subprogramme ARTANH(X). We cannot simply assume that the actual argument which replaces the dummy argument X will always lie between -1 and +1; this would be a dangerous assumption, indeed. Rather, we must test whether X satisfies this restriction, and we must transmit information to the superior programme if X fails to satisfy the restriction.

One way to do this is through the list of arguments: we add a second argument to the argument list, for example, we now define FUNCTION ARTANH(X,J), where X is the value of X, and J is purely an "indicator variable"; this new FUNCTION subprogramme returns the value of the inverse hyperbolic tangent of x if x lies between -1 and +1; in that case, J is set equal to 2; on the other hand, if the actual argument x falls outside the permitted range, then the value 0.0 is returned for the function ARTANH, and the indicator variable J is made equal to 1. The superior programme can then test whether J is 1 or 2; J=1 indicates a failure has occurred; J=2 means that it is all right to proceed.

This is a possible method. However, it is awkward, since J is not really an "argument" of the inverse hyperbolic tangent function. With such an "unnatural" calling sequence for the FUNCTION ARTANH, we are likely to make errors in invoking this function. Furthermore, the value of the indicator variable J must be tested rather quickly by the superior programme, otherwise there is a big chance that something else will be stored into this memory location, inadvertently, between the time the subprogramme ARTANH is invoked and the time the test is carried out on J.

A much better scheme is to make use of sense lights. For example, we may adopt the convention that all sense lights are "off" in the "normal state": to achieve this, we place the statement CALL SLITE(0) at the very beginning of the main programme. We then adopt the further convention that sense light number 1 indicates an arithmetic failure of some sort (for example, a FUNCTION subprogramme may have been called with an actual argument value X outside the permitted region for that function).

The FUNCTION subprogrammes are then written in such a way that sense light 1 is turned on if the argument of the function is outside the permitted region. For example, FUNCTION ARTANH(X) may appear as follows:

```
      FUNCTION ARTANH(X)
C     COMPUTE INVERSE HYPERBOLIC TANGENT WHEN ABS(X).LT.1.0
C     OTHERWISE, TURN ON SENSE LIGHT 1, AND MAKE VALUE=0.0
 1000 IF(ABS(X).LT.1.0) GO TO 1200
C     CRAZY ARGUMENT
 1100 CALL SLITE(1)
      ARTANH=0.0
      RETURN
C     ARGUMENT WITHIN RANGE
 1200 ... (ORDERS TO COMPUTE THE ARC TANH X)
      RETURN
      END
```

The superior programme may then, at some convenient point, test sense light 1, and take corrective action when sense light 1 is "on". The orders within the superior programme could be, for example.

```
      ...
      CALL SLITET(1,J)
      GO TO (3000,3100),J
C     THE SEQUENCE BELOW DOES CORRECTIVE ACTION FOR FAILURE
C        OF A FUNCTION
 3000 .......
      .......
C     THE SEQUENCE BELOW IS OBEYED IN THE 'NORMAL' CASE
 3100 .......
      .......
```

Note that the programme taking the corrective action need not be the immediately superior programme, which invoked FUNCTION ARTANH; nor need this corrective action be taken immediately after the invocation. We may find it more convenient to go on the assumption that things will be all right most of the time, and hence to test for sense light failure indications only at a much higher level subprogramme, perhaps even only in the main programme. Once a sense light has been turned on, it stays on no matter how often control may be transferred between programmes and subprogrammes, the sense light is turned off only through CALL SLITE(0) (this command should appear at the very beginning of the main programme) or as the result of a CALL SLITET(I,J) statement, which then allows us to use the value of J for a conditional branch, as above.

G. Communication between Subprogrammes. II. Common Regions of Memory.

The sense lights, though providing a means of communication independent of lists of arguments, give only four bits of information - each of four sense lights may be either "on" or "off". To communicate more information without using argument lists, FORTRAN provides the facility of COMMON regions of memory. There may be many different COMMON regions of memory, each labelled by an identifier name (up to 6 alphameric characters, the first of which is alphabetic). These are called "labelled COMMON regions". In addition, there may be exactly one "unlabelled COMMON region" of memory.

Each such region of memory is simply a certain number of bytes set aside, and accessible to all programmes and subprogrammes which contain a COMMON statement with that particular label for the COMMON region. For example, suppose that we have a number of subprogrammes, all of which require "work space" in which to do their calculations; in each case, the work area is not needed after the subprogramme has finished its job. We encountered one such example in the FUNCTION DETER (A,N,MDIM) which we wrote in Section D: the "work area" was called AVEC, and was a vector array of DIMENSION AVEC(900). This work area is used within FUNCTION DETER to evaluate the determinant. After the determinant evaluation is finished, we have no more need for these numbers, and they merely take up a precious 3600 bytes of memory (4 bytes per vector component of a REAL*4 vector), which might just as well be used by some other subprogramme.

The statement

COMMON/WORKA/AVEC(900)

can be used in FUNCTION DETER(A,N,MDIM) to *replace* DIMENSION AVEC(900). With DIMENSION AVEC(900), an area of 3600 bytes of storage is set up *within* the storage area allocated to FUNCTION DETER. The COMMON statement instead sets up 3600 bytes of storage in a COMMON storage area *labelled* WORKA. As far as this one subprogramme is concerned, nothing has altered - we still refer to AVEC(II), AVEC(KI), etc., and the fact that AVEC sits in a special region of memory does not matter.

However, now suppose that some other subroutine, say for matrix inversion, needs a work area for storing a 30-by-30 matrix, required during the computation. Let this matrix be given the identifier name BMAT. If SUBROUTINE INVERT(A,N,MDIM) contains the statement

DIMENSION BMAT(30,30)

then an area of 30x30x4 = 3600 bytes of storage is set aside for the array BMAT *within* the storage area allocated to SUBROUTINE INVERT. But if we replace that statement by

COMMON/WORKA/BMAT(30,30)

then the 3600 bytes of storage for BMAT are set aside in the special COMMON area labelled WORKA. Since this is the same COMMON label as before, we are now using the same 3600 bytes of storage for two different purposes - for AVEC within FUNCTION DETER, and for BMAT within SUBROUTINE INVERT. By assumption, both AVEC and BMAT can be "forgotten" after execution of the corresponding subprogramme. In this case, we are not using the COMMON storage area WORKA to communicate information between the subprogrammes DETER and INVERT; we are using the COMMON storage area simply to save machine storage space.

However, we can use such COMMON areas of storage for communication of information, as well. For example, the matrix array element BMAT(3,1) in SUBROUTINE INVERT occupies physically the same memory location as the vector array element AVEC(3) in FUNCTION DETER. Both occupy bytes number 9, 10, 11, and 12 of the COMMON area called WORKA. Thus, information can be passed between these two subprogrammes, if we wish to do so.

Note that the *label* of the COMMON area, in our example WORKA, is a *unique* identifier name, which identifies this area of memory. By contrast, the *variable names* (such as AVEC and BMAT) of variables stored within that COMMON area are *not unique,* and may differ from subprogramme to subprogramme. Neither the names, nor the types, nor the dimensions, of the variables in a COMMON area need agree from subprogramme to subprogramme. The one thing which must agree, under the FORTRAN language rules, is the *total amount of storage set aside* within a given labelled COMMON area of memory. That is, it would be *incorrect* to declare

COMMON/WORKA/JUNK(500)

within some other subprogramme: the name JUNK is all right, but with this statement we set aside only 2000 bytes of memory (assuming JUNK is of type INTEGER*4), whereas the earlier statements set aside 3600 bytes of memory in WORKA. To correct this, we can simply add a blank (unused) memory area, i.e., we write

COMMON/WORKA/JUNK(500),BLANK(400)

This sets aside the desired 3600 bytes of memory. The first 2000 bytes are occupied by JUNK(1), . . . , JUNK(500). The remaining 1600 bytes are occupied by BLANK(1), BLANK(2), . . . , BLANK(400); these are not actually used by the subprogramme, but this does not matter.

Note that JUNK(3), though occupying the same physical area of memory as AVEC(3) and BMAT(3,1), is not interpreted in the same way by the machine. JUNK is of type INTEGER*4 (first letter is a J), hence within this subprogramme, bytes 9, 10, 11, and 12 of WORKA are interpreted as the four bytes of a four-byte integer; whereas in the other subprogrammes, bytes 9, 10, 11, and 12 of WORKA are interpreted as the four bytes of a four-byte floating point number.

For reasons of machine efficiency in execution, it is dangerous to put variables of different lengths into the same labelled COMMON area. For example, let A be of type REAL*4, and DDT be of type REAL*8. Then the statement

COMMON/GROWL/A,DDT

sets aside 12 bytes of storage in the COMMON area labelled GROWL. The first 4 bytes are reserved for A, and the remaining 8 bytes are reserved for DDT. *However,* DDT is now "misaligned", in the sense that the first byte assigned to DDT, byte 5 of the area GROWL, is displaced from the first byte of GROWL by a multiple of 4, but *not* by an integral multiple of 8 (i.e., 5-1=4 is not divisible by 8). 8-byte numbers should have "displacements", in the above sense, divisible by 8; otherwise machine time is wasted needlessly.

Rather than remembering a lot of special rules and tricks, there is a simple *general rule* which takes care of all special cases: *Within any one subprogramme, any one labelled COMMON area should contain variables of the same length only.*

For example, the subprogramme TROUBL may use numbers of type REAL*4, INTEGER*4, REAL*8, and COMPLEX*8, which we may desire to put into COMMON storage areas. If so, we reserve a COMMON storage area with one label, say WORKA, for the variables of 4-byte length, and another COMMON storage area, say with label WORKB for the variables of length 8 bytes.

Note that this rule applies only within any one subprogramme. It may be convenient, in sub-programme SWEET, to use WORKA for variables all of type COMPLEX*16, and to use WORKB for variables of length 4-bytes - thereby perhaps using the available storage area to much better efficiency. This is perfectly all right.

Blank COMMON storage is set aside by a COMMON statement in which the label name, with its surrounding slashes, is omitted. Thus

COMMON CRIMNL(1000),THIEF(20,20),CRIME,ROBBER,COP

sets aside $4 \times (1000+400+1+1+1) = 5612$ bytes of memory in "blank COMMON", assuming the pre-defined type convention which makes all these variables of type REAL*4. The same would be achieved by supplying the two slashes for a label, with no actual label in between them:

COMMON //CRIMNL(1000),THIEF(20,20),CRIME,ROBBER,COP

Although we have emphasized, so far, that only the *label* (or absence of a label) of a COMMON storage area is unique, not the variable names within that area, this freedom is of practical use only for *work areas,* not for *communication areas.* Suppose we want to use the COMMON area labelled INFO to communicate information between a number of subprogrammes. It would be *very poor coding practice* to use different names for the variables within INFO, or different variable types, or different anything. On the contrary, the only safe procedure is to *copy the actual cards* setting aside this COMMON storage area, and insert the copied cards into all the subprogrammes which make use of this storage area. Any other procedure simply invites coding errors, and coding errors of a particularly nasty and hard-to-find type, at that! There are times to be clever, and there are times to be slow, plodding, and systematic. If it proves absolutely necessary to alter the assignment of variables within a communications area, *all* subprogrammes using this particular communications area should be recompiled; old relocatable binary cards should be not merely thrown out, but torn to pieces first, to avoid any chance of them being used ever again. Such precautions may seem extreme to the be-ginner; but they are based on bitter, bitter experience.

Blank COMMON, without any label, is particularly useful as a communications area in large pro-grammes; it often happens that a really large programme does not fit into the available memory space of the machine, and must be broken up into "links" of a "chain". The first "link" is loaded into memory, and executed. Then the second "link" of the programme is called in; the commands of the second link are written into the same memory area, thereby overwriting the commands of the first link; and the second link is executed. The third link is then called in, and so on. During all this time, blank COMMON stays in one area of memory, and can be used for communication of information between different links of this chain. Labelled COMMON, on the other hand, may or may not be allocated different regions of memory within different links (depending upon the "system" used in the in-stallation). Thus, programmers having to write such monster programmes are well advised to reserve blank COMMON as the main communications region, and to use labelled COMMON areas for work areas, and for communications within any one link of the chain, only. The fact that the total length of the *blank* COMMON area can alter from subprogramme to subprogramme is most helpful, too.

We now proceed to give the FORTRAN language rules for COMMON storage areas, in the form of a series of definitions.

DEF: A *COMMON list item* is one of

(1)   A simple variable identifier name,

(2)   the identifier name of an array variable, followed by dimension information for that array, in parentheses, or

(3)   the identifier name of an array variable, with dimension information for that array supplied in a separate DIMENSION statement (this third choice is not recommended).

Array dimensions must be given as unsigned integer constants, i.e., variable dimensions are not allowed for array variables in a COMMON area.

DEF: The COMMON storage area allocation statement has the form

COMMON/*LABEL*/*List*

where *LABEL* is a grammatically correct identifier name labelling the COMMON storage area, and unique to that area; and where *List* contains COMMON list items in sequence, separated by commas. Storage area is set aside in the COMMON area of label *LABEL* for the variables in the *List,* in sequence. Within any one programme or subprogramme, no two COMMON list items may have the same name, either within the same or within differently labelled COMMON regions. But different names may be used in different subprogrammes.

DEF: For *labelled COMMON* blocks, all COMMON blocks by the same label must have the same total size.

DEF: If the label is omitted (with or without the slashes), the allocation of storage is made to *blank COMMON.* This type of COMMON area need not have the same length in all subprogrammes.

DEF: The *dummy* arguments of a subprogramme must not be put into COMMON areas; but *actual* arguments may be in COMMON areas.

Note: The reason for this rule is understandable: dummy arguments are set (i.e., their addresses are supplied to the subprogramme) at the time the subprogramme is invoked. Thus, dummy arguments can not have fixed addresses in memory, as they would have were they in COMMON. Actual arguments may be taken from anywhere in memory, including from COMMON areas of memory.

DEF: No two variables in COMMON areas may be made EQUIVALENT. However, a variable in a COMMON area may be declared EQUIVALENT to a variable of some other name; the effect of this is to put the other variable into COMMON storage, also. However, certain *precautions* must be observed in EQUIVALENCE statements of this sort: COMMON areas must not be extended backwards implicitly (see below), and a labelled COMMON area must not be increased in length implicitly in one subprogramme, unless the same increase is made in all subprogrammes using the same labelled COMMON area.

Note: This rule requires explanation: the statements
COMMON/WORKA/A,B,C
EQUIVALENCE(A,C)

are *inconsistent;* the first demands that C be assigned a memory location 8 bytes down from A, the second demands that A and C be synonyms for the same memory location.

On the other hand, the statements

COMMON/WORKB/D,E,F
DIMENSION G(6)
EQUIVALENCE(F,G(1))

are quite permissible. G(1) is declared to be a synonym for F, and thus G(1) is allocated the same storage location as F. The whole vector array G is thus placed into the COMMON area labelled WORKB; this "implicitly extends" WORKB from a length of 12 bytes to a length of 32 bytes. If WORKB is used in some other subprogramme as well, WORKB must have a total length of 32 bytes in that other subprogramme, also.

The statements

COMMON/WORKC/D,E,F
DIMENSION G(6)
EQUIVALENCE (F,G(6))

are *incorrect,* since they have the effect of extending the COMMON area WORKC in a backwards direction: G(6) is a synonym for F, G(5) is thus a synonym for E, G(4) is a synonym for D; to store G(3), G(2), and G(1) as well, we require an additional 12 bytes *ahead* of D, thereby conflicting with the COMMON statement declaring D to be at the *start* of the COMMON storage area.

H. Communication between Subprogrammes. III. Block Data Subprogrammes.

One practical use of COMMON regions of memory is to store standard mathematical constants, such as $2^{1/2}$, $3^{1/2}$, π, e, etc. which are likely to be used in a number of different subprogrammes. It would be helpful to initialize such a COMMON block by means of a DATA statement, to avoid reading in a lot of standard numerical data every time the programme is executed.

Unfortunately, FORTRAN does not allow one to do this quite so simply. It turns out that *blank* COMMON can not be initialized at all (that is, all variables in blank COMMON must be set by means of READ statements or of arithmetic or logical assignment statements), and that *labelled* COMMON can be initialized only by means of a separate subprogramme, called a BLOCK DATA subprogramme.

For example, suppose we have a COMMON block labelled MATHCS for mathematical constants, used in a number of subprogrammes, with the defining statement

COMMON/MATHCS/ROOT2,ROOT3,PI,EBASE

and we wish to initialize these four standard mathematical constants. To do this, we must write a special subprogramme as follows:

```
BLOCK DATA
COMMON /MATHCS/ROOT2,ROOT3,PI,EBASE
DATA ROOT2,ROOT3,PI,EBASE/1.414214,1.732051,3.141593,2.718282/
END
```

The rules are:

1. The BLOCK DATA subprogramme must not contain any executable statements.

2. The BLOCK DATA statement must be the first statement of such a subprogramme. If an IMPLICIT type declaration is used, it must be the second statement of this subprogramme (not counting comment cards).

3. All elements of a COMMON storage area must be listed (thereby defining the total length of the storage area), even though not all of them need to be initialized.

4. Any number of COMMON blocks may be initialized within any one BLOCK DATA subprogramme.

Note: It is possible to initialize a variable by means of an explicit type declaration, rather than by means of a DATA statement; for example, we might write

REAL*4 ROOT2/1.414214/,ROOT3/1.732051/,PI/3.141593/,EBASE/2.718282/

instead of the DATA statement above. For the reasons listed in Chapter IX, this practice is not recommended.

Drill Exercises for Sections F through H:

8. What changes are necessary in FUNCTION DETER(A,N,MDIM) of Section D, in its second version, to put the vector array AVEC into a COMMON area labelled WORKA? What changes, if any, are required in the calling programme? Suppose the superior programme has a matrix array WHAT, of dimension 20-by-20, in a COMMON area labelled HORROR. What are the statements in the superior programme, necessary to reserve this storage, and to evaluate the determinant of WHAT, assuming that WHAT is actually a 16-by-16 matrix?

9. What statements are necessary to reserve a COMMON area called MESS of length 3600 bytes, as follows: in the main programme, MESS is used to store a vector, of type INTEGER*4, called JUNK, with 20 components, and a REAL*4 matrix array WHYNOT with dimension 25-by-25. In subprogramme WHOSIS, this storage area is used for JUNK plus a vector array QUACK of size 500. In subprogramme GURGLE, this storage area is used for a vector array KOOKIE of dimension 40. The first 20 components of KOOKIE are to occupy the same storage as the vector JUNK. Furthermore at the start of the execution phase, the entire COMMON storage area labelled MESS is to be cleared to zeros.

I. **Guides for Placing Declaration Statements.**

There are restrictions regarding the placing of declaration statements within a programme or subprogramme. For example, the IMPLICIT type declaration statement, if it appears at all, must be the first statement (other than comments) of a main programme, and must be the second statement (other than comments) of a subprogramme.

A useful rule is to place all declaration statements at the beginning of the programme, in the following sequence:

1. IMPLICIT type declaration,

2. Explicit type declarations, if any (avoid these!)

3. DIMENSION statements for arrays not in COMMON,

4. COMMON statements, with dimensions included where required,

5. EQUIVALENCE statements, first to variables in COMMON, then between variables none of which are in COMMON,

6. DATA statements.

Some people put all FORMAT statements (see Chapter XV) at the beginning of the programme also, in position (7) on the above list. We rather advise placing each FORMAT statement immediately after the READ or WRITE statement in which the FORMAT is first used. This makes the programme somewhat easier to follow; if one and the same FORMAT statement is used many times over, in different READ or WRITE statements, searching for the FORMAT statement may take some time; but if we place all FORMAT statements at the very beginning, we find ourselves "flipping back and forth" in the programme all the time, which is worse.

J. Multiple Entries to Subprogrammes.

Quite frequently, there are several things which we wish to do by subprogrammes, so similar that it would be a waste of memory space to duplicate a large number of commands. For example, suppose we wish to write a function generating routine for the inverse hyperbolic cosine of x, for which the mathematical formula reads

$$\text{arc cosh } x = \log_e(x + (x^2-1)^{\frac{1}{2}})$$

This is so similar to arc sinh x, see Section D, that the two function generating routines can well be combined into one subprogramme with two different *entry points,* one entry point for ARSINH, the other for ARCOSH. We set a constant which is +1 for ARSINH and -1 for ARCOSH, so that we compute SQRT(X**2+CON) which is either the square root of x^2+1 or the square root of x^2-1, as the case may be.

Some care is needed because the range of values of x for arc cosh x is restricted to X.GE.1.0; for otherwise, the square root of x^2-1 becomes imaginary. Thus, we must test, at the entry point ARCOSH, but not at the entry point ARSINH, whether X is really greater than or equal to unity. If it is not, we shall set the result equal to zero, and put sense light 1 "on", as a warning.

The name of the location which is finally loaded with the computed function value is the "standard name" as declared in the FUNCTION statement; in our case, the location finally loaded with the computed function value is the location called ARSINH, *even though* the actual value may be the one appropriate for arc cosh x(*) For this reason, it is necessary that all entry names used for a

(*)   What happens in the machine is this: when a RETURN statement is encountered, the content of the "standard name" location is loaded into an "arithmetic register", and this "arithmetic register" is used by the superior programme to obtain the function value. The superior programme does not have direct access to the storage locations, including such storage locations as ARSINH and ARCOSH, reserved within the area of core memory occupied by the subprogramme. The superior programme looks at the content of an arithmetic register. Since a RETURN statement can be reached, in principle, by starting from any one of several ENTRY statements, FORTRAN would not know which named storage location to use for loading up that arithmetic register. The way out, used by FORTRAN, is to load from the location of "standard name", the name declared in the FUNCTION statement, rather than in any of the alternative ENTRY statements.

FUNCTION subprogramme are of the same *type* as the "standard name" which appears in the FUNCTION statement. For instance, both ARSINH and ARCOSH are of type REAL*4, in the pre-defined type convention.

Since the value of X must be positive for ARCOSH, we lose nothing by retaining the final statement

ARSINH=SIGN(W,X)

for *both* the ARSINH and the ARCOSH computation. It is correct for ARSINH (see Section D), and does no harm for ARCOSH, since X is then positive, anyway.

The flow diagram and FORTRAN code follow:

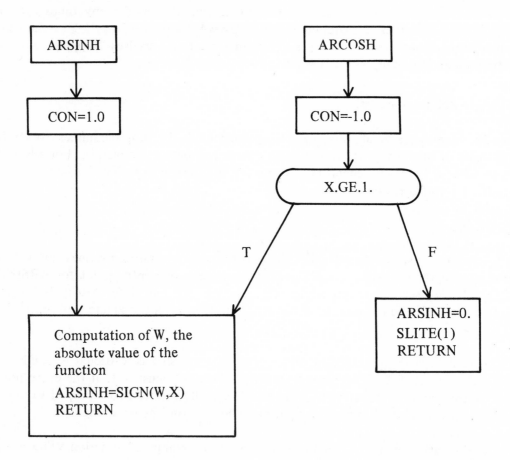

```
      FUNCTION ARSINH(X)
C     ARC SINH AND ARC COSH ROUTINE
      DATA ALOG2/.693147/
C     INITIATE ARSINH COMPUTATION
 1000 CON=1.0
      GO TO 1200
C
      ENTRY ARCOSH(X)
```

186

```
C        INITIATE ARCOSH COMPUTATION
 1100 CON=-1.0
C        TEST ARGUMENT VALUE
      IF (X.GE.1.0) GO TO 1200
C        CRAZY ARGUMENT.
      ARSINH=0.0
      CALL SLITE(1)
C        THIS TURNS SENSE LIGHT 1 ON
      RETURN
C        THIS IS THE FAILURE RETURN
C
C        NORMAL COMPUTATION
 1200 Y=ABS(X)
      IF(Y.GT.1.0E+4) GO TO 1500
      IF(Y.LT.0.01) GO TO 1300
      W=ALOG(Y+SQRT(Y**2+CON))
      GO TO 2000
 1300 W=Y-Y**3/6.0
      GO TO 2000
 1500 W=ALOG(Y)+ALOG2
C        PATHS REJOIN
 2000 ARSINH=SIGN(W,X)
      RETURN
      END
```

Notes: The flow diagram is clearer than the FORTRAN code for such a subprogramme. The reason is that a FORTRAN code, of necessity, has statements one after the other, in linear order, whereas a flow diagram can show parallel branches next to each other on the page.

There are two entry points, ARSINH and ARCOSH. If a superior programme contains a well formed arithmetic expression with ARSINH(U) in it, for example, then we enter at the entry point ARSINH, with the dummy variable X equal to U. If the superior programme contains an arithmetic expression with ARCOSH(V) in it, for example, then we enter at ENTRY ARCOSH, with the dummy variable X replaced by the actual argument V. In either case, we set the appropriate value of CON, but in the ARCOSH entry we also test whether X.GE.1.0, and leave with function value zero and sense light 1 on, if this condition is violated.

From statement 1200 on, the two paths are identical. The advantage gained by combining the two subprogrammes into one subprogramme with two entry points is represented by this joint section of the code, which would otherwise have been duplicated. Multiple entry points can save a great deal of memory space as well as programming effort.

Statement 1300 can not be reached from the ARCOSH entry point, since X, and hence Y, must be greater than or equal to 1.0 when we come from that point. Thus there is no need to make special provisions to avoid the use of the series expansion, i.e., statement 1300, for ARCOSH (for which the series would be quite inappropriate).

Having explained what is meant by multiple entry points, and given an example of their use, we now write down the FORTRAN language definitions for this feature:

DEF: Within any subprogramme (FUNCTION or SUBROUTINE type) it is possible to declare *alternative entry points* by statements of the form

ENTRY *NAME(ARGP1,ARGP2, . . . , ARGPM)*

where *NAME* is the name of an alternative entry point, and *ARGP1, ARGP2, . . . , ARGPM* are the dummy arguments for *that* entry point. These dummy arguments may differ in all respects (dummy identifier names, number, order, type) from dummy arguments for the main entry point, or for other alternative entry points. However, if two different entry points contain dummy arguments by the same dummy identifier name *ARG,* say, then the reference must be consistent (either by name or by value, and to a variable of the same type).

DEF: If the primary entry point is a FUNCTION statement, all alternative entry points refer to FUNCTION subprogrammes also; if the primary entry point is a SUBROUTINE statement, all alternative entry points refer to SUBROUTINE subprogrammes also. The subprogramme must be invoked, from superior programmes, consistent with these rules.

DEF: Each call must provide actual arguments agreeing in order, number, and type with the dummy argument list for *that* SUBROUTINE, FUNCTION, or ENTRY statement whose *NAME* is invoked by the superior programme. Dummy argument lists at other entry points are irrelevant.

DEF: During execution of a subprogramme, the occurrence of an ENTRY statement does not affect the flow of the programme.

Note: This explains the need for the statement GO TO 1200 in our example above, just before the statement ENTRY ARCOSH(X). Without the GO TO 1200, flow of control would proceed right past the ENTRY ARCOSH(X) statement, so that we would set CON=1.0, incorrectly, even for the primary entry, FUNCTION ARSINH(X); thus we would always compute the arc cosh x function, contrary to our intentions.

DEF: Reference to an ENTRY will not transmit new values for arguments not appearing in the dummy argument list for *that* entry point. Old values, from some previous entry to the subprogramme, will be used for all other dummy variables.

DEF: If new dimensions for an array with adjustable dimensions are to be passed to a subprogramme, the dummy array name (as well as the new dimensions) must appear in the dummy argument list of that ENTRY.

DEF: Arithmetic Statement Functions, if used, must appear before the first executable statement of the entire subprogramme.

DEF: A dummy argument name may not appear in any executable statement of the subprogramme unless it has been defined previously (as a dummy argument) in an ENTRY, SUBROUTINE, or FUNCTION statement.

10. Write a multiple-entry SUBROUTINE to combine the matrix operation subroutines of drill exercises number 4. The main entry point is to be called MATADD, with subsidiary entry points called MATSUB and MATMPY, respectively.

11. Write a double precision version of the FUNCTION subprogramme given in this Section, with entry points DRSINH and DRCOSH. The two entry points accept arguments DX of type REAL*8 and return function values of type REAL*8. Hint: Watch out for possible loss of precision!

CHAPTER XV

INPUT/OUTPUT OPERATIONS IN FORTRAN

In this Chapter we introduce, describe, and illustrate the standard FORTRAN language facilities for input/output operations, usually abbreviated to I/O. The "free" I/O we have been using so far is characteristic of student compilers (such as WATFOR); it is not part of the standard FORTRAN language, although there are indications that it may become so in the future. In any case, however, "free" I/O is limited in what it can do, particularly in producing easily readable, well "laid out" printed output, and in handling transfers of information to or from media other than the printer and the card reader (e.g., magnetic tapes, magnetic drums, magnetic disks). In this Chapter, we start from the simplest operation, printing a line of numbers, and work our way up in stages, all the way to direct access operations with magnetic disks and drums.

A. I/O Units. Logical Unit Numbers. The WRITE Statement. The FORMAT Statement

Modern machines have a number of "units" which can be used for transfer of information to or from magnetic core storage, and which are therefore called I/O units. So far, we have encountered the *card reader* (an input unit) and the *line printer* (an output unit). Besides these, there is generally a *card punch,* controlled directly by the machine: this can be used to let the machine punch output cards. These three devices are sometimes called "external" I/O units, because they communicate directly with the external world. In addition to these, there are "internal" I/O units, of various types. The most common are magnetic tapes, drums and disks; they are described later in this Chapter.

The WRITE statement of the FORTRAN language allows us to transfer information *from* magnetic core storage *to* any of these I/O units (except, naturally, the card reader); the READ statement allows us to transfer information *to* magnetic core storage *from* any of these I/O units (except, naturally, the printer and the card punch). In issuing a READ or WRITE command in FORTRAN, we must therefore specify which unit is to be used for the information transfer. In FORTRAN useage, the units are assigned "logical unit numbers". For example, the printer might be logical unit number 3; hence, specifying unit number 3 in a WRITE statement means that we wish the information to appear on the printer.

Unfortunately, the logical unit numbers are not the same everywhere. The correspondence between logical unit numbers and actual, physical I/O units is not part of the FORTRAN language, but rather is part of the "monitor system" of the particular installation. The two most common assignments for the external I/O units are: (*)

(*) With modern, fast machines, the I/O operations are often performed in stages; the input cards are transferred from the card reader to an "input tape"; the output appears initially on an "output tape", and is transferred to printer and/or card punch only later. This is of no practical importance to the FORTRAN programmer.

ACTUAL UNIT	LOGICAL UNIT NUMBER	
	ASSIGNMENT A	ASSIGNMENT B
CARD READER	1	5
CARD PUNCH	2	7
PRINTER	3	6

The existence of different logical unit number conventions at different installations is a major nuisance for programmers. The FORTRAN language is well-nigh universal (there are various "dialects" of FORTRAN, but these dialects are very similar), but unless special care is taken, a whole long programme may have to be revised when going from one installation to another, merely to alter all the READ and WRITE statements for different unit assignments.

An effective way of getting around this difficulty is to give *symbolic names* to the I/O units within the FORTRAN programme: for example, the integer variable NREAD may be used for the logical unit number of the card reader; the integer variable NPRINT may be used for the logical unit number of the line printer; and the integer variable NPUNCH may be used for the logical unit number of the card punch. These logical unit numbers can then be set by a single DATA statement:

Assignment A: DATA NREAD, NPRINT, NPUNCH/1,3,2/
Assignment B: DATA NREAD, NPRINT, NPUNCH/5,6,7/

Only this one DATA statement need then be altered when going to another installation.

This technique is good enough for small programmes. For big programmes, however, involving many subprogrammes, too much recompilation of subprogrammes is involved, since *every* (or nearly every) subprogramme will have to be revised by insertion of a new DATA statement. The preferred technique for large programmes is the use of labelled COMMON. Each programme or subprogramme contains the statement:

COMMON/IOUNIT/NREAD, NPRINT, NPUNCH

and the actual assignment is made by means of a BLOCK DATA subprogramme:

BLOCK DATA
COMMON/IOUNIT/NREAD, NPRINT, NPUNCH
DATA NREAD, NPRINT, NPUNCH/1,3,2/
END

In going to another installation, this single BLOCK DATA subprogramme is the only one which needs to be recompiled, with an appropriately altered DATA statement. (*)

Besides specifying the logical unit number of the I/O unit in a FORTRAN WRITE statement, it is also necessary to specify *what* is to be written, and *how* it is to be written. The "what" is a list of

(*)   It may appear peculiar that one has to go to such lengths to make a FORTRAN programme truly interchangeable between different computer installations. The reason is the complete absence of standardization for monitor systems, as opposed to standardization of FORTRAN compiler source languages. It is highly likely that the next major step in computer "software" will be standardization of the way the monitor system looks to the user (this of course has nothing to do with how the monitor system appears internally). The present tower of Babel in this field can not grow much higher without complete collapse. Already, ordinary programmers have to spend inordinate amounts of time to learn to use various sets of quite arbitrary conventions, which differ from computer manufacturer to computer manufacturer, and often from installation to installation even with the same machine.

variable identifiers, called an *I/O list*, which tells the compiler from which memory positions to take the numbers to be written. The "how" is another matter, about which we must now say something.

Inside the machine, numbers are stored as patterns of binary digits. This is not what we want to appear on the printed output. We want numbers in ordinary decimal form, numbers we can read and understand without special effort. Furthermore, we want, at the least, some blank spaces between the output numbers, so that the output numbers do not run into each other on the output page. There must be a way to tell the machine in what form we want the output to appear, including the number of blank spaces etc. In FORTRAN, this information is provided by a special statement, called the FORMAT statement. This statement must carry a statement number; the WRITE or READ statement contains not only the logical unit number of the I/O unit to be used, but also the statement number of the FORMAT statement to be used. Since we give only the statement number of the FORMAT statement within any READ or WRITE statement, it follows that one and the same FORMAT statement can be used by a number of different READ and/or WRITE statements.

With all this preface, let us now give the FORTRAN statements required to print out three numbers, the integer I, the REAL*4 number A, and the REAL*8 number DR.

```
        DATA NREAD, NPRINT, NPUNCH/1, 3, 2/
          .
          .
          .
        WRITE (NPRINT, 1200) I,A,DR
1200    FORMAT (I12, E16.7,D28.16)
          .
          .
          .
```

Let us explain this set of statements. The DATA statement was explained earlier. The WRITE statement contains the logical unit number of the printer in the symbolic form NPRINT, as well as the statement number 1200 of the FORMAT statement which is to be used. These two pieces of information are separated by a comma, and are enclosed in parentheses. The WRITE statement then contains an I/O list, consisting of the three identifier names I,A, and DR. Items in that list are separated by commas, but there is no comma before or after the list.

The FORMAT statement specifies *how* these variables are to be printed out. The FORMAT code I12 means that the first item in the list is to be converted from internal machine form to *decimal integer* form (this is the meaning of the letter I), and the number 12 means that this decimal integer is to occupy exactly 12 adjacent positions on the printed line. This quantity is called the "field width". Naturally, the decimal integer is not likely to have as many as 12 decimal digits. Suppose that the value of I is actually I=-425. Then the 12 adjacent positions on the printed line are arranged as follows: the first 8 positions are left blank, the 9th position contains the symbol "-", and the 10th, 11th and 12th positions contain the decimal digits 4, 2, 5, respectively. This is called "right-adjusted", that is, the actual value to be printed is pushed to the extreme right end of the "field", and the leftmost positions within the field are left blank.

The FORMAT code E16.7 means the following: The letter E stands for "exponential form" or "E-format", that is, the number is printed out as a decimal mantissa, followed by the letter E, followed in turn by a decimal exponent. (*) The number 16 is the field width. And the number 7

(*) This is similar to, but not identical with, the way floating point numbers are stored in the machine, as explained in Chapter VII. Within the machine, the mantissa is a binary number (not a decimal number), and the exponent is also a binary number; furthermore, the exponent is taken to be a power of 16, not a power of 10. Clearly a good deal of converting must be done to obtain the external, decimal form from the internal floating point form. The letter E in the Format code tells the machine to do this particular conversion.

is the number of decimal digits of the mantissa, *after* the decimal point. With this FORMAT code, the decimal number 362.57 would appear on the printed page as 0.3625700E 03, in the right-most 13 positions of the 16-position field. The left-most 3 positions are left blank, and so serve to space this printed number away from whatever came before.

The FORMAT code D28.16 means that the list item in question should be converted to D-format that is, exponential form for a REAL*8 number. The field width is 28, and the decimal mantissa is to have 16 decimal digits following the decimal point. If the actual number is 4735.678923, the symbols appearing on the printed page are 0.4735678923000000D 04, in the right-most 22 positions of the 28-position field. The left-most 6 positions of the field are left blank, and serve to space this printed number away from whatever came before.

Combining the information so far, the printed output line appears as follows (*)

```
    -425     0.3625700E 03          0.4735678923000000D 04
```

This is, in fact, exactly the same as would have been obtained from the WATFOR statement:

    PRINT, I,A,DR

with these values of I, A, and DR. The complexity of the standard FORTRAN I/O statements, illustrated by this example, is the reason for the existence of "free" I/O in student compilers, as well as for the fact that we have waited till Chapter XV before discussing I/O in FORTRAN.

We note that the I/O list and the FORMAT codes contain some *duplicate information*: the variable name A tells the compiler that this is a REAL*4 variable (using the pre-defined type convention); yet part of the function of the letter E in the format code E16.7 is to tell the compiler exactly the same thing! With duplicate information, there arises the problem of what happens when the two pieces of information are inconsistent (we use "when", not "if", quite deliberately). For example, suppose we have the inconsistent statements

    WRITE (NPRINT, 1250) A
    1250   FORMAT (I12)

The variable name A implies that this is a floating point number; the format code I12 says that the conversion operation, to decimal form, should be carried out assuming the existence of a 32-bit integer at that memory location. In such a case, *the format code overrides the type specification:* The bit pattern in memory location A is assumed to be a binary integer, which is converted to decimal integer form and printed out as a decimal integer in a field of width 12. Naturally, the number so printed out is not even remotely similar to the number we want to see. When the output numbers of your programme look crazy, one very likely reason is inconsistent FORMAT specifications!

There is no such duplication in "free" I/O: the type of A is taken from the type specification (pre-defined, implicit, or explicit, as the case may be); all numbers of type REAL*4 are printed out with the format code E16.7.

_____

(*)   The fact that the first item in the list, in this case the integer I, has one field position "stolen" (i.e., the actual field width is only 11, not 12) will be explained and discussed in Section C.

FORTRAN also provides a non-duplicating format code, called the G-format. With G-format, the type specification is taken from the type of the variable to be printed out, just as in "free" I/O; but the G-format allows more flexibility than "free" I/O.

This G-format, as well as other format codes for transferring numerical information, will be discussed in Section B.

We close the present section with the formal definition of the FORTRAN WRITE statement in its simplest form:

DEF: The simple form of the FORTRAN WRITE statement is

WRITE (n, m) *List*

where n is a positive integer constant, or integer variable name, denoting the logical unit number of the I/O unit to be employed; m is the statement number of the FORMAT statement to be employed; and *List* is a list of variable identifier names, separated by commas, specifying the memory locations whose contents are to be written onto I/O unit n.

In earlier versions of FORTRAN, the standard statement for output onto the line printer did not require a logical unit specification; it was:

DEF: PRINT m, *List* is equivalent to WRITE (n,m) *List* with n equal to the logical unit number of the line printer.

This form of the printing output statement is still recognized by G-level FORTRAN IV and by WATFOR. It is not recommended, for the following reasons:

1.   It is possible that this statement will not be recognized by future FORTRAN compilers.

2.   It is frequently desirable to retain the option of getting output in a form other than printed sheets of paper; for example, we may wish to get our output onto a magnetic tape (see Section L), so that it can be printed up more than once if desired, and so that it can be used as input for a later run. With the WRITE statement, all we need to do to achieve this is to alter the logical unit number assigned to NPRINT, to make it the logical unit number of some magnetic tape. But with the PRINT statement, we would have to alter the programme, with all that that involves.

The statement PRINT m, *List* must not be confused with the WATFOR statement PRINT, *List*. The FORTRAN statement PRINT m, *List* requires a FORMAT statement with statement number equal to m; whereas the WATFOR statement PRINT, *List* produces format-free printed output.

B.   FORMAT Codes for Transferring Numerical Information

DEF: The FORMAT code for transmitting *integers* is nIw where n is an unsigned integer constant called a duplication factor, and w is an unsigned integer constant called the field width. If n equals 1, it may be omitted; otherwise, n specifies the *number* of consecutive data items for which the format code Iw is to be used; thus 3I12, for example, is equivalent to I12,I12,I12. If the field width w is insufficient for the number of characters actually to be written, either a possible minus sign may be lost (if w suffices for the digits, but not for the sign), or else the field is filled with asterisks rather than decimal digits. If the field width w exceeds the number of characters to be written, the characters are placed in the right-most positions of the field, and leading blanks are supplied to the left.

Note: (1) The "duplication factor" n is most useful, since it happens very often that we wish to print out a line of similar items, e.g., a line of integers. With 9 integers to be printed, the format code

9I12, say, is a lot simpler to write than nine codes I12 next to each other, separated by commas; not only is it simpler, but less prone to error. Since FORMAT errors are annoyingly frequent, anything which reduces the chance of such errors is more than welcome.

(2)   The possibility of an insufficient field width w, and the specification of what is done in such a case: the largest integer that can be stored in the machine is $2^{31}-1 = 2147483647$, which has 10 decimal digits. If it is negative, a minus sign is needed in front (the plus sign for positive numbers is *not* written explicitly by the WRITE statement). Thus we need at most 11 field positions for an integer. The format specification I12 is therefore always "safe", leaving at least one blank character as a spacer in front of the printed integer. However, in many cases we know that the numbers to be printed out are nowhere near this big. For example, if they are of type INTEGER*2, they can not be bigger than $2^{15}-1=32767$, five decimal digits. Allowing for a possible minus sign and for at least one blank space in front, I7 would be a safe format code for such integers. I12 would space these integers out farther from each other, but this often interferes with easy reading of a table of numbers. Thus, we may choose, deliberately, to specify a smaller field width; but having done so, we may encounter actual numbers which do not fit within that field width. The proper thing for the machine to do in such cases is to avoid printing the "truncated" set of digits, since this would not warn the reader that the number is actually wrong: he would read 3546781, say, for a specification I7, without knowing that the actual number was -3546781, or perhaps -223546781. In the latter case, FORTRAN does the right thing: it prints a field full of asterisks, as many as the field width: *******, rather than printing out any digits at all. But in the former case, where there is enough room for the digits, but not enough room for the minus sign, FORTRAN just omits the minus sign. This is unfortunate, but true. *In reading output, be suspicious of any output number occupying the entire field width.* If in doubt what field width to specify, always opt for the bigger value of w.

DEF: The FORMAT code $nFw.d$ is used for transferring REAL*4 or REAL*8 numbers in ordinary decimal form. The unsigned integer constants n, w, and d are, respectively, the duplication factor, the field width, and the number of decimal places to be printed to the right of the decimal point. The field width w must be sufficient to allow for a possible minus sign in front, for the decimal digits in front of the decimal point, for the decimal point itself, and for the d decimal digits after the decimal point. If insufficient positions are reserved by d, the fractional portion is *rounded* to the d'th position. If excessive positions are reserved by d, zeros are filled in on the right.

Notes: The F-format is by far the most easily readable, and hence preferred, form of output for real numbers. It is amazing how much more easily the human eye "takes in" the printout

    -356.7235

than the alternative form

    -0.3567235E 03

Thus, if you have good reason to believe that the numbers to be printed out will be neither excessively large nor excessively small, by all means specify the F-format rather than the E or D-formats. (However, note the existence of the G-format, which may be best of all!)

    The format code 3F15.4 is equivalent to F15.4, F15.4, F15.4.

    The number -356.7235 would be printed out in just this form under format code F15.4, the "4" in the format code specifying four digits after the decimal point. With this number, 9 actual positions are used (minus sign, 3 digits before the decimal point, the decimal point itself, and four digits thereafter). The remaining 15-9=6 positions of the field are left blank, and precede the 9 positions used; that is, the number is again right-adjusted.

Beginners are often tempted to print out numbers to full machine accuracy, i.e., seven significant digits for REAL*4, 16 significant digits for REAL*8. This is not necessary, and is often quite undesirable: the numbers become hard to read and assimilate, and in any case their true accuracy is likely to be much less than the formal machine precision; a short discussion of round-off errors and their propagation appeared in Chapter X, and we saw there that quite a few significant digits tend to be lost during machine computation. So print out the number of digits you are really interested in, with perhaps one extra one as a "guard digit".

Note that the F-format *cannot* be used for complex numbers. We can overcome this difficulty by prior conversion to a pair of real numbers: let C be of type COMPLEX*8; we can write the statements

```
          CR=REAL(C)
          CI=AIMAG(C)
          WRITE (NPRINT, 1256) CR, CI
     1256 FORMAT (2F15.4)
```

CR contains the real part of C, CI the imaginary part, and we write out these two real numbers with the format specification 2F15.4. Again, the G-format is an easier way to do the same thing.

The main danger in using the F-format is that the numbers may become too large, or too small, to fit into this format. For example, with F15.4 as a format code, the number 0.00356723 would be printed out as 0.0036, since we have specified only four digits after the decimal point. The printed-out number is properly rounded, but contains only two significant digits. Conversely, the number 2.316×10^{25} would overflow the field width, since we would want 26 digits before the decimal point, then a decimal point, and four digits thereafter, a total of 26+1+4=31 positions for the field. Even when the number does not actually overflow the field width, the advantage of the F-format, easy readability, is lost if there are too many digits before the decimal point: the eye gets confused and loses count. (In hand-written numbers of large size it is conventional to insert commas every three decimal digits, e.g., 42,347,211.9872. There is no provision for this form of print-out in FORTRAN.)

One way to overcome these difficulties is to use the exponential format codes, E-format and D-format.

DEF: The FORMAT code *nEw.d* is used for transferring REAL*4 numbers in exponential form. The unsigned integer constants *n, w,* and *d* are, respectively, the duplication factor, the field width, and the number of decimal digits of the mantissa to the right of the decimal point. The field width *w* must suffice for at least one blank space in front, a possible minus sign, for a digit 0 before the decimal point, the decimal point, *d* digits after the decimal point, the letter E, one space or minus sign, and a two-digit decimal exponent; that is, *w* should be *at least* equal to *d*+8. The last decimal digit of the mantissa is rounded if *d* is less than 7; zeros are supplied in the low-order positions if *d* exceeds 7.

DEF: The FORMAT code *nDw.d* is used for transferring REAL*8 numbers in exponential form. The unsigned integer constants *n, w,* and *d* have the same meanings as before, and *w* should be at least equal to *d*+8. The code letter preceding the decimal exponent is a D, rather than an E. The last decimal digit of the mantissa is rounded if *d* is less than 16; zeros are supplied in the low order positions of the mantissa if *d* exceeds 16.

Notes: These are the format codes implied by the WATFOR "free" PRINT statement, and thus numbers in decimal exponential form should be quite familiar to you by now. The standard form for -356.7235, for example, is -0.3567235E 03, where the E 03 means that the mantissa is to be multiplied by 10^3=1000 to obtain the actual number. Since the mantissa is always adjusted to have its first non-zero digit immediately following the decimal point, it follows that *d in the format code is equal to the number of significant decimal digits printed out.* Thus, the E- and D-formats allow us to specify directly the number of *significant* digits which we wish to write out; but we pay quite heavily for this, by a much less readable form of print-out.

Although the standard form is used by many people, many others prefer a form in which the mantissa has exactly one non-zero decimal digit *before* the decimal point; that is

-3.567235E 02   rather than   -0.3567235E 03

The first form corresponds directly to the hand-written and rounded -3.57×10^2, which most people prefer to -0.357×10^3.

This alternative form can be achieved in FORTRAN by specifying a *scale factor* for the entire FORMAT statement. This scale factor is written as 1P, the 1 meaning that we shift things by one digit to the right, in the mantissa, and correspondingly decrease the exponent by 1. This code is written *before* the first nE$w.d$ or nD$w.d$ format code within the format statement, immediately to the left of it; for example, 1P5E16.4. Having been written down once, the scale factor 1P then applies to all subsequent format codes of the same format statement; for example, FORMAT (1P5E16.4,D26.12) is equivalent to FORMAT (1P5E16.4, 1PD26.12). If all real numbers in this format statement are in E- and/or D-format, this procedure leads to output which many people find more easily readable.

However, an *important warning* must be given: *the scale factor plays havoc with numbers in F-format.* With the WRITE statement, that is in output, the 1P code shifts the decimal point of a number in F-format, without any compensating change elsewhere (since there is no decimal exponent which can be used for compensation). Thus, *numbers in F-format are printed out 10 times bigger than they really are.* A 1P in a READ statement FORMAT causes real numbers in F-format to be decreased by a factor 10, before being stored into core storage. This is ideal for generating errors.

Sometimes, we may want to print out a line containing some numbers in exponential form, followed by some other numbers in F-format. To avoid the scale factor 1P being used for numbers in F-format a scale factor 0P can be used in front of the first nF$w.d$ specification in the FORMAT statement. For example, the statement

FORMAT (1P2E16.6, 0P3F15.4)

specifies that we wish to print out the first two numbers in the list in E-format, with scale factor 1; and the remaining three numbers in the list in F-format, *without* that undesirable displacement of the decimal point.

In our experience, the scale factor, if used at all, should be used with considerable caution. The only practical use we have found is the 1P in front of the E- or D-format codes; the more general scale factor nP is part of the FORTRAN language; but with the exception of n=1 (i.e., 1P) and n=0 (i.e., 0P), as illustrated above, nP should be avoided like the plague.

We mentioned earlier that with the format codes discussed so far, there is duplication of information supplied to the compiler, between the I/O list in the WRITE statement, and the format codes in the FORMAT statement: the variable type is specified twice, once by its name in the I/O list, then again by the code letter (I, F, E, or D) in the format code. This is neither necessary nor desirable. The FORTRAN language contains a "general" format code, called the G-format, which avoids this duplication. In our view, the G-format is the safest specification to use. It gives most of the advantages of the F-format, where that format makes sense, and still allows specification of the number of *significant* digits that we wish to output. The definition follows:

DEF: The FORMAT code $nGw.d$ is used for transferring information of any of the following types: INTEGER, REAL, COMPLEX, LOGICAL, of any of the permitted lengths (number of bytes). The unsigned integers n, w, and d represent, respectively, the duplication factor, the field width, and the number of *significant* digits to be written. The variable type is taken from the I/O list in the WRITE or READ statement. For INTEGER and LOGICAL variables, the ".d" need not be supplied, and is ignored if it is supplied. For REAL numbers, the last four positions in the field are reserved for a code letter (E or D), a blank or minus sign, and a two-digit decimal exponent. If the real number to be written has an absolute value either less than 0.1, or greater than 10^d, then the format code is equivalent to $nEw.d$ for REAL*4 variables, or to $nDw.d$ for REAL*8 variables. On the other hand, if the real number to be written falls in absolute value between 0.1 and 10^d, then the exponent positions (last four positions in the field) are left blank, and exactly d significant digits are printed out in F-format in the remaining positions of the field, right-adjusted. Variables of type COMPLEX*8 are treated as if they were two variables of type REAL*4, namely the real and imaginary parts of the number; similarly, variables of type COMPLEX*16 are treated as if they were two variables of type REAL*8. Variables of type LOGICAL are written out as single letters, T for .TRUE. and F for .FALSE., right-adjusted in the field.

Notes: It is clear that the G-format comes much closer to what we want to do, than any of the earlier format codes. The G-format code should be used in most cases. However, there are exceptions: if we want to produce a table of numbers, the F-format is easier to read than the G-format, as illustrated below: Let the first three numbers be 12.45, -345.6, and 1.378, all of them having four significant digits. Suppose these are to appear underneath each other, as a column in a table of numbers. With the format code G12.4, the column reads

```
    12.45
   -345.6
    1.378
```

whereas the format code F12.3 leads to the column

```
    12.450
   -345.600
     1.378
```

Most people find the second form easier to "see" at a glance. The G-format shifts the decimal point to wherever it belongs inside the number, whereas the F-format shifts the number so as to keep the decimal point in the same print position within the field, and supplies rightmost zeros as needed.

As against this one disadvantage, the G-format code has a number of significant advantages. There is no duplication of information, and hence no danger of clashes between the FORMAT statement and the I/O list. The number of significant digits is specified, so if right-most zeros appear, they are significant (or at least, they are wanted by the programmer who hopes they are significant). Complex numbers can be transferred (we must merely remember to use a duplication factor of 2 for each complex number, since it is printed as two real numbers), and so can logical variables.

Drill Exercises for Sections A and B:

1. Find the FORTRAN language errors in the following WRITE statements. Assume that the variable NPRINT has been initialized to the appropriate value (3 or 6, depending upon the installation) in a DATA statement appearing earlier.

   (a) WRITE (NPRINT, 1001,) A,B,Q

   (b) WRITE (NPRINT, 1002), A,B,Q

   (c) WRITE (NPRINT, 1003) A,Q,V,

   (d) WRITE (NPRINT, 1004) 40.1, 25.7, 32.8

   (e) WRITE (NPRINT, 1005) (A(I),I=1,1,500,1)

   (f) WRITE (NPRINT, 1006) SQRT(A**2+B**2)

2. Write FORMAT statements to achieve the following:

   (a) 10 integers to a line of 120 character line-length

   (b) 5 real numbers to a line, in exponential format, with 6 significant digits

   (c) same as (b), except a non-zero digit before the decimal point of the mantissa

   (d) 2 integers; followed by two real numbers, 6-digit precision, in exponential form with a non-zero digit before the decimal point; followed by two real numbers in F-format; all to fit on a line of line length 120 characters.

   (e) 5 numbers to a line, of any type; we want 6 figure accuracy for floating point numbers.

3. Check the following FORMAT statements for errors:

   (a) 1009 FORMAT (35I10)

   (b) 1010 FORMAT, 1P5E20.7)

   (c) 1011 FORMAT, (5F18.7)

   (d) 1012 FORMAT (5F10.9)

   (e) 1013 FORMAT (1P5E15.9)

   (f) 1014 FORMAT (5F12.9)

   (g) 1015 FORMAT (5F11.9)

C. Layout Control. Messages, as part of the FORMAT

There is more to printing out than print-out of numbers. We would like to be able to control the way information appears on successive lines of a table, to skip lines if required, to skip to the start of a new page if required, and we would like to print out messages telling us what the printed numerical information means. All this can be done through use of the FORMAT statement.

The length of a printed line depends on the particular line printer used by the computer installation. Many installations use printers with 120 positions in a line; another, somewhat larger, standard line length is 132 positions.

If the sum of the field widths w specified within a FORMAT statement exceeds the allowable line length, then we exceed the "maximum permissible record length" for a line image record. This is diagnosed as an error, and causes termination of job execution - i.e., the programme is thrown off the machine.

To prevent this, we are allowed to specify a "carriage return" within the FORMAT statement (or, more generally, an "end-of-record" for whatever record it is: line image record, card image record, etc.). The symbol for this is a slash / within the FORMAT statement. Each slash generates one end-of-record, i.e., one carriage return if the record is a line image for the printer. Thus a single slash means the end of one line and the start of the next line. Two slashes next to each other leave one blank line, and more generally, k adjacent slashes within the FORMAT statement leave k-1 blank lines in the output.

Furthermore, each WRITE statement results in starting a new record, i.e., starting a new line on the printer. Thus k slashes at the very beginning of a FORMAT statement leave k blank lines, not k-1 blank lines.

An additional, and related, feature is the existence of the *printer control character* which is always the *first character of the line image record in the machine*. This tends to be confusing at first, but is simple enough to understand: The line image of a printed line of h characters, say, is a character string of length h+1 inside the machine (we defined character strings in Chapter VII). The *first* of these h+1 characters is the "printer control character"; this character represents a coded instruction to the line printer, rather than a symbol to be printed. The remaining h characters appear on the actual printed line.

The FORMAT statement defines the character string inside the machine; thus to print out a line of h characters, we must specify h+1 characters within the FORMAT statement. The first of these characters is the printer control character, which thereby gives us control over the action of the printer. The simplest way to specify the printer control character within the FORMAT statement is to enclose it in apostrophes, e.g.,

FORMAT ('1',1P5E16.6)

The 1 inside the apostrophes is the printer control character; the printed line contains 5 real numbers in E-format, with a scale factor 1P. The meaning of the printer control characters is given in the Table below:

MEANING OF PRINTER CONTROL CHARACTERS

CHARACTER	ACTION OF PRINTER
blank	One line shift
0	Two line shifts
1	One page shift, i.e., start a new page
+	Suppression of line shift and/or page shift; i.e., we can "over-print" the line printed before.

The blank control character is the "normal" choice; it starts a new line. If a slash / is followed by a blank control character, the slash produces a carriage return (think of a typewriter!) and the blank control character produces one line feed: hence we start at the left end of a new line. If several slashes follow each other immediately, blank control characters between them are understood, and need not be supplied.

The control character '1' is not recommended for student programmes, since there is a limit on the number of output pages permitted (printer paper costs money!); starting a new page means that you are that much closer to exceeding the maximum number of pages. On the other hand, for production programmes, especially those producing tables of numbers, it is often most desirable to start a certain part of the output at the top of a page.

The control character '+' should be avoided by beginners. It can be used by more experienced programmers to produce special effects.

If the programmer fails to specify a control character within the FORMAT statement, the first character of the line image is "stolen" and interpreted as being the control character. For example, we mentioned in Section A that the FORMAT statement

FORMAT (I12,E16.7,D28.16)

produces a printed line with a field width of 11, not 12, for the first number printed. The reason is that we have failed to specify a printer control character. Thus, the initial blank produced by the I12 format code is "stolen" and interpreted as a blank control character. If we want the fields to be correct, we must supply the printer control character explicitly, thus:

FORMAT (' ',I12,E16.7,D28.16)

Note that the printer control character applies to printed output only, not to other forms of I/O. It is most dangerous to omit the printer control character - some characters, not given in the Table above, cause the printer to "go crazy"; for example, to go into a never-ending loop of page feeds: the line printer proceeds to spit out blank pages, one after another in rapid succession, until the operator stops the process manually. (*)

The printer control character is one example of *characters supplied by the FORMAT statement,* as opposed to characters resulting from the conversion of machine numbers to external, decimal form. This particular character appears only as the first character of the line image within the machine, and

(*) This is not possible in WATFOR. Control characters other than the ones in the Table are replaced by blank control characters, automatically.

does not appear as such as part of the printed line. But other FORMAT-supplied characters appear as "messages" on the actual print-out. For example, consider the statements:

```
      IMPLICIT REAL*8(D)
      DATA NREAD,NPRINT,NPUNCH/5,6,7/
         .
         .
      WRITE (NPRINT, 3214) J, A,DR
3214 FORMAT (' J=',I12,'A=',E16.7,'DR=',D28.16)
         .
```

If the numerical values of J, A and DR are as specified at the end of Section A, the print-out appears as follows:

```
J=           -425A=    0.3625700E 03DR=        0.4735678923000000D 04
```

We note that the first character supplied (the blank before the J in ' J=') does not appear explicitly; it is the printer control character. The other characters do appear. But this print-out can hardly be tolerated. We clearly want spaces before the A= and DR= character strings. One way to achieve this is to supply the spaces as part of these strings:

```
3214 FORMAT (' J=',I12,'   A=',E16.7,'   DR=',D28.16)
```

with the result:

```
J=           -425   A=    0.3625700E 03   DR=        0.4735678923000000D 04
```

An alternative way is the *X-format code,* which is of form nX, and has the effect of supplying exactly n blank characters to the line image. Thus, an equivalent FORMAT statement to the one just before is:

```
3214 FORMAT (' J=',I12,3X,'A=',E16.7,3X,'DR=',D28.16)
```

This produces the same printed line as before, with three blank spaces before A= and before DR=.

We repeat what we said earlier: messages within the printed output are most important; purely numerical output, without any indication of what the numbers mean, is an abomination which must not be tolerated. It takes time and effort to supply messages, but this time and effort is well-spent.

Messages appearing as part of a FORMAT statement are "fixed messages", i.e., the same message is printed out whenever this FORMAT statement is invoked by a WRITE statement. (See, however, Section J for an amendment). In Section E we shall describe an alternative method, allowing variable messages, with the message appearing as an item in the I/O list, rather than as a fixed message within the FORMAT statement. However, the disadvantage of "fixed" messages should not be exaggerated; in fact, most of the practically useful messages might just as well be fixed. Only occasionally do we feel the urgent need for variable messages.

The character strings for messages can be supplied in two alternative forms within the FORMAT statement:

1. Enclosed within apostrophes, as above; in that case, an internal apostrophe must be "coded" as two adjacent apostrophes; i.e., 'DON''T' appears on the printed page as DON'T

2. The format code nH followed immediately by exactly n characters; blank characters are part of the count. Apostrophes are *not* "coded" in this method, e.g., the above character string could also be written as 5HDON'T

In practice, the counting of characters needed with the nH format code is amazingly effective at generating errors, and bad errors at that: If n is too large by 1, the next character in the FORMAT statement becomes part of the message, and is lost as a control character. For this reason, it is desirable to put a comma after each character string, even though this comma is not necessary under the FORTRAN language rules: if the comma is "eaten" as part of the character string, the comma appears as part of the message, but nothing fatal happens. If the n in nH is too small by 1, the effect is usually fatal: unless the last character of the actual message is a blank, this last character will be interpreted as part of the next format code, and is likely to be quite incomprehensible to the compiler; hence sudden death!

For these reasons, the character strings in apostrophes are preferred. But they have a danger, too! We may overrun the available line length without knowing it, again with sudden death as the result.

There is no royal road to writing correct FORMAT statements; no matter how experienced the programmer, every FORMAT statement must be watched and checked. Letting the machine find FORMAT errors for you is much too expensive: there is sudden death of execution after the first FORMAT error found; you correct that one, submit another run, and promptly get stopped by the next wrong FORMAT statement; and so on, one FORMAT error after another until you have used up your time allocation on the machine. It is clear that "free" I/O is a much better choice for most purposes, not just for student teaching; and that it is hence just a matter of time before "free" I/O becomes a normal part of the FORTRAN language.

As the last format code for layout control, we discuss the "tab" or T-format code.

DEF: The format code Tw, where w is an unsigned integer constant less than 256, has the effect of placing the *subsequent* information so that it starts in position w of the I/O record. If the I/O record is used as the line image record of a printed line, the subsequent information appears starting in column w-1 of the printed line (since position 1 of the line image record is the printer control character).

As an *example*, consider the FORMAT statement

```
3214 FORMAT (' J=',I12,T19,'A=',E16.7,T40,'DR=',D28.16)
```

This specifies that the characters A=, followed by a number in format code E16.7, should appear within the I/O record starting at position 19 (hence should appear on the printed line itself starting in position 18); and that the characters DR=, followed by a number in format code D28.16, should appear within the I/O record starting at position 40 (hence should appear on the printed line itself starting at position 39). The net result is exactly the same as the output given earlier.

In principle, it is not necessary to keep these "tabs" in sequence; for example, T40 might appear within a FORMAT statement *before* T19. However, it is bad coding practice to make use of that sort of freedom, and it can easily lead to errors. For example, the sequence of statements

```
      WRITE (NPRINT,3214)J,A,DR
 3215 FORMAT (' J=',I12,T40,'DR=',D28.16,T19,'A=',E16.7)
```

gives rise to quite wrong and misleading output! To see the reason, we must understand just how the I/O list in the WRITE statement interacts with the specifications in the FORMAT statement. The procedure followed by the machine is this: we proceed to scan the FORMAT statement, putting character information etc. into the line image as we go along, until we come to the first format code for a numerical conversion. We use that format code for converting the first number in the I/O list. We then scan the FORMAT statement further, again putting character information etc. into the line image as we go along, until we come to the format code for the next numerical conversion. We use that format code to convert the second number in the I/O list. And so on.

Now apply this procedure to the two statements above: We start by putting the characters ' J=' into the line image (without the surrounding apostrophes), and we use format code I12 to convert the first number in the I/O list, i.e., the number stored in location J. We then notice T40, so we store what follows into locations 40 ff within the line image. The first characters so stored are 'DR='. Next, we see a format code for a numerical conversion, and we use that format code to convert the second number in the I/O list, i.e., the number stored in location A(!). This is not at all what is wanted: Location A contains a REAL*4 number, whereas the format code specifies a REAL*8 conversion operation (D-format); furthermore, the identifying characters, i.e., the message 'DR=', do not correspond to the number which follows. Going on, the characters 'A=' are placed starting in position 19 of the line image all right, but the number appearing immediately thereafter is the value of the third number in the I/O list, i.e., the value of DR, truncated to REAL*4 because we have specified an E-format code. Conclusion: keep the tab-codes in sequence!

At this stage, we can understand that *it is possible to omit the I/O list altogether in the WRITE statement.* When this is done, we still proceed to construct a line image, based on the character and tab information in the FORMAT statement, appearing before the first numerical conversion format code (if any) in the FORMAT statement. When we come either to the end of the FORMAT statement, or to the first numerical conversion format code without accompanying list item in the I/O list, we close the line image, and put out the line onto the printer.

The most important use of this kind of WRITE statement is for *table headings*. The "tab" feature is particularly helpful here. For example, consider the statements:

```
      WRITE (NPRINT,3216)
 3216 FORMAT ('1',T32,'TABLE OF TRIGONOMETRIC FUNCTIONS'//' ',
     1T5,'X',T25,'SIN',T45,'COS',T65,'TAN',T85,'COT')
```

No I/O list appears in the WRITE statement; yet two lines are produced and printed out as a result of the FORMAT statement, with a blank in between. The '1' at the beginning tells the printer to skip to the head of a new page. At the top of that page, the heading TABLE OF TRIGONOMETRIC FUNCTIONS appears starting in position 31 of the printed line. Then there is a blank line, and the line below that contains the column headings of the table: X in position 4, SIN in positions 24-26, COS in positions 44-46, TAN in positions 64-66, and COT in positions 84-86.

At a later stage in the programme, probably within a DO loop, we might have statements computing X, followed by

```
      S=SIN(X)
      C=COS(X)
      T=TAN(X)
      U=COTAN(X)
      WRITE (NPRINT,3345) X,S,C,T,U
 3345 FORMAT (' ',F8.4,2X,4F20.6)
```

This prints out X with four places after the decimal point, the decimal point itself appearing just below the table heading letter X; the other four numbers are printed out with 6 places after the decimal point, with the decimal point itself appearing just below the appropriate table heading. (You should verify these statements!)

The second major use of WRITE statements without an I/O list is for warning messages in case of programme failure of some kind, for example:

```
      WRITE (NPRINT,9999)
 9999 FORMAT ('0MATRIX ILL-CONDITIONED. GIVE ME BETTER DATA,PLEASE.'
     1////)
      STOP
```

Note the character 0 as the printer control character: it will space this line down by one step, i.e., leave a blank line before it, for easier visibility.

Still another use of the list-free WRITE statement is to leave a vertical space in a table of numbers. For example, we might write a DO loop to compute the table of trigonometric functions above, with loop index K; near the end of the loop, we put the statements:

```
      IF (MOD(K,5).EQ.0) WRITE (NPRINT, 3350)
 3350 FORMAT (' ')
 4000 CONTINUE
```

Here, 4000 is the CONTINUE statement for the DO loop; the statements preceding it have the effect of inserting a blank line whenever the loop index K is divisible by 5.

Drill Exercises for Section C:

4. Write the FORMAT statements to go with the WRITE statement

    WRITE (NPRINT, 1009) M,A,B,C,D,E,F,G

    if it is desired that the output appear as follows:

    (a) as it would be printed out by the WATFOR statement
         PRINT, M,A,B,C,D,E,F,G

    (b) the integer M in a field of width 15, followed by A, B and C in G-format, 6 significant figures, each with a field width of 25; then start a new line containing the remaining numbers in F-format, with three figures after the decimal point; the field for D should be right underneath the field for A, the field for E right underneath the field for B, and so on.

(c) on the first line of a new page, we want the message: NEW ITERATION, then a blank line, then a line with the message M= followed by the value of M; then another blank line, followed by a line with the values of A, B, and C, each preceded by an appropriate message, then another blank line, then the values of D, E, F, and G each preceded by an appropriate message; the format codes are to be as in (b), and proper alignment is desired.

5.   The statement WRITE (NPRINT, 1004) is meant to produce a table heading for a table of values of M, X, Y, Z produced by the WATFOR statement PRINT, M, X, Y, Z (the PRINT statement appearing inside a DO loop). Write a suitable FORMAT statement with statement number 1004.

D.   Repetitions: Implied DO Loops, Repeated Format Codes, Repeated Formats

FORTRAN provides a number of methods designed to avoid having to write lengthy I/O lists and lengthy FORMAT statements. In this Section, we discuss these features.

The first feature was introduced already in Chapter XIII; this is the *implied DO loop* in the I/O list. For example, let VEC be a vector array: then the statement

WRITE (NPRINT, 1201) (VEC(I),I=1,5)

is equivalent to

WRITE (NPRINT, 1201) VEC(1), VEC(2), VEC(3), VEC(4), VEC(5)

More than one quantity may appear within such an implied DO loop, for example, let H be another vector. The statement

WRITE (NPRINT, 1202) J,A, (VEC(I), H(I), I=1,3)

is equivalent to

WRITE (NPRINT, 1202) J, A, VEC(1), H(1), VEC(2), H(2), VEC(3), H(3)

DEF: The general form of *an implied DO loop list item* in an I/O list is

($List, I=m_1, m_2, m_3$)

where *List* is any valid I/O list, *I* is the name of an integer variable, and m_1, m_2, m_3 are either unsigned integer constants or names of integer variables. The rules for m_1, m_2, and m_3 are as for the corresponding quantities in DO loops (see Chapter XI). The List is transmitted exactly as often as the DO loop DO n $I=m_1, m_2, m_3$ would be traversed, and with exactly the same values of the loop variable *I*.

Notes:

1.   The items in the list may or may not depend on the value of the loop variable *I*. For example, the list (A, VEC(I), I=1, 5, 2) is equivalent, by the above definition, to

A, VEC(1), A, VEC(3), A, VEC(5)

corresponding to the three values of I in the DO loop DO n I=1, 5, 2, that is I=1, then I=3, finally I=5. Since the list element A does not depend upon I at all, it is simply repeated three times.

2.   The loop index I may itself appear in the list. For example, the list item may be as follows (I, VEC(I), I=1, 5, 2). With this list, the value of I is transmitted each time around the implied DO loop, just before the value of VEC(I). (*)

3.   The above definition is recursive, in the sense that the *List* in the implied DO loop list item may itself contain other implied DO loops. In this way, we can organize loops within loops. For example, let ARRAY be a matrix array, and let VEC be a vector array. Then the list item

(VEC(I), (ARRAY(I,J), J=1, 3), I=1, 5, 2)

is equivalent to the explicit list

VEC(1), ARRAY(1,1), ARRAY(1,2), ARRAY(1,3), VEC(3), ARRAY(3,1), ARRAY(3,2),
ARRAY(3,3), VEC(5), ARRAY(5,1), ARRAY(5,2), ARRAY(5,3)

Here, the inner loop is (ARRAY(I,J), J=1,3), which is equivalent to the expanded list ARRAY(I,1), ARRAY(I,2), ARRAY(I,3). This is enclosed in the outer loop on I, where I takes the values 1, 3, and 5 in turn.

4.   It is apparent that the implied DO loop facility allows us to specify quite lengthy I/O lists. Furthermore, by making use of the fact that m_1, m_2, and m_3 are allowed to be variable names rather than just constants, we can specify these lists flexibly;   for example, the list item (VEC(I), I=1,K) specifies the transmission of K numbers, whatever the current value of K is in the machine. It would not be possible to specify such a list directly, item by item, but the implied DO loop allows this flexibility.

Having given the definition and some discussion of implied DO loops in the I/O list, we now turn our attention to methods for simplifying and shortening the FORMAT statements. FORTRAN allows several forms of "repetition":   a single format code may be repeated a number of times, by means of the duplication factor n in format codes such as nIw, $nFw.d$, and so on. Furthermore, *groups* of format codes may be repeated, as illustrated by the following example:

```
FORMAT (' ',2(I12,F16.7),I20)
```

is equivalent to

```
FORMAT (' ',I12,F16.7,I12,F16.7,I20)
```

This facility is "limited" in the sense that at most two levels of parentheses, in addition to the outer parentheses required by every FORMAT statement, are permitted. That is, we may write:

```
FORMAT (' ',2(I7,2(F15.5,F12.5)),I7)
```

(*)   This form is permissible in WRITE lists, but not in READ lists. In a READ statement, we would be asking the machine to *input* a value for I, at the same time that the implied DO loop *specifies* a set of consecutive values for I; this is inconsistent.

but no more nesting of parentheses than this is permitted. The equivalent expanded form of the above FORMAT statement is

```
   FORMAT (' ',I7,F15.5,F12.5,F15.5,F12.5,I7,F15.5,F12.5,
  1 F15.5,F12.5,I7)
```

where we have spilled over onto a continuation card. The advantage gained from the use of repeated groups of format codes should be apparent.

The "group" (F15.5,F12.5) in the above example may be convenient, in particular, for easily readable output of complex numbers: The real and imaginary parts appear next to each other, with a bit of blank space in between, but the bigger field width (15) for the first format code means that additional blank space is left before the real part, thereby setting off the complex number as one unit.

Incidentally, just why is the above example *unsuitable* for a printer with a line length of 120?

Another form of repetition occurs when the FORMAT statement does not contain enough specifications for all the numbers in the I/O list of the WRITE statement. For example, consider the sequence:

```
   DATA NREAD,NPRINT,NPUNCH/5,6,7/
   DIMENSION A(125)
      .
      .
   WRITE (NPRINT,3215) A
3215 FORMAT (' ',5G18.6)
      .
      .
```

Here the FORMAT statement contains numerical conversion information for only 5 numbers, whereas the I/O list contains 125 numbers to be converted (the entire vector array A). In such a case we produce a line image record containing the first five numbers on the I/O list in converted form; we then close the record, and start with the same FORMAT statement all over again, for the next five numbers; and so on. The result is that we print out line after line, each line containing 5 components of the vector A, until the vector array A is exhausted.

This rescanning of a FORMAT statement in case of a too long I/O list does not necessarily include the entire FORMAT statement; rather, *if the FORMAT statement contains parenthesized groups of format codes, then the rescan commences at the first-level left parenthesis that precedes the end of the FORMAT statement.* Parts of the FORMAT statement preceding this last first-level left parenthesis are not rescanned.

This feature can be used to include heading information within the FORMAT statement, thus:

```
   DIMENSION A(125)
   WRITE (NPRINT, 3216) A
3216 FORMAT(' ',T25,'THE COMPONENTS OF VECTOR A ARE'/(' ',5G18.6))
```

208

The effect of this is to precede the table of components of A by a line with the table heading. This table heading is *not* rescanned again, rather, the rescan of the FORMAT statement starts at the first-level parenthesis immediately following the slash.

Although quite legitimate, a table of this form would be somewhat hard to read: with 125 components to be printed, and 5 components to a line, there are 25 lines of print, and nothing is easier than to lose track of what component it is we are looking at. It would be better to label each vector component by the component number, for easy reading. This can be achieved by using the implied DO loop feature of the I/O list:

```
      DIMENSION A(125)
      .
      WRITE (NPRINT,3217)(I,A(I),I=1,125)
 3217 FORMAT (' ',T25,'THE COMPONENTS OF THE VECTOR A ARE'
     1 /(' ',5(I4,G18.6)))
      .
```

With this form of printout, each vector component is preceded by its number. The heading is output first, and the rescan after the first numerical line starts at the same left parenthesis as before (the one immediately after the slash); note that the left parentheses followed immediately by the format code I4 is a second-level parenthesis, not a first level parenthesis!

Drill Exercises for Section D:

6. Construct the WRITE and FORMAT statements for the following: The matrix array A, of dimension 4-by-4, is to be printed out row by row, each row preceded by the row number; the entire print-out is to be preceded by a heading, saying MATRIX ARRAY A in one line, then a blank line, then a line containing the headings ROW NO, COLUMN 1, COLUMN 2, COLUMN 3, and COLUMN 4 in appropriate places. The matrix elements are to be printed out to 7 significant digits.

7. Print out the diagonal elements (indices I=J) of the matrix array D, dimension 40-by-40, each preceded by its order number. Provide suitable heading information in the print-out.

8. Construct WRITE and FORMAT statements for printing out all the *odd*-numbered rows of the matrix array B, of dimension 7-by-7. Each row is to be preceded by the row number, and suitable heading information is to appear before the print-out.

9. Print out the even-numbered rows of the matrix array C, dimension 20-by-20, starting with row N and ending with row M (assume that N and M are even). Since it is not possible to have 20 numbers next to each other on a printed line, print out each row as a set of four lines, five matrix elements to a line; the first line of each group of four lines is to contain the row number; the other three lines in each group are to be indented suitably. Suitable heading information is to be provided, including the values of N and M.

10. Print out those elements of the matrix array E, dimension 40-by-40, which lie on and below the diagonal (i.e., for which I.GE.J in E(I,J)). The print-out is to appear row by row, with each complete row preceded by the row index. Watch out for too long lines! (Hint: this cannot be done entirely by means of implied DO loops in a single WRITE statement; the list can be specified in that way, but the associated FORMAT statement cannot be written as a single FORMAT statement; use an outer DO loop on the row index I to solve this exercise).

11. The checkerboard array KB(I,J), dimension 8-by-8, described in problem 7 of Chapter XIII, is to be printed out on a page in a square array, with vertical and horizontal distances of 1 inch. The whole display is to cover an 8-by-8 inch area of paper. Assume that the printer prints 10 characters to the inch, horizontally, and that there are 6 lines to the inch, vertically. Allow a 2 inch margin on the left side of the printed sheet. Provide suitable heading information.

E. Format Codes for Non-Numerical Items in the I/O List

Besides numbers, the I/O list may contain non-numerical information, such as LOGICAL variables and strings of characters. Furthermore, there are occasions when we do *not* wish to carry out any conversion at all, but want to look at the bit pattern actually in the machine at that memory location.

DEF: The FORMAT code nLw is used to transmit logical information. The unsigned integer constants n and w are, respectively, the duplication factor and the field width. In a WRITE statement, the character T is written to denote .TRUE., F is written to denote .FALSE., in either case right-adjusted within the field of width w.

Note: The format code nGw, when used to convert a variable of type LOGICAL, will do exactly the same thing, but without danger of inconsistency with the type of the item in the I/O list. Thus, nGw is preferable to nLw.

DEF: The FORMAT code nZw is used to transmit information in unconverted, hexadecimal form. The unsigned integers n and w are, respectively, the duplication factor and field width. There are two hexadecimal characters per byte of information (see Chapter VII), thus w should be at least 8 for transfer of a 4-byte memory location, at least 16 for transfer of an 8-byte memory location, and so on. If the field width w exceeds this minimum, the information is right-adjusted within the field, and left-most blanks are supplied if it is a WRITE operation; left-most zeros are supplied if it is a READ operation.

Note: The Z-format can be most helpful in debugging a code, particularly when the bug is really nasty. With the Z-format, and only with this format, can we find out exactly what is stored inside the machine. No conversion, no monkey business; we get precisely the bit pattern actually in core memory. There are times when it is absolutely essential to know just what the machine has in its core memory. Beginning programmers are likely to underestimate the value of such information, and they have difficulty interpreting hexadecimal printout; naturally, one needs to know a bit of the actual machine language to interpret this. But in more advanced programming, one tends to become increasingly suspicious of what is actually going on inside the machine, and correspondingly more eager to go to some trouble to find out.

DEF: The FORMAT code nAw is used to transmit information in character form. The unsigned integer constants n and w are, respectively, the duplication factor and the field width. Each character transmitted occupies one position in the field, hence w should be at least equal to the number of characters (number of bytes) contained in the item within the I/O list. If w is below this minimum, the left-most w characters will be transmitted. If w is above the minimum, then the line image produced by a WRITE statement contains the correct number of characters, right-adjusted in the field of width w, with left-most leading blanks supplied for the rest of the field.

One use of the A-format code is the transmission of messages as part of the I/O list, thereby giving us the option of *variable messages,* as opposed to the fixed messages contained within the FORMAT statement itself. The set of messages to be used can be initialized by a DATA statement. For example, suppose we wish to print out one of three different messages, which are respectively:

ITERATION PROCEEDING.
ITERATION IN TROUBLE.
ITERATION HOPELESS.

The longest of these messages, the first, contains 21 characters. If we store the message in a matrix of type REAL*4 called SSAGE(*), a convenient dimension statement is

DIMENSION SSAGE(6,3)

Each column of this matrix contains six numbers of type REAL*4, hence 24 bytes of information. Thus each column contains enough information for a 24 character message, and there are three columns, one for each of the three messages. We now initialize the matrix SSAGE by the DATA statement

```
      DATA SSAGE/'ITERATION PROCEEDING.   ITERATION IN TROUBLE.   ',
     1'ITERATION HOPELESS.      '/
```

The DATA statement, combined with the DIMENSION statement for SSAGE, reads in the entire matrix in FORTRAN sequence, i.e., by columns. This is what we want.(**)

Now suppose that we compute, somewhere in the programme, an iteration number N, an error size EPSLON, and a number K which equals 1 if everything is going all right, 2 if the error is increasing and 3 if the error has continued to increase for a number of iterations. We might then wish to print out, at the end of each iteration, the following

```
      WRITE(NPRINT,2525) N,EPSLON,(SSAGE(I,K),I=1,6)
 2525 FORMAT (' ITERATION NO.',I5,3X,'ERROR=',G10.3,2X,6A4)
```

If N=13, EPSLON= 0.00235, and K=1, the printed line reads:

ITERATION NO.   13   ERROR= 0.235E-02 ITERATION PROCEEDING.

With the same N and EPSLON, but K=2, the printed line reads:

ITERATION NO.   13   ERROR= 0.235E-02 ITERATION IN TROUBLE.

(*) In standard FORTRAN, we may use any type for storing such messages. In WATFOR, however, use of the
     A-format code is restricted to variable names typed as REAL*4.

(**) This form of the DATA statement is permitted in IBM FORTRAN, but not at present in WATFOR. Rather, WATFOR demands that the data be broken up into four-byte groups, one such group for each element of the matrix array SSAGE. Each four-byte group must be enclosed by separate apostrophes, and there must be commas between adjacent four-byte groups, e.g., 'ITER', 'ATIO', 'N PR', 'OCEE', 'DING', and so on. It is hoped that WATFOR will be modified soon in this respect.

Note that we have used a mixture of fixed messages and variable messages. Fixed messages, such as 'ITERATION NO.' and 'ERROR=', are best put within the FORMAT statement. Variable messages are best handled by means of the technique just described.

Drill Exercises for Section E:

12. Same as problem 11, except that the positions on the checkerboard are to be marked with:

    WM for "white man"
    WK for "white king"
    BM for "black man"
    BK for "black king"
    . . for an empty square

13. The vector arrays WIDTH, HEIGHT, and DRAG, each containing 25 components, are to be printed out in tabular form. Each row of the table is to have 4 columns, each column of field width 20. The first column should contain a value of WIDTH, the second a value of HEIGHT, the third a value of DRAG; the fourth column should contain a message, namely: O.K. if DRAG is less than 0.01, SOSO if DRAG is between 0.01 and 10.0, and BAD! if DRAG exceeds 10.0. Table headings for the four columns should be supplied. A vertical space is to appear after every 5 lines of the table.

F.   Punching Output Cards

In elementary programming, there is little occasion for getting output information in other than printed form. Since the card punch attached to the computer is a particularly slow device (perhaps 2 punched cards per second, compared to perhaps 16 printed lines per second), computer installations generally discourage the use of punched cards as an output medium.

Nonetheless, in more advanced programming, output in card form can be very valuable. The point is that output cards prepared by one programme can be used as input cards for the next programme. Printed output, on the other hand, can not be used as input information with present computers.

Another use of punched card output is for restart of the computation in case of machine failure. In scientific computations, often a great deal of computation is done for a small set of input numbers. Furthermore, it is likely that the computation is in the form of an iterative loop, approximating closer and closer to the final solution. It can be most annoying if, after two hours on the computer, the calculation is terminated by the monitor system because of a machine fault (for example, a failure in the printer!), and we lose everything done during those two hours. In such computations, we should *at least* print out intermediate information every ten minutes or so, thereby enabling us to make a restart of the calculation at a later stage, not having to go back to the very beginning, only to the values of the last printed-out checkpoint. Naturally, it is important to print out *all* the information necessary for such a restart.

However, if the restart information is a bit lengthy, say more than 25 numbers, the preparation of input cards for such a restart can become a serious problem. People make errors in punching cards from printed information! The more numbers that are to be punched, the greater is the chance for errors.

It is therefore good practice to produce such restart information in card form *as well as* in printed-out form. Both forms are required, since cards are easy to feed back into the computer, but are hard to read.

The FORTRAN WRITE statement can be used for punching output cards just as easily as for printing output on the line printer. We merely specify the logical unit number of the output card punch, rather than the logical unit number of the line printer. We shall use the symbolic name NPUNCH for the logical unit number of the output card punch; we refer to Section A of this Chapter for a discussion of these unit numbers.

Although there is little to say about the WRITE statement, we must say several things about the associated FORMAT statement for card output.

First of all, a card has 80 columns, whereas a printed line has at least 120 positions within the line. Thus an output "card image record" must be no more than 80 characters long, otherwise we exceed the maximum permissible record length.

Second, there is nothing in card output corresponding to the printer control character in line printing. The 80 characters in the card image record appear finally as 80 columns punched on the output card.

For both these reasons, FORMAT statements suitable for printed output are rarely, if ever, suitable for punched card output.

There are other considerations in card output: for one, we shall have little occasion for "reading" the cards ourselves - the cards are to be read by a machine, not by humans. Hence there is no advantage whatever in leaving a lot of blank spaces (empty columns) on the card. On the contrary, information should be tightly packed, thereby decreasing the number of cards which must be punched.

In spite of this desire, however, some columns on the card must be set aside for *identification of the card* itself. Cards can easily get out of order, with disastrous results for the restart. It is conventional to use columns 73-80 (the last 8 columns of the card) for identification. The identification consists of a name, followed by a sequence number of the card. The beginning 72 columns can be used, for example, for 6 real numbers in format code 1P6E12.5. This particular format code gives 6 significant figures (the scale factor 1P makes the figure before the decimal point significant, rather than an insignificant zero) for each number, and specifies the minimum field width (12) for this purpose; we need one field position for the sign, 7 for the mantissa (this includes the decimal point), and 4 for the exponent code (say, E-16), 12 field positions in all.

When such a set of cards is read in again, for a restart, the identification of every input card should be checked before the information on this card is accepted. Beginners may think such precautions excessive. The experienced programmer smiles a wry smile, and inserts even more precautions.

If the cards get out of order, the fact that the sequence number of each card is coded onto the card is most useful: there are devices, called "card sorters", which enable us to put such a set of cards into proper order mechanically. (*)

(*)   The sorting is done column by column, one column at a time. The inexperienced user is likely to start with the column corresponding to the most significant digit of the sequence number, then sort separate bundles of cards for the next digit of the sequence number, and so on. The preferred procedure is to sort the entire deck of cards, first by the *least* significant digit of the sequence number, then by the digit to the left of that, and so on until we finally reach the most significant digit of the sequence number. After such a sort, the cards are in correct sequence.

As an illustration, we give, below, a short programme segment for punching a set of 6 output cards, each containing one row of a 6-by-6 matrix called ATRIX. The name ATRIX appears as identification, plus a three-figure sequence number (two of these figures are wasted for such a short set of cards).

```
      DIMENSION ATRIX(6,6)
      DATA NREAD,NPRINT,NPUNCH/5,6,7/
      .
      WRITE (NPUNCH, 1984) ((ATRIX(I,J),J=1,6),I,I=1,6)
 1984 FORMAT (1P6E12.5,'ATRIX',I3)
```

Note that there is no "printer control character". The characters ATRIX appear in columns 73 to 77, inclusive, and the sequence number I of the card (which is also the row number of the row stored on the card) appears in columns 78-80.

In addition to the FORTRAN IV WRITE statement, G-level FORTRAN IV and WATFOR also recognize an earlier FORTRAN statement for punching output cards, namely:

DEF: PUNCH *n,List* is equivalent to WRITE (NPUNCH,*n*) *List* where NPUNCH is the logical unit number assigned to the card punch.

Just as for printing output, the more general statement WRITE is preferred.

Drill Exercises for Section F:

14. Restart information for a certain long job consists of the following items: the integers I,J,K, each of them between 1 and 999; the double precision real numbers DA,DB, and DC, and a double precision real matrix DMAT, dimension 15-by-15. Write a programme segment which will punch that information onto cards in efficient form, whenever I is divisible by 5. The cards are to carry the identification characters SCR, followed by the value of I, followed by a 2-digit card sequence number. The identification information is to appear in columns 73-80 of the card.

15. Arrange to punch out a single card which specifies the present position of the checkerboard at move number NMOVE of game number NGAME. The first 64 columns of the card contain coded characters, namely 1 for a black king, 2 for a black man, 3 for an empty square, 4 for a white man, and 5 for a white king. These symbols are to appear in row-by-row sequence on the checkerboard. The checkerboard position is described by the matrix KB described in Chapter XIII, problem 7. The values of NGAME and NMOVE are to appear in columns 65 through 72, both as four-digit integers. Columns 73 through 80 are to contain the characters CHECK followed by the value of KARDNO. The value is to be increased by 1 after each output operation.

G.   Reading Input Data under FORMAT Control

While FORMAT control has some significant advantages over "free" I/O in input operations, there is less advantage in FORMAT controlled *input.* The usual format-controlled input is from cards fed into the card reader.(*) Each card is one "input record", of maximum record length equal to 80 (80 columns on each card).

DEF: The form of the format-controlled FORTRAN input statement is

READ (n,m) *List*

where n is a positive integer constant, or integer variable name, denoting the logical unit number of the I/O unit to be employed; m is the statement number of the FORMAT statement controlling the input; and *List* is a list of variable identifier names, separated by commas, specifying the memory locations which are to be loaded with the information read from I/O unit number n.

As an example of format-controlled input of numbers, let us suppose that we wish to input numerical data for the variables A, I, and J, from one input card, and we wish to load the vector array B, with 15 components, from cards each of which contains five components of the vector.

The programme segment might read:

```
      DIMENSION B(15)
      DATA NREAD,NPRINT,NPUNCH/5,6,7/
        .
      READ (NREAD,2187) A,I,J,B
2187  FORMAT (F10.6,2I5/(5F10.6))
        .
```

Let us describe the input cards implied by this. The value of A *must* be in F-format, and *must* appear in the first 10 columns of the first card read. The only leeway FORTRAN allows us is that the decimal point *need not* appear in the position implied by F10.6 as an output format code (i.e., it need not be in column 4 of the card); the actual position of the decimal point within this field of width 10 overrides the format code information. The value of the integer I *must* appear, right-adjusted, in the next field, i.e., in columns 11-15 of the card. The value of the integer J *must* appear, again right-adjusted, in the following field, i.e., in columns 16-20 of the card. The slash denotes an "end-of-record", that is, the end of one card for card input. Thus, the first five components of the vector B appear on the following card, in format code 5F10.6; the first number must appear in columns 1-10, the next in columns 11-20, ..., the fifth in columns 41-50. No "spill-over" is allowed. The numbers need not be right-adjusted within their fields, nor need the actual decimal point be in the fourth position within the field (as would be implied by the same format code in output).

It should be noted that we have adopted a "standard convention" of a field width of 5 for integers, a field width of 10 for floating point numbers in F-format. In view of the rigidity of the "field" allocations in format-controlled input, some definite convention must be adopted by the programmer, to minimize wrongly punched input cards.

For data cards to be punched by the programmer, F-format is preferable to E- or D-format. It is usually possible to arrange it so that input numbers are of a magnitude accessible to F-format (i.*e*., neither extremely large nor extremely small); this is desirable in any case, to make the input

(*) In most modern machine installations, the cards read by the card reader are transferred to an "input tape", and actual reading at execution time is done from that tape, rather than straight from the card reader. This is of no concern to the FORTRAN programmer.

cards easier to read and check for errors. For example, lengths which would come out to be very small numbers if expressed in centimetres (say, atomic distances) should appear on data cards in some other units (e.g., Angstrom units, 10^{-8} cm) so that the data numbers are of a reasonable magnitude; conversion from these other units to the units actually used in the calculation (say, to centimetres), should then be carried out immediately following the READ operation and the echo check (echo check *first* however!).

Format-controlled input is not recommended for data cards to be punched by people, rather than by the machine. The person making up the data cards needs to watch the input fields like a hawk. Most errors are "fatal" errors, i.e., result in reading in a completely erroneous set of numbers, or in complete termination of execution on the grounds of a "format error", i.e., a card with punchings badly inconsistent with the specifications in the FORMAT statement. Furthermore, the same information must be read, in the same sequence, and from the same fields on each card, every time the READ statement is executed. For example, the READ statement given before is incapable of resetting just one component of the vector B; rather, each time we come to this READ statement in the execution phase, we must input exactly four separate data cards; the first card must contain the values of A, I, and J in the correct fields, the second card must contain B(1) through B(5), the third card must contain B(6) through B(10), and the fourth card must contain B(11) through B(15). There is no flexibility whatever. Even though B(3) may be the only component of B which has altered, we must still read in all these four cards.

On the other hand, format-controlled input is most suitable for data cards punched out by the machine itself in a previous run, as explained in Section F. The machine is not likely to get columns wrong on the card. Some checks are necessary, nonetheless: the cards might be out of order, cards might be missing, and occasionally the machine might mispunch a card altogether.

In addition to the FORTRAN IV READ statement, G-level FORTRAN IV and WATFOR also recognize an earlier FORTRAN version of the format-controlled READ statement, namely:

DEF: READ *n,List* is equivalent to READ (NREAD,*n*) *List*

where NREAD is the logical unit number assigned to the card reader. Just as for printing output and punching output cards, the more general FORTRAN IV version of the READ statement is to be preferred.

Drill Exercises for Section G:

16. A matrix W has 5 rows and 8 columns. Data cards contain two numbers each, which are to be read into columns 5 and 6, one pair for each row.

17. The matrix array WHACKO has dimension 15-by-19. Data cards appearing 7 to a card are to be stored into the even-numbered rows of WHACKO, row by row.

18. Write a SUBROUTINE READER, with appropriate arguments, to read in the data cards punched out in problem 14. Card identification and card sequence numbers should be checked, with an error termination message containing the card image of the bad card.

19. Same for the data cards of problem 15, except no check on KARDNO since there is only one card to be read. Print out the message RESTART OF GAME NO ... AT MOVE NO ..., followed by a line THE PRESENT POSITION and the position itself (Note: remember problem 12!)

H. Reading Input Data Under NAMELIST Control

A more flexible, and preferable, form of data input is provided by the NAMELIST option of FORTRAN. In this option, the I/O list is declared separately as a NAMELIST, with a list identifier name. The READ statement then contains the list identifier name in place of the statement number of a FORMAT statement, and allows flexible input of some or all items of the NAMELIST.

DEF: The NAMELIST declaration statement has the form

NAMELIST /*Name*/*List*

where *Name* is an identifier name (at most 6 alphameric characters, the first of which is alphabetic) assigned to the I/O list *List*, which consists of variable or array identifier names, separated by commas. Neither a dummy variable name nor a dummy array name may appear in the list; nor may "implied DO loops" be used in such a list.

As an example, let us construct a NAMELIST for the quantities read in the example of the preceding section. The declaration statement could be

DIMENSION B(15)
NAMELIST/BABEL/A,I,J,B

This assigns the identifier name BABEL to this NAMELIST.

DEF: To read items belonging to a NAMELIST of name *Name,* the FORTRAN statement is

READ (*n,Name*)

where *n* is a positive integer constant, or integer variable name, denoting the logical unit number of the I/O unit to be employed. The input data read as a result of execution of this FORTRAN command must be prepared in a special form, for which the rules appear below.

As an example, the READ statement would now be:

READ (NREAD,BABEL)

and would cause read-in of a set of input cards from the card reader, during the execution phase.

The input cards themselves are the really new thing. The *first column of every card is ignored.* The beginning of the data group is denoted by the appearance of the symbol & (ampersand) in column 2 of the first card of the group, followed immediately by the namelist name *Name*. This prevents us from reading in cards for the wrong namelist. In our example, the first input card must have the characters &BABEL in columns 2-7 inclusive, to identify this group of input cards as belonging to the namelist of name BABEL. Later columns of that card, as well as later input cards of the group, contain a number of 'data items'. Each 'data item' is of one of two forms:

1. *Variable name* = FORTRAN constant

2. *Array name* = a set of FORTRAN constants, separated by commas

For example, the first (and in this case, only) card of our input group might contain:

```
&BABEL   J=64,   B(3)=23.17,    &END
```

This data card tells the machine to store the number 64 into location J, and to store the number 23.17 into location B(3). The &END declares that this is the end of this particular input group. Thus, we have read only *two* numbers from the *List* with list identifier name BABEL. Furthermore, each number read in is preceded immediately by the name of the memory location into which it is stored. This is tremendously important in minimizing errors.

Furthermore, unlike format-controlled input, there are no fixed fields on the card. Blanks are simply ignored.

A comma appears after every list item on the card; a comma after the last item is optional.

The data items on the input card need not appear in the same order as the list items in the NAMELIST declaration. For example, another group of input cards for the same READ statement might be:

```
&BABEL   J=32,   A=14.89,
B=23.16,54.75,6*1.5,7*0.0,   I=4,   &END
```

Here we have two input cards, each starting with punches in column 2. We read data in the sequence J,A,B,I, even though the namelist declaration contained the list in the sequence A,I,J,B. This is permitted, since each data item is in any case preceded by the variable or array identifier.

This example also illustrates the use of an array name, B, rather than a variable name, such as B(3) in the preceding example. If we specify an array name, we must provide enough constants to fill the whole array (in our present case, 15 constants). To make this easier, the use of a duplication factor is allowed, i.e., '6*1.5,' above is equivalent to '1.5,1.5,1.5,1.5,1.5,1.5,' on the data card, and similarly for 7*0.0.

Constants used in these data items may be integer, real, complex, logical, or literal FORTRAN constants, as described in Chapter VIII. If the constants are of type LOGICAL, the letter T may be used in place of .TRUE., and the letter F in place of .FALSE.

Compared to "free" input of numbers, NAMELIST-controlled input has the advantage that the numbers need not correspond, in precise sequence, to the list items of the I/O list in the READ statement. That is, the "free" input statement READ,A,I,J,B differs from the NAMELIST-controlled input in that exactly 18 numbers must be read from the input cards, the first to be stored into location A, the second into location I, the third into location J, the fourth into location B(1), ..., and the eighteenth into location B(15). No variation is permitted in either the number of items input, or in their sequence.

As against this, the namelist name and the symbols &END must appear in input cards for NAMELIST-controlled input; and each data item input must specify its "destination" within core memory explicitly, by a variable name or array name. This, however, is really an advantage, since it has the effect of decreasing the number of errors.

If input cards without namelist name, or with the wrong namelist name, are encountered in the input card stream, they are simply ignored. We "flush through" card after card, until we reach a card with the correct namelist identification, starting with a & in column 2.

The namelist names are unique, i.e., no two namelists may have the same name. But the variable names appearing within these namelists are not unique; that is, one and the same variable (or array) name may appear in several namelists; also, if the programme uses EQUIVALENCE statements, synonyms may appear within the same namelist, or within different namelists, quite freely. However, the actual names used on the input cards must be as in the NAMELIST declaration. That is, we must *not* use a data item K=67 in our example above, *even if* the equivalence statement

EQUIVALENCE (I,K)

appears within the programme. We can use the data item K=67 if and only if the variable name K itself appears in the NAMELIST declaration statement. Synonyms are not good enough in this context.

Several list names and associated I/O lists may be declared in a single NAMELIST declaration, e.g.,

NAMELIST/BABEL/A,I,J,B,/FUSION/I,J,K,MESS,KRISIS

Note that the variable names I and J belong to *both* lists. It is cleaner coding to use a new NAMELIST declaration statement for every such list.

DEF: Besides NAMELIST-controlled input, FORTRAN also allows NAMELIST-controlled *output*. The FORTRAN statement is

WRITE (*n,Name*)

where *n* is the logical unit number of the I/O device, and *Name* is a previously declared namelist name.

With NAMELIST-controlled output, the *entire list* is output each time the WRITE statement is encountered. The heading information *&Name* appears on one line (or on one card), each non-array item appears on a line (or card) to itself, and the termination message &END appears on the last line (or card). For most purposes, this form of output cannot be recommended: if simplicity of programming is the main consideration, "free" output is a better choice; if easily readable appearance of the output is desired, format-controlled output allows much more flexibility of layout and messages.

However, there are two special uses for which NAMELIST-controlled output is preferred:

1. For punching of cards which are to be read by the machine, in a later run, with a NAMELIST-controlled READ statement.

2. For debugging output, as explained in Chapter XVI. For such output, "free" output is not explicit enough, and format-controlled output is too much of a nuisance to organize.

Drill Exercises for Section H:

20. Declare a NAMELIST of name GETIT containing the variables I,J,K,A,B,C, the vector array VEC with dimension 20, and the matrix array GEE with dimension 35-by-35. Write down a suitable set of input cards which will result in making J and K equal to 5, B equal to 0, clear the entire array VEC to zero, and set all of GEE equal to 1.0, except for GEE(1,1) which is to equal 3.5, and GEE(35,35) which is to equal 6.8. Also write down the input statement.

219

21. Declare a suitable NAMELIST and give the output statement necessary to have the machine punch up a set of output cards containing the values of J, VEC(1), and GEE(2,3), in a form suitable for later input under control of the input statement of exercise 20. (Assume the WRITE and READ statements appear in *different* subprogrammes).

I. Use of the A-FORMAT for Character Manipulation

Although FORTRAN is a language designed specifically for numerical computations, not for manipulation of strings of characters, the A-FORMAT code provides a facility for character manipulation within FORTRAN. By use of the A-format, we can read character strings into the machine from input cards, and we can use ordinary FORTRAN commands to perform manipulations on these character strings. Since FORTRAN, in its WATFOR implementation, requires characters in A-format to be stored in 4-byte words, we could store up to four characters to each word. However, this would be awkward for character manipulation, since then we would need to "unpack" a word in order to get at any one character of the string. Hence, if character manipulation is intended, characters should be stored one to a word, even though this wastes 3 bytes of the 4 in the word.

To illustrate the type of character manipulation possible within FORTRAN, we shall write a programme segment to read data cards containing unsigned integer constants; the integers may appear anywhere on a card (not in specific "fields"); any symbol other than a decimal digit (in particular, blanks and/or commas) is taken to be a "separator", that is, we assume the integer constant is finished as soon as we reach a symbol on the card, other than a decimal digit; the end of the input is signalled by the appearance of the symbol string &END on a card. The integers are to be stored in vector array INTS, and the number actually input into that array is to be stored into location KOUNT. Up to 500 integers can be stored; we must test for KOUNT.GE.500, however, and print out a message when this happens. The end of a card is always a "separator", i.e., integers are not allowed to "spill over" from one card to the next.

In spite of these simple specifications, the FORTRAN programme is surprisingly involved. This reflects the fact that FORTRAN is not oriented toward character manipulation; but it also illustrates that character manipulation *can* be done; for modest amounts of character manipulation, it pays to learn how to do it in FORTRAN, rather than learning an entirely different language just for that purpose!

In order to test whether a given character CHAR is one of the decimal digits, we reserve a vector array DIGIT of dimension 10, with DIGIT(1)='0', DIGIT(2)='1', ..., DIGIT(10)='9'. Note that DIGIT(2) is the *character* '1', not the *number* 1. Nonetheless, with this method of storage, there is a simple relation between the character DIGIT(K) and the numerical digit which it represents: the numerical digit equals K-1.

In order to reconstruct an integer N from a sequence of decimal digits, consider the set of characters '476'. In our search, we look at the first character and find that it equals DIGIT (5). We therefore put

N=5-1=4

We then look at the next character and find that it is DIGIT(8). The numerical value of this digit is 8-1=7, and therefore we advance N by means of the assignment statement:

$$N=10*N+7$$

which stores the number 10*4+7=47 into location N. Finally, we look at the last character and find that it equals DIGIT(7). The numerical value of this digit is 6, and we advance N by

$$N=10*N+6$$

which produces the number 10*47+6=476 and stores it into location N. We have thus succeeded in constructing the *number* 476 from the *string of characters* '476'.

The general procedure is easily seen from this special example: we search through the vector array DIGIT(K), from K=1 to K=10, comparing each member of the array with the character CHAR under study. If CHAR.EQ.DIGIT(K), we execute the command

$$N=10*N+K-1$$

thereby updating the number N. This works for all digits except the very first digit read. And it works even for that very first digit provided that storage location N was cleared to zero to start with.

We need to "remember" whether we are in the process of constructing an integer, or whether we are just searching through the character string for the first decimal digit of an integer. We shall use a "switch" in location KSW to tell us that. KSW=1 shall mean that we are just searching; KSW=2 shall mean that we are in the process of reconstructing an integer.

Besides searching for possible integers, we must also search for the character string &END. We shall do this by searching first for the symbol &; if we find such a symbol, we test whether there is enough room on the card image for three more symbols following it. If there is, i.e., if the & appears no later than column 77 of the card, then we search through the next three characters for the characters E, N, and D, respectively. We do this efficiently by defining a vector array FINIS of dimension 3, with FINIS(1)='E', FINIS(2)='N', and FINIS(3)='D'.

With these preliminary remarks out of the way, we now show the flow diagram and the code based on this flow diagram. To keep the complexity of the flow diagram within bounds, we do not show all operations in full detail: the FORTRAN code contains the details, after all.

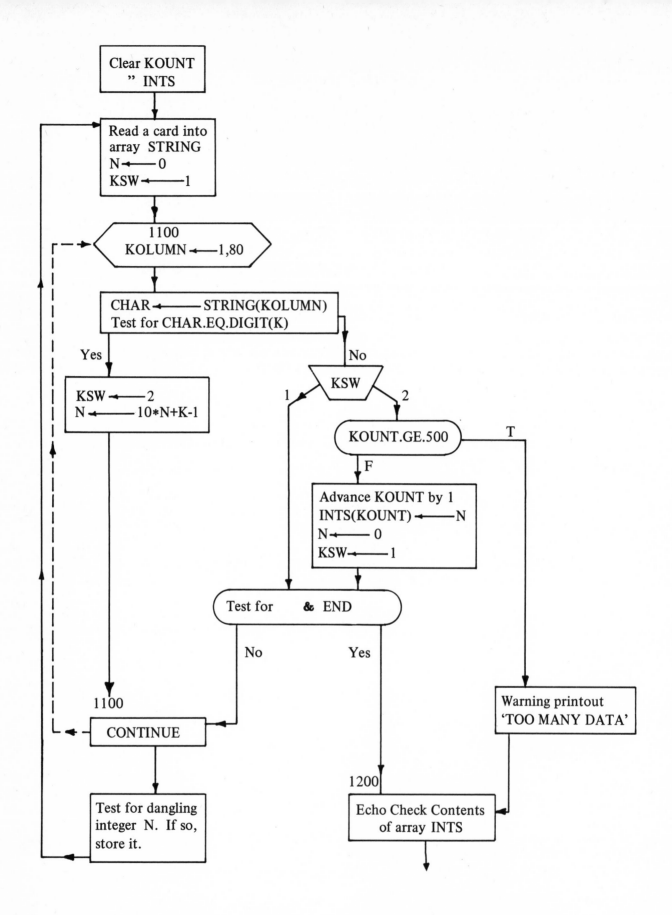

```
C          PROGRAMME TO READ INTEGERS IN FREE FORMAT
C          INTEGERS MAY BE IN ANY COLUMN OF THE CARD, BUT MUST BE
C              ON ONE CARD
C          END OF INPUT SIGNALLED BY THE CHARACTERS '&END'
C          INTEGERS STORED INTO ARRAY INTS, COUNT KEPT IN KOUNT
C          ALLOW UP TO 500 INTEGERS, TEST FOR EXCESS
C
           DIMENSION INTS(500),DIGIT(10),STRING(80),FINIS(3)
           DATA NREAD,NPRINT,NPUNCH/5,6,7/
           DATA AMPSND/'&'/,FINIS/'E','N','D'/
           DATA DIGIT/'0','1','2','3','4','5','6','7','8','9'/
C
 1000 KOUNT=0
C          NOW CLEAR THE ARRAY INTS
           DO 1010 I=1,500
           INTS(I)=0
 1010 CONTINUE
C          READ ONE DATA CARD INTO ARRAY STRING
 1020 READ (NREAD,1021)STRING
 1021 FORMAT (80A1)
C          NOTE A1, NOT A4. A4 WOULD STORE 4 CHARACTERS INTO ONE WORD.
C          WE WANT TO STORE ONE CHARACTER PER WORD.
C
C          NOW ANALYZE THE CARD IMAGE, COLUMN BY COLUMN
C          KSW=1 MEANS NOT A DECIMAL DIGIT, KSW=2 MEANS A DECIMAL
C            DIGIT
C
           N=0
           KSW=1
           DO 1100 KOLUMN=1,80
           CHAR=STRING(KOLUMN)
C          NOW TEST WHETHER CHAR IS A DECIMAL DIGIT
           DO 1030 K=1,10
           IF(CHAR.EQ.DIGIT(K)) GO TO 1050
C          NOTE THE LOGICAL IF. WHY WOULD THE ARITHMETIC IF FAIL??
 1030 CONTINUE
C          IF WE GET HERE, THE CHARACTER WAS NOT A DIGIT
           GO TO (1040,1035),KSW
C          THE BRANCH BELOW IS FOR THE CASE THAT WE HAVE JUST
C              FINISHED AN INTEGER
 1035 IF(KOUNT.GE.500) GO TO 1180
           KOUNT=KOUNT+1
           INTS(KOUNT)=N
           N=0
           KSW=1
C          BRANCHES REJOIN. TEST WHETHER CHAR IS AN '&'
 1040 IF(CHAR.NE.AMPSND) GO TO 1100
C          IT IS AN AMPERSAND &. IS IT THE START OF A &END?
           IF(KOLUMN.GT.77) GO TO 1100
C          COLUMN NUMBER IS .LE.77 TEST FOR END
           DO 1045 J=1,3
           KOL=KOLUMN+J
           IF(STRING(KOL).NE.FINIS(J)) GO TO 1100
```

```
      1045 CONTINUE
C          IF WE GET TO THIS POINT, IT WAS INDEED &END
           GO TO 1200
C
C          WE ARE SENT TO THIS POINT ON DISCOVERY OF DIGIT NUMBER K
      1050 KSW=2
           N=10*N+K-1
      1100 CONTINUE
C          THIS ENDS THE LOOP ON KOLUMN=1,80
C          IF WE GET HERE, WE HAVE FINISHED A CARD.
C          WERE WE IN THE PROCESS OF CONVERTING AN INTEGER?
           GO TO (1020,1120),KSW
C          YES, WE WERE. STORE THAT NUMBER. FIRST TEST KOUNT.
      1120 IF(KOUNT.GE.500) GO TO 1180
           KOUNT=KOUNT+1
           INTS(KOUNT)=N
C          NO NEED TO RESET N AND KSW. IT WILL BE DONE AFTER 1020
           GO TO 1020
C          THIS READS THE NEXT CARD
C
C          WE GET TO THIS POINT IF THERE WERE TOO MANY DATA
      1180 WRITE (NPRINT,1181) N
      1181 FORMAT (' TOO MANY DATA. LAST NUMBER READ WAS',I12/)
C
C          THIS IS THE ECHO CHECK, TO TELL US WHAT HAS BEEN STORED
C          THE ORDER NUMBER IN ARRAY INTS PRECEDES EACH ARRAY
C            ELEMENT
C
      1200 WRITE (NPRINT,1201) (K,INTS(K),K=1,KOUNT)
      1201 FORMAT (' THE INTEGERS IN ARRAY INTS ARE'//(' ',5(I10,I12,',')))
             .
             .
             .
             .
```

Study of the flow diagram together with the FORTRAN code should show what we have done, and why. Note that we have moved STRING(KOLUMN), the character being tested, into a location called CHAR, for easier manipulation. In such storage-to-storage transfers, it is essential that the "source" and "destination" locations have the same *type* within the FORTRAN conventions. Otherwise, FORTRAN organizes an implied conversion, which is the last thing we want for character transfers.

Since the characters are stored in memory locations assigned type REAL*4 by the pre-defined type convention, an arithmetic IF statement can *not* be used to test for equality of two characters: If the set of 32 bits in such a storage location is handled as if it were a floating point number, and subtracted from the contents of a similar storage location, it is too easy to get floating point overflow during the arithmetic operation. A logical IF statement does not carry out arithmetic operations, just a straight bit-by-bit comparison.

Programming Exercises for Section I:

1. Write SUBROUTINE PLOT(XVEC, YVEC, XMIN, XMAX, YMIN, YMAX, K) which does the following: DIMENSION XVEC(K), YVEC(K) are vectors containing the x- and y-coordinates, respectively, of K points to be plotted on a "graph" produced by the printer. XMIN and XMAX are the boundaries of the x-axis on the graph, and these boundaries are divided into 100 intervals (100 print positions). YMIN and YMAX are the boundaries on the y-axis, and this segment is divided into 50 intervals (50 effective lines on the page). We skip to a new page at the start of the graph - plotting operation. We then go down line by line, putting the symbol * into a line if and only if there is some point X(I), Y(I) whose coordinates are within the little rectangle defined by this print position. If you want to be diligent about it, also supply printed numbers for various values of y on the y-axis, to the left of the graph, and printed numbers underneath the x-axis for values of x. Also, keep track of points which fall outside the graph, and print out their coordinates at the bottom of the page, or on the next page.

2. Modify the subroutine of problem 1 so that it does the following: if both XMIN and XMAX are zero, these quantities are computed by another SUBROUTINE SCALE(UVEC,UMIN,UMAX,K) so that all the x-coordinates fall within the range of the x-axis on the graph, and furthermore the lowest x on the graph and the highest x on the graph are integers; similarly, if both YMIN and YMAX are zero on entry, values of YMIN and YMAX are computed so that all the given y-coordinates fall on the graph, and lowest and highest values of y on the graph are integers.

Drill Exercises for Section I:

22. A set of input cards has English sentences punched, one sentence to a card. Commas may appear in a sentence, but no other punctuation, nor are hyphens used. The last card of the set has &END in columns 2 through 5. Write a programme segment which counts the number of times the sentence KILROY WAS HERE appears (note: you may assume every sentence starts in column 2 of a card, and words are separated by single blanks).

23. Write a programme segment which punches out copies of the input cards, but with all duplicate cards deleted. Assume that there are no more than 500 different sentences on the cards. The input cards themselves are as in exercise 22.

J. FORMAT Information Stored in Arrays, and Read In at Execution Time

There are several ways in which FORMAT information can be altered at execution time.

The first and simplest way is to issue a READ statement with an associated FORMAT containing character strings. For example, we may use the statements

```
      DATA NREAD,NPRINT,NPUNCH/5,6,7/

      READ (NREAD,1200)
 1200 FORMAT ('
     1     ')
```

The FORMAT statement simply contains a blank character string of 60 characters, enclosed in apostrophes. The 60 characters are all blanks; 57 of them are on the first card of the FORMAT statement, the remaining 3 on the continuation card. More characters can be used if desired, up to 80.

225

When execution time comes, and this particular statement is reached, the next "record" on logical unit number NREAD is examined; in practice, one "record" is one card in the card reader. The first 60 characters in that record are extracted (i.e., the characters in columns 1 through 60, inclusive, of this input card), and are placed into the space between the apostrophes in the FORMAT statement; the rest of the input record (the input card) is simply skipped. Note that it is not necessary to leave the space between apostrophes blank, as we have done above: it doesn't matter, since all that information gets overwritten anyway.

If the same programme contains, at a later point, the statement

WRITE (NPRINT,1200)

the line which is output on the line printer contains the message read in by the READ statement above. This feature is quite useful for identifying information for a given computer run; for example, the input card for the READ statement might contain the character string, in columns 1 through 60 inclusive:

```
1JOHN SMITH. TEST RUN ON DATA FROM FLIGHT 312, TIME-SMOOTHED
```

The result of the WRITE command is then a skip to a new page on the printer (printer control character= 1) and the message

```
JOHN SMITH. TEST RUN ON DATA FROM FLIGHT 312, TIME-SMOOTHED
```

appearing on the first line of that new page

For production running of large programmes, such identifying information for each run is *indispensable*. It is hard to believe, but only too true, how quickly one can lose track of the masses of paper spit out by a computer, so that one no longer knows which numbers refer to what input, and why.

It is not necessary, but it is desirable, to restrict the FORMAT statement purely to a character string, and the corresponding READ statement to have a blank I/O list, as above. If an I/O list is specified in a READ statement, and if the FORMAT statement contains character strings within it, then the right number of characters are read into these character strings, and the numbers are read, converted, and stored into the locations specified in the I/O list, in the sequence specified in the FORMAT statement. However, it is too easy to make mistakes in preparing the input cards with this form of input. It is safer to do one thing at a time. With all I/O operations, "better safe than sorry" is the right motto.

The simple method above is restricted to character strings within the FORMAT statement. To allow more flexibility, it is also possible to use a vector array to store FORMAT information. In that case, the identifier name of this array replaces the statement number m in the standard forms

READ (n,m) *List* and WRITE (n,m) *List*

For example, we may assign the array name FMT to our FORMAT information, and use a DATA statement to initialize this information, as follows:

```
DIMENSION FMT(18)
DATA NREAD,NPRINT,NPUNCH/5,6,7/
  .
DATA FMT/44H(' MERRILY WE ROLL ALONG'//' I,J,K=', 3I12) /
WRITE (NPRINT,FMT) I,J,K
  .
```

This set of statements is equivalent to

```
DATA NREAD,NPRINT,NPUNCH/5,6,7/
  .
WRITE (NPRINT,1200) I,J,K
1200 FORMAT (' MERRILY WE ROLL ALONG'//' I,J,K=', 3I12)
```

Note that the array FMT is a vector array (this is *necessary* in this case, even though the "vector" may be declared to have only one component). Since FMT is of pre-defined type REAL*4, each component of the vector is four bytes long, and can thus be used to store 4 characters. With declared dimension 18 for FMT, we can accommodate up to 4x18 = 72 characters in this array. The characters must *include* the outer parentheses of the equivalent FORMAT statement, but must *exclude* the characters 'FORMAT'. In the DATA statement above, the 44H introduces a character string of length 44 characters.

In this form, we have gained nothing by declaring an array FMT rather than using a statement number, e.g., 1200, for the equivalent FORMAT statement.

However, we can now issue a READ command, using the A-format code, to *load* the array FMT at execution time, thus:

```
      READ (NREAD,1100) FMT
1100    FORMAT (18A4)
```

When this command is reached at execution time, 18 groups of four characters each are read from an input card, and stored into locations FMT(1), FMT(2), ..., FMT(18), respectively. The statement

WRITE (NPRINT,FMT) *List*

encountered after this READ statement, uses the newly stored information in array FMT as the format information for the writing operation. Naturally, care must be taken that the nature of the *List* in the WRITE statement is consistent with the format information at present contained in array FMT.

The input card for the READ statement above should contain the outer parentheses of the desired new FORMAT, plus everything in between. It should *not* contain apostrophes outside these parentheses.

Drill Exercise for Section J.

24. Input data for least squares analysis are: ITEMS, the number of items, KREE, the degree of the polynomial which is to be fitted to the data items, and the values of X(I) and Y(I) for I=1,2,..., ITEMS. One laboratory prepares these data as follows: the first card has ITEMS and

KREE, in fields of 5 each; subsequent cards each contain a value of X and a value of Y, in fields of width 10. A second laboratory "packs" the input card more tightly: The first card contains, in addition to ITEMS and KREE, 6 decimal numbers in fields of width 10 each, which are to become X(1),Y(1),X(2),Y(2),X(3), and Y(3) in the machine. All subsequent cards have seven numbers on them (except perhaps the last card of the set), which are alternatively values of X and of Y. Write a programme segment which will enable either set of data to be read into the machine. Describe the first card to be read by your programme.

K. The 'END=' and 'ERR=' Options

The FORTRAN language includes options in READ commands, allowing the programmer (rather than the system) to take recovery action on the occurrence of certain types of trouble.

DEF: The general form of the FORTRAN READ command is

READ (a,b,END=c,ERR=d) *list*

where: a is an unsigned integer constant or an integer variable, giving the logical unit number of the I/O unit to be used

b is either a statement number or the array name of the FORMAT statement describing the data being read, *or* a NAMELIST name

c is the statement number to which transfer is made upon encountering the end of the data set.

d is the statement number to which transfer is made upon entering an error condition in data transfer

list is an I/O list, consisting of variable or array names, separated by commas.

Compared to the things discussed earlier in this Chapter, the new features are the END=c and ERR=d options.

Under normal monitor system control, execution is terminated on encountering the end of the data set in a READ statement (for example, no more data cards in the card reader, even though the programme calls for more data to be read). If we use the option END=2300, for example, then an end-of-data condition results in transfer of control to statement number 2300 of *our* programme; we are no longer thrown off the machine.

The manual goes on to say: "No indication is given as to the number of items in the list (if any) read before encountering the end of the data set." Thus, we are not thrown off the machine, *but* neither are we given sufficient information to initiate a meaningful recovery action! It is to be hoped that this particular FORTRAN language specification will be improved in the future. At present, the only thing to do, in most programmes, is to initiate a "holding" rather than a "recovery" action: we proceed, at statement number *c,* to print out messages telling us what happened, and to output data for a later restart of the programme, either onto punched cards (see Section F) or onto a private tape (see Section L).

Similarly, if we include the option ERR=9000, for example, the occurrence of a reading error will no longer throw us off the machine; rather, control will be transferred to statement number 9000 of *our* programme; as against this, "no indication is given as to which input record or records are in error; only that an error occurred".

The END=c and ERR=d parts of the READ command are options, one or both of which may be omitted. Furthermore, if both are included, they can appear in either order, i.e., either as shown, or with ERR=d preceding END=c.

At present, these options exist only for READ, not for WRITE. It is hoped that such options will be improved, and made more widely available, in the future.

L. Reading and Writing Magnetic Tapes

So far, we have been discussing I/O operations with *external* devices such as line printers, card readers, and card punches. In addition to these, modern computers have *internal* units, such as magnetic tapes, magnetic drums, and magnetic disks, with other types of devices likely in the future.

These "internal" devices are in essence "auxiliary memory", ways for the machine to remember, and use in later computations, large masses of information which can not be kept in core memory, either because all of core memory is not big enough, or because the whole job cannot be done in one run on the machine, and hence intermediate results must be retained by the programmer from one run to the next. Even if the whole job can be done in one machine run, but that machine run is a long one, it is most desirable to load up an internal memory device, such as a tape, with full restart information, every ten minutes or so. If there is a machine failure during the run, not all is lost; the only machine time lost is the (less than 10 minutes) time since the last "core dump"; as soon as the fault on the machine has been taken care of, we can restart the run by loading up core memory from this dump tape, and off we go as if nothing had happened.

In commercial data processing, tapes and disks are used to keep large "files", for example, a file of all customers of an insurance company, with their policies, premium rates, bonus rates, expiry dates, etc. Such files are "created", in the first place, by making up a set of input cards, reading these cards into the machine core memory, and then transferring from core memory to tape, a few cards at a time.

In scientific computing, information on tape is not usually created in this way. If large masses of data are to be stored on tape, for example, radar signals for an entire rocket flight, this is done directly by attaching a magnetic tape drive to the radar set, and storing the incoming radar signals onto tape in "real time". Once such a tape has been created, the computer analysis of the data can take much more time than the actual rocket flight; that is, only the creation of the tape file is done in "real time", not its use. On the other hand, there are also cases in which the computing itself must be done in "real time", for example, if the computer is to analyze the flight data while the flight is still going on, to produce information for guidance of the rocket, this information to be transmitted to the rocket in flight. In such "real time" applications, naturally speed of computation is the main consideration.

Another way in which large masses of information are stored onto tapes in scientific computing is in large iterative computations. For example, suppose we wish to study the air flow around an airplane wing in supersonic flight. The differential equations are complicated, and are usually solved by some iterative technique. We start with a very crude approximation, based on some simple formula which can be programmed, and we improve this approximation step by step. If the three-dimensional space around the wing is replaced, for numerical purposes, by a discrete set of "net points", we need a huge number of such net points in order to get reasonable accuracy. We must store the results at all these net points, from one approximation, in order to generate, from these stored results, the values in the next approximation. Core memory is entirely inadequate for such storage, so we are forced to go out onto tape.

Magnetic tapes attached to computers are similar to those used in tape recorders except that computer tapes are wider, more sturdy, and much longer. A typical computer tape is ½ inch wide and 2400 feet long. Information is stored in magnetic spots across the tape, 9 bits of information in a line running across the width of the tape; 8 of these 9 bits contain one byte of information, and the ninth bit is a check bit. These bytes of information are stored very close to each other along the length of the tape, at densities ranging from 200 to 800 bytes per inch length of the tape. Thus, a 2400 foot tape can be used to store between 5 and 90 million bytes of information, compared to core memories ranging from 0.1 to 1 million bytes.

Reels of tape can be mounted and dismounted, labelled, and stored away as "private tapes" for future use. Furthermore, there is a plastic ring which fits into a groove on the posterior surface of the tape reel. If this plastic ring is taken out, and the tape reel without the ring is mounted on a tape drive, then the "writing head" in the tape drive is disabled: the tape can be read, but it is impossible to write onto it. Such a tape is said to be "file-protected". This is a very useful precaution, since it prevents fools (for example, oneself) destroying the valuable information on the tape by a mistaken WRITE command.

Information on a tape is segmented into "records", with "record gaps" between adjacent records on the tape. Groups of records are combined into "files", with a "tape mark" or "end of file mark", at the end of each file.

The speed with which a tape can be read and written depends on the tape drive used, as does the density of information on the tape. Typical speeds are 20000 to 90000 bytes per second. This is slower than core-to-core transfers (close to a million bytes per second), but very impressive compared to the speed of reading a punched card (not much more than 1000 bytes per second).

However, the high speed of transfer of information to and from tape can be misleading. The records appear on the tape, one after the other. It is most time-consuming to have to space forward, or back, across a large number of records, to get to the record you really want. The tape must unwind from one reel, and wind onto another reel. This takes time, and meanwhile the computer just waits. With bad programming, these waiting times can be enormous, up to minutes, and the high speed of information transfer becomes merely a bad joke. Careful planning is essential here: one must plan, from the start, to write the information onto the tape in such a sequence that the records can be used afterwards in the same sequence. It may be necessary to "rewind" the tape to the very beginning for each new use (say, at the beginning of each iteration), but rewinding is a fast operation, comparatively speaking, and it is possible to issue a REWIND order well before the rewound tape has to be used; the REWIND order merely *starts* the rewinding; control then returns to the computer programme, and further computations can be carried out while the rewinding is in progress.(*)

DEF: In FORTRAN, the simplest way to write one record onto a tape is to issue a FORMAT-free WRITE command

WRITE (*n*) *list*

(*) A warning is in order: two REWIND commands in quick succession *will* stop the machine from further computing: the second REWIND command finds the tape drive "busy" (with the first rewind), and this causes the computer to wait.

where n is the logical unit number assigned to a data set on a tape, and *list* is a standard I/O list.
n may be an unsigned integer constant, or an integer variable name. The effect of this command is to
write one "record"(*) onto this data set, in so-called "internal form", that is, each byte on the tape
is the image of one byte of information in core, taken from the *list*.

DEF: To read a record written in this way, we issue the FORMAT-free command

READ (n) *list*

If the *list* corresponds in size (number of bytes) to the record written on the tape at that point, we
read the record and store the information into the memory locations specified in the *list*. If the
number of bytes in the list exceeds the record size, an I/O error condition is diagnosed, and programme execution stops. If the number of bytes in the list is less than the length of the record, we
read the required number of bytes from the record, and space the tape forward to the beginning of
the next record. In particular, if the list is omitted altogether, the command READ (n) spaces the
data set n forward by one record.

DEF: In order to space data set number n backwards by one record, the FORTRAN command is
BACKSPACE n.

DEF: To bring data set number n back to the beginning of the very first record, the FORTRAN
command is REWIND n.

DEF: After writing the last record of a data set, the end of the data set is marked onto the medium
(e.g., tape) by the FORTRAN command

END FILE n

This command results in an end-of-file mark (tape mark) to be written onto the tape. The monitor
system sees to it that a programmer, in reading the same tape later on, cannot simply read forward
across such an end-of-file mark.

We have been a bit vague in these definitions, talking sometimes about a "tape", sometimes about
a "data set", with logical unit number n. The commands just defined apply to "data sets", which may
or may not be stored on a tape. One physical tape may be used to store several data sets; other
devices (e.g., magnetic disks) may be used to store data sets.

Clearly, the monitor system must be told, in some way, that FORTRAN logical unit number
n, whatever it is, corresponds to a data set of a certain type, on a particular device (e.g., on a tape),
with a particular label, etc. This is done by means of a "system control card", which is read by the
monitor system, not by the FORTRAN compiler. These system control cards are, at present, a
major bugbear to programmers (not just beginning programmers, either!). They are not part of a
standard language, such as FORTRAN. Rather, system control cards differ from manufacturer to
manufacturer, from machine to machine, from installation to installation. Do not, repeat not, attempt
to write your own system control cards. Every computer installation provides this service, by necess-

(*)   FORTRAN-written "logical records" do not correspond precisely to actual "physical records" on the tape.
One logical record may be broken up, by the FORTRAN system, into a number of physical records on the
tape. The FORTRAN programmer need not worry about this distinction. To the programmer, a "record" on
tape is one FORTRAN logical record, never mind about physical records.

ity, since the amount of detail required to write system control cards is an intolerable burden on the ordinary user, more intolerable because of the lack of standardization. It is to be hoped that there will be, in the future, a standardization of systems control cards similar to the already existing standardization of compiler source languages, such as FORTRAN; that is, not complete uniformity (there are "dialects" of FORTRAN), but something other than the existing tower of Babel.

When writing and reading records from tape, it is most desirable to put identifying information, such as the *record number* of the record in question, into each such record. The *list* in the WRITE and READ commands above should, therefore, contain a variable NRECRD as its first item; this variable should be increased by one whenever a record is written. When a record is read, the record number read in should be checked against the number the programmer expects to be reading. Since there are usually a large number of similar records on a tape, this precaution is essential to make sure that the information just read into core memory is what we really wanted to read.

FORTRAN tape transfers take longer, and space on the tape is used less efficiently, than with tape transfers coded in assembly language (see Chapter XVII). If speed of transfer and/or total information size is really important, assembly language subroutines for reading and writing tape should be used. Beginning programmers are in no position, however, to write and debug such routines.

Besides records in "internal form", FORTRAN also allows a programmer to write records onto a tape, and read them off again, in "character form", also called "external form" or "BCD form". This second form of information storage on the tape takes more space than the internal form, for the same amount of information. However, "external form" is preferable if the information on tape is to be transferred directly to an external medium (e.g., if we wish to print up the information on the tape, on the line printer).

DEF: In order to write records onto a tape in *external form,* we issue a WRITE command *with* a FORMAT statement number specified:

WRITE (*n,m*) *list*

where *n* is the logical unit number of the data set in question, and *m* is either the statement number of a FORMAT statement or the name of a vector array containing the stored FORMAT statement (see Section J for the latter); *list* is the usual I/O list.

This command is in exactly the same form as writing onto a line printer, or punching cards on a card punch. The only differences are:

1. Logical unit number *n* must be specified by a systems control card to be the tape we want.

2. There is no limitation to the record size of any one record (whereas card image records can be no more than 80 bytes, and printer line images are limited to 120 bytes, or 132 bytes, etc., depending upon the actual line printer used in the installation).

With this form of WRITE command, the information in the FORMAT statement controls the number of records that is written. Each slash within the FORMAT statement marks the end of one record, just as it does for writing onto the printer. The only difference is that, in one case, a "record" means one printed line, whereas here a "record" means one FORTRAN (logical) record on a tape.

DEF: In order to read records in *external form,* the FORTRAN command is

READ (*n,m*) *list*

where *n* is the logical unit number of the data set in question, and *m* is either the statement number of a FORMAT statement, or the name of a vector array containing the stored FORMAT statement; *list* is an I/O list in standard form.

Note: This READ command is exactly the same form as for reading input cards under FORMAT control (see Section G). The number of records so read is controlled by the information in the FORMAT statement, each slash indicating the start of a new record to be read. When reading cards, unit number *n* is the card reader, and the records read must be no more than 80 characters long (80 columns on the card, each record is one card). When reading tape, the records may be of any length, provided that the record length specified does not exceed the length of the record actually on the tape at that point. If the record length specified is less than the length of the record on the tape (in particular, if the *list* is missing altogether, or if there are consecutive slashes in the FORMAT statement), then the tape is spaced forward to the beginning of the next record. If the record length in the READ statement exceeds the length of the record on the tape at that point, an I/O error is diagnosed, and execution of the programme is terminated by the monitor system.

The FORTRAN commands BACKSPACE *n,* REWIND *n,* and END FILE *n* can be used with records written in either internal form or external form. It is not advisable to "mix" these forms on one data set, even if the monitor system allows it. For most scientific uses of magnetic tape, internal form is preferable.

Drill Exercises for Section L:

25. A large programme contains information required for restarting in two COMMON storage areas: the first is labelled INTS and contains 325 integers; the second is labelled FLOATS and contains 15000 floating point numbers of four-byte length. Write a SUBROUTINE SAVER without arguments to do the following: Test sense light 1; if it is off, test the first integer in INTS; if this integer is divisible by 20, dump the two COMMON storage areas onto a tape with logical unit number NTAPE, which is set equal to 13 by a DATA statement. On the other hand, if sense light 1 was on, load the two COMMON storage areas from the tape, and return control to the superior programme with sense light 2 on. Before returning control, print out a message RESTART WAS NECESSARY. PROGRAMME RESTARTED WITH I= ..., where ... is the first integer stored in the COMMON area called INTS.

26. A tape contains coordinates x, y, z of a rocket at successive times, 0.01 seconds apart. The last set of coordinates has z=0.0, indicating that the rocket flight has terminated by the rocket diving into the ocean (sea-level is considered zero). Write a programme to compute the total distance travelled by the rocket. The information on the tape is stored in "internal" form, with the record number NREC and the values of X, Y, Z at one time forming one record.

27. With the same input tape as in exercise 26, write a programme to compute, at the start of each new second, the speed at that moment (that is, the speed during the 0.01 second immediately following the whole second), and to store that information onto another tape, in external form, for possible later print-out.

Programming Exercises for Section L:

3. Given a 700-by-700 matrix on a tape, write a SUBROUTINE subprogramme to produce the square of this matrix on a second tape. Each record contains one whole column of the matrix, preceded by the record number. Try to optimize machine time, if necessary by using additional tapes during the calculation.

4. Same as 3, but the matrix is N-by-N, with N anything up to 1000.

5. Similar to 4, but we want to compute the determinant of the matrix.

M. Reading and Writing Drums and Disks. Direct Access I/O

Computer drums are cylindrical drums, with the curved surface of the cylinder coated with magnetic material. There are a number of "read-write heads" next to each other, each such head capable of reading and writing information onto one "track" on the drum surface. These tracks are in the shape of circles, around the curved surface of the drum, next to each other. A typical time for one complete rotation of the drum is 0.02 seconds, and every bit of information on the drum can be assessed in a time no longer than this (on the average, in half that time). This contrasts with tape access times of up to minutes, if one has to space forward or back over many records.

Drum storage space is generally less than space on a tape; and unlike tapes, drums can not be mounted and dismounted easily; thus it is impossible to have your own private drum, whereas you can have your own private tape. Information on the drum can not usually be retained from one computer run to the next, but rather is used for intermediate information storage (as an extension of core memory) during any one computer run.

Magnetic disks, so-called, are really *sets* of thin, horizontal circular disks, mounted on the same spindle, with magnetic surface coating on the upper and lower surface of each horizontal disk. Read-write heads, mounted on horizontal access arms, are pushed in between each pair of circular disks; these access arms can move in or out, in unison, thereby enabling the read-write heads to access different circular tracks on the magnetic surfaces. Since the heads may have to move to access a particular bit of information on the disk, the access time is longer than for drums, up to several tenths of a second. However, this time can be decreased to typical drum times (a few hundredths of a second) by careful programming, to avoid unnecessary motion of the read-write heads.

Compared to tapes, magnetic disks have much shorter average access times, and allow random access without long times for spacing forward or back. Compared to drums, magnetic disks, at least in their most common form, have the advantage of being demountable, so that it is possible to have one's own private disk, with information stored for later use, just as one can have one's private tape. One word of warning, however: Unlike tapes, present disks do not have a mechanical method of file-protection, i.e., it is impossible to protect the information on a disk by making it "read-only" information. Programming serves as a protection of sorts, but is less certain than taking out the ring from a tape reel.

Transfer of information to and from drums or disks *may* be programmed in the same way as for tapes, i.e., as a sequence of logical records. A set of tracks on a disk may be assigned a "logical unit number" by an appropriate system control card (do not, repeat not, attempt to do this yourself; ask an expert in your installation!). A given physical disk unit may thus contain a number of different FORTRAN logical units.

In such "sequential files", a REWIND command gets us back to the start of the first logical record within the data set on disk, corresponding to FORTRAN logical unit number n. Each READ command gets us forward one logical record and each BACKSPACE command gets us back one logical record. Unlike tape commands, the REWIND is now a "fast" command, executed in at most a few tenths of a second. But spacing forward or backwards over a number of logical records within the data set is still "slow"; we are not really using the disk to best advantage by sequential file programming.

FORTRAN allows writing and reading "random access files" on a disk or drum, as an alternative to "sequential files". Each random access file requires the following information for its definition:

1. The logical unit number n of the unit on which the file is to be found (this refers to a specific set of tracks on a disk, usually, and systems control cards are needed to tell the system, as apart from the FORTRAN compiler, about this logical unit number).

2. The maximum number of logical records which can be written onto this random access file; call this number m.

3. The maximum size of each such record, expressed in various ways, depending upon item (4) below. Call this number r.

4. A control character, call it f, which specifies whether we read and write under FORMAT control. This character may be one of: E, L, U.

    (a) E indicates that we require FORMAT control, as specified by a FORMAT statement for each WRITE or READ command. In this case, r is measured in characters, or bytes (one character corresponds to one byte of information).

    (b) L indicates that data may be written and read in either way, with or without FORMAT control. In this case, the maximum record length r is measured in groups of 4 bytes each.

    (c) U indicates that all the records in this random access file are to be written, and read, in internal form, without FORMAT control. In this case, r is measured in groups of 4 bytes each.

5. A *marker variable name* for this random access file, call it *Marker*. This must be a variable name of type INTEGER*4. At the conclusion of each READ or WRITE operation, the value of this variable equals the record number of the *next* record to which the read-write head points: at the conclusion of a FIND operation, the value of the marker variable equals the record number of the record found. The marker variable tells the programmer just which record he is ready to look at, at any moment.

DEF: To define a FORTRAN random access file, the standard statement is

DEFINE FILE $n(m,r,f,Marker)$

where the parameters are as explained above.

For example, the statement

DEFINE FILE 11(50,100,U,K11)

defines a file on logical unit number 11 (a systems control card is needed to establish logical unit number 11 as a set of tracks on a specific disk); this random access file can contain up to 50 logical records, each of which is up to 400 bytes long (4 times 100, since U means we measure record length in groups of four bytes each); the records are to be written and read in internal (machine) form, not in external (character) form. The READ and WRITE statements for these records must not make reference to FORMAT statements. Finally, the name of the marker variable for this file is K11; that is, memory location K11 in core storage will contain the record number of the next record to which the read-write head points at any moment. It is possible to place memory location K11 into a COMMON area of core memory, thereby making the value of K11 accessible to a number of different sub-programmes. Alternatively, the value of K11 may be used as the actual argument to replace a dummy argument of a sub-programme being invoked by the main programme.

In a large programme, consisting of a main programme and a number of subprogrammes, the DEFINE FILE statement for any one random access file should appear exactly once, for example, in the main programme. The subprogrammes must be given the number of the file (the logical unit number n) and the name of the marker variable, nothing more. This information can be transmitted to subprogrammes either via shared COMMON areas, or by means of argument lists.

The DEFINE FILE statement need not appear in the main programme; it may instead appear in a subprogramme. But wherever it does appear, its appearance must precede, logically, the first executable statement which accesses that file; that is, the first READ or WRITE or FIND statement referring to the file by that logical unit number.

One DEFINE FILE statement can be used to define several random access files; if so, commas must be placed between the sets of defining information for the various files. This practice is not recommended.

DEF: The standard statement for writing onto a random access file *under FORMAT control* is

WRITE $(n'k,j)$ *list*

where

n is the logical unit number on which the file has been defined.

k is an integer constant, or arithmetic expression of integer type, representing the number of the record within this file. Note that an apostrophe ' *must* separate n and k; this is how FORTRAN tells that this is a random access command.

j is either the statement number of a FORMAT statement, or the name of a vector array in which the FORMAT information is stored (see Section J).

list is a standard I/O list.

Under FORMAT control, one or more records may be written, starting with record number k. The number of records written is as defined by the FORMAT statement, each slash indicating the end of one record.

DEF: The standard statement for writing onto a random access file *in internal form* is

WRITE ($n'k$) *list*

where n and k are as above. Exactly one logical record is written onto the file, namely record number k, and this record contains the information specified in the I/O list *list,* in internal form.

DEF: The standard statements for *reading* records from a random access file are as above, with READ replacing WRITE. The number k defines the first record to be read.

It is possible to place the read-write head into position for accessing record number k of logical unit n, *before* the READ or WRITE operation, while the machine is doing useful computing. This can save considerable machine time. The FORTRAN command to do this is:

FIND ($n'k$)

This command initiates the FIND operation. We can then, at a later stage, test the content of the marker variable to see whether we have found the desired record; or we can simply, at that stage, give the READ or WRITE command which we want executed; if the record has not yet been found, the machine then waits until the read-write head is properly positioned. The FIND statement is optional, not mandatory.

Programming Exercises for Section M:

6.   Same as programming exercise 4 after Section L, but use random access techniques rather than sequential file techniques.

7.   Same as programming exercise number 5 (evaluation of the determinant of a large matrix), but using random access techniques.

CHAPTER XVI

PROGRAMME PLANNING AND DEBUGGING

The beginner imagines that writing a programme is all there is to computer programming. This is incredibly far from the truth. Experienced programmers find that the time needed to write the FORTRAN code is a small fraction of the total time required, perhaps one third of the total time, or even less. All the rest of the time is spent in *programme planning* and in *debugging*.

Programme planning involves a number of things: What numerical technique should be used? What are the storage space requirements for each numerical technique available; how much machine time will be required? Will we need to use auxiliary storage? And if so, should we use tapes, or disks? Is random access essential, or can we programme the job so that sequential access does not lose us time?

How should the programme be broken up into subprogrammes? (Only very inexperienced programmers write single, long programmes; the more experienced the programmer, the more and shorter subprogrammes he uses).

Shall we need to go to double precision arithmetic? In all subprogrammes, or only in some? If so, which subprogrammes require double precision working?

Will the number of subprogrammes be high enough to warrant the use of COMMON storage? If so, how many different labelled COMMON blocks shall we need? Shall we require BLOCK DATA initialization subprogrammes for some of these labelled COMMON blocks?

What data shall we need to read in? What checking can we do on these data to guard against incorrectly punched data cards? What action should we take when incorrect data are encountered?

Will the computation take enough machine time to warrant intermediate output of restart information, in case of machine failure during the run? If so, can this information be put onto output cards, or is there so much of it that a dump tape will be required?

What checks, against numerical troubles such as loss of significant figures, must we built into the computation? What should we do in case of trouble? Should we guard against machine malfunctions, such as I/O errors, which throw the run off the machine? What is the best method to "beat the monitor system" in such cases?

What output do we want? In what form do we want the output (printed paper, punched cards, magnetic tape, disk)?

All these questions, and many more, are asked by the experienced programmer when planning a programme. The answers to these questions determine how the programme is "laid out", and all these questions should be answered, after careful thought, *before* the very first FORTRAN command is written.

But the most important question, and the one requiring most planning, still has not been asked. It is this: HOW DO WE DEBUG THE CODE?

All programmes, without exception, are crawling with "bugs". The experienced programmer knows this, and plans the debugging operation as an integral part of planning the programme itself. Generally, debugging a programme takes longer, and is incomparably more difficult, than writing the FORTRAN code for the programme.

The simplest species of "bug" is a straightforward language error which can be, and is, picked up by the compiler. Such errors are flagged in the output, and were discussed in Chapter VI. These must be corrected, and the new card deck submitted for further machine running, until no more language errors are flagged by the compiler.

It would be foolhardy, however, to take it for granted that the programme is *right* at this moment. Far from it! Now we must deal with the really vicious bugs. Remember, the machine obeys the instructions you have given it. It does precisely what you *tell* it to do, not what you *want* it to do.

The absence of compiler-flagged statements means that your programme talks grammatically correct FORTRAN. But it is entirely possible to talk grammatically correct English and still say complete nonsense. The same is true of grammatically correct FORTRAN.

The first essential in debugging is to *echo-check every number read into the machine.* The word "echo-check" refers to immediate output of all input numbers. Every READ statement for reading external data should be followed *immediately* by a WRITE statement, for output of these numbers onto the printer. One should *not* use the same FORMAT for reading and echo-checking, for two reasons:

1. Reading of input data is best done by using a NAMELIST, nor a FORMAT-controlled READ statement.

2. In any case, all output, including the echo-check, should contain messages telling what the output numbers mean. While NAMELIST-controlled output does do this, it is generally a bit awkward for "normal", as opposed to "debugging", output.

Immediate echo-checking is essential to know what numbers the machine actually read into the storage positions involved; this is not at all the same as the numbers the programmer *thinks* he gave the machine to read! The echo-checking must be done immediately, rather than later on, for two reasons:

1. The computation might never get as far as that later point; thus, delayed echo-checking may leave you ignorant of the very input numbers which caused failure of the programme.

2. The contents of the storage locations used for input of numbers might alter during execution of the programme, either deliberately or as the result of a bug; in that case, delayed echo-checking

gives you misleading information, namely the values of these numbers at the point you do the echo-check, rather that at the time the numbers were actually read in.

The second essential in debugging is *clean coding*. Tricky, fancy codes are extraordinarily difficult to debug. Remembers, you are looking for errors which you made yourself, so you have a strong psychological bias against "seeing" the error. This is bad enough. No need to make your job any harder than it need be, by being fancy about your coding. Draw up a clean flow chart, and follow it when writing the code. Put plenty of *comments* into the code. Comments do not affect the working of the programme; but they have an enormous effect on the debugging process, by reminding you just what you meant to do at each stage. A particularly useful device is to put a large number of comment cards at the beginning of each programme and subprogramme. These comments should answer the following questions:

1. What is this programme designed to do?

2. What input data, if any, does it need? In what FORMAT? From which input medium? In which sequence? What conditions must the input data satisfy? What happens if these conditions are violated? If this is a subprogramme, how is the failure "told" to the superior programme? If by sense light, which sense light?

3. What subprogrammes, if any, does this programme require? What do these subprogrammes do, what are their dummy arguments and entry sequences?

4. What COMMON storage, if any, is used by this programme? What, if anything, does this programme *assume* to be in COMMON areas?

5. What tapes, disks, etc., are used by this programme? What FORTRAN logical unit numbers are assigned to them? What are the system control cards which should appear elsewhere in the card deck, to go along with these assignments? What, if anything, does this programme *assume* to be stored onto these data sets, before it starts? What, if anything, does this programme *write* onto these data sets? In what form?

6. What forms of failure can occur during execution of this programme or subprogramme? What action is taken in each such case?

7. What debugging output has been programmed in? Where are these statements?

All these questions should be answered clearly and precisely in the comment cards appearing at the beginning of each programme or subprogramme. This may mean a hundred comment cards, or more, for a fairly short subprogramme. A beginner thinks: "But I know all that, anyway. I wrote the programme. Why do I need to remind myself?" The experienced programmer knows that he is bound to forget half these things, long before the programme is finally debugged; so he spends the time to make up all these comment cards, the more the merrier. He knows from bitter experience that such comments are worth their weight in gold later on.

The third essential in debugging, even more important than echo-checking and clean coding, is *extensive debugging output,* that is, output of numbers which appear during the course of the calculation but are not themselves final results worth printing out in a production run. This is the "debugging output" mentioned as item (7) in the list just above.

For example, suppose we wish to debug the Simpson's rule FUNCTION subprogramme of Chapter XIV, Section D. The only result we really want finally, is the function value set into location SIMPSN, and returned to the superior programme by execution of the RETURN statement at the end. But we shall never be able to debug this subprogramme if this is all the information available to us on the printed output. All we get is a crazy number which means nothing, and has no relation to the number we want to get.(*) That is to be expected, naturally. But what do we do now? What information do we have to tell us *why* the output number is crazy? The answer is: we have *no* meaningful information, and there is *nothing* we can do! We have failed to include debugging output, and we are now paying the price for this cardinal sin in computing.

All right, so let us go back, and *plan our debugging* from the start. Given that the programme has bugs in it (never was there a safer assumption!), what information do we require to locate the bugs? First of all, the parameter values: no use trying to check what happened, without knowing what actual argument values were used in the subprogramme. So, right after the first executable statement of the subprogramme (statement number 1000, see Section D of Chapter XIV), we arrange to output the values of A, B, and N, the dummy arguments. For this purpose NAMELIST-controlled output is ideally suited; we insert the statements:

```
C********DEBUGGING
      NAMELIST/SI1000/AP,BP,NP
      DATA NPRINT/6/
      AP=A
      BP=B
      NP=N
      WRITE (NPRINT,SI1000)
C********END DEBUGGING
```

Explanation:

1. The comment cards are used to "flag" the debugging statements within the programme. The statements are arranged in such a way that these comments, and everything between them, can be eliminated later on, without affecting the remainder of the programme.

2. The namelist name SI1000 is constructed as follows: SI is a reminder of the subprogramme name, SIMPSN; and the '1000' tells us that this particular debugging print-out occurred adjacent to statement number 1000 of subprogramme SIMPSN.

3. FORTRAN does not allow output of dummy argument values under NAMELIST control. We therefore define ordinary storage locations with names AP, BP, and NP, and set their contents equal to A, B, and N, respectively, for the NAMELIST printout. This has the slightly unfortunate result that the printout gives AP=1.23, say, rather than A=1.23. But if we follow a standard convention of using a letter P at the end (for 'primed'), this is no real trouble.

4. The NAMELIST-controlled output is in the following form:

(*) The programme given in Chapter XIV, Section D, is actually debugged already. But it didn't work in its first form, either! No programme ever does.

241

```
&SI1000
AP     =-0.1230000E-01
BP     =-0.4370000E-02
NP     =              16
&END
```

The first line identifies the source of the output, the subsequent lines tell what the numbers mean, and the final line tells us that this particular debugging output has come to an end. This is precisely what we want, and is the reason for preferring NAMELIST-controlled output for debugging.(*)

All right, so now we *know* what numbers the programme was operating on. What else do we need to know? Well, there is a loop, on the loop variable I, for accumulation of EVNSUM and ODDSUM, each of which are sums of FUN(X) at the appropriate points. We had better check how these sums are accumulated. There is no need to check for *every* value of I in the loop from I=1 to I=MMIN1; let us check at the first few values, the last few values, and perhaps one value in the interior of the loop. Note that the loop ends at statement 1200 CONTINUE, and that all paths in the loop lead to statement number 1150, just before it. So we insert our debugging printout between statements 1150 and 1200, as follows:

```
C********DEBUGGING
      NAMELIST/SI1150/I,J,X,FUNP,EVNSUM,ODDSUM
      IF((I.LT.4).OR.(I.EQ.MMIN1/2).OR.(I.GT.MMIN1-4)) GO TO 1160
      GO TO 1200
 1160 FUNP=FUN(X)
      WRITE (NPRINT,SI1150)
C********END DEBUGGING
```

This will cause print-out of the loop variable I, the "switch" J, the values of X, FUN(X), EVNSUM, and ODDSUM, for I=1,2,3, for I=7 (assuming N=16, as we know from the previous print-out), and for I=13, 14, and 15. Note that we again had to set a printable variable FUNP, since FUN(X) involves the dummy argument name FUN, which is the name of a FUNCTION subroutine.

Is this enough? By no means. We still need to check what the subprogramme returns at the end. So, just before the RETURN statement, statement 1300, we insert

```
C***** DEBUGGING
      NAMELIST/SI1200/H,ENDSUM,EVNSUM,ODDSUM,VALUE
      VALUE=SIMPSN
      WRITE (NPRINT,SI1200)
C***** END DEBUGGING
```

Well, that is probably enough as a start. It will give us at least a fighting chance to find out what is wrong with FUNCTION SIMPSN, and to fix it.

(*)   In some FORTRAN systems, there are special "DEBUG packages" written for this purpose. In our opinion, NAMELIST-controlled output does all that needs to be done, usually.

Also, let us consider what function FUN(X) we should use here. For debugging purposes, it pays to choose FUN(X) so that we know the correct answer. For example, we know that Simpson's rule should give the exact value of the integral for an integrand which is a polynomial of degree no more than 3. So we define:

```
      FUNCTION FUN(X)
C     SIMPLE POLYNOMIAL FOR DEBUGGING THE SIMPSON'S RULE
C        PROGRAMME
C     THE INTEGRAL OF THIS, FROM X=1 TO X=3, IS 116.
      FUN=1.+2.*X+3.*X**2+4.*X**3
      RETURN
      END
```

Note the comments. Note also that it does not pay to insert a debugging statement into this sub-programme, since the value of FUN(X) is printed out, along with X, at namelist SI1150.

The last essential in debugging is *full recomputation,* by hand or electric desk-machine, of several special cases. Every intermediate number should be checked by hand, as well as the final result.

You may ask, why use an electronic computer at all, if we have to check the beast every step of the way? The answer is that, once a programme has been fully debugged, this programme can be used over and over again for many sets of input data. Also, "full checking" does not mean that we check every time around every loop. For example, we organized debugging print-out for the loop in FUNCTION SIMPSN, not for every value of I, but only for a few values at the beginning, a few values at the end, and one value in the middle. We need to check only those values by hand; other values should then be all right.(*)

Since a numerical integration rule, such as Simpson's rule, gives only an approximation in general, not the precise value, it will be necessary to make sure that the discrepancy between the exact result and the machine result is consistent with the error estimate for Simpson's rule. If the discrepancy is too large, it is certain to be the result of a coding bug.

If all tests have succeeded, all numbers have been checked, and exhaustive recomputations have been completed, then one can no longer say with certainty that the programme is still full of bugs. It is merely very likely.

(*)   Sometimes these turn out to be "famous last words".

CHAPTER XVII

MACHINE LANGUAGE AND ASSEMBLY LANGUAGE

A. Introduction

After learning the FORTRAN language, many people still feel a desire to know "what really goes on inside the machine". It is the purpose of this Chapter to answer this question, to the extent that it can be answered in a few pages. At the same time, we shall be able to indicate what the differences are between three types of language, to wit:

1. Compiler source language, e.g., FORTRAN

2. Assembly language

3. Basic machine language.

In order to discuss assembly language and basic machine language, it is necessary to pick a particular computer as an example. This could be a purely imaginary machine, invented purely for this one purpose. We prefer, for a number of reasons, to pick an actual machine, namely the IBM 360 series of computers. Naturally, machine language and assembly language on other computers are different. But the basic ideas are the same, and once the basic ideas have been understood, learning the particular language is fairly simple.

Before getting into the discussion of machine language, we review quickly some of the material of Chapter VII, concerning the organization of storage space in the computer. The unit of core storage is the "byte", a group of 8 adjacent binary digits. These are represented by 8 tiny magnetic rings, each of which can be magnetized clockwise or counterclockwise, indicating a binary digit of 0 or 1, respectively. It is not convenient to write down 8 adjacent binary digits all the time. Therefore, we combine four binary digits at a time into one *hexadecimal digit*. For example, the 8 binary digits 01101001 are written as two adjacent groups of 4 binary digits: 0110 1001; the first group of four binary digits is represented by the single hexadecimal digit *6*, the second by the single hexadecimal digit *9*, so that the 8 binary digits are represented by two hexadecimal digits: *69*. We shall follow the practice, in this Chapter, of italicizing hexadecimal digits, to distinguish them from decimal or binary digits. The hexadecimal digits are: *0, 1, 2, 3, 4, 5, 6, 7, 8, 9, A, B, C, D, E, F.* The hexadecimal digit *F* stands for the group of four binary digits 1111. The hexadecimal digit *F* must not be confused with the alphabetic character F.

Each byte of core storage in the machine has its own address. These addresses are 24-bit numbers (1 bit = 1 binary digit), or in hexadecimal form, numbers with 6 hexadecimal digits. The possible addresses range from 0 to $2^{24}-1 = 16^6-1 = 16,777,215$, thus allowing addressing of up to 16 million bytes of core storage. Most actual machines do not have that much core storage, usual sizes ranging from 0.1 million to 1 million bytes. If we specify the address of a non-existent byte of core, the machine recognizes the mistake and interrupts the calculation with an "addressing exception".

B. Basic Components of the Machine

The basic components of a computing machine are:

1. Core storage

2. Registers

3. Arithmetic Unit

4. Control Unit

5. I/O Units

Core storage has been discussed already. The *registers* are special storage locations, with particularly fast operation times. In the IBM 360 there are 16 *general purpose registers,* numbered hexadecimally *0, 1, ..., F*; each of these registers can be used to store 32 binary digits, or 4 bytes, of information. There are also 4 *floating point registers,* with hexadecimal numbers *0, 2, 4, and 6,* respectively. Each of these can be used to store 64 binary digits, or 8 bytes, of information.

The *arithmetic unit* is the part of the machine which actually performs calculations. The registers are attached directly to the arithmetic unit. In an addition of two integers, at least one of the integers must be stored in a general purpose register before the addition takes place. As a result of the addition, the content of this register is replaced by the value of the sum. Thus, to add two integers, two operations are necessary: first, one of the integers must be loaded into a general purpose register, from core storage; then, the addition is performed by the arithmetic unit. The sum now appears in that general purpose register. If we want to store away this sum for later use, we need yet a third operation: the content of this register must be stored into a conventional location in core memory.(*) If the numbers to be added are floating point numbers, not integers, the process is similar, except that the floating point registers are used, not the general purpose registers.

The *control unit* deciphers the machine instructions stored in core memory, and organizes the execution of each instruction by whatever other unit is appropriate, e.g., by the arithmetic unit or by one of the I/O units.

The instructions are themselves stored in core memory. In principle, though not in usual practice, the instructions can be "loaded into core" by punching up a set of appropriate punched cards, putting them into the card reader attached to the machine, and then pressing a button on the machine saying "load". We shall assume that this has been done, and that the instructions sit somewhere in core memory already.

The control unit keeps track of the address, in core, of the next instruction to be obeyed. For "ordinary" instructions, this next instruction address is advanced by the appropriate amount as each

(*) A transfer from core storage to a register is called "loading" the register; a transfer from register to core storage is called "storing" the content of the register into core.

instruction is executed, so the control unit goes through the stored instruction one by one. When a "jump" instruction (similar to GO TO in the FORTRAN language) is encountered, the control unit alters the next instruction address to coincide with the address in core memory specified by that jump instruction, so that the next instruction obeyed is taken from that new region of core memory.

We shall not discuss *I/O units* in this Chapter. The physical I/O units are the line printer, the card reader, the card punch, tape drives, disk drives, etc., and their associated electronic circuitry. But the programming of the operation of these devices is impossible for the ordinary programmer, who is forced to make use of standard systems programmes for this purpose.

C.   Some Machine Instructions in Basic Machine Language

To illustrate basic machine language, we shall now give a few machine instructions as they actually appear in the core memory of the machine. We shall assume that the instructions have already been loaded into core memory, i.e., we are not concerned with the "initial programme loading" phase of the operation.

Before discussing the instructions themselves, we first state how core memory is addressed within an instruction.(*) The actual address is a 24-bit binary number, which could be expressed by means of 6 hexadecimal digits. This is not the way addresses are actually specified within machine instructions. Rather, each address is expressed as a *sum* of two hexadecimal numbers:

$a = b + d$

b = the last 24 bits stored in a general register, called the *base register*

d = the last 12 bits (last 3 hexadecimal digits) of the instruction

This last number, d, is called the "displacement" from the base address, whereas b is called the "base address". Since d is a 12-bit number, the displacements range from 0 to $2^{12}-1 = 4095$. Most subprogrammes are shorter than that.

Within the instruction itself, we specify the displacement directly; but the base address is not specified as such; rather, we specify the number of the *base register*, a single hexadecimal digit. It is conventional to use general register number F for this purpose. Then the base address, b, is obtained by looking into that register, and this base address b is added to the displacement d to give the actual address a.

For example, if the last four hexadecimal digits of the instruction are *F013*, then the F tells us to look for our base address in register number F, and *013* is the value of the displacement. Let us suppose that register number F contains the number *00000A17* at this moment. Then the actual address computation goes as follows:

base address	$b = 000A17$	or,	in decimal form,	10×16^2	+	1×16	+	7	=	2583
displacement	$d = \quad 013$	"	" " "			1×16	+	3	=	19
actual address	$a = 000A2A$	"	" " "	10×16^2	+	2×16	+	10	=	2602

This address computation is organized by the control unit of the machine: the control unit first sees that it must look in register number F, drags out the last 6 hexadecimal digits (the last 24 binary

(*)   We simplify the situation here, by assuming that a certain feature, called the "index register", is not used. We shall not use it in our example, in Section D.

246

digits) from that register, and then calls on the arithmetic unit to perform the addition $b+d$.

The advantage of this method of address specification is that it makes the programmes *relocatable* in core memory. The base address b specifies the address in memory where the *first* meaningful command of the programme is stored; the displacements d are then *relative to this point*. If we wish to load the programme into a different part of core memory, we can do so freely: all that is required is to make sure that the base register is loaded correctly with the new base address. By contrast, if addresses were specified directly as 24-bit numbers, all addresses within a subprogramme would have to be redone in order to relocate the subprogramme.

Now let us show some actual machine orders, in machine form. We shall use register F as our base register, and we shall indicate the displacement digits (3 hexadecimal digits) by three dots.

The *load* instruction has the form $58R0F...$, where 58 is the "operation code" (saying that this is a load instruction), R is the hexadecimal number of the register which is to be loaded, 0 implies that we are not using the indexing feature, F specifies that register F is the base register, and the dots are three hexadecimal digits specifying the displacement. The address a computed in the way given above is the address in core of the number to be loaded into register number R. The number in core is a four-byte number; the address a is the address of the first of these four bytes. a must be divisible by 4, otherwise the instruction is considered invalid.

The *store* instruction has the form $50R0F...$ where 50 is the operation code for a "store" instruction, R is the hexadecimal number of the register containing the number to be stored, and the address a of the destination in core is computed in the usual way. This is the address of the first of four bytes of core memory. This address a must be divisible by 4, otherwise the instruction is considered invalid.

The *add* instruction (fixed point) has the form $5AR0F...$, where $5A$ is the operation code for "fixed point addition"; one of the summands is taken from register number R, the other summand is taken from core memory at an address a computed in standard fashion. As a result of this instruction, the value of the sum appears in register R.

The *unconditional jump* instruction has the form $47F0F...$, where 47 is the operation code for "jump", the first F indicates that the jump is unconditional, 0 implies we are not using the indexing feature, the second F says that the base register is register number F, and the dots are the displacement. The address a is computed in usual fashion. The effect of this instruction is that the "next instruction address" within the control unit is set equal to a. Thus, the next instruction obeyed by the machine is the instruction stored at address a in core memory.

The *jump on zero* instruction has the form $4780F...$, where the digit 8 indicates that the jump is a conditional jump, with a particular condition. If this instruction appears in a code, immediately after an *add* instruction, the jump occurs if and only if the value of the sum was zero. If the sum differed from zero, the control unit merely proceeds to the next instruction in normal sequence, as if nothing had happened.

The last machine instruction which we shall need is *branch and link*. It has the form $05RS$, where R and S are two hexadecimal digits. When the control unit encounters this instruction, it does the following:

1. The core address of the *next* instruction is placed in register number R

2. If $S=0$, this next instruction is obeyed. If S differs from 0, a jump occurs to the address stored in general register number S.

This instruction has two main uses:

(i) In order to "invoke" a subprogramme, we load the entry address of that subprogramme into register number S, and execute *05RS*. The effect is that general register number R contains the *return address* for the subprogramme.

(ii) In order to *set a base register*, we execute the instruction *05R0*, where R is the number of the register we wish to use as a base register. R is then loaded with the address of the immediately following order, which is the first meaningful order of the programme, and corresponds to zero displacement. If register F is to be the base register, then we execute the command *05F0* just before the first meaningful order of the programme.

These are all the instructions we shall require for the little "programme" of Section D. Needless to say, the actual variety of machine instructions is very much larger, and there are many things which we have omitted altogether. The full set of machine instructions for the IBM 360 is given in the manual "Principles of Operations", in coded form.

D. A Short Programme Segment in Basic Machine Language

Let us suppose that a FORTRAN programme starts with the statements:

```
      DATA M,N/5,28/
1000  IF((M+N).EQ.0) GO TO 1010
      M=M+N
1010  ...
```

where the dots indicate the next instruction. Let us see what we need to do to code this in basic machine language.

First, we must decide which general register to use as a base register for the programme. It is usual to employ register number F for this purpose, and we shall do so. To make sure that the programme is properly "relocatable", we must set this base register, by a branch and link instruction *05F0*, the very first thing we do.

Second, we shall need a register for carrying out the addition (at least one of the two numbers must be in a register, remember). We shall use register number *1* for that purpose.

Third, we must assign storage locations to the variables M and N, and we must initialize the contents of these locations to the decimal integers 5 and 28, respectively. Since we must work in machine language, this means the machine numbers *00000005* and *0000001C*, respectively. We shall put the storage spaces for M and N just before the next instruction, FORTRAN statement number 1010, in memory. (This is *not* what FORTRAN does: it puts storage locations for variables used in the programme, at the very end of the programme instructions, i.e., after the last machine instruction of the programme).

We now set out, in tabular form, the things which we wish to do, and as much of the machine

248

language instructions as we can supply at this stage: since we do not know, as yet, what the addresses are, we shall leave the "displacement" digits blank for the time being, to be filled in later.

Displacement from base address	Instruction code of instruction	Length of instruction (in bytes)	Meaning of the instruction
	05F0	2	Set the base register F
000	5810F...	4	Load M into register 1
004	5A10F...	4	Add N to this
008	4780F...	4	Branch on zero to statement 1010
00C	5010F...	4	Otherwise, store register 1 into M
010	47F0F...	4	Unconditional jump to statement no. 1010
014	00000005	4	Location for M, set to 5
018	0000001C	4	Location for N, set to 28
01C	...	...	Statement number 1010 here

Having gone this far, we can now fill in the missing displacement digits, to supply the correct addresses in each case. For example, the address which should appear in the *add* instruction, instruction code *5A*, is the address of the variable N. Looking at the table, we see that N is stored at a point displaced *018* bytes from the base address. Thus the displacement digits for this *add* instruction should be *018,* and the whole instruction has the machine code *5A10F018.*

Using the same reasoning for all the other instructions, the completed code reads:

05F0 5810F014 5A10F018 4780F01C 5010F014 47F0F01C 00000005 0000001C...

This is how this code would appear in machine memory, one instruction after the other. If we ask for a "hexadecimal dump" of what is in the machine, this is how the print-out would look. In this form, the code is "relocatable", i.e., it may appear anywhere in core memory and still will execute correctly; all that is required is that the first instruction obeyed by the machine should be the instruction *05F0* of this sequence. This sets the base register correctly, and everything afterwards is automatic.

Notice that this code is *not* what would be compiled by the FORTRAN compiler. The store instruction *5010F014,* makes use of the fact that the quantity we wish to store, namely the sum M+N, is at this moment contained in general register number *1,* and hence need not be recomputed. The FORTRAN compiler is not that clever; it compiles one statement at a time, and does not make use of what happened in earlier statements. Thus, FORTRAN will compile the statement M=M+N of our little programme as three machine instructions: *load* M into register *1, add* the value of N to this, and *store* the contents of register *1* into the location reserved for M. The first two of these three instructions are redundant.

This sort of inefficiency is inevitable in the translation process, if the translation is carried out by a machine. What a human programmer can do almost automatically, may be very difficult to describe to the machine in terms the machine can understand. Even if the FORTRAN compiler could be written in such a way as to carry out such "optimization" of the object programme, it is not certain that one would gain very much by it: the compilation process itself would then take much longer, and we may lose on time of compilation more than we gain by efficiency of the object programme. This would certainly be true in the compilation of student exercises: the gain in execution time would come nowhere near the loss in compilation time.

E. Assembly Language

There are a number of very awkward features of a machine language programme.

1. We must remember the operation codes of all the instructions, in hexadecimal form, e.g., *05* for *branch and link, 58* for *load*, etc. It would be nice to have *mnemonic operation codes*, e.g., BALR for branch and link to a register, L for load, etc.

2. The figuring out of addresses, particularly in hexadecimal form, is a major nuisance. We would like to be able to define *symbolic addresses*, e.g., use the letter M for the location of the variable M, the character string S1000 for statement number 1000 of the FORTRAN programme, and so on. Let the machine do the bookkeeping!

3. Since some one general register will be used as the base register in a number of instructions, we would like to be able to specify this once and for all, without having to write it in again, for every new instruction.

4. The instructions should appear in "readable" form, not as a sequence of hexadecimal digits which must be "decoded" step by step. In particular, we would like to be able to add *comments* to each instruction. Comments are of major help in a FORTRAN programme. They are *absolutely indispensable* in a machine language or assembly language programme.

Assembly language satisfies the above requirements. The instructions are written, in assembly language, one instruction to a line (which is then punched up on a single card). The operation code appears in mnemonic form:

Operation Code in Machine Language	Meaning of Command	Mnemonic Operation Code in Assembly Language
05	Branch and Link (register)	BALR
58	Load	L
5A	Add (fixed point)	A
478	Branch on zero	BZ
50	Store	ST
47F	Branch (unconditional)	B
	"Define a Constant"	DC

The last of these is *not* a machine instruction, rather it is an instruction to the *assembly programme* which looks at assembly language statements and translates them into machine code. The instruction

M   DC   F'5' says the following to the assembly programme: "This memory location is to be assigned the symbolic name M. A constant value is to be stored into this memory location. This constant is a full-word (4 byte) integer (this is the meaning of the code letter F), and its value equals the decimal integer 5." This is the way in which assembly language satisfies the second of our requirements above.

To satisfy the third requirement, there is an assembly language instruction

USING *, 15

which tells the assembly programme to use register 15 (decimal form; register number F in machine language) henceforth, until further notice, as the base register for the programme.

The layout of an assembly language card is as follows:

1. Symbolic addresses, if any, appear starting in column 1 of the card; names for such symbolic addresses must be no more than 8 alphameric characters, the first of which is an alphabetic character. An asterisk in column 1 indicates a comment card.

2. Operation codes, in mnemonic form, appear starting in column 10 of the card.

3. Other information for the instruction, e.g., the number of a register to be employed, and/or an address in symbolic form, appears starting in column 16 of the card, and continues until we reach the first blank column on the card.

4. Anything appearing thereafter on the card is taken to be a comment, i.e., reproduced on the output listing of the programme, but not translated into machine language in any way.

Let us now give the machine language code for the preceding section, as it would appear in assembly language:

```
          BALR   15,0       SET THE BASE REGISTER
          USING  *,15       TELL THE ASSEMBLY PROGRAMME THAT
*                           15 IS THE BASE REGISTER
S1000     L      1,M        LOAD THE VALUE OF M INTO REGISTER 1
          A      1,N        ADD THE VALUE OF N TO THIS
          BZ     S1010      BRANCH ON ZERO, TO STATEMENT NUMBER
*                           1010
          ST     1,M        STORE CONTENTS OF REGISTER 1 INTO
*                           LOCATION M (THE SUM M+N)
          B      S1010      BRANCH (UNCONDITIONAL) TO STATEMENT
*                           NUMBER 1010
M         DC     F'5'       LOCATION FOR M, SET TO CONSTANT VALUE 5
N         DC     F'28'      LOCATION FOR N, SET TO CONSTANT VALUE 28
S1010     ...    ....       STATEMENT NUMBER 1010 STARTS HERE
```

Compared to machine language, assembly language is a lot easier to read and to write. But compared to FORTRAN, the above coding is by no means as simple as the FORTRAN statements

```
      DATA M,N/5,28/
1000  IF((M+N).EQ.0) GO TO 1010
      M=M+N
1010  ...
```

In this particular case, we have nothing to show for the effort of writing in assembly language rather than in FORTRAN. The only "gain" is the fact that the statement M=M+N has been translated into a single instruction, rather than into three instructions as FORTRAN would do. And this gain is more than counterbalanced by the time we have had to put in ourselves, to programme in a much more difficult language; furthermore, in a language appropriate to only *one* machine, whereas the FORTRAN code can be used on *every* machine.

F. When to Use Assembly Language

Most FORTRAN programmers have neither the time nor the inclination to learn assembly language programming. This is particularly true of programmers who use more than one machine: learning a new language for every new machine can soon become an intolerable strain. Just as soon as one learns to use one particular assembly language in really fluent fashion, that language goes "out of fashion" - because the machine has become obsolete, and is being replaced by a bigger, better, and faster computer, with an entirely different assembly language!

However, this does *not* mean that FORTRAN programmers should ignore assembly language programming altogether.(*) Judicious use of *assembly language subprogrammes* can do wonders for the execution time of the full programme, even though *most* of the full programme remains purely a FORTRAN programme.

The subprogrammes which take most time in execution are the ones farthest down in the hierarchy, the "low man on the totem pole" subprogrammes. It is likely that they carry out most of the actual computation (the innermost loops), and most of the machine time is spent on them.

Most installations provide service subroutines for keeping track of machine time during execution of a programme. A FORTRAN subroutine call can often be used, e.g., CALL CLOCK(TIME) which then sets the variable TIME to the present time, expressed in some convenient units such as seconds, The FORTRAN programmer should enquire what the name and calling sequence of the CLOCK routine is at his installation (and set up a mighty scream if there is no such routine available at all). CALL statements such as the above, followed by NAMELIST-controlled printout, should then be inserted at a number of points in the programme. The statements might be:

```
C*****  TIMING
        NAMELIST/SI2315/TIME
        CALL CLOCK(TIME)
        WRITE (NPRINT, SI2315)
C*****  END OF TIMING
```

If this set of statements appears near statement number 2315 of a subprogramme SIMPSN, for example, the resulting print-out will inform us of the time, every time we pass this point. *Note,*

(*) They, and everyone else almost, can ignore basic machine language programming. Basic machine language programming is done only by systems programmers, and by them only once: to write the first, simplest version of the assembly programme. This accepts, and translates into machine language, a subset of the full assembly language. The rest of the assembly programme is then written by a "bootstrap" method, using the first version of the assembly programme to produce a better, more flexible version, and so on, until the assembly programme is complete. The FORTRAN compiler is written in assembly language, not in basic machine language.

however, that the process of *printing out the time itself takes time,* and thus our measurement of time distorts the true time values. This can be overcome by writing a slightly more elaborate SUBROUTINE, which prints out the time interval elapsed since the last time the subroutine was called, in such a way that the time taken for the I/O operation is not counted as part of the elapsed time.

Having a clocking routine of some sort available, the next step is to insert timing statements at various places in the main programme, to find out how long the first-level subprogrammes take in execution. Next, move one step down: into the first-level subprogramme taking most of the time, insert clocking statements to time the second-level subprogrammes, as well as "suspect" operations such as I/O operations on sequential files (magnetic tapes). Keep going in this way, until you have a good idea where the time is really being spent. Chances are that this is in one or two very low-level subprogrammes.

At this stage, it is time to consult someone who knows how to programme in assembly language, for an opinion of how much time can be saved by rewriting this subprogramme, or these few subprogrammes, in assembly language. Sometimes, this may not even be necessary: it is often possible, by a judicious rewriting of the FORTRAN language programme, to force the FORTRAN compiler to produce a much more efficient object programme. This should be tried first, since it takes little time and effort, and can be done by the FORTRAN language programmer. But if this is impossible, or does not give enough gain in speed, then assembly language programming is called for, and is well worth the effort.

Naturally, as soon as some of the subprogrammes are in assembly language, the programme as a whole is no longer transferable to another machine. Therefore, the FORTRAN versions of these subprogrammes should not be discarded - they might come in very handy later on.

Drill Exercise:

Assume that the time can be obtained by CALL CLOCK(TIME). Write a SUBROUTINE CLOCKR(N) with the following specifications:

1. When entered with N.LE.0, we print out the value of N and the message CLOCK SET. We call CLOCK(TIME) and set OLDTIM=TIME, then RETURN

2. When entered with N.GT.0, we call CLOCK(TIME), compute ELAPSE=TIME-OLDTIM, print out the message: CLOCKR ENTERED WITH N=... ELAPSED TIME=... where the dots represent the values of N and ELAPSE. We call CLOCK(TIME) once more, to obtain the time *after* the printing operation, and set OLDTIM=TIME. Then we RETURN.

The typical entry, from a superior programme, would now be as follows:

```
N=2315
CALL CLOCKR(N)
```

The value of N chosen should be such as to remind us where in the programme this timing occurred: for example, the above might appear near statement number 2315 of the programme.

APPENDIX A

A DICTIONARY OF FORTRAN IV

The purpose of this dictionary is to give typical examples of all types of FORTRAN IV statements. The formal definitions, restrictions, coding considerations etc. are not given here; rather, a Chapter and Section reference is given for each statement. The typical examples given here suffice to answer the questions arising most frequently in actual coding, to wit: is a comma required in a certain position? are parentheses required? and so on.

In addition to this Dictionary, the Table of Built-In Functions in Chapter XII, Section A, should be consulted for standard names of the built-in functions.

Term or Statement	Typical Example		Definition
.AND.	(A.GT.B).AND.(B.GT.C)		III,B
Arithmetic IF	IF(A-B) 1100, 1200, 1300		XI,A
Arithmetic Statement Function	FUN(X)=X**3-(X+2.0)**2 Y=A+B*FUN(C)	(def.) (use)	XII,B
ASSIGN statement	ASSIGN 1200 TO J		XI,B
Assigned GO TO	GO TO J, (1100, 1200)		XI,B
BACKSPACE	BACKSPACE NTAPE BACKSPACE 14		XV,L
BLOCK DATA subprogramme	BLOCK DATA		XIV,H
Built-in Functions, Table			XII,A
CALL statement	CALL MATMPY(A,B,C,MDIM)		XIV,E
CHARACTER type code	IMPLICIT CHARACTER*25($) CHARACTER*25 $BILL(3)/'SS', 'TT', 'UU'/		IX,F
COMMON statement	COMMON/PEST/A,B,C(2,2) COMMON D, E, F(3,4)		XIV,G
COMPLEX type code	IMPLICIT COMPLEX*8(C), COMPLEX*16(Z) COMPLEX*16 ZETA(3), ETA/(0.D0, 1D0)/		IX,C IX,E

Term or Statement	Typical Example	Definition
Computed GO TO	GO TO (1100, 1200, 1300),J	XI,B
CONTINUE	1100 CONTINUE	XI,C
DATA statement	DATA A, B/10.5, 14.7/	IX,D
DEFINE FILE	DEFINE FILE 15(50, 1000, U, NREC5)	XV,M
DIMENSION	DIMENSION VECTOR (15), ARRAY(25,35)	XIII,A,E,H
DIMENSION, adjustable	DIMENSION ARRAY(MDIM, MDIM)	XIV,B,D
Direct Access Commands	see: DEFINE FILE, FIND, READ, WRITE	XV,M
DO	DO 1100 K=2, 26, 4	XI,C,D
DOUBLE PRECISION	DOUBLE PRECISION DOTARD, DOLT	IX,E
END	END	V,B and XIV,D
END= option	READ(NREAD, 1100, END=1200, ERR= 1300)	XV,K
END FILE	END FILE NTAPE END FILE 14	XV,L
ENTRY	ENTRY ARCOSH(X)	XIV,J
.EQ.	A.EQ.B	III,B
EQUIVALENCE	EQUIVALENCE (A,B), (C(5), D(3,1))	XIII,F
ERR= option	READ(NREAD, 1100, END=1200, ERR=1300)	XV,K
EXTERNAL	EXTERNAL ARSINH, ARCOSH	XIV,C
.FALSE.		III,B and X,E
FIND	FIND(NFILE'NRECD)	XV,M
FORMAT	1400 FORMAT ('0A AND B ARE', 2G21.7)	XV,A,B,C,D, E,J
FORMAT codes A	18A4	XV,E,I
D	3D27.14	XV,B
E	3E17.6	XV,B
F	3F17.6	XV,B
G	4G21.8	XV,B
H	5HDON'T	XV,C
I	5I12	XV,B
L	3L5	XV,E
P	1P3E16.7	XV,B
T	T19	XV,C
X	15X	XV,C
Z	3Z16	XV,E
FUNCTION subprogramme	FUNCTION ARSINH(X) (def) Y=A+B*ARSINH(C) (use)	XIV,A,B XIV,A,C,D
.GE.	A.GE.B	III,B

Term or Statement	Typical Example	Definition
.GT.	A.GT.B	III,B
GO TO, assigned	GO TO J, (1100, 1200, 1300)	XI,B
GO TO, computed	GO TO (1100, 1200, 1300),J	XI,B
GO TO, unconditional	GO TO 1200	III,A
IF, arithmetic	IF(A-B) 1100, 1200, 1300	XI,A
IF, logical	IF(A.GT.B) GO TO 1300	III,C
IMPLICIT	IMPLICIT REAL*8(D), COMPLEX*16(Z)	IX,C
INTEGER type code	IMPLICIT INTEGER*4(A-Z) INTEGER*4 MONKEY(3,4)/12*5/	IX,C IX,E
.LE.	A.LE.B	III,B
LOGICAL type code	IMPLICIT LOGICAL *1($) LOGICAL*1 JUDGE(200)/100*T, 100*F/	IX,C IX,E
Logical IF	IF(A.GT.B) GO TO 1300	III,C
.LT.	A.LT.B	III,B
NAMELIST	NAMELIST/BABEL/A,B,C (def) READ (NREAD, BABEL) (use) WRITE (NPRINT, BABEL) (use)	XV,H
.NE.	A.NE.B	III,B
.NOT.	.NOT.(A.GT.B)	III,B
.OR.	(A.LT.B).OR.(C.LT.D)	III,B
PAUSE	PAUSE 'MOUNT DATA TAPE 7'	XI,E
PRINT (FORTRAN II)	PRINT 1100,A,B,C	XV,A
PRINT (WATFOR)	PRINT,A,B,C	IV,A
PUNCH (FORTRAN II)	PUNCH 1100, A,B,C	XV,F
READ commands: (WATFOR) (FORTRAN II) FORMAT-controlled NAMELIST - controlled sequential file Direct access file	READ, A,B,C READ 1100, A,B,C READ (NREAD, 1100) A,B,C READ (NREAD,BABEL) READ (NTAPE) A,B,C (internal form) READ (NTAPE, 1100) A,B,C (external form) READ (NFIL'NRECD) A,B,C (internal) READ (NFIL'NRECD, 1100) A,B,C (external)	IV,B XV,G XV,G XV,H XV,L XV,M
REAL type code	IMPLICIT REAL*8(D) REAL*4 KLOT, MONKEY(5)/1.0, 4*5.0/	IX,C IX,E
RETURN	RETURN RETURN 2 (SUBROUTINE only)	XIV,B,E XIV,E

Term or Statement	Typical Example	Definition
REWIND	REWIND NTAPE REWIND 14	XV,L
Statement Function	see: Arithmetic Statement Function	XII,B
STOP	STOP	III,A
.TRUE.		III,B and X,E
Unconditional GO TO	GO TO 1200	III,A

WRITE commands
    FORMAT - controlled
    NAMELIST - controlled
    sequential file
 	
    direct access file
	
	WRITE (NPRINT, 1100) A,B,C
	WRITE (NPRINT, BABEL)
	WRITE (NTAPE) A,B,C (internal form)
	WRITE (NTAPE, 1100) A,B,C (external form)
	WRITE (NFILE'NRECD) A,B,C (internal form)
	WRITE (NFILE'NRECD, 1100) A,B,C
	       (external form)
		
		XV,A
		XV,H
		XV,L
		
		XV,M

APPENDIX B

WATFOR DIAGNOSTIC MESSAGES AND HINTS

In this Appendix, we give the diagnostic message codes printed out by the WATFOR/360 compiler; next to each message code is the actual diagnostic message. For those messages which are not self-explanatory, further explanations are given, as well as hints for possible action.

ASSIGN STATEMENTS AND VARIABLES

AS-2   ATTEMPT TO REDEFINE AN ASSIGNED VARIABLE IN AN ARITHMETIC STATE-MENT. Not likely to occur, since ASSIGN and the assigned GO TO should not be used, except in special circumstances.

AS-3   ASSIGNED VARIABLE USED IN AN ARITHMETIC EXPRESSION. See above comment.

AS-4   ASSIGNED VARIABLE CANNOT BE HALF WORD INTEGER. See above comemnt.

AS-5   ATTEMPT TO REDEFINE AN ASSIGN VARIABLE IN AN INPUT LIST. See above comment.

BLOCK DATA STATEMENTS

BD-0   EXECUTABLE STATEMENT IN BLOCK DATA SUBPROGRAM. Remove the interloper.

BD-1   IMPROPER BLOCK DATA STATEMENT. Nothing should follow BLOCK DATA.

CARD FORMAT AND CONTENTS

CC-0   COLUMNS 1-5 OF CONTINUATION CARD NOT BLANK. The compiler assumes that a card with something punched into column 6 is meant to be a continuation card. A continuation card must not have punchings earlier than column 6. Only first cards, not continuation cards, are allowed to have statement numbers. Did you perhaps punch a normal FORTRAN card starting in column 1 instead of column 7?

CC-1   TOO MANY CONTINUATION CARDS (MAXIMUM OF 5). This is a WATFOR convention. Some FORTRAN compilers allow up to 9 continuation cards. Long statements requiring many continuation cards are poor coding practice.

CC-2   INVALID CHARACTER IN FORTRAN STATEMENT. '?' INSERTED IN SOURCE LISTING. A character not belonging to the 49 character set of FORTRAN has been found on the card. This character has been replaced by ? in the line above. The most likely cause is overpunching, i.e. punching two separate characters into one column of the card. You must look at the actual holes punched into the card, not just at the typed interpretation along the top edge of the card. See V,A.

CC-3   FIRST CARD OF A PROGRAMME IS A CONTINUATION CARD. PROBABLE CAUSE - STATEMENT PUNCHED TO LEFT OF COLUMN 7. The FORTRAN statement must appear starting in column 7. If it spills over into column 6, and is the first statement of a programme, this diagnostic results.

CC-4   STATEMENT TOO LONG TO COMPILE (SCAN STACK OVERFLOW). The WATFOR compiler cannot handle this statement; break it up into shorter statements.

CC-5   BLANK CARD ENCOUNTERED. A blank card is not a valid FORTRAN source language programme card. Remove it!

CC-6   KEYPUNCH USED DIFFERS FROM KEYPUNCH SPECIFIED ON THE JOB CARD. The job card specification is either KP=29 or KP=26, for a model 29 or model 26 punch, respectively. KP=29 is understood if this specification is omitted. Look at the punch you are using! Do not repunch the whole programme; rather, alter the KP= specification on the job card.

CC-7   FIRST CHARACTER OF STATEMENT NOT ALPHABETIC. All valid FORTRAN statements start with alphabetic characters; why doesn't yours?

CC-8   INVALID CHARACTER(S) CONCATENATED WITH FORTRAN KEYWORD. A standard FORTRAN command is followed by unexpected material as listed after the code symbol CC-8.

CC-9   INVALID CHARACTERS IN COLUMNS 2-5. STATEMENT NUMBER IGNORED. PROBABLE CAUSE - STATEMENT PUNCHED TO LEFT OF COLUMN 7. See comment to CC-3; this was *not* the first statement of the programme, hence the slightly different diagnostic.

COMMON

CM-0   VARIABLE PREVIOUSLY PLACED IN COMMON. Within any one programme or sub-programme, one variable identifier name must not appear in two different COMMON blocks, nor twice in the same COMMON block.

CM-1   NAME IN COMMON LIST PREVIOUSLY USED AS OTHER THAN VARIABLE. If you follow the instructions in Chapter XIV, Section I, this diagnostic is most unlikely. Names of other sub-programmes, be they FUNCTION or SUBROUTINE sub-programmes, must not be put into COMMON storage areas.

CM-2   SUBPROGRAMME PARAMETER APPEARS IN COMMON STATEMENT. The dummy argument names of a FUNCTION or SUBROUTINE sub-programme must not be put into COMMON.

CM-3   INITIALIZING OF COMMON SHOULD BE DONE IN A BLOCK DATA SUBPROGRAMME. You have attempted to initialize a variable in COMMON by means of an ordinary DATA statement. Tut-tut! See Chapter XIV, Section H.

CM-4   ILLEGAL USE OF COMMON BLOCK OR NAMELIST NAME. Names of COMMON storage areas and names of namelists must not be used as variable names, nor as sub-programme names.

FORTRAN TYPE CONSTANTS

CN-0   MIXED REAL*4, REAL*8 IN COMPLEX CONSTANT. The real part and imaginary part of a complex constant must have the same length. 0. is REAL*4; use 0.D0 if you want a REAL*8 zero.

CN-1 INTEGER CONSTANT GREATER THAN 2,147,483,647 (2**31-1)

CN-3 EXPONENT ON REAL CONSTANT GREATER THAN 99

CN-4 REAL CONSTANT HAS MORE THAN 16 DIGITS, TRUNCATED TO 16. This is a warning, not necessarily an error message. You have asked for more significant digits than the IBM 360 can store in double precision.

CN-5 INVALID HEXADECIMAL CONSTANT. Students should avoid hexadecimal constants!

CN-6 ILLEGAL USE OF DECIMAL POINT. The exponent of a floating point number should be an integer, without a decimal point.

CN-8 CONSTANT WITH E-TYPE EXPONENT HAS MORE THAN 7 DIGITS, ASSUME D-TYPE. Did you really want more than 7 significant digits? If not, why did you write them? If so, use D instead of E.

CN-9 CONSTANT OR STATEMENT NUMBER GREATER THAN 99999 Statement numbers cannot exceed 99999, nor can the corresponding numbers in, say, a GO TO statement.

COMPILER ERRORS

CP-0 COMPILER ERROR DETECTED IN PHASE RELOC. This one wasn't your fault! Tell this to the manager of the Computing Centre. Make sure to preserve the complete computer output and the input card deck, unchanged. Bring both of them with you.

CP-1 COMPILER ERROR DETECTED IN PHASE LINKR. See CP-0.

CP-2 COMPILER ERROR. DUPLICATE PSEUDO STATEMENT NUMBERS. See CP-0.

CP-4 COMPILER ERROR DETECTED IN PHASE ARITH. See CP-0.

DATA STATEMENT

DA-0 REPLICATION FACTOR GREATER THAN 32767, ASSUME 32767. This is the factor in a DATA statement, saying you want the same number repeated more than 32767 times. Did you really mean that?

DA-1 NON-CONSTANT IN DATA STATEMENT. The initial values set by a DATA statement, and appearing within the slashes /.../, must be valid FORTRAN constants.

DA-2 MORE VARIABLES THAN CONSTANTS IN DATA STATEMENT. Each variable name appearing in a DATA statement must have at least one constant corresponding to it (not all elements of an array need be initialized, but at least one element must be, for each array name that appears). You have broken this rule.

DA-3 ATTEMPT TO INITIALIZE A SUBPROGRAMME PARAMETER IN A DATA STATEMENT. Values of dummy arguments must not be set by a DATA statement within the subprogramme. They may be set by an assignment statement, however.

DA-4 NON-CONSTANT SUBSCRIPTS IN A DATA STATEMENT INVALID IN /360 FORTRAN. A vector array element VEC(4) can be set in a DATA statement, but not VEC(J).

DA-5 EXTENDED DATA STATEMENT NOT IN /360 FORTRAN. No implied DO loops in a DATA statement.

DA-6 NON-AGREEMENT BETWEEN TYPE OF VARIABLE AND CONSTANT IN DATA STATEMENT. No implied conversions allowed in a DATA statement!

DA-8   VARIABLE PREVIOUSLY INITIALIZED. LATEST VALUE USED. CHECK COMMON/ EQUIVALENCED VARIABLES. You have attempted to initialize the same memory location twice over; perhaps you have forgotten synonyms declared by means of EQUIVALENCE statements.

DA-7   MORE CONSTANTS THAN VARIABLES IN DATA STATEMENT. You have lost count!

DA-9   INITIALIZING BLANK COMMON NOT ALLOWED IN /360 FORTRAN. The variable you have attempted to initialize has been assigned to blank (unlabelled) COMMON storage. Use an assignment statement to initialize it.

DA-A   INVALID DELIMITER IN CONSTANT LIST PORTION OF DATA STATEMENT. The list of constants in a DATA statement should contain constants separated by commas. The invalid symbol or symbols is listed with this diagnostic.

DA-B   TRUNCATION OF LITERAL CONSTANT HAS OCCURRED. A literal constant (character string) is too long for the space into which it is meant to be stored. Some of the characters have been chopped off.

DIMENSION STATEMENTS

DM-0   NO DIMENSIONS SPECIFIED FOR A VARIABLE IN A DIMENSION STATEMENT.

DM-1   OPTIONAL LENGTH SPECIFICATION IN DIMENSION STATEMENT IS ILLEGAL. An adjustable dimension can be used only if (1) this is a subprogramme, (2) the array name is one of the dummy arguments, and (3) the variable dimension name is also one of the dummy argument names.

DM-2   INITIALIZATION IN DIMENSION STATEMENT IS ILLEGAL. Use a separate DATA statement.

DM-3   ATTEMPT TO RE-DIMENSION A VARIABLE. Any one array name can be dimensioned only once in a programme or subprogramme.

DM-4   ATTEMPT TO DIMENSION AN INITIALIZED VARIABLE. If you had stuck to the recommendations of Chapter XIV, Section I, this would not have happened to you!

DO LOOPS

DO-0   ILLEGAL STATEMENT USED AS OBJECT OF DO. The last statement in the range of a DO loop (statement number n of DO n ...) must be an *executable* statement *other than* GO TO, PAUSE, STOP, RETURN, IF, or another DO.

DO-1   ILLEGAL TRANSFER INTO THE RANGE OF A DO LOOP. Have you forgotten to insert, in your programme, the final CONTINUE statement for a DO loop? If so, the compiler thinks the DO loop is still going strong.

DO-2   OBJECT OF A DO STATEMENT HAS ALREADY APPEARED. The final statement of a DO loop (statement number n in DO n ...) must come *after* the DO statement. You should have kept your statement numbers in strictly increasing sequence.

DO-3   IMPROPERLY NESTED DO-LOOPS. Have you forgotten a CONTINUE statement?

DO-4   ATTEMPT TO REDEFINE A DO-LOOP PARAMETER WITHIN RANGE OF LOOP. Within the range of DO n $I=m_1$, m_2, m_3 none of I, m_1, m_2, or m_3 may appear to the left of an assignment statement. Did you forget to close the loop with a CONTINUE statement?

DO-5   INVALID DO-LOOP PARAMETER. In DO n $I=m_1, m_2, m_3$ I must be a simple variable name of type INTEGER. All of m_1, m_2, and m_3 must be either variable names of type INTEGER, or unsigned integer constants greater than 0. No well-formed arithmetic expressions are permitted, nor names of array variables.

DO-6   TOO MANY NESTED DO'S (MAXIMUM OF 20). How on earth did you get that diagnostic in a student programme? Two or three nested loops are all you should ever need.

DO-7   DO-PARAMETER IS UNDEFINED OR OUTSIDE RANGE. One of m_1, m_2, m_3 is a variable name which has not been assigned a value heretofore, or which is negative or zero.

DO-8   THIS DO LOOP WILL TERMINATE AFTER FIRST TIME THROUGH. This is a warning message, not necessarily an error. However, if you really want the loop to be traversed only once, why write it as a loop at all?

DO-9   ATTEMPT TO REDEFINE A DO-LOOP PARAMETER IN AN INPUT LIST. Similar to DO-4, except one of I, m_1, m_2, m_3 appears in the list of a READ statement within the range of the DO loop (rather than to the left of an assignment statement). Did you want the READ statement inside the loop, anyway? Maybe you forgot to close an earlier loop with a CONTINUE statement.

EQUIVALENCE AND/OR COMMON

EC-0   TWO EQUIVALENCED VARIABLES APPEAR IN COMMON. EQUIVALENCE is allowed between one variable in COMMON and another variable not in COMMON; but not between two variables both of which are within COMMON blocks.

EC-1   COMMON BLOCK HAS A DIFFERENT LENGTH THAN IN A PREVIOUS SUBPROGRAMME. Labelled COMMON blocks with the same label must have the same total length (number of bytes) in all subprogrammes.

EC-2   COMMON AND/OR EQUIVALENCE CAUSES INVALID ALIGNMENT. EXECUTION SLOWED. This is a warning message only; the programme will work, but machine time is being wasted through improper alignment. Avoid putting variables of different length into the same COMMON block; use differently labelled COMMON blocks for variables of 4-byte, 8-byte, and 16-byte lengths.

EC-3   EQUIVALENCE EXTENDS COMMON DOWNWARDS. See the end of Section G, Chapter XIV.

EC-7   COMMON/EQUIVALENCE STATEMENT DOES NOT PRECEDE PREVIOUS USE OF VARIABLE. Don't ignore the good advice in Chapter XIV, Section I, next time!

EC-8   VARIABLE USED WITH NON-CONSTANT SUBSCRIPT IN COMMON/EQUIVALENCE LIST. The subscripts appearing in such lists must be unsigned integer constants greater than 0. Adjustable dimensions may appear only in a DIMENSION statement.

EC-9   A NAME SUBSCRIPTED IN AN EQUIVALENCE STATEMENT WAS NOT DIMENSIONED. Don't ignore the good advice in Chapter XIV, Section I, next time!

END STATEMENTS

EN-0   NO END STATEMENT IN PROGRAMME - END STATEMENT GENERATED. You forgot to put an END statement at the end of your FORTRAN source language programme. WATFOR has been kind enough to fix it up for you, but do not let it happen again!

EN-1 END STATEMENT USED AS STOP STATEMENT AT EXECUTION. This is permissible, but very poor coding practice. If you want the computation to stop at that point, put an explicit statement STOP just ahead of the END statement.

EN-2 IMPROPER END STATEMENT. An unexpected character has been added to the word END.

EN-3 FIRST STATEMENT OF SUBPROGRAMME IS END STATEMENT. Not much of a subprogramme, that one! Perhaps you got your deck of cards shuffled a bit?

EQUAL SIGNS

EQ-6 ILLEGAL QUANTITY ON LEFT OF EQUAL SIGN. The quantity to the left of the equal sign must be a variable name; it must not be a constant, nor a wfae.

EQ-8 ILLEGAL USE OF EQUAL SIGN. Did you use A=B instead of A.EQ.B for a comparison?

EQ-A MULTIPLE ASSIGNMENT STATEMENTS NOT IN /360 FORTRAN. A "multiple assignment statement" is, for example, A=B=3.0 as an attempt to set both A and B equal to 3.0. WATFOR will accept this, but it is considered ungrammatical standard FORTRAN. Avoid writing ungrammatical FORTRAN, even when WATFOR permits it.

EQUIVALENCE STATEMENTS

EV-0 ATTEMPT TO EQUIVALENCE A VARIABLE TO ITSELF

EV-1 ATTEMPT TO EQUIVALENCE A SUBPROGRAMME PARAMETER. Dummy arguments of a subprogramme must not appear within an EQUIVALENCE statement.

EV-2 LESS THAN 2 MEMBERS IN AN EQUIVALENCE LIST. Did you leave out a parenthesis?

EV-3 TOO MANY EQUIVALENCE LISTS (MAX=255)

EV-4 PREVIOUSLY EQUIVALENCED VARIABLE RE-EQUIVALENCED INCORRECTLY

POWERS AND EXPONENTIATION

EX-0 ILLEGAL COMPLEX EXPONENTIATION. Complex**integer is the only permitted form involving complex numbers.

EX-2 I**J WHERE I=J=0   Undefined

EX-3 I**J WHERE I=0, J.LT.0   The result would be infinity.

EX-6 0.0**Y WHERE Y.LE.0.0   The result would be infinity.

EX-7 0.0**J WHERE J=0   Undefined.

EX-8 0.0**J WHERE J.LT.0   The result would be infinity.

EX-9 X**Y WHERE X.LT.0.0, Y.NE.0.0   You probably want an integer exponent, anyway. Why not leave out that decimal point?

ENTRY STATEMENT

EY-0 SUBPROGRAMME NAME IN ENTRY STATEMENT PREVIOUSLY DEFINED. Each ENTRY statement must provide a different subprogramme name. The subprogramme name must not be used as a variable name etc. elsewhere in the subprogramme.

EY-1 PREVIOUS DEFINITION OF FUNCTION NAME IN AN ENTRY IS INCORRECT

EY-2   USE OF SUBPROGRAMME PARAMETER INCONSISTENT WITH PREVIOUS ENTRY POINT. If a dummy argument, say X, is used at two different entry points, it must be used consistently: as a variable of the same type, same length, same number of dimensions, etc.

EY-3   ARGUMENT NAME HAS APPEARED IN AN EXECUTABLE STATEMENT, BUT WAS NOT A SUBPROGRAMME PARAMETER. If X, say, is a dummy argument name for one entry point, it must not be used as if it were a "local" memory location at another entry point earlier on. Once a dummy variable, always a dummy variable.

EY-4   ENTRY STATEMENT NOT PERMITTED IN MAIN PROGRAMME

EY-5   ENTRY POINT INVALID INSIDE A DO-LOOP. No ENTRY statement may appear inside the range of a DO-loop. Did you forget to close an earlier DO-loop by means of a CONTINUE statement?

EY-6   VARIABLE WAS NOT PREVIOUSLY USED AS A PARAMETER - PARAMETER ASSUMED. A variable name has been used as a local name heretofore, and now suddenly appears as a dummy variable name in an ENTRY statement.

FORMAT

FM-0   INVALID CHARACTER IN INPUT DATA. A card read during execution of a READ statement was not a valid data card. The particular character to which the master programme objects is given along with the message. This could be either an invalid form for data (see Chapter IV, Section B for data cards in WATFOR; Chapter XV, Sections G and H for data cards in standard FORTRAN), or an end-of-job card, or the job card of the next student job in the batch. In the latter two cases, this is not a significant error, and merely means there were no more data to be read. If one of your own data cards had an invalid character, you must look at the card itself, i.e., at the holes punched into the card, not merely at the typewritten interpretation along the top edge of the card. The computer has objected to the holes in the card, not to the typing on the card.

FM-2   NO STATEMENT NUMBER ON A FORMAT STATEMENT. Supply that number!

FM-5   FORMAT SPECIFICATION AND DATA TYPE DO NOT MATCH. An inconsistency between the variable type in the list of the READ or WRITE statement, and the type conversion code specified as a format code (for example, F or E for a variable of type INTEGER). Use G-format!

FM-6   INCORRECT SEQUENCE OF CHARACTERS IN INPUT DATA. A data card has commas or decimal points misplaced or repeated. See also comments for FM-0.

FM-7   NON TERMINATING FORMAT

FT-0   FIRST CHARACTER OF VARIABLE FORMAT NOT A LEFT BRACKET. Stay away from using variable formats!

FT-1   INVALID CHARACTER ENCOUNTERED IN FORMAT

FT-2   INVALID FORM FOLLOWING A SPECIFICATION. The specification numbers following the format code letter do not agree with that letter; for example, a letter I followed by 12.5 instead of just I12 by itself.

FT-3   INVALID FIELD OR GROUP COUNT

FT-4   A FIELD OR GROUP COUNT GREATER THAN 255

FT-5   NO CLOSING BRACKET ON VARIABLE FORMAT.   See FT-0

FT-6   NO CLOSING QUOTE IN A HOLLERITH FIELD   'INSERT THAT QUOTE'

FT-7   INVALID USE OF COMMA

FT-8   INSUFFICIENT SPACE TO COMPILE A FORMAT STATEMENT (SCAN-STACK OVER-FLOW). Your programme as a whole is too long, or else the FORMAT statement is too long. Try shortening it.

FT-9   INVALID USE OF P-SPECIFICATION. P-specification should not be used for integers.

FT-A   CHARACTER FOLLOWS CLOSING RIGHT BRACKET. Better count those brackets!

FT-B   INVALID USE OF PERIOD (.)

FT-C   MORE THAN THREE LEVELS OF PARENTHESES. Don't be so fancy!

FT-D   INVALID CHARACTER BEFORE A RIGHT BRACKET

FT-E   MISSING OR ZERO LENGTH HOLLERITH ENCOUNTERED. A "Hollerith field" is another name for a character string within a FORMAT statement. Character strings of length zero, i.e., '' and/or 0H, are not permitted.

FT-F   NO CLOSING RIGHT BRACKET. Count those brackets!

FUNCTIONS AND SUBROUTINES

FN-0   NO ARGUMENTS IN A FUNCTION STATEMENT.   A FUNCTION subprogramme must have at least one dummy argument.

FN-3   REPEATED ARGUMENT IN SUBPROGRAME OR STATEMENT FUNCTION DEFINITION   Dummy arguments of a subprogramme or statement function must have different names. This *could* be due to omission of a DIMENSION statement for an array variable name to the left of the equal sign in an assignment statement.

FN-4   SUBSCRIPTS ON RIGHT HAND SIDE OF ARITHMETIC STATEMENT FUNCTION. PROBABLE CAUSE - VARIABLE TO LEFT OF = NOT DIMENSIONED.

FN-5   MULTIPLE RETURNS ARE INVALID IN FUNCTION SUBPROGRAMMES   The statement RETURN I can be used only in SUBROUTINE subprogrammes.

FN-6   ILLEGAL LENGTH MODIFIER IN TYPE FUNCTION STATEMENT   We recommend strongly that the type of the FUNCTION name be declared by means of an IMPLICIT type declaration right after the FUNCTION statement, not within the FUNCTION statement itself.

FN-7   INVALID ARGUMENT IN ARITHMETIC OR LOGICAL STATEMENT FUNCTION   Did you omit a DIMENSION statement for the variable on the left of an arithmetic or logical assignment statement?

FN-8   ARGUMENT OF SUBPROGRAMME IS SAME AS SUBPROGRAMME NAME   The name of the subprogramme must not be used as the name of a dummy argument.

GO TO STATEMENTS

GO-0   STATEMENT TRANSFERS TO ITSELF OR TO A NON-EXECUTABLE STATEMENT

GO-1   INVALID TRANSFER TO THIS STATEMENT

GO-2   INDEX OF COMPUTED 'GO TO' IS NEGATIVE OR UNDEFINED

GO-3   ERROR IN VARIABLE OF 'GO TO' STATEMENT   The index variable for a computed GO TO must be of type INTEGER; the statement number in an unconditional GO TO must be an unsigned integer constant.

GO-4   INDEX OF ASSIGNED 'GO TO' IS UNDEFINED OR NOT IN RANGE   Avoid the assigned GO TO. The computed GO TO is logically equivalent, and should be used in preference. The index variable of the *computed* GO TO appears *after* the list of statement numbers in parentheses.

HOLLERITH CONSTANTS   *(Meaning: Character Strings)*

HO-0   ZERO LENGTH SPECIFIED FOR H-TYPE HOLLERITH   Avoid 0H specification.

HO-1   ZERO LENGTH QUOTE-TYPE HOLLERITH   Avoid " specification.

HO-2   NO CLOSING QUOTE OR NEXT CARD NOT CONTINUATION CARD   Supply that closing quote.

HO-3   HOLLERITH CONSTANT SHOULD APPEAR ONLY IN CALL STATEMENT   IBM/360 FORTRAN IV does not permit character strings in assignment statements, such as A='DISASTER'. Character strings can be used as actual arguments of a SUBROUTINE subprogramme, in a CALL statement.

HO-4   UNEXPECTED HOLLERITH OR STATEMENT NUMBER CONSTANT   A "statement number constant" is an actual argument such as &1200 replacing a dummy argument * of a SUBROUTINE subprogramme. No such should have appeared at this point. Are you perhaps using a wrong keypunch? A + on one keypunch may be the same as a & on another keypunch.

IF STATEMENTS (ARITHMETIC AND LOGICAL)

IF-0   STATEMENT INVALID AFTER A LOGICAL IF   The statement S in the logical IF(P) S must not be one of : i) specification statement, ii) DO statement, iii) another logical IF statement.

IF-3   ARITHMETIC OR INVALID EXPRESSION IN LOGICAL IF   The logical expression P in IF(P) S was ill-formed! Did you use A=B instead of A.EQ.B?

IF-4   LOGICAL, COMPLEX, OR INVALID EXPRESSION IN ARITHMETIC IF   The well-formed arithmetic expression W in IF(W) n_1, n_2, n_3 was of dominant type COMPLEX, or ill-formed altogether as an arithmetic expression.

IMPLICIT STATEMENT

IM-0   INVALID MODE SPECIFIED IN AN IMPLICIT STATEMENT   The permissible modes are INTEGER, REAL, COMPLEX, LOGICAL, and, in WATFOR only, CHARACTER. Did you misspell one of these words?

IM-1   INVALID LENGTH SPECIFIED IN AN IMPLICIT OR TYPE STATEMENT   The permitted lengths are: 2 and 4 for INTEGER, 4 and 8 for REAL, 8 and 16 for COMPLEX 1 and 4 for LOGICAL, and (in WATFOR only) between 1 and 120, inclusive, for CHARACTER.

IM-2   ILLEGAL APPEARANCE OF $ IN A CHARACTER RANGE   Although $ is counted as an 'alphabetic' character, it is not considered to be the 27th character, immediately following Z. Thus IMPLICIT REAL*8(A-Z,$) is valid, but IMPLICIT REAL*8(A-$) is invalid.

IM-3   IMPROPER ALPHABETIC SEQUENCE IN CHARACTER RANGE   The character range (B-G) is all right, but (G-B) is wrong. Keep them in alphabetical order!

IM-4   SPECIFICATION MUST BE SINGLE ALPHABETIC CHARACTER, FIRST CHARACTER USED   A statement such as IMPLICIT COMPLEX*16(CD) would be very useful, but is not grammatically correct FORTRAN. WATFOR would assume that the first character alone is meant, i.e., replace the above by IMPLICIT COMPLEX*16(C). If you want both C and D as initials, you must write (C,D) or (C-D), not just (CD).

IM-5   IMPLICIT STATEMENT DOES NOT PRECEDE OTHER SPECIFICATION STATE-MENTS   The IMPLICIT statement must be the first (non-comment) statement of a main programme; it must be the second (non-comment) statement of a subprogramme.

IM-6   ATTEMPT TO ESTABLISH THE TYPE OF A CHARACTER MORE THAN ONCE Any one initial can appear only once in the lists of initials in an IMPLICIT statement. The offending initial is also given.

IM-7   /360 FORTRAN ALLOWS ONLY ONE IMPLICIT STATEMENT PER PROGRAMME

IM-8   INVALID ELEMENT IN IMPLICIT STATEMENT   Check that all parentheses and commas are in their correct places.

IM-9   INVALID DELIMITER IN IMPLICIT STATEMENT   Check that all parentheses and commas are in their correct places. Don't replace commas by periods. Don't use a final, or initial, comma.

INPUT/OUTPUT

IO-0   MISSING COMMA IN I/O LIST OF I/O OR DATA STATEMENT

IO-2   STATEMENT NUMBER IN I/O STATEMENT NOT A FORMAT STATEMENT NUMBER There is no FORMAT statement with that statement number in the programme.

IO-3   BUFFER OVERFLOW - LINE TOO LONG FOR DEVICE   You have attempted to punch a card with more than 80 columns, or to print a line with more than 120 (or perhaps 132) characters. Fix that FORMAT statement!

IO-6   VARIABLE FORMAT NOT AN ARRAY NAME   The most likely cause of this diag-nostic is omission of the comma in the WATFOR command READ, *List* or PRINT, *List*. The compiler thinks you wanted to do something much more fancy (using a variable FORMAT statement) and issues this diagnostic, whereas all you really did was to omit one comma.

IO-8   INVALID ELEMENT IN INPUT LIST OR DATA LIST   These lists must contain variable names, *not* constants, subprogramme names, arithmetic expressions, etc.

IO-9   TYPE OF VARIABLE UNIT NOT INTEGER IN I/O STATEMENT   You have used a variable name for the logical unit number, and that variable name is not of type INTEGER. Did you use PRINTR instead of NPRINT, for example?

IO-A   HALF-WORD INTEGER VARIABLE USED AS UNIT IN I/O STATEMENTS   That variable name for the logical unit number must be of type INTEGER*4, not of type INTEGER*2.

IO-B   ASSIGNED INTEGER VARIABLE USED AS UNIT IN I/O STATEMENTS   You have been warned to avoid ASSIGN statements and assigned GO TO statements. Listen next time!

IO-C   INVALID ELEMENT IN AN OUTPUT LIST   Same as IO-8, except this refers to the
         list in a WRITE statement.

IO-D   MISSING OR INVALID UNIT IN I/O STATEMENT   You either forgot to specify the
         logical unit number altogether, or you have specified it incorrectly. Did you check on the
         standard I/O unit assignments for your computer installation?

IO-E   MISSING OR INVALID FORMAT IN READ/WRITE STATEMENT

IO-F   INVALID DELIMITER IN SPECIFICATION PART OF I/O STATEMENT   The
         valid delimiters are parentheses, commas, and (for direct-access I/O statements only)
         the apostrophe, e.g., WRITE (NFILE'NRECRD, 1200) .... Do not replace commas by
         periods or semi-colons, etc.

IO-G   MISSING STATEMENT NUMBER AFTER END= OR ERR=

IO-H   /360 FORTRAN DOES NOT ALLOW END/ERR RETURNS IN WRITE STATEMENTS

IO-J   INVALID DELIMITER IN I/O LIST   Did you place a comma at the very end of the
         list in a READ or PRINT or WRITE statement? If so, remove it. Otherwise, start searching
         for invalid delimiters, i.e., things other than commas and parentheses, in the interior of the
         I/O list.

IO-K   INVALID DELIMITER IN STOP, PAUSE, DATA, or TAPE CONTROL STATEMENT

JOB CONTROL CARDS

JB-1   JOB CARD ENCOUNTERED DURING COMPILATION.   Did you forget to put a
         $ENTRY (or //DATA or its equivalent) card after your FORTRAN source programme?
         This card has to be there, even if the job does not require actual data cards. Otherwise
         the compiler thinks the job card of the next student job is a part of your source language
         programme. As such, it is invalid.

JB-2   INVALID OPTIONS SPECIFIED ON JOB CARD   Did you forget to leave blank
         spaces before your name? Students should not specify job card options at all (other than
         KP=26 for a model 26 key punch).

JB-3   UNEXPECTED CONTROL CARD ENCOUNTERED DURING COMPILATION   See
         comment, JB-1.

JOB TERMINATION

KO-0   JOB TERMINATED IN EXECUTION BECAUSE OF COMPILE TIME ERROR
         WATFOR attempts execution even if errors were diagnosed during compilation. But when
         execution reaches an erroneous source language statement, you are executed rather than
         your faulty programme.

KO-1   FIXED POINT DIVISION BY ZERO

KO-2   FLOATING POINT DIVISION BY ZERO

KO-3   TOO MANY EXPONENT OVERFLOWS   One is too many. See Chapter XIV, Section
         D.

KO-4   TOO MANY EXPONENT UNDERFLOWS   See Chapter XIV, Section D.

KO-5   TOO MANY FIXED-POINT OVERFLOWS   Your large integers are showing. One
         integer arithmetic overflow is "too many". But see Chapter XIV, Section D.

KO-6   JOB TIME EXCEEDED

KO-7   COMPILER ERROR - INTERRUPTION AT EXECUTION TIME, RETURN TO SYSTEM
This one was not your fault. Preserve this output, as well as the input card deck, and show them to the manager of your computer installation.

KO-8   INTEGER IN INPUT DATA IS TOO LARGE (MAXIMUM IS 2147483647)

LOGICAL OPERATIONS

LG-2   .NOT. USED AS A BINARY OPERATOR   The negation operator .NOT. is a unary operator, wanting to operate on only one logical quantity, located to its right. You have placed the operator .NOT. between two operands, incorrectly.

LIBRARY ROUTINES

LI-0   ARGUMENT OUT OF RANGE DGAMMA OR GAMMA.   (1.382E-76 .LT.X.LT. 57.57). The mathematical function generating routine for the gamma function must have an argument value x within the stated range. Yours was outside that range.

LI-1   ABSOLUTE VALUE OF ARGUMENT .GT. 174.673 FOR SINH, COSH, DSINH, OR DCOSH

LI-2   SENSE LIGHT OTHER THAN 0, 1, 2, 3, 4 FOR SLITE, OR OTHER THAN 1, 2, 3, 4 FOR SLITET

LI-3   REAL PORTION OF ARGUMENT .GT. 174.673 FOR CEXP OR CDEXP

LI-4   ABS(AIMAG(Z)) .GT. 174.673 FOR CSIN, CCOS, CDSIN, OR CDCOS OF Z

LI-5   ABS(REAL(Z)) .GE. 3.537E+15 FOR CSIN, CCOS, CDSIN, OR CDCOS OF Z

LI-6   ABS(AIMAG(Z)) .GE. 3.537E+15 FOR CEXP OR CDEXP OF Z

LI-7   ARGUMENT .GT. 174.673 FOR EXP OR DEXP

LI-8   ZERO ARGUMENT FOR CLOG, CLOG10, CDLOG, OR CDLOG10

LI-9   NEGATIVE OR ZERO ARGUMENT FOR ALOG, ALOG10, DLOG, or DLOG10

LI-A   ABS(X) .GE. 3.537E+15 FOR SIN, COS, DSIN, OR DCOS OF X

LI-B   ABSOLUTE VALUE OF ARGUMENT .GT. 1, FOR ARSIN, ARCOS, DARSIN, OR DARCOS

LI-C   NEGATIVE ARGUMENT FOR SQRT OR DSQRT

LI-D   BOTH ARGUMENTS OF DATAN2 OR ATAN2 ARE ZERO

LI-E   ARGUMENT TOO CLOSE TO A SINGULARITY (POINT AT WHICH THE FUNCTION BECOMES INFINITE) OF TAN, COTAN, DTAN, OR DCOTAN

LI-F   ARGUMENT OF ALGAMA OR DLGAMA IS OUT OF RANGE. PERMISSIBLE RANGE: 0.0.LT. X.LT. 4.29E+73

LI-G   ABSOLUTE VALUE OF ARGUMENT .GE. 3.537E+15 FOR TAN, COTAN, DTAN, OR DCOTAN

LI-H   FEWER THAN TWO ARGUMENTS FOR ONE OF THE MINIMUM OR MAXIMUM ROUTINES (MIN0, AMIN1, AMIN0, ETC.)

MIXED MODE

MD-2 RELATIONAL OPERATOR HAS A LOGICAL OPERAND The relational operators, .EQ., .NE., .GE., etc. must appear between two well-formed *arithmetic* expressions. You have broken this rule.

MD-3 RELATIONAL OPERATOR HAS A COMPLEX OPERAND The relational operators .EQ., .NE., .GE., etc. must appear between two well-formed arithmetic expressions of dominant type INTEGER or REAL, but not COMPLEX. You have a COMPLEX type expression there.

MD-4 MIXED MODE - LOGICAL WITH ARITHMETIC An "ill-formed" expression indeed.

MD-6 WARNING - SUBSCRIPT IS COMPLEX A subscript may be any wfae of dominant type INTEGER or REAL, but not COMPLEX.

MEMORY OVERFLOW

MO-0 SYMBOL TABLE OVERFLOWS OBJECT CODE. SOURCE ERROR CHECKING CONTINUES Your programme is too long to fit into machine memory. The rest of the source programme will be checked for FORTRAN language errors, but will not be translated into machine language, nor executed.

MO-1 INSUFFICIENT MEMORY TO ASSIGN ARRAY STORAGE. JOB ABANDONED. Do you really need these huge matrices and vectors? Be more modest!

MO-2 SYMBOL TABLE OVERFLOWS COMPILER, JOB ABANDONED. This is a later stage of the trouble diagnosed under MO-0. Now it has gotten so bad that even checking of the remainder of the source language programme for language errors has become impossible.

MO-3 DATA AREA OF SUBPROGRAMME TOO LARGE - SEGMENT SUBPROGRAMME The WATFOR compiler dislikes subprogrammes which are too long. You had better humour it, by breaking up the subprogramme into several shorter subprogrammes.

MO-4 GETMAIN CANNOT PROVIDE BUFFER FOR WATLIB

PARENTHESES

PC-0 UNMATCHED PARENTHESIS

PC-1 INVALID BRACKET NESTING IN I/O LIST You have fouled up your nested implied DO loops. Count those parentheses!

PAUSE, STOP STATEMENTS

PS-0 STOP WITH OPERATOR MESSAGE NOT ALLOWED. SIMPLE STOP ASSUMED. The full FORTRAN allows an operator message after STOP, e.g., STOP 'GOOD NIGHT, OPERATOR'. WATFOR does not allow this.

PS-1 PAUSE WITH OPERATOR MESSAGE NOT ALLOWED. TREATED AS CONTINUE. WATFOR does not permit a student to stop operation of the machine with a PAUSE statement (with or without operator messages). In WATFOR, PAUSE is the same as CONTINUE.

RETURN STATEMENT

RE-0 FIRST CARD OF SUBPROGRAMME IS A RETURN STATEMENT Not much of a subprogramme, that one! Did you get your deck of cards shuffled?

RE-1 RETURN I, WHERE I IS ZERO, NEGATIVE, OR TOO LARGE I must lie between 1 and the number of asterisks in the dummy argument list of the SUBROUTINE subprogramme.

RE-2 MULTIPLE RETURN NOT VALID IN FUNCTION SUBPROGRAMME   No RETURN I is allowed in a FUNCTION subprogramme.

RE-3 VARIABLE IN MULTIPLE RETURN IS NOT A SIMPLE, INTEGER VARIABLE

RE-4 MULTIPLE RETURN NOT VALID IN MAIN PROGRAMME

ARITHMETIC AND LOGICAL STATEMENT FUNCTIONS

SF-1 PREVIOUSLY REFERENCED STATEMENT NUMBER ON STATEMENT FUNCTION
Probable cause: Variable on left of = was not dimensioned.

SF-2 STATEMENT FUNCTION IS THE OBJECT OF A LOGICAL IF STATEMENT
Probable cause: An array variable was not dimensioned.

SF-3 RECURSIVE STATEMENT FUNCTION, NAME APPEARS ON BOTH SIDES OF =
Probable cause: An array variable was not dimensioned.

SUBPROGRAMMES

SR-0 MISSING SUBPROGRAMME   Possible cause: An array variable was not dimensioned, hence presumed to be the name of a FUNCTION subprogramme.

SR-2 SUBPROGRAMME ASSIGNED DIFFERENT MODES IN DIFFERENT PROGRAMME SEGMENTS   The type of a FUNCTION name is the type of the value of that function; it must be the same type wherever the function value is used.

SR-4 INVALID TYPE OF ARGUMENT IN SUBPROGRAMME REFERENCE   One of the actual arguments of the subprogramme is of a type different from the type of the corresponding dummy argument in the subprogramme definition.

SR-5 SUBPROGRAMME ATTEMPTS TO REDEFINE A CONSTANT, TEMPORARY, OR DO PARAMETER   When a subprogramme alters one of its dummy argument values (e.g., by an assignment statement with the dummy argument name to the left of the = sign) the corresponding actual argument is altered upon return of control to the superior programme. In the present case, this actual argument was either a FORTRAN constant, or a temporary location (from evaluation of an actual argument which is a wfae), or one of the looping parameters of some DO loop.

SR-6 ATTEMPT TO USE SUBPROGRAMME RECURSIVELY   The subprogramme calls upon itself.

SR-7 WRONG NUMBER OF ARGUMENTS IN SUBPROGRAMME REFERENCE   The number of actual arguments disagrees with the number of dummy arguments.

SR-8 SUBPROGRAMME NAME PREVIOUSLY DEFINED - FIRST REFERENCE USED
You have given the same subprogramme name to two different subprogrammes. The first subprogramme by that name is being used.

SR-9 NO MAIN PROGRAMME

SR-A ILLEGAL OR BLANK SUBPROGRAMME NAME

SUBSCRIPTS

SS-0 ZERO SUBSCRIPT OR DIMENSION NOT ALLOWED

SS-1   SUBSCRIPT OUT OF RANGE   The numerical value of a subscript exceeds the number in the corresponding DIMENSION statement.

SS-2   INVALID VARIABLE OR NAME USED FOR DIMENSION   A subroutine name, logical variable name, or a character string has been used as a subscript.

STATEMENTS AND STATEMENT NUMBERS

ST-0   MISSING STATEMENT NUMBER   The missing number is given, also the line in which this statement number is used.

ST-1   STATEMENT NUMBER GREATER THAN 99999

ST-3   MULTIPLY-DEFINED STATEMENT NUMBER   You have used the same statement number for two or more FORTRAN statements.

ST-4   NO STATEMENT NUMBER ON STATEMENT FOLLOWING TRANSFER STATEMENT The statement immediately following a GO TO statement, or an arithmetic IF statement, or a STOP statement, or a RETURN statement *must* be numbered. An unnumbered statement in such a position can never be reached during execution of the programme.

ST-5   UNDECODEABLE STATEMENT   The WATFOR compiler could make no sense out of this mess.

ST-7   STATEMENT NUMBER SPECIFIED IN A TRANSFER IS THE NUMBER OF A NON-EXECUTABLE STATEMENT

ST-8   STATEMENT NUMBER CONSTANT MUST BE IN A CALL STATEMENT   The form &1200 is a "statement number constant" for statement number 1200. This form is permitted only within a CALL statement, as an actual argument replacing one of the dummy arguments *. Are you in trouble with the wrong type of key punch? What is + on one keypunch can be & on another keypunch.

ST-9   STATEMENT SPECIFIED IN A TRANSFER STATEMENT IS A FORMAT STATEMENT

ST-A   MISSING FORMAT STATEMENT   The statement number of the missing FORMAT statement is given along with this diagnostic.

SUBSCRIPTED VARIABLES

SV-0   WRONG NUMBER OF SUBSCRIPTS   The number of subscripts disagrees with the number of subscripts specified in the DIMENSION statement.

SV-1   ARRAY NAME OR SUBPROGRAMME NAME USED INCORRECTLY WITHOUT LIST An array name appears without subscripts in parentheses, or a subprogramme name appears without its list of actual arguments, in parentheses.

SV-2   MORE THAN 7 DIMENSIONS NOT ALLOWED

SV-3   DIMENSION TOO LARGE   In WATFOR, the subscript of an array variable must not have more than 8 digits.

SV-4   VARIABLE WITH VARIABLE DIMENSIONS IS NOT A SUBPROGRAMME PARAMETER   Only those variable names which appear on the list of dummy arguments may be assigned variable (adjustable) dimensions.

SV-5   VARIABLE DIMENSION NEITHER SIMPLE INTEGER NAME NOR SUBPROGRAMME PARAMETER   The identifier name of a variable (adjustable) dimension must be the name of a simple (non-array) variable of type INTEGER; furthermore, that particular name must appear in the list of dummy arguments.

SYNTAX ERRORS (ERRORS DETECTED IN ATTEMPTING TO DECODE ONE STATEMENT)

Note: All these diagnostics represent reasonable guesses, on the part of the compiler, as to the nature of the error you have made. Usually more detailed information appears after the code symbol itself. Only you can tell whether the erroneous statement is really in error in that particular fashion, or whether the compiler has jumped to conclusions. See Chapter VI, Section A.

SX-0   MISSING OPERATOR   The rest of the statement demands an operator, none there.

SX-1   SYNTAX ERROR - SEARCHING FOR SYMBOL, NONE FOUND

SX-2   SYNTAX ERROR - SEARCHING FOR CONSTANT, NONE FOUND

SX-3   SYNTAX ERROR - SEARCHING FOR SYMBOL OR CONSTANT, NONE FOUND

SX-4   SYNTAX ERROR - SEARCHING FOR STATEMENT NUMBER, NONE FOUND

SX-5   SYNTAX ERROR - SEARCHING FOR SIMPLE INTEGER VARIABLE, NONE FOUND

SX-C   ILLEGAL SEQUENCE OF OPERATORS IN EXPRESSION

SX-D   MISSING OPERAND OR OPERATOR

I/O OPERATIONS

UN-0   CONTROL CARD ENCOUNTERED ON CARD READER DURING EXECUTION. In attempting to read a data card, we have come upon a control card instead (probably the end-of-job card of your job, or the job card of the next job in the batch). This is the *usual* termination message if you have run out of data cards; special programming is needed to avoid this (e.g., see the programming exercises for Chapter V). Another possible cause is an incorrectly written FORMAT statement.

UN-1   END OF FILE ENCOUNTERED   See Chapter XV, Section L

UN-2   I/O ERROR   This is a machine error, not your fault. Preserve the output as well as the input card deck, and show both to the Computer Manager.

UN-3   DATA SET REFERENCED FOR WHICH NO DD CARD SUPPLIED   You have used a non-standard logical unit number in your FORTRAN programme, without supplying the monitor system control card (DD card) required to tell the monitor system what this logical unit number means. Have you enquired about the standard logical unit assignments for card reader, line printer, and card punch at your installation?

UN-4   REWIND, END FILE, BACKSPACE COMMANDS MUST NOT BE GIVEN TO THE CARD READER, LINE PRINTER, OR CARD PUNCH

UN-5   ATTEMPT TO READ THE CARD READER AFTER IT HAS COME TO THE END OF THE FILE

UN-6   LOGICAL UNIT NUMBER IS NEGATIVE, OR ZERO, OR TOO LARGE FOR THIS INSTALLATION

UN-7   TOO MANY PAGES OF OUTPUT

UN-8   ATTEMPT TO DO SEQUENTIAL I/O ON A DIRECT ACCESS FILE   Once a certain logical unit number has been defined as the number of a direct access file (by a DEFINE FILE statement), that unit number must not be used with ordinary (sequential) I/O

UN-9   YOU HAVE ATTEMPTED TO WRITE ONTO THE CARD READER, OR TO READ FROM THE LINE PRINTER OR CARD PUNCH

UNDEFINED VARIABLES, I.E., VARIABLES WHICH HAVE BEEN ASSIGNED NO VALUES SO FAR

UV-0   UNDEFINED VARIABLE - SIMPLE VARIABLE   The variable name appears also. This is the name of a storage location into which nothing has been stored as yet, but nonetheless you have attempted to use the contents of this storage location.

UV-1   UNDEFINED VARIABLE - EQUIVALENCED, COMMONED, OR DUMMY PARAMETER   See UV-0

UV-2   UNDEFINED VARIABLE - ARRAY MEMBER   See UV-0

UV-3   UNDEFINED VARIABLE - ARRAY NAME WHICH WAS USED AS A DUMMY PARAMETER   See UV-0

UV-4   UNDEFINED VARIABLE - SUBPROGRAMME NAME USED AS DUMMY PARAMETER   See UV-0

UV-5   UNDEFINED VARIABLE - ARGUMENT OF THE NAMED LIBRARY SUBPROGRAMME   See UV-0

UV-6   VARIABLE FORMAT CONTAINS UNDEFINED CHARACTER(S)

VARIABLE NAMES

VA-0   ATTEMPT TO REDEFINE TYPE OF A VARIABLE NAME   The offending variable name is given after the code symbol VA-0. In this diagnostic, "type" refers to one of: simple variable name, array variable name, subprogramme name, or COMMON block name.

VA-1   SUBROUTINE NAME OR COMMON BLOCK NAME USED INCORRECTLY   Names of SUBROUTINE subprogrammes and labels of labelled COMMON blocks must not be used as if they were variable names.

VA-2   VARIABLE NAME LONGER THAN SIX CHARACTERS. TRUNCATED TO SIX. This is a very common error, and WATFOR is a "forgiving" compiler: all but the first six characters have been removed from the name you supplied, and this truncated name is used henceforth. The programme might even work.

VA-3   ATTEMPT TO REDEFINE THE MODE OF A VARIABLE NAME

VA-4   ATTEMPT TO REDEFINE THE TYPE OF A VARIABLE NAME   The offending variable name is given, following the code symbol VA-4. In this diagnostic, "type" means one of INTEGER, REAL, COMPLEX, or LOGICAL.

VA-6   ILLEGAL USE OF A SUBROUTINE NAME   You have used the name of a SUBROUTINE programme as if it were the name of some other sort of variable (e.g., simple variable, array variable, function name, COMMON block name).

VA-8   ATTEMPT TO USE A PREVIOUSLY DEFINED NAME AS FUNCTION OR ARRAY Have you placed the DIMENSION statement for an array variable later than the first point at which this array variable is used in the programme?

VA-9   ATTEMPT TO USE A PREVIOUSLY DEFINED NAME AS A STATEMENT FUNCTION Possible cause: omission of a DIMENSION statement for an array variable.

VA-A   ATTEMPT TO USE A PREVIOUSLY DEFINED NAME AS A SUBPROGRAMME NAME

VA-B   NAME USED AS A COMMON BLOCK PREVIOUSLY USED AS A SUBPROGRAMME NAME   This refers to the label of a labelled COMMON area.

VA-C   NAME USED AS A SUBPROGRAMME NAME WAS PREVIOUSLY USED AS A COMMON BLOCK LABEL

VA-D   ILLEGAL DO-PARAMETER, ASSIGNED OR INITIALIZED VARIABLE IN SPECIFIC-ATION   One of the parameters in a DO statement, i.e., either the loop variable, or the initial value, or the termination test value, or the loop increment, has a variable name which has already appeared as the name of a variable in an ASSIGN statement, or which has appeared in a DATA initialization statement.

VA-E   ATTEMPT TO DIMENSION A CALL-BY-NAME PARAMETER   See Chapter XIV, end of Section B. A true array is referenced "by name" anyway, so there is no need to insist on this by placing slashes around the array name. If there are slashes, the compiler assumes that the name is the name of a simple (non-array) variable, and gets confused when a DIMENSION statement appears for a variable of that name.

EXTERNAL STATEMENT

XT-0   INVALID ELEMENT IN EXTERNAL LIST   One of the names in the list following the EXTERNAL declaration is not a grammatically correct subprogramme name.

XT-1   INVALID DELIMITER IN EXTERNAL STATEMENT   The names in the list must be separated by commas; there is *no* comma before the first name, and *no* comma after the last name, of that list.

XT-2   SUBPROGRAMME NAME APPEARED PREVIOUSLY IN AN EXTERNAL STATEMENT

APPENDIX C

ANSWERS TO DRILL EXERCISES

CHAPTER I   (FORTRAN source language programmes only are given here; control cards must be supplied in addition)

1.
```
READ,A,B,C
V=A*B*C
PRINT,A,B,C,V
STOP
END
```

2.
```
READ,A,B,C
V=A*B*C
S=2.0*(A*B+B*C+C*A)
PRINT,A,B,C,V,S
STOP
END
```

3.
```
READ,DEBT,PAYMNT,PERCNT
CHARGE=0.01*PERCNT*DEBT
REDUCE=PAYMNT-CHARGE
RESIDU=DEBT-REDUCE
PRINT,DEBT,PAYMNT,PERCNT,CHARGE,REDUCE,RESIDU
STOP
END
```

4.
```
READ,R1,R2
R=R1*R2/(R1+R2)
PRINT,R1,R2,R
STOP
END
```

5.
```
READ,RATE,HOURS,SURATE,TXRATE
GROSS=RATE*HOURS
SUDDCT=SURATE*GROSS
TXDDCT=TXRATE*GROSS
PAY=GROSS-SUDDCT-TXDDCT
PRINT,RATE,HOURS,SURATE,TXRATE,GROSS,SUDDCT,TXDDCT,PAY
STOP
END
```

```
6.    READ,RATE,HOURS,OVTIME,SURATE,TXRATE
      GROSS=RATE*HOURS+1.5*RATE*OVTIME
      SUDDCT=SURATE*GROSS
      TXDDCT=TXRATE*GROSS
      PAY=GROSS-SUDDCT-TXDDCT
      PRINT,RATE,HOURS,OVTIME,SURATE,TXRATE,GROSS,SUDDCT,TXDDCT,PAY
      STOP
      END

7.    READ,U,A,T
      S=U*T+0.5*A*T**2
      PRINT,U,A,T,S
      STOP
      END

8.    READ,A,B
      AREA=3.14159*A*B
      PRINT,A,B,AREA
      STOP
      END
```

CHAPTER II

1. KILLER (integer), 123GO (starts with non-alphabetic character), K123 (integer), DASTARD (more than 6 characters), PROFESSOR (ditto), MAD (integer), LOTTERY (more than 6 characters), LOTTRY (integer), WHATINHELL (more than 6 characters), BE WARY (interior blank).

2. 23, -23 are integers.

3. a)   (A-(B/(C+D)))   A-B/(C+D)

    b)   ((A-B)/(C+D))   (A-B)/(C+D)

    c)   ((A/(C+D))-B)   A/(C+D)-B

    d)   ((A/C)-(B/D))   A/C-B/D

    e)   ((A/(C+(B/D)))-E)   A/(C+B/D)-E

    f)   (((A-B)*(D-F))/((A-C)*(D-G)))   (A-B)*(D-F)/((A-C)*(D-G))

    g)   (((((3.0*(X**4))-(2.0*(X**2)))+(1.34*X))-2.5)
              3.0*X**4-2.0*X**2+1.34*X-2.5

4. (c), (e), (f), (g)

5. (e)

CHAPTER III

1. a)   (A.GT.B).AND.((C.LT.3.0).OR.(D.EQ.5.0))

    b)   (A.GT.2.0*B).AND.(A.LT.4.0*C)

    c)   (X.GT.A).OR.(X.GT.B).OR.(X.GT.C)

    d)   (X.GT.A).AND.(X.GT.B).AND.(X.GT.C)

    e)   (X.NE.A).AND.(Y.NE.B).AND.(Y.NE.C).AND.(Y.NE.D)

    f)   (X.GT.1.5).AND.(X.LT.2.3).AND.((Y.LT.1.5).OR.(Y.GT.2.3))

g)   (X.LT.1.5).AND.(Y.LT.1.5).OR.(X.GT.2.3).AND.(Y.GT.2.3)

2.   a)   Either X is less than or equal to Y, or Y is less than Z, or both

b)   Z lies between Y and X

c)   Either $2 \leqslant X \leqslant 4$,   or $1.5 < Y < 5.6$,   or both

d)   X lies outside the closed interval from 2 to 4

e)   same as d; the two logical expressions are equivalent

3.   a)   A=B should be replaced by A.EQ.B

b)   Parentheses are needed around A.GT.B

c)   A statement number in numerical form is needed instead of C

d)   periods missing in A.EQ.B

e)   right parenthesis missing

f)   names too long; right parenthesis missing

4.   a)
```
          IF(F.LE.0.0) GO TO 1200
          IF(C.GE.D) GO TO 1100
          BIG=D
          GO TO 2000
     1100 BIG=C
          GO TO 2000
     1200 IF(C.GE.D) GO TO 1300
          SMALL=C
          GO TO 2000
     1300 SMALL=D
     2000 ...
```

b)
```
          TEST=C
          IF((B.GT.2.5).AND.(B.LT.3.5)) TEST=D
```

c)
```
          Y=0.0
          IF(X.EQ.0.0) Y=0.5
          IF((X.GT.0.0).AND.(X.LT.1.0)) Y=X
          IF(X.GE.1.0) Y=1.0
```

5.   (b) is the only valid one.

6.   a)   likely to be an unending loop, since A will never equal 10.0, exactly, in the machine.

b)   the statements between GO TO 1100 and statement number 1100 can never be reached in execution of the programme.

7.   (a)   and   (b) yes   (c) no. Solution:
```
                              IF(A.GT.1.0) GO TO 2500
                              IF(A.GE.0.0) GO TO 2000
                              GO TO 1500
```

8.   (a)   and   (b) yes.   (c) no. Same solution, except omit the final GO TO 1500.

CHAPTER IV

1. 4.19,   4190,   0.00419,   0.00419,   4190   0.9999

2. 3.76E+15   -3.76E+15   3.76E-15   -3.76E-15

3. a)   correct
    b)   wrong value: .476E+2
    c)   minus sign missing: -.537E+3
    d)   decimal point missing: 436.
    e)   exponent missing: 74.8E0
    f)   correct

4. Two statements after statement number 1600, replace the command GO TO 3700 by the commands

    PRINT,X1
    GO TO 1000

    The preceding statement, X2=X1, can now be omitted, and should be omitted for the sake of clean coding.

5. a)   The symbol = is not a logical comparison operator. .EQ. must be used.

    b)   Using the rule that logical expressions are read from left to right, the bracketed form of this is

    IF(((A.EQ.B).EQ.C).EQ.0.0) STOP

    The innermost quantity to be evaluated is (A.EQ.B); this is a *logical* expression, with value either .TRUE. or .FALSE. It must not be compared, by means of the comparison operator .EQ., with C, which is an *arithmetic* quantity. The expressions on *both* sides of every operator .EQ. must be *arithmetic* expressions. The above is an "ill-formed" expression, i.e., grammatically incorrect FORTRAN.

    c)   A well-formed logical expression but not the one we want: suppose A=B=1.0 and C=0.0: the expression takes the value .TRUE., but this is not a case in which we really want to stop the calculation!

    d)   Correct

    e)   Only the outermost parentheses need be retained in either statement.

    f)   The warning does not apply because we are looking at numbers just as they have been read into memory, not at numbers resulting from some calculation. If the number 0.0 appears on a data card, the number stored into memory is 0.0, and the comparison A.EQ.0.0, say, gives .TRUE. as an answer.
    On the other hand, if we read a data card with values of E and F, these being + 23.6 and -23.6, respectively, the comparison (E+F).EQ.0.0 may give .FALSE. as an answer! Conversions occur from decimal form to internal machine form, and roundoff errors occur in addition; thus the value of E+F inside the machine may be some small number (such as 10^{-6}) rather than a true zero.

6. a)   READ,A,B,C   b)   READ,A,B,C
        READ,D,E   READ,D,E
        PRINT,A,B,C,D,E   PRINT,E,D,C,B,A

CHAPTER VII (OPTIONAL)

1.   a)   *69=105*   b)   *C3 = 195*   c)   *D31 = 3377*

2.   a)   17   b)   256   c)   2560
     d)   427   e)   2737

3.   a)   *00000001*   b)   *0000000C*
     c)   *000000F0*   d)   *000007C0*

4.   a)   k=66,   f=25/256,   number = 25
     b)   k=64,   f=25/256,   number = 25/256
     c)   k=0,   f=25/256,   number = $25/(16)^{66}$

CHAPTER VIII

1.   c)   omit decimal pt.   d)   omit comma   g)   omit decimal pt.
     h)   too large;   a,b,e,f are correct

2.   b)   need decimal pt.   d)   omit comma   e)   3.E0   f)   exponent too large
     g)   E, not D   i)   omit at least one zero;   a,c,h,j,k are correct

3.   a)   4-byte;   use +0.D0   g)   exponent too large;
   others are correct.

4.   b)   decimal pt. needed for real part   e)   mixed lengths
     g)   (4.7,0.);   others are correct.

5)   d)   mixed lengths   e)   mixed lengths   f)   mixed lengths;(3.1D2,0.D0)
     g)   imag. part is integer   h)   mixed lengths
     j)   exponent missing after second D
   others are correct.

6.   a)   5HDON'T   b)   'DON''T, PLEASE'
     c)   same as b   d)   same as b
     f)   13H, not 12H   h)   should be same as g, omit one apostrophe;
   others are correct.

CHAPTER IX

1.   IMPLICIT REAL*8(A-H), COMPLEX*16(O-Z),LOGICAL($)
   first statement of main programme
   second statement of subprogramme

2. DATA ALPHA,BETA,GAMMA,DELTA/4*1D0/
   DATA OMEGA/(-5D-1,.8660254038844385)/,ZI/(0D0,1D0)/
   DATA $TEST/T/

3. b) and d) imply conversion, the latter a truncation to 2, rather than rounding to 3

4. REAL*8 PRICE
   COMPLEX*16 BESSEL

5. IMPLICIT INTEGER*4(A-T),LOGICAL(U-Z)
   REAL*8 FRED,NURK,NONG,NING/3*1.D0,0.D0/

CHAPTER X

1. a) -2   b) -4
   c) -2   d) -2

2. a) REAL, -5.0, yes   b) INTEGER,4, no
   c) REAL, 10.0, yes   d) REAL, 2191.0, no
   e) REAL, 4.111111, yes   f) REAL, 343.2500, yes

3. a) 272000   b) 128000
   c) overflow   d) 0
   e) 2   f) overflow
   g) overflow

4. a) invalid   b) .TRUE.
   c) .TRUE.   d) .TRUE.
   e) invalid   f) invalid

5. a) negative**real is forbidden; 0**real is forbidden

   b) X.GT.$X illegal for .GT.; $CD**2 illegal (no arithmetic comparisons or arithmetic operations
      with logical variables)

CHAPTER XI

1.
```
      READ,A,INDEX
      GO TO (1100,1200,1300),INDEX
      DIRT=A
      GO TO 1400
 1100 A1=A
      GO TO 1400
 1200 A2=A
      GO TO 1400
 1300 A3=A
 1400 ...        (next statement in all cases)
```

2. a) omit comma after statement number
    b) K+3 cannot be used. Correct form: KPLUS3=K+3
                                                DO 3400 I=1,KPLUS3
    c) The increment A is not of type INTEGER, in the pre-defined convention
    d) The word TILL must not appear
    e) The word FOR must not appear
    f) Omit the final comma
    g) The loop variable must be of type INTEGER
    h) The name of the loop variable can not be used as a termination test value - this would amount
        to redefining the termination test value within the loop, and is forbidden

3.
```
        READ,A,INDEX
        IF(INDEX-2) 1100,1200,1300
   1100 A1=A
        GO TO 1400
   1200 A2=A
        GO TO 1400
   1300 A3=A
   1400 ...      (next statement in all cases)
```

4. a) loop increment is negative
        loop variable is redefined within the loop (statement 2000)
        the last statement transfers control inside the range of a DO loop
        the last statement uses the value of a DO loop variable after normal termination of the loop;
        actually, I is undefined there.

    b) the last statement of a DO loop is itself another DO - illegal.

    c) the loop variable I also appears as the loop increment
        DO loop finishes on an IF statement
        the statement K=I+6 uses the value of I after normal completion of the DO loop, when I is
        actually undefined
        the very last statement transfers control into the range of a DO loop

5. a) invalid: the integer must be unsigned
    b) invalid: the message must be inside apostrophes
    c) valid
    d) invalid: the integer must be no more than 5 figures long
    e) valid (but unduly optimistic!)

CHAPTER XII

1. a) A*SIN(PSI)-B   b) A*SIN(PSI-ALPHA)
    c) SIN(SQRT(LOG(U**2-V**3)))   d) COTAN(EXP(U)+SQRT(V))
    e) TANH(ATAN(U)+ARCOS(V))   f) A*SIN(AMAX1(U,V,W))

2. Use IMPLICIT REAL*8(D) at the start; then:
    a) DA*DSIN(DPSI)-DB   b) DA*DSIN(DPSI-DALPHA)
    c) DSIN(DSQRT(DLOG(DU**2-DV**3))) d) DCOTAN(DEXP(DU)+DSQRT(DV))

e)   DTANH(DATAN(DU)+DARCOS(DV))   f)   DA*DSIN(DMAX1(DU,DV,DW))

3.   Use IMPLICIT COMPLEX*8(C) at the start; then:

a)   CA*CSIN(CPSI)-CB   b)   CA*CSIN(CPSI-CALPHA)

c)   CSIN(CSQRT(CLOG(CU**2-CV**3)))   d)   CCOTAN(CC)=CCOS(CC)/CSIN(CC)
                                              CCOTAN(CEXP(CU)+CSQRT(CV))

e)   there is not built-in complex ATAN or ARCOS routine

f)   the "maximum" of three complex numbers has no meaning (the set is not ordered)

4.   Use IMPLICIT COMPLEX*16(C) at the start; then   b)   CA*CDSIN(CPSI-CALPHA)

a)   CA*CDSIN(CPSI)-CB   d)   CDCOTN(CC)=CDCOS(CC)/CDSIN(CC)

c)   CDSIN(CDSQRT(CDLOG(CU**2-CV**3)))   CDCOTN(CDEXP(CU)+CDSQRT(CV))

e) and f) same reasons as before.

5.   a)   The arithmetic statement function definition must come *before* the first executable state-
          ment of the programme, i.e., before the statement I=1.

     b)   Types are badly out of joint, unless type declaration statements are made. CDEXP is itself
          of type COMPLEX*16, and expects an argument of that type also. Unless the identifier
          names EXPSQ, X, and Z are declared to be of type COMPLEX*16 (and, in WATFOR, unless
          the name CDEXP is also declared of type COMPLEX*16), something is wrong. Even then,
          X is the wrong type of argument for the built-in function SIN; the built-in function CDSIN
          should be used. Furthermore, in the last statement, no actual argument is given for the arith-
          metic statement function EXPSQ.

     c)   (Bet you didn't find it!) One right hand parenthesis is missing at the end of the arithmetic
          statement function definition.

CHAPTER XIII

1.   a)   2.0   e)   4
     b)   5.0   f)   4
     c)   -1.0   g)   2.0
     d)   3   h)   9.0

2. a.)
```
      TEMP=A(15)
      DO 1200 I=1,14
      A(16-I)=A(15-I)
 1200 CONTINUE
      A(1)=TEMP
```

   b)
```
      TEMP=B(N)
      B(N)=B((N+1)/2)
      B((N+1)/2)=TEMP
```

c)

```
      NMIN1=N-1
      DO 1200 I=1,NMIN1,2
      TEMP=C(I)
      C(I)=C(I+1)
      C(I+1)=TEMP
 1200 CONTINUE
```

3.

```
      DIMENSION KOOKOO(8,8)
      DATA KOOKOO/64*0.0/
      DO 1200 I=1,7,2
      DO 1050 J=2,8,2
      KOOKOO(I,J)=I-J
 1050 CONTINUE
      IP=I+1
      DO 1100 J=1,7,2
      KOOKOO(IP,J)=IP+J
 1100 CONTINUE
 1200 CONTINUE
```

4. a)

```
      DO 1200 I=1,15
      B(I)=C*A(I)
 1200 CONTINUE
```

b)

```
      DO 1200 I=1,15
      A(I)=A(I)+B(I)
 1200 CONTINUE
```

c)

```
      DO 1200 I=1,15
      B(I)=A(I)-B(I)
 1200 CONTINUE
```

d)

```
      C=0.0
      DO 1200 I=1,15
      C=C+A(I)*B(I)
 1200 CONTINUE
```

e)

```
      C=0.0
      DO 1200 I=1,15
      C=C+A(I)**2
 1200 CONTINUE
      C=SQRT(C)
```

5.

```
      ANSWER=1.0
      DO 1200 I=1,N
      ANSWER=ANSWER*(1.0+X(I))
 1200 CONTINUE
```

6.

```
      MOP=M/2
      DO 1200 J=1,MOP
      TEMP=B(J)
      B(J)=B(MOP-J)
      B(MOP-J)=TEMP
 1200 CONTINUE
```

7. a)
```
      KWP=0
      KWK=0
      DO 1200 I=1,8
      DO 1100 J=1,8
      IF(KB(I,J).EQ.1)KWP=KWP+1
      IF(KB(I,J).EQ.2)KWK=KWK+1
 1100 CONTINUE
 1200 CONTINUE
```

b)
```
      KBP=0
      KBK=0
      DO 1200 I=1,8
      DO 1100 J=1,8
      IF(KB(I,J).EQ.-1)KBP=KBP+1
      IF(KB(I,J).EQ.-2)KBK=KBK+1
 1100 CONTINUE
 1200 CONTINUE
```

c)
```
      KOUNT=0
      DO 1300 I=1,8
      IF(KB(I,I).EQ.2)KOUNT=KOUNT+1
 1300 CONTINUE
```

d)
```
      KOUNT=0
      DO 1200 J=1,7
      JPLUS1=J+1
      DO 1100 I=JPLUS1,8
      IF(KB(I,J).EQ.-1)KOUNT=KOUNT+1
 1100 CONTINUE
 1200 CONTINUE
```

e)
```
      KOUNT=0
      DO 1200 I=1,8
      DO 1100 J=1,8
      IF(I.EQ.J) GO TO 1100
      IF(KB(I,J).EQ.1)KOUNT=KOUNT+1
 1100 CONTINUE
 1200 CONTINUE
```

f)
```
      KOUNT=0
      DO 1200 I=3,8
      DO 1100 J=1,8
      IF(KB(I,J).NE.1) GO TO 1100
      IF(J.LE.2) GO TO 1050
      IF(KB(I-1,J-1).LT.0.AND.KB(I-2,J-2).EQ.0) GO TO 1080
 1050 IF(J.GE.7) GO TO 1100
      IF(KB(I-1,J+1).LT.0.AND.KB(I-2,J+2).EQ.0) GO TO 1080
```
285

```
      GO TO 1100
1080  KOUNT=KOUNT+1
1100  CONTINUE
1200  CONTINUE
```

8. a)
```
      DIMENSION A(9,9),V(9)
      EQUIVALENCE (A(1,1),V(1))
```

  b)
```
      DIMENSION A(9,9),V(9)
      EQUIVALENCE (A(1,9),V(1))
```

  c)
```
      DIMENSION A(9,9),V(9)
      EQUIVALENCE (A(82),V(1))
```

  d)
```
      DIMENSION CARDS(4,13),QUEENS(4),QINGS(4),ACES(4)
      EQUIVALENCE(CARDS(1,11),QUEENS(1))
      EQUIVALENCE(CARDS(1,12),QINGS(1))
      EQUIVALENCE(CARDS(1,13),ACES(1))
```

9. a) 1.0   b) 2.0   c) 3.0   d) 3.0   e) 1.0

10. a) array requires 2000000000 memory locations, each of four bytes length!

   b) more than seven subscripts declared; the comma at the very end is wrong, too.

   c) more than 6 characters in array name; also, a dimension of unity is redundant and should be avoided. DIMENSION VECA1(3,3) would suffice.

CHAPTER XIV

1. a)
```
      FUNCTION ZIGZAG(X)
      U=ABS(X)
      V=AMOD(U,2.0)
      IF(V.GT.1.0) GO TO 1100
      ZIGZAG=V
      RETURN
1100  ZIGZAG=2.0-V
      RETURN
      END
```

  b)
```
      FUNCTION SQWAVE(X)
      U=ABS(X)
      V=AMOD(U,2.0)
      IF(V.EQ.0.0) GO TO 1020
      IF(V-1.0) 1010,1020,1030
1010  SQWAVE=1.0
```

```
      GO TO 1040
1020 SQWAVE=0.0
      GO TO 1040
1030 SQWAVE=-1.0
1040 IF(X.LT.0.0) SQWAVE=-SQWAVE
      RETURN
      END
```

c)

```
      FUNCTION KWAD(C)
      COMPLEX*8 C
      X=REAL(C)
      Y=AIMAG(C)
      K=1
      IF(Y) 1010,1000,1020
1000 K=0
      GO TO 1040
1010 K=3
1020 IF(X*Y) 1030,1000,1040
1030 K=K+1
1040 KWAD=K
      RETURN
      END
```

d)

```
      FUNCTION SMALL(VEC,N,MDIM)
      DIMENSION VEC(MDIM)
      SMALL=VEC(1)
      IF(N.EQ.1) GO TO 1300
      DO 1200 I=2,N
      IF(VEC(I).LT.SMALL)SMALL=VEC(I)
1200 CONTINUE
1300 RETURN
      END
```

e)

```
      FUNCTION TRACE(A,N,MDIM)
      DIMENSION A(MDIM,MDIM)
      TRACE=0.0
      DO 1100 I=1,N
      TRACE=TRACE+A(I,I)
1100 CONTINUE
      RETURN
      END
```

f)

```
      FUNCTION VERDCT(WTNESS,N,MDIM)
      IMPLICIT LOGICAL(V,W)
      DIMENSION WTNESS(MDIM)
      J=0
      DO 1100 I=1,N
```

```
      IF(WTNESS(I))J=J+1
1100  CONTINUE
      VERDCT=(J-N/2).GT.0
      RETURN
      END
```

2.   6.0,   2.0,   3.0,   4.0

3.
```
      SUBROUTINE HERMIT(C,N,MDIM)
      IMPLICIT COMPLEX*8(C)
      DIMENSION C(MDIM,MDIM)
      DO 1200 I=1,N
      DO 1100 J=1,N
      CTEMP=CONJG(C(I,J))
      C(I,J)=CONJG(C(J,I))
      C(J,I)=CTEMP
1100  CONTINUE
1200  CONTINUE
      RETURN
      END
```

4. a)
```
      SUBROUTINE MATADD(A,B,C,N,MDIM)
      DIMENSION A(MDIM,MDIM),B(MDIM,MDIM),C(MDIM,MDIM)
      DO 1200 I=1,N
      DO 1100 J=1,N
1050  C(I,J)=A(I,J)+B(I,J)
1100  CONTINUE
1200  CONTINUE
      RETURN
      END
```

  b)   Same as (a) except MATSUB and

```
1050  C(I,J)=A(I,J)-B(I,J)
```

  c)   Same as (a) except MATMPY and

```
1050  TEMP=0.0
      DO 1060 K=1,N
      TEMP=TEMP+A(I,K)*B(K,J)
1060  CONTINUE
      C(I,J)=TEMP
      statement 1100 follows
```

5.
```
      SUBROUTINE MATOP(A,B,C,N,MDIM,OPER)
      DIMENSION A(MDIM,MDIM),B(MDIM,MDIM),C(MDIM,MDIM)
1000  CALL OPER(A,B,C,N,MDIM)
      RETURN
      END
```

The EXTERNAL statement is required in the calling programme; it is not required in SUB-ROUTINE MATOP. (The character string OPER in statement 1000 above can only be the name of a SUBROUTINE subprogramme, by the language rules of FORTRAN; nothing else can be in that position within a CALL statement.)

6.
```
      SUBROUTINE PUTIN(X,K,VEC,N,MDIM,*)
      DIMENSION VEC(MDIM)
      NPLUS1=N+1
      IF(K.GT.NPLUS1.OR.NPLUS1.GT.MDIM) RETURN 1
      IF(K.EQ.NPLUS1) GO TO 2000
      NPLUS2=N+2
      MOVE=N-K+1
      DO 1200 I=1,MOVE
      VEC(NPLUS2-I)=VEC(NPLUS1-I)
C     EXPLAIN THIS CODING !
 1200 CONTINUE
 2000 VEC(K)=X
      N=NPLUS1
      RETURN
      END
```

7.
```
      SUBROUTINE REMOVE(K,VEC,N,MDIM,*)
      DIMENSION VEC(MDIM)
      IF(K.GT.N.OR.N.GT.MDIM) RETURN 1
      N=N-1
      IF(K.EQ.N+1) RETURN
      DO 1100 I=K,N
      VEC(I)=VEC(I+1)
 1100 CONTINUE
      VEC(N+1)=0.0
      RETURN
      END
```

8. a) Replace the DIMENSION statement by

```
      DIMENSION A(MDIM,MDIM)
      COMMON/WORKA/AVEC(900)
```

b) No changes are required in the calling programme

c) The calling programme contains the statements

```
      COMMON/HORROR/WHAT(20,20)
      ...
      DET=DETER(WHAT,16,20)
      ...
```

9. In the main programme:

```
      COMMON/MESS/JUNK(20),WHYNOT(25,25),BLANK(255)
```

In the subprogramme WHOSIS:

```
COMMON/MESS/JUNK(20),QUACK(500), BLANK(380)
```

In subprogramme GURGLE:

```
COMMON/MESS/KOOKIE(40),BLANK(860)
```

To initialize to zero:

```
BLOCK DATA
COMMON/MESS/JUNK(20),BLANK(880)
DATA JUNK/20*0/,BLANK/880*0.0/
END
```

(Note the last 20 components of KOOKIE are initialized to floating point zeros, which may or may not agree with integer zeros in the machine).

10.
```
      SUBROUTINE MATADD(A,B,C,N,MDIM)
      DIMENSION A(MDIM,MDIM),B(MDIM,MDIM),C(MDIM,MDIM)
      INDEX=1
      GO TO 1000
C
      ENTRY MATSUB(A,B,C,N,MDIM)
      DIMENSION A(MDIM,MDIM),B(MDIM,MDIM),C(MDIM,MDIM)
C     NOTE THIS IS NECESSARY TO RESET DIMENSION INFORMATION
C          FOR THIS ENTRY
      INDEX=2
      GO TO 1000
C
      ENTRY MATMPY(A,B,C,N,MDIM)
      DIMENSION A(MDIM,MDIM),B(MDIM,MDIM),C(MDIM,MDIM)
      INDEX=3
C     PATHS JOIN
 1000 DO 1200 I=1,N
      DO 1100 J=1,N
C     NOW BRANCH OUT DEPENDING UPON THE VALUE OF INDEX
      GO TO (1010,1020,1030),INDEX
 1010 C(I,J)=A(I,J)+B(I,J)
      GO TO 1100
C     NEXT COMES THE MATSUB BRANCH
 1020 C(I,J)=A(I,J)-B(I,J)
      GO TO 1100
C     LAST COMES THE MATMPY BRANCH
 1030 TEMP=0.0
      DO 1060 K=1,N
      TEMP=TEMP+A(I,K)*B(K,J)
 1060 CONTINUE
      C(I,J)=TEMP
C     ALL THREE BRANCHES REJOIN NOW
 1100 CONTINUE
 1200 CONTINUE
```

```
      RETURN
      END

11.
      FUNCTION DRSINH(DX)
      IMPLICIT REAL*8(D)
      DATA DLOG2/0.69314718055994453/
 1000 DCON=1.0D0
      GO TO 1200
C
      ENTRY DRCOSH(DX)
 1100 DCON=-1.0D0
      IF(DX.GE.1.0D0) GO TO 1200
C     FAILURE RETURN
      DRSINH=0.0D0
      CALL SLITE(1)
      RETURN
C
 1200 DY=DABS(DX)
      IF(DY.GT.1.0D8) GO TO 1500
C     NOTE 10**8 FOR THIS TEST, NOT 10**4. EXPLAIN!
      IF(DY.LT.1.0D-4) GO TO 1300
C     NOTE 10**(-4) FOR THIS TEST, NOT 0.01. EXPLAIN!
C     NORMAL CASE
      DW=DLOG(DY+DSQRT(DY**2+DCON))
      GO TO 2000
C     SMALL DY
 1300 DW=DY-DY**3/6.0D0
      GO TO 2000
C     LARGE DY
 1500 DW=DLOG(DY)+DLOG2
 2000 DRSINH=DSIGN(DW,DX)
      RETURN
      END
```

CHAPTER XV

1. a) no comma should appear after statement number of FORMAT statement

   b) no comma should appear before the first item of the list

   c) no comma should appear after the last item of the list

   d) the list must contain variable names, not actual numbers

   e) the implied DO loop is written incorrectly; perhaps I=1,1500,1 is meant

   f) ⟩ the list must contain simple variable names, not arithmetic expressions (note: this statement would actually work in WATFOR, but not in standard FORTRAN).

2. The statement number and the character string FORMAT are omitted below:
   a) (10I12)
   b) (5E20.6)
   c) (1P5E20.5)
   d) (2I15,1P2E20.5,0P2F20.8) is a possible choice

e) (5G20.6) *note:* The widths in (b)-(e) are flexible, could be chosen as high as 24 for a line of length 120

3. a) excessive line length

   b) comma should be replaced by (

   c) omit the comma

   d) field width of 10 is too small for 9 digits after the decimal point

   e) field width of 15 is too small for 9 digits after the decimal point

   f) field width barely adequate; numbers are not spaced out properly.

   g) field width inadequate; possible minus signs are lost, and the numbers run into each other

4. a)
```
 1009 FORMAT (' ',I12,7E16.7)
```
   for a printer with 132 or more positions
```
 1009 FORMAT (' ',I12,6E16.7/' ',E16.7)
```
   for a printer with 120 positions

   b)
```
 1009 FORMAT (' ',I15,3G25.6/' ',T16,4F25.3)
```

   c)
```
 1009 FORMAT ('1NEW ITERATION'/'0M=',I15/'0A=',G25.6,4X,'B=',G25.6,4X,'C
     1=',G25.6/'0D=',F25.3,4X,'E=',F25.3,4X,'F=',F25.3,4X,'G=',F25.3)
```

5.
```
 1004 FORMAT (T12,'M',T22,'X',T38,'Y',T54,'Z'/)
```

6.
```
      WRITE (NPRINT,1401) (I,(A(I,J),J=1,4),I=1,4)
 1401 FORMAT (' ',T40,'MATRIX ARRAY A'/'0  ROW NO',12X,'COLUMN 1',12X,'C
     1OLUMN 2',12X,'COLUMN 3',12X,'COLUMN 4'//(I8,4G20.7))
```

   Alternative solution to problem 6 :
```
      WRITE (NPRINT,1401) (K,K=1,4),(I,(A(I,J),J=1,4),I=1,4)
 1401 FORMAT (' ',T40,'MATRIX ARRAY A'/'0  ROW NO',4(12X,'COLUMN',I2)//(
     1I8,4G20.7)
```

7.
```
      WRITE (NPRINT,1402) (I,D(I,I),I=1,40)
 1402 FORMAT (' ',T30,'DIAGONAL ELEMENTS OF MATRIX D, WITH ORDER NUMBERS
     1'//(5(I8,G16.7)))
```

8.
```
      WRITE (NPRINT,1403) (I,(B(I,J),J=1,7),I=1,7,2)
 1403 FORMAT (' ',T30,'ODD NUMBERED ROWS OF MATRIX B'/'0  ROW NO',8X,'CO
     1LUMN 1',8X,'COLUMN 2',8X,'COLUMN 3',8X,'COLUMN 4',8X,'COLUMN 5',8X
     2,'COLUMN 6',8X,'COLUMN 7'//(I8,7G16.7))
```

   Alternative solution to problem 8 :

```
      WRITE (NPRINT,1403) (K,K=1,7),(I,(B(I,J),J=1,7),I=1,7,2)
 1403 FORMAT (' ',T30,'ODD NUMBERED ROWS OF MATRIX B'/'0  ROW NO',7(8X,'
     1COLUMN',I2)//(I8  ,7G16.7))
```

9.
```
      WRITE (NPRINT,1404) N,M,(I,(C(I,J),J=1,20),I=N,M,2)
 1404 FORMAT (' ',T20,'EVEN NUMBERED ROWS OF MATRIX B, BETWEEN ROWS NO',
     1I5,5X,'AND',I5//(I8,5G20.7/8X,5G20.7/8X,5G20.7/8X,5G20.7/))
```

10.
```
      WRITE (NPRINT,1405)
 1405 FORMAT (' ',T20,'ELEMENTS OF MATRIX E ON AND BELOW THE DIAGONAL'/)
      DO 1408 I=1,40
      WRITE (NPRINT,1407) I,(E(I,J),J=1,I)
 1407 FORMAT (I8,5G20.7/(8X,5G20.7))
 1408 CONTINUE
```

11.
```
      WRITE (NPRINT,1409) ((KB(I,J),J=1,8),I=1,8)
 1409 FORMAT ('1',T20,'CHECKERBOARD. 1=MAN, 2=KING, +=WHITE, -=BLACK',(/
     1////11X,8I10))
```

12.
```
      DIMENSION SYMBOL(5)
      DATA SYMBOL/'BK','BM','..','WM','WK'/
      WRITE (NPRINT,1501) ((SYMBOL(KB(I,J)+3),J=1,8),I=1,8)
 1501 FORMAT ('1',T20,'CHECKERBOARD. W=WHITE, B=BLACK, M=MAN, K=KING',(/
     1////11X,8A10))
```

13.
```
      DIMENSION SSAGE(3)
      DATA SSAGE/'O.K.','SOSO','BAD!'/
      WRITE (NPRINT,1502)
 1502 FORMAT ('1',11X,'WIDTH',14X,'HEIGHT',16X,'DRAG',17X,'COMMENT'/)
      DO 1505 I=1,25
      K=1
      IF(DRAG(I).GT.0.01) K=2
      IF(DRAG(I).GT.10.0) K=3
      WRITE (NPRINT,1503) WIDTH(I),HEIGHT(I),DRAG(I),SSAGE(K)
 1503 FORMAT (' ',3G20.7,16X,A4)
      IF(MOD(I,5).EQ.0) WRITE (NPRINT,1504)
 1504 FORMAT (' ')
 1505 CONTINUE
```

14.
```
      IMPLICIT REAL*8(D)
      DIMENSION DMAT(15,15),DVEC(225)
      EQUIVALENCE (DMAT(1,1),DVEC(1))
      ...
      IF(MOD(I,5).NE.0) GO TO 1630
      WRITE (NPUNCH,1601) I,J,K,DA,DB,DC,I
```

```
 1601 FORMAT (3I3,1P3D21.15,'SCR',I3,'1')
      DO 1604 L=1,223,3
      LP=L+2
      KARD=(L+5)/3
      WRITE (NPUNCH,1602) (DVEC(M),M=L,LP),I,KARD
 1602 FORMAT (9X,1P3D21.15,'SCR',I3,I2)
 1604 CONTINUE
 1630 ...
```

15.

```
      DIMENSION KB(8,8),LVEC(5)
      DATA LVEC/1,2,3,4,5/
      ...
      WRITE (NPUNCH,1605) ((LVEC(KB(I,J)+3),J=1,8),I=1,8),NGAME,
     1NMOVE,KARDNO
 1605 FORMAT (64I1,2I4,'CHECK',I3)
      KARDNO=KARDNO+1
```

16.

```
      READ (NREAD,1701) (W(I,5),W(I,6),I=1,5)
 1701 FORMAT (2F10.5)
```

17.

```
      READ (NREAD,1702) ((WHACKO(I,J),J=1,19),I=2,14,2)
 1702 FORMAT (7F10.5)
```

18.

```
      SUBROUTINE READER(I,J,K,DA,DB,DC,DVEC)
      IMPLICIT REAL*8(D)
      DIMENSION IVEC(3),DVOC(3),DVEC(225)
      DATA CARDID/'SCR'/,NREAD,NPRINT,NPUNCH/5,6,7/
C     PREPARE TO READ IN THE FIRST CARD
 1000 KARD=1
      NONG=1
C     KARD WILL BE COMPARED WITH THE CARD NUMBER READ IN.
C     NONG=1 MEANS EVERYTHING O.K. NONG=2 MEANS FAILURE SOMEWHERE.
C     NOW START TO READ IN CARD. ALL CARDS ARE READ BY THE
C     STATEMENT WHICH FOLLOWS. DUMMY LOCATIONS ARE USED
C     FOR FLEXIBILITY.
 1010 READ (NREAD,1015) IVEC,DVOC,CORDID,II,KORD
 1015 FORMAT (3I3,1P3D21.15,A3,I3,I2)
C     NOW CARRY OUT TESTS, SUITABLE FOR ALL CARDS.
      IF(CORDID.EQ.CARDID) GO TO 1025
      WRITE (NPRINT,1020)
 1020 FORMAT (' INCORRECT CARD IDENTIFICATION')
      NONG=2
 1025 IF(KORD.EQ.KARD) GO TO 1035
      WRITE (NPRINT,1030)
 1030 FORMAT (' THIS CARD IS OUT OF ORDER')
      NONG=2
C     NOW BRANCH OUT, DEPENDING UPON WHETHER THIS IS CARD NO.1
 1035 IF(KARD.NE.1) GO TO 1100
C     THIS IS THE FIRST CARD OF THE SET. ONE MORE TEST.
      IF(IVEC(1).EQ.II) GO TO 1045
```

```
      WRITE (NPRINT,1040)
 1040 FORMAT (' VALUES OF I ON THE CARD DISAGREE')
      NONG=2
 1045 GO TO (1050,1200),NONG
C     NORMAL FIRST CARD. DISTRIBUTE THE NUMBERS READ.
 1050 I=IVEC(1)
      J=IVEC(2)
      K=IVEC(3)
      DA=DVOC(1)
      DB=DVOC(2)
      DC=DVOC(3)
      KARD=KARD+1
      GO TO 1010
C     THIS GOES BACK TO READ CARD NUMBER 2
C
C     THE SEQUENCE BELOW DOES FURTHER TESTS ON THE LATER CARDS.
 1100 IF(I.EQ.II) GO TO 1110
      WRITE (NPRINT,1105)
 1105 FORMAT (' VALUE OF I ON THIS CARD DISAGREES WITH VALUE ON FIRST CA
     1RD OF THIS SET')
      NONG=2
 1110 IF(IVEC(1).EQ.0.AND.IVEC(2).EQ.0.AND.IVEC(3).EQ.0) GO TO 1120
      WRITE (NPRINT,1115)
 1115 FORMAT (' NON-ZERO I,J,K ON A CARD OTHER THAN THE FIRST CARD')
      NONG=2
 1120 GO TO (1130,1200),NONG
C     NORMAL LATER CARD
 1130 DO 1140 KOOK=1,3
      DVEC(3*KARD+KOOK-3)=DVOC(KOOK)
C     CHECK THAT ADDRESS WITHIN DVEC, PLEASE!
 1140 CONTINUE
      KARD=KARD+1
C     NOW TEST WHETHER WE HAVE READ ALL CARDS OF THE SET (76 CARDS)
      IF(KARD.LE.76) GO TO 1010
      RETURN
C     THERE HAS BEEN A FAILURE. PRINT OUT CARD IMAGE.
 1200 WRITE (NPRINT,1205) IVEC,DVOC,CORDID,II,KORD
 1205 FORMAT (' CARD IMAGE OF BAD CARD',5X,3I3,1P3D21.15,A3,I3,I2//)
      STOP
      END


19.
      SUBROUTINE READER(KB,NGAME,NMOVE)
      DIMENSION CHOCK(2),KB(8,8),SYMBOL(5),KVEC(64),CHICK(2)
      DATA CHOCK/'CHECK'/,SYMBOL/'BK','BM','..','WM','WK'/
      DATA NREAD,NPRINT,NPUNCH/5,6,7/
 1000 NONG=1
      READ (NREAD,1005) KVEC,NGAME,NMOVE,CHICK,KARDNO
 1005 FORMAT (64I1,2I4,A4,A1,I3)
C     CHECK THE IDENTIFICATION
      DO 1010 I=1,2
      IF(CHICK(I).EQ.CHOCK(I)) GO TO 1010
      WRITE (NPRINT,1007)
 1007 FORMAT (' CARD IDENTIFICATION IS WRONG')
```

```
            NONG=2
 1010 CONTINUE
C     CHECK THAT ALL VALUES OF KVEC ARE IN PERMISSIBLE RANGE
      DO 1020 I=1,64
      IF(1.LE.KVEC(I).AND.KVEC(I).LE.5) GO TO 1020
      WRITE (NPRINT,1017) I,KVEC(I)
 1017 FORMAT (' COMPONENT NUMBER',I5,'   OF POSITION VECTOR HAS AN IMPOS
     1SIBLE VALUE, EQUAL TO',I12)
      NONG=2
 1020 CONTINUE
      GO TO (1100,1200),NONG
C     CARD WAS O.K. PRINT OUT APPROPRIATE MESSAGE.
 1100 WRITE (NPRINT,1110) NGAME,NMOVE,(SYMBOL(KVEC(I),I=1,64)
 1110 FORMAT ('1RESTART OF GAME NO.',I5,' AT MOVE NO.',I5//' PRESENT  PO
     1SITION.  W=WHITE, B=BLACK, M=MAN, K=KING'/(//////11X,8A10))
C     NOW SET THE VALUES IN ARRAY KB FROM KVEC VALUES
      DO 1120 I=1,8
      DO 1119 J=1,8
      KB(I,J)=KVEC(J+8*(I-1))-3
C     NOTE THE PECULIAR ORDER NUMBER WITHIN KVEC. KVEC IN ROW ORDER!
 1119 CONTINUE
 1120 CONTINUE
      RETURN
C     THE SEQUENCE BELOW IS FOR A FAILURE
 1200 WRITE (NPRINT,1201) KVEC,NGAME,NMOVE,CHICK,KARDNO
 1201 FORMAT (' CARD IMAGE OF BAD CARD',5X,64I1,2I4,A4,A1,I3)
      STOP
      END
```

20.
```
      DIMENSION VEC(20),GEE(35,35)
      NAMELIST/GETIT/I,J,K,A,B,C,VEC,GEE
```
   the input statement in the source programme is
```
      READ (NREAD,GETIT)
```
   a possible data card is (the first '&' must be in column 2)
```
 &GETIT J=5,K=5,B=0.0, VEC=20*0.0,GEE=3.5,1223*1.0,6.8,&END
```

21.
```
      DIMENSION VEC(20),GEE(35,35)
      NAMELIST/GETIT/J,VEC(1),GEE(2,3)
      WRITE (NPUNCH,GETIT)
```

22.
```
      DIMENSION SENTCE(20),QILROY(4)
C     STORING 4 CHARACTERS TO A WORD IS POSSIBLE HERE, AND
C         QUICKER
      DATA QILROY/'KILROY WAS HERE'/,FINIS/'&END'/
      DATA NREAD,NPRINT,NPUNCH/5,6,7/
 1000 KOUNT=0
 1010 READ (NREAD,1015) SENTCE
 1015 FORMAT (1X,19A4,A3)
C     WHAT WOULD BE WRONG WITH (1X,20A4) ??
      IF(SENTCE(1).EQ.FINIS) GO TO 1100
C     TEST FOR KILROY WAS HERE
```

296

```
      DO 1020 I=1,4
      IF(SENTCE(I).NE.QILROY(I)) GO TO 1010
1020 CONTINUE
C     IF WE GET TO THIS POINT, KILROY WAS REALLY HERE
      KOUNT=KOUNT+1
      GO TO 1010
C     WE GET HERE AFTER READING THE CARD &END
1100 WRITE (NPRINT,1105) KOUNT
1105 FORMAT (' THE MESSAGE    KILROY WAS HERE    APPEARED',I10,'  TIMES').
      STOP
```

23.

```
      DIMENSION OLDSTC(20,500),SENTCE(20)
      DATA FINIS/'&END'/,NREAD,NPRINT,NPUNCH/5,6,7/
1000 INDEX=1
C     THIS INDEX EQUALS 1 FOR THE FIRST CARD ONLY.
      KOUNT=0
C     THIS WILL BE A RUNNING COUNT OF DISTINCT SENTENCES
C
C     START OF READING LOOP
1010 READ(NREAD,1015) SENTCE
1015 FORMAT (1X,19A4,A3)
C     WAS THIS THE FIRST CARD?
      GO TO (1020,1025),INDEX
C     YES, IT WAS... SKIP OVER DUPLICATION TEST!
1020 INDEX=2
      GO TO 1100
C     NO, IT WAS NOT... TEST FOR DUPLICATION.
1025 DO 1040 K=1,KOUNT
      DO 1035 J=1,20
      IF(SENTCE(J).NE.OLDSTC(J,K)) GO TO 1040
1035 CONTINUE
C     IF WE GET TO THIS POINT, IT WAS A DUPLICATE CARD
      GO TO 1010
1040 CONTINUE
C     IF WE GET TO THIS POINT, THE MESSAGE ON THE CARD IS NEW
1100 KOUNT=KOUNT+1
      WRITE (NPUNCH,1015) SENTCE
C     NOTE USE OF SAME FORMAT AS BEFORE, FOR A CARD COPY
      DO 1110 J=1,20
      OLDSTC(J,KOUNT)=SENTCE(J)
1110 CONTINUE
C     NOW TEST FOR THE &END CARD
      IF(SENTCE(1).NE.FINIS) GO TO 1010
      STOP
```

24.

```
      DATA NREAD,NPRINT,NPUNCH/5,6,7/
      DIMENSION FMT(18), X(100),Y(100)
      READ(NREAD,1100) FMT
1100 FORMAT (18A4)
      READ (NREAD,FMT) ITEMS,KREE,(X(I),Y(I),I=1,ITEMS)
```

for the first laboratory, their data cards are preceded by the card
(2I5/(2F10.5))

for the second laboratory, their data cards are preceded by the card

`(2I5,6F10.5/(7F10.5))`

Note that FMT could have a smaller dimension, but better to play it safe.

25.

```
      SUBROUTINE SAVER
      COMMON/INTS/JUNK(325)/FLOATS/PUNK(15000)
      DATA NREAD,NPRINT,NPUNCH/5,6,7/,NTAPE/13/
 1000 CALL SLITET(1,J)
      GO TO (1100,1200),J
C     SENSE LIGHT 1 WAS ON
 1100 REWIND NTAPE
      READ(NTAPE) JUNK,PUNK
      CALL SLITE(2)
      WRITE (NPRINT,1105) JUNK(1)
 1105 FORMAT ('1RESTART WAS NECESSARY, PROGRAMME RESTARTED WITH I=',I9/)
      RETURN
C     SENSE LIGHT 1 WAS OFF
 1200 IF(MOD(JUNK(1),20).NE.0) GO TO 1300
      REWIND NTAPE
      WRITE (NTAPE) JUNK,PUNK
 1300 RETURN
      END
```

26.

```
      DATA NREAD,NPRINT,NPUNCH/5,6,7/,NTAPE/13/
      DIMENSION XNEW(3),XOLD(3)
 1000 DIST=0.0
      KREC=0
      REWIND NTAPE
 1100 KREC=KREC+1
      READ (NTAPE) NREC,XNEW
      IF(NREC.EQ.KREC) GO TO 1110
 1103 WRITE (NPRINT,1105) NREC,KREC
 1105 FORMAT ('0RECORD NO',I10,' READ FROM TAPE, INSTEAD OF NO', I10//)
      STOP
 1110 IF(NREC.EQ.1) GO TO 1150
      TEMP=0.0
      DO 1120 I=1,3
      TEMP=TEMP+(XNEW(I)-XOLD(I))**2
 1120 CONTINUE
      DIST=DIST+SQRT(TEMP)
      IF(XNEW(3).LE.0.0) GO TO 1200
 1150 DO 1160 I=1,3
      XOLD(I)=XNEW(I)
 1160 CONTINUE
      GO TO 1100
C     WE REACH THE POINT BELOW WHEN NREC.NE.0.AND.XNEW(3). LE.0.0
 1200 TIME=FLOAT(NREC)*0.01
      WRITE (NPRINT,1205) TIME,DIST
 1205 FORMAT ('0COMPUTED DISTANCE, FOR A FLIGHT TIME OF',F10.2,'  SECOND
     1S IS',F16.6/)
      REWIND NTAPE
      STOP
```

27.
```
       DATA NREAD,NPRINT,NPUNCH/5,6,7/,NTAPE1,NTAPE2/13,14/
       DIMENSION XNEW(3),XOLD(3)
 1000 REWIND NTAPE1
       REWIND NTAPE2
       KREC=0
C      HEADING INFORMATION ONTO TAPE NTAPE2
       WRITE (NTAPE2,1005)
 1005 FORMAT ('1SPEEDS OF THE ROCKET (COLUMN 1) AT SELECTED TIMES (COLUM
     1N 2)'//)
C      READ RELEVANT TWO RECORDS ON TAPE NTAPE1
 1010 KREC=KREC+1
       READ (NTAPE1) NREC,XOLD
       IF(NREC.EQ.KREC) GO TO 1030
C      READ FAILURE
 1020 WRITE (NPRINT,1021) NREC,KREC
 1021 FORMAT ('0RECORD NO',I10,'READ FROM TAPE INSTEAD OF NO',I10//)
       STOP
 1030 IF(XOLD(3).LE.0.0.AND.NREC.NE.1) GO TO 1100
       KREC=KREC+1
       READ (NTAPE1) NREC,XNEW
       IF(NREC.NE.KREC) GO TO 1020
       IF(XNEW(3).LE.0.0) GO TO 1100
C      NOW COMPUTE SPEED
       TEMP=0.0
       DO 1040 I=1,3
       TEMP=TEMP+(XNEW(I)-XOLD(I))**2
 1040 CONTINUE
       SPEED=SQRT(TEMP)*100.0
       TIME=0.01*(NREC-2)
       WRITE (NTAPE2,1045) SPEED,TIME
 1045 FORMAT (' ',2G20.7)
C      NOW SPACE FORWARD OVER THE NEXT 98 RECORDS
C      REMEMBER TO CHECK FOR THE LAST RECORD ON TAPE NTAPE1
       DO 1060 I=1,98
       KREC=KREC+1
       READ (NTAPE1) NREC,XOLD
       IF(NREC.NE.KREC) GO TO 1020
       IF(XOLD(3).LE.0.0) GO TO 1100
 1060 CONTINUE
       GO TO 1010
C      WE GET TO THIS POINT WHEN XOLD(3).LE.0.0.AND.NREC.NE.1
 1100 REWIND NTAPE1
       SPEED=-1.0
       TIME=-1.0
       WRITE (NTAPE2,1105) SPEED,TIME
 1105 FORMAT (' ',2G20.7,' THIS IS ALL, BOYS! CHEERIO!')
C      WHEN READING THE TAPE LATER, WE CAN TEST FOR NEGATIVE SPEED
       END FILE NTAPE2
       REWIND NTAPE2
       WRITE (NPRINT,1110) NTAPE2
 1110 FORMAT (' COMPUTATION OF SPEEDS COMPLETED, INFORMATION IS NOW ON T
     1APE',I10//)
       STOP
```

```
        SUBROUTINE CLOCKR(N)
C       USES SUBROUTINE CLOCK(TIME) TO FIND TIME
C       PRINT OUT N AND ELAPSED TIME IF N.GT.0
C       MERELY SETS OLDTIM, PRINTS N, IF N.LE.0
        DATA NREAD,NPRINT,NPUNCH/5,6,7/
 1000 IF(N.LE.0) GO TO 1100
C       N.GT.0 BRACH...
        CALL CLOCK(TIME)
        ELAPSE=TIME-OLDTIM
        WRITE (NPRINT,1010) N,ELAPSE
 1010 FORMAT (' CLOCKR ENTERED WITH N=',I10,8X,'ELAPSED TIME=', F12.3)
        GO TO 1200
C       N.LE.0 BRACH...
 1100 WRITE (NPRINT,1110) N
 1110 FORMAT (' CLOCKR ENTERED WITH N=',I10,8X,'CLOCK SET.')
C       PATHS REJOIN...
 1200 CALL CLOCK(TIME)
        OLDTIM=TIME
C       IN THIS WAY, THE TIME TAKEN FOR PRINTOUT IS NOT COUNTED IN ELAPSE
        RETURN
        END
```

APPENDIX D

DIALECTS OF FORTRAN

As mentioned at the beginning of Part B of the book, there are many "dialects" of the FORTRAN language. To give an exhaustive description of all dialects would take a great deal of space, and would not be worth the effort, since the dialects are by no means stable; on the contrary, manufacturers tend to consider "their own" FORTRAN as a selling point, and as soon as one dialect of FORTRAN acquires some "gimmick" or other, other dialects try to go it one better.

Rather than giving exhaustive lists, we shall point out the main sources of variation between dialects of FORTRAN, and give some discussion under each heading. The main sources of variation are three:

1. Major variations, which happen only rarely. The step from FORTRAN I to FORTRAN II was one such, the step from FORTRAN II to FORTRAN IV another.

2. Differences between machine hardware, resulting naturally in differences in the translated (object) programme produced from a given source programme; the main point here is the number of bits per machine word.

3. The desire of each manufacturer to have some special selling point for "his" FORTRAN.

1. Major Variations

There is little doubt that the two major variations, from FORTRAN I to FORTRAN II and from FORTRAN II to FORTRAN IV, have both been significant improvements. In the first of these steps, the main change was the introduction of subprogramme facilities: in FORTRAN I, the entire programme had to be written as one main programme, whereas FORTRAN II allowed the writing of FUNCTION and SUBROUTINE subprogrammes.

The step from FORTRAN II to FORTRAN IV was equally major, and we now mention the main differences between these dialects of FORTRAN. From the point of view of a programmer wishing to convert a FORTRAN II to a FORTRAN IV programme, the most annoying (and least defensible) difference is the renaming of all standard built-in function subprogrammes. In FORTRAN II, built-in functions had names ending with the letter F, for example, SINF(X) rather than SIN(X). Furthermore functions whose *value* was an integer had an *initial* letter X to their name, for example XMODF(I,J) rather than MOD(I,J).

Another difference is the replacement of certain standard FORTRAN II statements by calls on standard subroutine subprogrammes in FORTRAN IV. Thus the FORTRAN II statement SENSE LIGHT 2 is replaced, in FORTRAN IV, by CALL SLITE(2). Of particular interest are the statements checking for arithmetic failures during computation. In FORTRAN II, specific IF statements were provided for this, namely

301

IF DIVIDE CHECK *n, m*
IF QUOTIENT OVERFLOW *n, m*
IF ACCUMULATOR OVERFLOW *n, m*

In each case, control was transferred to statement number *n* in the presence of the failure condition stated, and to statement number *m* in the absence of the failure condition.

FORTRAN IV does not recognise special statements of this type. In most systems (including WATFOR) standard SUBROUTINE subprogrammes are provided. In WATFOR the statement CALL DVCHK(*J*) tests for the presence of a divide check (division by zero) condition: *J* is set to 1 if a divide check has occurred, *J* is set to 2 otherwise. In either case, the divide check indicator is returned to "O.K.". The value of *J* can then be used in a computed GO TO statement: GO TO *(n,m),J* where *n* is the first statement number of the programme segment dealing with a divide check failure, *m* is the first statement number for normal continuation of calculation.

Similarly, the statement CALL OVERFL(J) tests for the presence of an arithmetic overflow or underflow condition. *J* is set equal to 1 if an arithmetic overflow has occurred; it is set to 2 if neither overflow nor underflow occurred; and it is set to 3 if an underflow has occurred. In any of these cases, the overflow and underflow indicators are reset to "O.K." See Chapter XIV, Section D for further discussion of these interrupt conditions.

A number of features of FORTRAN IV were not available in FORTRAN II. These include:

the IMPLICIT type declaration
the DATA and BLOCK DATA facilities
existence of labelled (in addition to blank) COMMON storage
possibility of array dimension declarations inside a COMMON and/or explicit type declaration
    statement
NAMELIST and NAMELIST-controlled I/O
logical IF (FORTRAN II had only the arithmetic IF)
the ENTRY statement, and multiple return points in SUBROUTINE subprogrammes
the uniform READ and WRITE statements

Only the last of these points needs more elaboration: In FORTRAN II, separate I/O statements were provided for different I/O devices, for example,

PRINT *m, List* for output onto the printer,
WRITE OUTPUT TAPE *n, m, List* for writing tape number *n* under FORMAT control, *m* being
    the number of the FORMAT statement,
WRITE TAPE *n, List* for writing tape number *n* in internal form
WRITE DRUM *n, List* for writing on drum number *n*

Similar statements existed in FORTRAN II for reading various devices.

In FORTRAN IV, the only READ statement is READ and the only WRITE statement is WRITE. The device is referred to by means of a logical unit number; the result is that the FORTRAN IV READ and WRITE statements are largely device-independent; the FORTRAN IV language need not be amended as soon as some new information storage device is invented.

On the other hand, the difficulty has not been eliminated at all; it has merely been shifted to

302

another point: it is now much more difficult than ever in the past to make up the *monitor system control cards* which are required to inform the monitor system of the correspondence between logical unit numbers in FORTRAN and actual physical devices attached to the machine. We shall have more to say about this in Appendix E.

2. Machine-dependent Aspects of the FORTRAN Language.

The most important variation between different computing machines, in this connection, is the number of binary digits per machine "word". The IBM 7090 and 7094 have 36 bits per word. Thus the maximum size of a full-word integer is $2^{35}-1$. The IBM/360 is organized by bytes (groups of 8 bits), and the arithmetic unit of the machine is built to handle integer arithmetic for 4-byte integers; thus, the maximum size of an integer in the IBM/360 is $2^{31}-1$. The CDC 1604 and CDC 3600 have 48-bit words, thus the maximum size of an integer is $2^{47}-1$.

Machine hardware affects not only the maximum size of an integer, but the provisions for floating point arithmetic and floating point number storage. The number of bits allowed for the mantissa of a single-precision floating point number varies, and so does the number of bits allowed for the exponent of such a number; usually, the maximum size of the exponent for a double-precision floating point number is the same as for a single-precision floating point number, but of course the mantissa has considerably greater length.

The Table below gives these machine-dependent factors, for a few machines:

TABLE

MACHINE	Largest Integer (Full Word)	Largest Integer Subscript	Largest Decimal Exponent	Approximate No. of decimal Digits in the Mantissa	
				Single Precision	Double Precision
IBM 7090 7094	$2^{35}-1$	$2^{15}-1$	38	8	16
IBM/360	$2^{31}-1$	$2^{31}-1$	75	7	16
UNIVAC 1107 1108	$2^{35}-1$	$2^{16}-1$	38	8	21
PHILCO 2000	$2^{39}-1$	$2^{39}-1$	616	10	21
HW 1800	$2^{44}-1$	$2^{44}-1$	76	12	20
CDC 1604 3600	$2^{47}-1$	$2^{47}-1$	308	10	25
SDS 9300	$2^{23}-1$	$2^{23}-1$	77	12	19
GE 635	$2^{35}-1$	$2^{18}-1$	38	8	17

These differences between machines are, of necessity, reflected in the FORTRAN IV language definitions: FORTRAN integers may range up to $2^{47}-1$ in CDC FORTRAN, only up to $2^{23}-1$ in SDS

FORTRAN. In some machines, index register arithmetic uses only halfword integers, not full word integers; for example, in the IBM 7090 and 7094 FORTRAN subscripts are restricted more severely than other FORTRAN integers: subscripts can go up to 2^{15}-1 only.

A particularly important distinction between machines, for serious computing, is the presence or absence of rounding in all floating point operations. The number of significant digits in single-precision and double-precision floating point arithmetic means very little unless one knows whether

    i)   the machine hardware is capable of doing rounding

    ii)   the FORTRAN-compiled object programme makes actual use of this capability

In this author's view, *a computer and/or FORTRAN compiler which does not round all floating point arithmetic operations is completely unsuitable for serious computation.* Unfortunately, too few computer users are aware of the importance of rounding, and some manufacturers have adjusted to their customers' ignorance. The FORTRAN language rules say nothing about rounding; but in practice, the presence or absence of rounding makes an enormous difference to what can or cannot be done with the machine.

3. Minor Variations

In addition to the major changes of Section 1, and the machine-dependent (and hence unavoidable) variations of Section 2, there are a number of other variations between the FORTRAN languages implemented by various manufacturers. Rather than giving a complete list (which would go out of date rapidly, anyway) we shall give a few examples to indicate what sort of differences there are.

The maximum number of characters in an identifier name is 6 in "standard" FORTRAN. CDC FORTRAN and SDS FORTRAN allow up to 8 characters.

The maximum number of array subscripts is 7 in IBM FORTRAN, and in UNIVAC FORTRAN. There is no upper limit in SDS FORTRAN, whereas some other dialects of FORTRAN are restricted to no more than 3 subscripts of an array.

The largest statement number is 99999 in IBM/360 FORTRAN, but is 32767 in IBM 7090 and IBM 7094 FORTRAN. It is one or another of these two numbers in most dialects of FORTRAN.

Mixed mode arithmetic is permitted in IBM/360 FORTRAN, as well as in the FORTRAN compilers for the UNIVAC 1107 and 1108, for the CDC 1604 and 3600 and 6600, and for the SDS 9300. It is forbidden in some other dialects of FORTRAN.

The rules for DO loops were discussed in Chapter XI, where it was pointed out that explicitly coded loops are less restricted than normal FORTRAN DO loops. Some manufacturers implement more general forms of the DO loop. For example, in SDS FORTRAN the DO loop parameters m_1, m_2, and m_3 can be any well-formed arithmetic expressions, with numerical values which may be positive, negative, or zero (except for the increment m_3, which must not be zero but is allowed to be negative). Furthermore, if m_1 exceeds m_2 and m_3 is positive, then the loop is *not* traversed even once (as it would be in standard FORTRAN).

The handling of multiple return statements RETURN *I* in SUBROUTINE subprogrammes is not standardized, and neither is the handling of multiple entries (i.e., the ENTRY statement).

Manufacturers tend to consider "their" FORTRAN as a sales point; each variation from ASA standard FORTRAN is advertised as a positive achievement. In our view, the proliferation of dialects of FORTRAN, far from being an advantage, is a positive hindrance to serious programming. Special features may sound nice to the inexperienced users; but the experienced programmer knows enough to avoid them like the plague. It is much more important to have a programme which will work on all machines which have FORTRAN compilers, than to have a programme which is slightly shorter or neater at the expense of compatibility.

Given the competitive situation in the computing field, it would obviously be visionary to insist that all manufacturers should implement an identical version of FORTRAN; nor, in the long run, would this be a good thing, since some (but not all) of the "special features" do prove themselves and become accepted as part of standard FORTRAN.

However, we feel that it is right and proper to *demand that manufacturers provide an option in their FORTRAN compilers, called, say OPTION ASA STANDARD.* If a programmer asks for that option, any source language statement inconsistent with ASA standard FORTRAN is flagged as an error. With this option, the serious programmers who need compatibility more than they need gimmicks, can make sure that their programme is in fact compatible with standard FORTRAN. Other programmers, who wish to use all the special features provided by the manufacturer's "own" FORTRAN, simply do not ask for this option.

ORGANIZATION OR LARGE CLASSES IN COMPUTING, MONITOR SYSTEMS.

In this Appendix, we start with a discussion of the technical problems of organizing really large classes in elementary computing; we then go on to say something about monitor control systems.

1. Organization of Large Classes in Computing.

At the University of New South Wales, elementary computer programming is part of the first year mathematics subject, taken by all students in the Faculties of Science, Applied Science and Engineering. Even without the other Faculties, this means a group of some 2000 students. With such numbers, efficient organization becomes essential; an inefficiency, at any point, is likely to produce a complete breakdown. We now proceed to summarize our practice and provide reasons for our choice of certain alternatives.

We have found it best to let the *students punch their own cards,* without any special schedule of hours for this. The card punch room is open all day, from early morning till late at night and students are free to come in and use the punches. Naturally, students are slow at punching cards, and professional keypunch operators would be much faster. But quite a number of keypunches can be rented for the salary of one keypunch operator. The students are highly motivated, with the result that every keypunch is used by students for much more than an eight hour day. A large number of keypunches can be supervised, for student use, by one trained person (who need not be a professional keypunch operator himself - in fact, it is more useful if that person knows a bit about FORTRAN coding and the meaning of diagnostic messages). Putting together all these factors, free use of the keypunch room by students is economically a sound proposition; it is also paedagogically preferable; since it is impossible to let the students run the computer itself, at least let them operate a keypunch.

With beginning students, interactive techniques ("on-line consoles", "time-sharing") are incredibly expensive. A beginning student needs to study the diagnostic messages in his output for quite some time, before he understands what he should do to correct the errors. During all that time, the on-line console is occupied by the student, and not available to some other student. By contrast, printed output from a batch run can be taken away and studied at leisure. In time-shared operation, it is likely that there are many transfers to and from disk storage. The compiler may have to be called in from disk over and over again. The time required for this is not negligible at all.

For these reasons, we insist on *batch processing for large classes in computing.* With batch processing, the question of turnaround time arises. At first sight, people tend to opt for the shortest possible turnaround time, perhaps several batch runs a day. In our opinion, this has most unfortunate side effects. If there is a deadline for a batch run during the day, the students crowd into the card punch room prior to that deadline, and the room is nearly empty for some time after the deadline. This is a most inefficient utilization of expensive equipment. Quite apart from that, programming can become almost an "addiction" for a small fraction of students, who then neglect everything else to the detriment of their University career as a whole. We therefore run only one student batch run every 24 hours, and that at night. The students know that the time of submission of the job has no influence on when it will be run; this evens out the pressure on the keypunches. We also limit the number of separate jobs that can be submitted by a student for any one batch run; this, together with the overnight turnaround time, tends to provide a natural limitation on overenthusiasm by a minority of students.

The layout of the job card, suggested in Chapter V, is convenient for this form of running. All the information which the WATFOR compiler actually looks at is pre-punched onto the card. The additional punching done by the students is in fields treated as comment fields by the compiler. The accounting and analysis of the job card information should be done, ideally, by the programme which transfers the input cards to an input tape; it can be done, also, on the output tape at the time that tape is printed up. One important error which requires watching is overpunching of the job card by students, thereby producing an illegal card; in some systems, such a card stops the computer run altogether; thus, all these cards must be eliminated *before* the batch is processed by the machine.

Computing exercises must be spaced in time; if there is one deadline (say the end of term) for a number of exercises, students tend to wait till the last week or two, and then overload the keypunches in their frantic attempts to catch up. A separate deadline for each exercise is preferable. If there are parallel tutorial (or recitation) sections, separate deadlines for separate tutorial groups are also of great help.

Copying of a successful exercise by other students is hard to control, and we have not found a way of preventing this practice altogether. As a result, we do not base our mark in computing directly upon these exercises; rather, completion of the exercises is necessary to be admitted to the examination; the examination contains some questions on FORTRAN programming. A student who has merely copied the computing exercises is most unlikely to give correct answers to the questions on the examination.

Stealing of computer output from successful runs can become quite a problem, also. We have been forced, at times, to have the *compulsory* exercises handed back to small groups by tutors, rather than allowing students to pick up their output from alphabetical pidgeon holes accessible to other students.

WATFOR allows certain control card options, by which a student can nominate his own limit on execution time and on pages of output. These must be inhibited by suitable alteration of the compiler, otherwise students go wild on both counts. 3 or 4 pages of output, and a few seconds of execution time, are quite adequate limits for student jobs (the time can be cut down, of course, for a high-speed machine).

2. Monitor Systems

While FORTRAN is a reasonably standardized language, with dialects which resemble each other quite closely, the very opposite is true of the monitor systems programmes and the languages used for monitor systems control cards. *In our view, standardization of the monitor systems control card language is a matter of the very highest priority in the field of electronic computation.* The present state of affairs is utter and incredible confusion; each manufacturer provides one, or even several, monitor systems programmes for every computing machine which he manufactures. The language appropriate to each monitor system is different, not merely in the way that dialects of FORTRAN differ from each other, but basically and completely different. CDC FORTRAN differs slightly from IBM FORTRAN. But there is not the slightest resemblance between control cards under the CDC SCOPE system and control cards for the OS/360 system for the IBM/360. Furthermore, different control cards are needed for OS/360, DOS/360 and BOS/360, all of which are used on the IBM/360 series. None of these control cards are similar to the IBSYS control cards on the IBM 7090, 7094, or 7044 machines; and these control cards in turn differ completely from earlier operating system control cards on the IBM 7090.

Not only have control card languages altered, but they have altered for the worse. The changes have been in the direction of increasing complication and increasing demands on the programmer to specify all sorts of things which could be, and should be, purely optional.

Student programmes need, logically speaking, only *two* system control cards: the job card, which tells the system that a new job is about to start, and which gives information about whose job it is; and the card $ENTRY (or //DATA or whatever it may be) which signals the end of the translation process and the start of the execution phase. *Any system which demands more than these two control cards for a simple student job is a bad system.*

Options are fine, but they should remain optional. When *every* programmer is asked to specify, by means of complicated systems control cards, precisely what "options" he wants to use (when in fact he couldn't care less), then the "options" are no longer optional but mandatory, and the system is a bad system.

INDEX